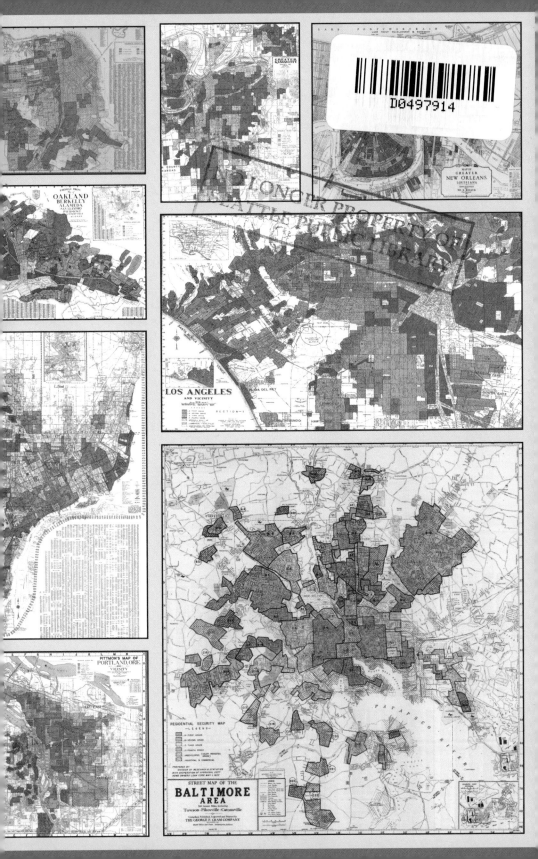

FREEDOM TO
DISCRIMINATE

FREEDOM TO DISCRIMINATE

HOW REALTORS CONSPIRED TO SEGREGATE HOUSING AND DIVIDE AMERICA

GENE SLATER

Heyday, Berkeley, California

Library of Congress Cataloging-in-Publication Data

Names: Slater, Gene, 1949- author.
Title: Freedom to discriminate : how realtors conspired to segregate housing and divide America / Gene Slater.
Description: Berkeley, California : Heyday, [2021] | Includes bibliographical references and index.
Identifiers: LCCN 2021010218 (print) | LCCN 2021010219 (ebook) | ISBN 9781597145435 (cloth) | ISBN 9781597145442 (epub)
Subjects: LCSH: Discrimination in housing--United States--History--20th century. | Discrimination in housing--Law and legislation--United States. | Real estate agents--United States--Attitudes. | Real estate business--Moral and ethical aspects--United States. | African Americans--Housing--Law and legislation. | African Americans--Segregation--History--20th century. | United States--Race relations.
Classification: LCC HD7288.76.U5 S54 2021 (print) | LCC HD7288.76.U5 (ebook) | DDC 363.5/1--dc23
LC record available at https://lccn.loc.gov/2021010218
LC ebook record available at https://lccn.loc.gov/2021010219

Cover Photo: *Ticky Tacky Houses in Daly City* (1968), photograph by Robert A. Isaacs, courtesy of the San José Museum of Art
Endpapers: Home Owners' Loan Corporation maps, from Robert K. Nelson, LaDale Winling, Richard Marciano, Nathan Connolly et al., "Mapping Inequality," *American Panorama*, ed. Robert K. Nelson and Edward L. Ayers, https://dsl.richmond.edu/panorama/redlining.
Cover Design: Ashley Ingram
Interior Design/Typesetting: Ashley Ingram

Published by Heyday
P.O. Box 9145, Berkeley, California 94709
(510) 549-3564
heydaybooks.com

Printed in East Peoria, Illinois, by Versa Press, Inc.

10 9 8 7 6 5 4 3 2 1

FSC
www.fsc.org
MIX
Paper from responsible sources
FSC® C005010

If an individual wants to discriminate against Negroes or others in selling or renting his house, he has a right to do so.

Ronald Reagan, 1966[1]

Restrictions and freedom are two facets of the same social factor. I must be restricted so that you can have freedom. Also, you must be restricted so that I may have liberty. The responsibility of government is to keep the restrictions sufficiently strong to assure to all equal freedom.

W. Byron Rumford, 1966[2]

There are such things in the world as human rights. They rest upon no conventional foundation, but are external, universal, and indestructible. Among these, is the right of locomotion . . . the right which belongs to no particular race, but belongs alike to all and to all alike.

Frederick Douglass, 1869[3]

CONTENTS

Martin Luther King at March on Washington, 1963

L. H. "Spike" Wilson, President, California
Real Estate Association, 1963

INTRODUCTION: Gettysburg 1964

> The world has never had a good definition of the word liberty, and the American people, just now, are much in want of one. We all declare for liberty; but in using the same *word* we do not all mean the same *thing*. . . . Here are two, not only different, but incompatible things, called by the same name—liberty. And it follows that each of the things is, by the respective parties, called by two different and incompatible names—liberty and tyranny.
>
> Abraham Lincoln, 1864[1]

Alone in his room at the Willard Hotel, at midnight on the night before the March on Washington, as Martin Luther King weighed his aides' often-conflicting advice on what he should, or should not, say the next afternoon, he had a specific, if almost unattainable, idea of what he wanted his speech to achieve. It needed to be "a sort of Gettysburg Address," he had quietly told a Black journalist a few days earlier.[2] To accomplish in a very different time and place what Lincoln had done almost exactly one hundred years before, King sought to persuade the vast majority of Americans, white and Black, that the nation's purpose depended on the principle that all men are created equal, not as some vague generality but as the active task of government; that American freedom had not been accomplished at the Revolution but was a promise still to be fulfilled, "a promissory note to which every American [is] heir";[3] and that such freedom was inextricable, that the freedom of white Americans depended on that of Black Americans.

To make the parallels to Lincoln's famous speech indelible, to enshrine the cause of civil rights in the noblest legacy of America's past,

King began by echoing the martyred president's words. Standing on the marble steps of the Lincoln Memorial—the gleaming pillars, brooding statue, and late afternoon sun behind him; the banked microphones and hot, travel-wearied crowd before him—he offered his vision as the completion of Lincoln's own: "Five score years ago, a great American in whose symbolic shadow we stand today signed the Emancipation Proclamation. But one hundred years later the Negro is still not free."

King's words and message drew on Lincoln's: on the rededication of America to the nation's "unfinished work." He wanted to make those long-familiar phrases—engraved on the monument's walls, recited by schoolchildren to symbolize the nation's purpose—new and urgent, the business of today. "We have . . . come to this hallowed spot, to make real the promises of democracy . . . that . . . this nation will . . . live out the true meaning of its creed: 'We hold these truths to be self-evident, that all men are created equal.'"[4]

The power of King's address would be borne out not only by the judgment of history—as the most important American speech of the twentieth century, second in our history only to Lincoln's[5]—but immediately by the fears of those diametrically opposed to King's ideas. The FBI's assistant director of domestic intelligence immediately wrote to J. Edgar Hoover, "We must mark him now, if we have not done so before, as the most dangerous negro of the future of this nation."[6] To those committed to the racial status quo and to preventing government action that would change it, nothing was more dangerous about the civil rights movement than its enlistment of Lincoln and the Declaration of Independence and their claims on the vocabulary of American freedom.

What proved to be the most effective ideological response to the civil rights movement's ideal of freedom was developed in these same months not by Southern segregationists, Republican politicians, or *National Review* intellectuals but by a source whose crucial role then is often forgotten today: the nation's realtors. To perpetuate residential discrimination, realtor organizations helped create an opposite vision of American freedom from King's. They made the right to discriminate the core of American freedom—while using the race-neutral language of the civil rights movement to insist on that right.

Thus, nine months after the March on Washington, Spike Wilson, leader of California realtors, invoked Lincoln too. This Fresno broker and president of his local Kiwanis Club quoted the Gettysburg Address in a campaign designed not to support King and the civil rights movement but to oppose them. Wilson's vision of American freedom answered King's in a 1964 ballot initiative that proved crucial to the future of both these visions.

"Gettysburg 1964," Wilson called the battle over Proposition 14, a California constitutional amendment that would permanently *ban* the state or any city from ever limiting housing discrimination.[7] "Now we are engaged in a great war over civil rights testing whether equal rights for all can be achieved without losing freedom of choice, freedom of association and . . . private property rights," Wilson announced in launching the realtors' campaign. "We are involved in a great battle for liberty and freedom. We have prepared a final resting place for the drive to destroy individual freedom."[8]

Wilson's message was designed to boost the morale of California's forty thousand realtors—half of all those in the country—and affirm the noble purpose of those working on the front line in the campaign for Proposition 14. For brokers who might doubt the morality of opposing minority rights or worry that their efforts could be seen as self-serving or on the wrong side of history, "Gettysburg 1964" made clear that the realtors' cause was that of American freedom itself.

The realtors' national association designed the California vote to be the turning point in their "great war" against fair housing laws across the country. "If Californians say, 'Yes, we want our full freedom restored!' the people in other states will take heart and fight the same battle for freedom there," Wilson proclaimed. "If they say, 'No, we believe the privileges of minorities are more important than the rights of majorities,' such laws will blanket the United States."[9]

The key to success, Wilson realized, was to challenge the idea of freedom at the heart of the civil rights movement. At a time when freedom as a domestic issue meant the struggle for equal rights—when news stories about freedom showed children attacked by police dogs in Birmingham—and at the height of support for civil rights, no prominent political leader would endorse Proposition 14 for fear of seeming racist. Republican presidential candidate Barry Goldwater, willing to vote against the 1964 federal civil rights bill, refused to take a position. Ronald Reagan, who campaigned for Goldwater and would run for governor of California two years later, was unwilling to support Proposition 14 until after it was approved. So controversial was the proposition that it overshadowed for *Time* magazine the "piddlin' contest" of the presidential election.[10] No state constitution, even in the deep South, had ever permanently protected discrimination. To win an overwhelming majority for such a measure—in a state whose voters had chosen a liberal legislature and a liberal governor who had made fair housing his highest priority—realtors had to counter King's vision of freedom with their own.

The division between these visions was sharp and far reaching. For King and civil rights advocates, housing discrimination was the greatest obstacle to freedom outside the South.[11] Denial of this right closed the door to many others. Being confined to a few, limited, tightly bounded neighborhoods created a sense of imprisonment that African Americans knew from lifelong experience. "The evils of segregation and discrimination in housing [cause] segregated schools, segregated jobs . . . , and a segregated society," the NAACP spelled out, in bitterly opposing Proposition 14.[12] Freedom, in this view, was clear and simple: a universal promise that government would secure rights for all Americans.

By contrast, realtors described freedom not as something to be achieved but preserved. Such traditional freedom, they claimed, had long included, at its very heart, the owner's choice of whom to sell or rent to—the right to discriminate. This right had long preceded the American Revolution, realtors argued. That this right had never been mentioned until the civil rights movement threatened it only proved how fundamental it was. Being *protected* against discrimination was not a right at all but a special privilege. "Militant minorities have organized and vocalized for equal rights," Wilson warned, "until equal rights have become special privileges and this forgotten man lies neglected. He is the great, passive majority."[13]

A former Sacramento news editor, Wilson argued for the absolute rights of owners in terms of America's promise to all. Proposition 14 carried the dreams, he said, of his great-great-grandfather James Wilson, a signer of the Declaration, and his mother, a Greek immigrant who came to America, like millions of others, for "something promised only here

. . . the rights and freedoms of individual American property owners."[14]

To appeal to the white majority while arguing that Proposition 14 was not against any minority, Wilson emphasized that realtors were in favor of the same rights for all races—the right of owners to discriminate: "We're trying to do something to help everyone—to protect their property rights." Realtors argued that they, not civil rights advocates, were the ones in favor of color-blind freedom.

Their campaign was not against minorities, realtors declared, but government oppression. "Am I anti-Negro? By God I am not. I am their champion," Wilson insisted.[15] By making state bureaucrats the enemy, realtors could be on the side of the underdog, the individual owner. Realtors therefore consistently referred to fair housing—laws prohibiting discrimination—as "forced housing," compelling owners to sell or rent to whoever paid the full asking price regardless of their race or religion. Proposition 14 was thus not about race but "the rights of the individual."[16] That a Fresno real estate broker invoked the Gettysburg Address to answer Martin Luther King was neither surprising nor peripheral to the realtors' campaign, but at its core.

The stakes could hardly have been higher. Residential discrimination was so intense and systemic that in the Bay Area—then as now one of the most liberal parts of the country—only 50 out of 325,000 new homes in the 1950s were sold on an open-occupancy basis without regard to race.[17] Of six hundred brokers in Palo Alto, only three would even consider showing African Americans a home in a white area.[18] Real estate boards systematically excluded every African American broker. Newspapers grouped real estate ads in columns marked "restricted" or "unrestricted," determined not by the individual seller but the local real estate board. Far from being abstract arguments, these opposing visions of freedom would have direct, immediate impacts on where people could live—and would powerfully affect support for all types of civil rights.

For in describing American freedom as belonging to each individual separately, rather than as something shared, realtors undermined King's fundamental political premise at the March on Washington. The future of civil rights, King recognized, depended on the shared recognition of a common stake, of "white brothers [who] have come to realize that their destiny is tied up with our destiny . . . that their freedom is inextricably bound to our freedom."[19] Realtors argued the opposite: "Granting one group of citizens rights . . . necessarily takes away equivalent rights from the rest of the citizenry," as if this were simple arithmetic.[20] If white Americans saw freedom in this atomized way, if granting rights to minorities did not strengthen but diminished their own, it would become almost impossible for the civil rights movement to challenge any type of racial discrimination in the North.

King recognized the dangers of the realtors' ideology. Taking time away from pressing struggles in the South, he rushed to San Francisco and Los Angeles to inveigh against the dangers of Proposition 14. At a Freedom Rally in Fresno, a few miles from Wilson's office, King warned what would happen if the realtors succeeded. "If this initiative passes, it will defeat all we have been struggling to win."[21] King's terms echoed those of his speech at the March on Washington. But he was now defending his vision of freedom not against Southern defenders of Jim Crow but against Northern advocates of color-blind American freedom.

The results stunned politicians of both parties. Cast as racially neutral, the realtors' idea of embattled freedom—freedom endangered by liberal government—resonated with the vast majority of voters. In the same election in which Lyndon Johnson defeated Barry Goldwater by the largest margin in American history, on the same state ballot where Goldwater received barely 40 percent of the vote, 65 percent supported Proposition 14.[22]

In a political message that would not be lost across the rest of the country, 75 percent of white voters supported the realtors' initiative. Proposition 14 won by almost as wide a margin among union members, the longtime core of the Democratic Party, five to one, as among Republicans.[23] Many white Californians who saw themselves as racial moderates, and generally supported the federal Civil Rights Act of 1964,[24] found in the realtors' vision of American freedom a nonracial reason, expressed in terms of the country's deepest values, to oppose the extension of civil rights.

At the very moment when liberalism in America seemed most dominant, the realtors showed how conservatives could succeed. That the realtors' idea of freedom had triumphed in a non-Southern state, a political bellwether for the nation as a whole, made California a megaphone.

Proposition 14 showed how freedom could be used virtually everywhere to oppose civil rights and indeed liberal government itself.

Although Proposition 14's legal influence would prove relatively short lived—state and federal supreme courts ruled it unconstitutional—the realtors' campaign had a lasting effect on the nation's political landscape. It propelled the rise of former actor Ronald Reagan, transformed the language of freedom in a way that became a template for modern conservatism, and contributed to the way that many, perhaps most, Americans understand freedom today.

King, who called passage of Proposition 14 "a tragic setback for integration throughout the country,"[25] did not live to see a federal fair housing law. When Congress finally approved such a law days after his assassination, it was largely gutted by the memory of Proposition 14. No government administrative enforcement mechanism was provided. To this day, an estimated four million housing discrimination complaints each year go uninvestigated, and fair housing remains largely unenforced.[26]

In 1984, the Heritage Foundation looked back at what had been crucial to conservative success in dealing with civil rights: "For twenty years, the most important battle in . . . civil rights. . . . has been for control of the language. . . . It is the rhetoric of civil rights that justifiably appeals to Americans' . . . inherent sense of fairness. . . . Americans oppose . . . 'segregation' and 'racism'; they favor 'equality' [and] opportunity. The secret to victory . . . has been to control the definition of these terms."[27] The realtors had grasped that the essential word to redefine, the key to victory, was *freedom.* Eric Foner, a progressive historian and leading scholar on American freedom, similarly recognized the lasting importance of the realtors' 1964 redefinition of this one key word.[28]

King's warning about the impact of the realtors' idea of freedom proved prophetic. His "I Have a Dream" speech is so widely celebrated and the origins of the realtors' redefinition of freedom so little known, it is easy to forget which has generally dominated American politics since the 1960s.[29]

"Gettysburg 1964" was a pivotal moment in a far larger story. It represented both the culmination of a sixty-year effort by the nation's realtors to divide where Americans can live and a germinal moment in the rise of a conservative movement that would transform our politics. The nation's polarization today is driven by an idea of freedom rooted in the history of residential segregation. This larger story shows the origins and features of an idea of freedom designed to divide America.

SEGREGATING AMERICA'S NEIGHBORHOODS

This book shows the deep connection between two features of our modern history that have rarely been looked at together: the establishment and defense of residential segregation in every city in the country, and the creation of a conservative idea of American freedom in the 1960s that has shaped our political debates ever since. Both were designed to divide Americans. Both reflected the work of the country's organized real estate industry—the nation's realtors—to sell homes, maintain their business practices, and define a particular version of the American dream. Tracing this work from the inside—from the industry's own documents, many examined here for the first time—helps us see these two defining features of modern America in a new and holistic way.

Instead of the story of twentieth- and twenty-first-century America gradually reducing barriers, this account helps explain the opposite. It shows how America's neighborhoods went from being racially mixed to intensely segregated, how racial and political divisions were systematically widened, and how new ideas of American freedom were invented to successfully counter those of World War II and the emerging civil rights movement. It spells out the power of those new ideas to continue housing segregation long after it officially ended and to transform America's political parties, pushing the country further and further to the right. This is a story of innovation: of how the common good, community progress, the New Deal, freedom of choice, and individual rights were used to limit where Americans could live and to increasingly polarize the country.

Housing segregation, far from being a narrow issue whose impacts were as isolated as those it excluded, dramatically reshaped the country for all Americans. All-white neighborhoods were first created not in the South but in Berkeley, a mile from the University of California. Residential segregation was not the norm in American cities at the beginning of the twentieth century but a new marketing tool for early realtors to sell house lots. The realtors' commitment to racial homogeneity drove their design of federal programs and—by financing only developments far from any minorities—the layout of every metropolitan area. The neighborhoods where most Americans live today, and who their neighbors are, are the result of that commitment.

Restricting the country's vast free-market economy required enormous effort. To racially divide every housing market in America and patrol and enforce these boundaries, the real estate industry had to organize and police itself and enlist many of the country's leading lawyers, economists, public officials, newspapers, universities, lenders, and courts. This racial system was so effectively organized that by 1960—long after the U.S. Supreme Court prohibited court enforcement of the racial covenants realtors had invented—African Americans remained excluded from 98 percent of new homes and 95 percent of neighborhoods.[30]

The realtors' need to justify this racial system transformed America's values. The residential system they created not only drew on existing prejudice but required and fostered it. Every white resident had to view any minority not as an individual but as a threat to his home, community, and the American dream. Inventing a "scientific" law that "undesirable human elements" depreciate property values, realtors built this axiom into vast federal programs.

When even the real estate industry's own appraisers discredited this property-value axiom, realtors needed a new set of arguments to publicly defend this same racial system. To counter the civil rights movement's argument that American freedom depended on treating people as individuals rather than as groups to be discriminated against, the real estate industry designed a counteridea of individual freedom as the right to a "traditional" community. This vision of color-blind freedom, placing the right to discriminate at the heart of American freedom, provided a road map for the rise of conservatism.

This book thus reveals, step-by-step, how the real estate industry constructed many of our most intractable divides—social, geographic, economic, and ideological. Modern American history is, in many ways, the story of these divides. Racially separate neighborhoods were not peripheral to the creation of today's America but at its core.

THE LASTING POWER OF JUSTIFICATIONS

If this perspective seems unfamiliar, it may be because this history has not been told from the inside as a single narrative of what it took to create and perpetuate this new system. The myths realtors promoted to make this racial system seem inevitable are still widely accepted today. Most Americans, both Black and white, came to accept the realtors' myth that American cities had always been racially divided, that segregation was normal, natural, and historical—not a twentieth-century invention to sell homes.

The realtors similarly explained residential segregation as simply a result of prejudice. But racism was just as intense at the beginning of the 1900s before residential segregation began. It took a newly organized real estate industry to invent and maintain organized segregation. If these had not been myths, realtors would not have worked so hard— would not have had to work at all—to stop minorities from moving into white neighborhoods.

In looking at segregation not as something normal but as a construct that had to be explained and defended, this history focuses on the *justifications* for dividing America's neighborhoods: on how and why they were created, and their impact on where people lived and on America's values. These justifications were not separate from this racial system but intrinsic to how it worked: how the real estate industry enlisted its own members and government itself to enforce segregation. The extraordinary effort realtors put into these justifications belies their claim that housing segregation was simply a result of racial prejudice.

The realtors' central challenge, in fact, was how to continue segregation in the face of America's changing values. Continuing racially divided housing markets depended, generation after generation, on transforming one American ideal after another to defend discrimination. Realtor leaders redefined progress, the Golden Rule, free markets, freedom of association, and, ultimately, individual freedom itself to keep neighborhoods segregated.

Such justifications helped realtors see themselves not as upholding white supremacy but as politically, ethically, and ideologically carrying out the American dream. With the rise of the civil rights movement, realtors urgently needed nonracial or, better still, antiracial arguments that spoke—as realtor leaders explicitly instructed their members—always about freedom and never about race. Realtors and the voters they sought to convince in states across the country wanted to be told, a dissident realtor recognized, "that what we have been doing to the minority members in our communities is right—is accepted—is morally good."[31]

These justifications had a lasting effect. Housing segregation officially ended in 1968; realtor organizations no longer opposed fair housing. But if segregation of African Americans at each income level remains almost as intense as it was fifty years ago, this is a testament to the lasting political consequences of the realtors' vision of freedom. Only strong government action could have overcome the economic and social forces realtors had long put in place—racially exclusive suburbs, organized prejudice, and informal discriminatory pressures. But strong governmental action is precisely what the political impact of the realtors' arguments has long prevented. The popularity of the realtors' appeal to individual freedom weakened not only the 1968 law itself but efforts to enforce it ever since.[32]

The realtors' redefinition of American freedom has only become more important over time on issues far removed from housing or even race. The idea that freedom belongs separately to each individual—that freedom, like private property itself, depends on the right to exclude others—became part of our political vocabulary. The technique the realtors perfected, of identifying and elevating a single narrow right as American freedom itself, as an absolute without regard to the rights of others, could be tellingly employed on virtually any issue: gun control, abortion, contraception, gay marriage, or corporate campaign contributions. Our political debates today are driven by an idea of freedom created to defend all-white neighborhoods half a century ago.

How this happened, how a racial system that officially ended in the 1960s came to shape our politics today in ways that few Americans are aware of—this concern is at the heart of this book and the reason for its urgency.

OPPOSING IDEAS OF FREEDOM

This book, in fact, began as a question: Why is freedom used so regularly and insistently by conservatives to oppose civil rights? This question led in turn to others. How had freedom come to be used in this way? Had this always been the case? What did conservatives mean by American freedom that extensions of civil rights would violate?

At the heart of these questions is a paradox—one that haunts our politics and polarizes the country, but is rarely put in words. Americans from opposite ends of the political spectrum, who disagree about almost everything, agree that freedom is the country's most important value. The natural assumption has been that those on opposing sides of our debates are talking about the same principle—that when Ronald Reagan, say, spoke of freedom, he was referring to at least the same general idea from the Declaration of Independence as Jimmy Carter.

Freedom to Discriminate shows that this assumption is wrong, that the differences between modern conservative and liberal views of freedom are neither incidental nor matters of emphasis. American politics over the last fifty years has been driven by two *mutually incompatible* visions of freedom.

This explains why, on issue after issue—immigration, voting rights, gender rights, policing, discrimination—what liberals see as essential freedoms, natural rights that any government should guarantee, seem to conservatives like deliberate attacks on freedom itself. Each side sees the other as threatening to destroy American freedom. These differences are not willful or perverse. They reflect that, to oppose Martin Luther King and the civil rights movement, the nation's realtors created a new definition of American freedom that made the right to discriminate essential.

Why did the realtors' redefinition of freedom offer a model for American conservatism as a whole—on issues far beyond neighborhoods or race? What differentiated their arguments from those of Southern segregationists, *National Review* intellectuals, and conservative politicians? The realtors' internal documents show how they constructed their vision and thus the features that would make it successful far beyond their own fight against fair housing.

A central answer—and a key theme of this history—was that the realtors invoked individual freedom to maintain community conformity. Realtors used libertarianism to justify its seeming opposite, conformity to locally dominant beliefs. Here was a way to unite the two separate and competing strands of conservatism, to link libertarians and social conservatives in the defense of American freedom.

By defining as "freedom" what government seemed to be taking away from "ordinary Americans," the realtors helped create a polarizing, transcendent view of what was at stake in American politics. This would provide a compelling reason, far beyond economics, for millions of union members, Catholics, and white ethnic Americans who had long been part of FDR's coalition to see, in issue after issue, why they should define themselves as conservatives.

Timeliest of all, the realtors' redefinition of American freedom offered a unifying ideology for something new in twentieth-century America: a national conservative political party. Such a party had first been proposed by Southern Democrats in the late 1940s as a way to protect Jim Crow. White Southerners would abandon the national Democratic party in return for a pledge from probusiness Northern Republicans to protect local racial customs.[33] Republicans in turn would become a national majority. Goldwater's success in the South made such a party possible. But a party devoted to limiting federal regulation of business and civil rights needed a publicly acceptable ideology that could work in both the North and the South.

The realtors' vision of color-blind freedom, which had proven so successful in California, could unite Southerners, working-class Northern Democrats, and conservative and moderate Republicans in a new national majority party—one very different from the party whose congressmen had voted 80 percent in favor of the Civil Rights Act. Over time, the internal dynamics of such a party pushed it further and further toward those who most ardently embraced this vision as the *only* meaning of American freedom. The hyperpolarization of American politics is a natural result.

Yet the power, importance, and origin of these two opposite meanings of freedom are often unrecognized—as if both were the same fundamental value rooted in the country's history. Partly this is by design.

Realtors worked hard to portray their vision of freedom as not new at all. Wrapping their proposition in the language of the Bill of Rights, realtors explained that the owner's right to discriminate had only been left out of the original Bill of Rights and Constitution because it *underlay* those documents; it was what the American Revolution had been fought for. This right to discriminate was therefore fundamental and absolute; no government could limit it. That the realtors' vision of freedom has become so much a part of our political landscape is a measure of its success.

The use of the same word *freedom* has made it hard to recognize the deep-seated and intentional differences between these two visions. One vision has been based on the fundamental idea that freedom for all Americans is inseparable, that freedom for others is necessary to one's own. "To be a free society," a fair housing advocate argued, "we cannot justify denial of this same right, which we enjoy, to any person by reason of his race or property."[34] The other view rejected this basic premise and, in line with the realtors, saw freedom as a zero sum, an individual possession like private property itself. Granting rights to others would only diminish one's own.

Each side has, naturally, seen its vision of freedom as freedom itself. Realtors and conservatives argued that they were truly committed to American freedom, while their opponents sacrificed freedom for equality.[35] But this conservative motto assumed that freedom meant the same thing to both sides. The difference in modern politics, as on Proposition 14, is between those who believe in the *inseparability* of all Americans' ability to exercise freedom versus those who do not.

Conversely, civil rights advocates and liberals have viewed realtors and modern conservatives as rejecting the obvious and long-standing meaning of American freedom from the Declaration of Independence. George Lakoff, a leading liberal expert on framing political ideas, attacked conservatives for having stolen the original, progressive meaning of freedom while denying that they have done so. "What I am calling progressive freedom is simply freedom in the American tradition . . . the ideal of freedom which has been cherished, defended and extended over more than two centuries. What contemporary conservatives call freedom . . . is a radical departure . . . outside the mainstream of American history and American life today."[36] For Lakoff, the conservative view of freedom was illegitimate. In the struggle over Proposition 14—and today—civil rights advocates and liberals had a similarly hard time responding to the realtors' vision of freedom because it did not seem like freedom at all. They therefore dramatically underestimated the power of the realtors' argument and why it would prove so influential.[37]

That these diametrically opposite views presumed a singular correct version of American freedom reflected what was at stake: who would successfully claim the meaning of this central word. Freedom was the high ground, as Eric Foner has long noted,[38] the key asset to be seized.

Recognizing how opposite these visions are, and how the conservative vision was precisely designed to undermine that of the civil rights movement, can not only illuminate the past but also shape the future. It can provide us a way to change our political debates, by recognizing that the choices we face reflect two opposite meanings of American freedom—inclusive freedom, designed to equalize and balance rights, and exclusive freedom, based on the right to discriminate.

AN UNCLAIMED LEGACY

Yet if the realtors had such a significant impact on the conservative idea of freedom and ultimately the country's political landscape, why is this so rarely mentioned or studied? One reason is that those on both sides of the battle over fair housing had little reason to talk about the realtors' idea of freedom or its impacts. After they lost their battle over fair housing in 1968, realtors quickly sought to distance themselves from their past defense of racial segregation. Liberals and civil rights advocates, too, had little reason to want to talk about Proposition 14. They attributed this painful setback in the triumphalist story of 1960s civil rights gains to simple racial bias that might diminish over time, not to the positive appeal of an alternative vision of freedom. In the histories of civil rights struggles, the realtors' arguments, and particularly their idea of freedom, have rarely been considered important in themselves.

Nor has the realtors' ideological vision been featured in histories of modern conservatism. Such histories have largely taken a top-down perspective, focusing on conservative intellectuals and their relationships to the candidacies of Goldwater, Nixon, and Reagan. Later historians, taking a bottom-up approach, have studied Southern suburban segregationists and their role in the Southernization of the Republican Party[39] and the grassroots activism of suburban homeowners in California stimulated by Proposition 14,[40] without focusing on the realtors' redefinition of freedom itself.

To the extent that the realtors' vision of freedom has been considered, it has largely been discounted on two grounds: motivation and backlash. Proposition 14 opponents and most historians since have largely dismissed the realtors' idea of freedom as only a cover for racism, as unimportant in itself.[41] But while racial concerns and fears of change and loss drove the war against fair housing, opponents who underestimated the impact of realtors translating those concerns into a vision of freedom did so at their peril. They failed to recognize how compelling this vision was to vast numbers of voters, and its impact on American politics.

It has been equally tempting to centrist political analysts who deeply influenced Bill Clinton in the 1990s to see the vote on Proposition 14 as a "backlash" to excessive liberal and minority demands.[42] The idea of backlash, however, ignores the long history of realtor resistance to racial integration, a history that goes back to the founding of the realtor movement in the early 1900s. As many historians have found, resistance by realtors in the 1960s was not to sudden extreme demands but to any potential change whatsoever.[43]

Moreover, the idea of backlash itself—with Proposition 14 often cited, along with George Wallace's 1964 Northern campaign, as the defining early example—implies a natural, automatically occurring, popular reaction rather than one contingent on active agency. The Proposition 14 campaign, however, reflected realtors' organized and deliberate efforts to arouse fears and emotions and to frame these in terms of loss of freedom. Without an initiative campaign, the quiet work of the state commission investigating complaints—eighty cases in its first eighteen months, including only two against homeowners—might well have continued without becoming the leading issue in California politics. In the two states, Colorado and Massachusetts, where realtor organizations cooperated with rather than led campaigns against fair housing, there was almost no controversy. If fair housing became by far the most divisive issue in California in 1964, it was because the realtors chose to make it so.

Indeed, throughout the last year of his life, when Martin Luther King repeatedly criticized the growing popularity of this idea of white backlash, he cited Proposition 14 as his prime example. This "so-called 'white backlash'" was "not something that just came into being because of shouts of Black Power, or because Negroes engaged in riots in Watts. . . . The fact is that the state of California voted a Fair Housing bill out of existence before anybody shouted Black Power, or before anybody rioted in Watts."[44] The chronology demonstrated the point King wanted to make.

"Backlashing," as King called it, to emphasize its active, organized nature, was simply "a new name for an old phenomenon":

> Ever since the birth of our nation, white America . . . has been torn between . . . a self in which she proudly professed the great principles of democracy and a self in which she sadly practiced the antithesis of democracy. . . . This tragic duality has . . . [caused] America to take a step backward simultaneously with every step forward on the question of racial justice. . . . The step backward has a new name today. It is called the "white backlash." But the white backlash is nothing new. It is the surfacing of old prejudices, hostilities and ambivalences that have always been there.[45]

In pushing for fair housing, civil rights advocates did not create such prejudice and fear, but rather exposed them.[46] White opposition to fair housing was a reason not to stop such efforts but to continue them.

But in framing the realtors' campaign in terms of past resistance to change, King sought to discount what made Proposition 14's vision of freedom new and influential. Like many observers, he looked at the realtors' argument through the lens of the past. To "talk eloquently against open housing and . . . in the same breath . . . contend that they are not racist,"[47] King argued, simply masked the same long-standing "premises that came into being to rationalize slavery."[48] What made the realtors' campaign new, however, was its claim to freedom. Their "crusade for freedom" recast the discussion King wanted Americans to have.

Yet despite the success of the realtors' vision of American freedom, its history has rarely been studied. The most incisive scholarly analyses have focused on the immediate problems the realtors' arguments posed for fair housing advocates, rather than their long-term impacts on American politics.[49] Indeed, the very success of the realtors' idea suggested that there was nothing to study, that this idea of freedom simply existed. The realtors had done everything possible to foster that impression.

As a result, the most fundamental divisions of our country—the idea of Black neighborhoods and white neighborhoods, that neighborhoods belong to a race, our polarized ideas of freedom—are taken for granted as if they were natural features of the country, rather than the result of enormous, deliberate efforts.

Indeed, as I wrote this book, what stood out from more than forty years of serving as a senior advisor on affordable housing for federal agencies, states, and local governments—of designing homeownership programs with realtors in South Central Los Angeles; advising on federal mortgage insurance programs and the assets of failed savings and loans; and helping design what became the Treasury's program financing 110,000 homes for first-time buyers after the 2009 financial crisis—is how little of the history of residential segregation and its impacts is known not only by the general public but also by the leaders of the public agencies charged with improving our cities and housing.

Because this legacy is unclaimed and the impact of the realtors' vision of freedom largely overlooked, this history can let us look at our current divides in a new light. For those concerned with housing segregation, it shows the central role and responsibility of the real estate industry—and how the ideology realtors developed to defend their role remains, so many decades later, the great obstacle to ending it. For those who have supported this conservative vision of American freedom, this book shows how and why it was created. For those disturbed by this vision, this history shows how it was constructed and the importance of offering a clear alternative, of not leaving the conservative vision unopposed.

Finally, this history shows that redefining the country's highest purpose as the right to live in a conforming community challenges the very idea of a common, unifying vision of American freedom—Lincoln's great purpose in the Gettysburg Address. This redefinition makes those who disagree not compatriots but enemies of freedom, only fellow conservatives "freedom-loving Americans,"[50] and the protection of such absolute rights more important than democracy. By its terms, this idea of individual freedom, designed to justify divided neighborhoods, drives Americans further and further apart.

REALTORS AND REALTOR ORGANIZATIONS

Realtors were, and are, members of a private business trade organization, one of the oldest, largest, and most successful in the country. This organization consisted of local real estate boards, such as the Los Angeles Realty Board (LARB), and of statewide associations, such as the California Real Estate Association (CREA), joined together in the National Association of Real Estate Boards (NAREB). These names were changed in the 1970s because of the events described in this history. They are currently the Beverly Hills Greater Los Angeles Association of Realtors, the California Association of Realtors, and the National Association of Realtors. Officers at each level have always been elected annually.

The term *Realtor* was first used and trademarked in the late 1910s. For simplicity, members of organized real estate boards prior to that date are referred to as realtors or early realtors; organizations are referred to by the names they used from the 1910s through 1970. Although realtors were only a minority of all real estate brokers, they controlled 80 to 90 percent of all sales.

Although boards and associations had their own policies, all were subject to NAREB's Code of Ethics and standards of practice. Positions were coordinated through the work of joint committees. Positions and views in this book described as those of "realtors" were those consistent across these bodies, and so referred to by spokesmen at the time. Individual members sometimes dissented quietly and, more rarely, openly, often with severe consequences for their ability to earn a living.[51]

That much of this history focuses on the relationship between California and national realtors reflects the state's outsize role in NAREB's membership and NAREB's devoting its own resources to the battle in California, to making it Gettysburg. Similarly, this history often emphasizes discrimination in homeownership. Discrimination in private rental housing was just as severe; but while realtors played major roles in rental property management and ownership, in their arguments against fair housing they usually focused on homeowners and homeowner rights, for political and ideological reasons.

All realtor organizations today stress how different they are from their predecessors in dealing with fair housing. "Fair Housing for All" is on the letterhead of the California Association of Realtors. "Committed to fair housing," the letterhead reads. "We acknowledge the past as we fight for a more equitable future."[52]

This book plumbs the power of that past. It is a history of the concerted efforts of realtor organizations from 1903 to 1968 to organize and justify residential segregation, and the impacts of their decades of actions then on the divisions we face as Americans today.

Part One.

Limiting Individual Freedom for the Common Good: Early 1900s–Early 1920s

To grasp why in 1961 the realtors' national president declared "forced" housing "the greatest challenge facing America"[1]—and why for realtors this was not hyperbole but simple truth—requires understanding the physical, economic, and racial world realtors had helped create. America's realtors in the 1960s were agents not only of individual clients but of the system of real estate their predecessors established long before.

The beliefs that drove the realtor movement were set at the very beginning. These deep-seated assumptions—about organizing real estate, rooting out fraud, and creating segregation, all in the name of the public good—remained at the heart of all their views, and gave their vision of freedom in the 1960s its distinctiveness and effectiveness. Realtors, over time, changed the language they used to defend these deep values, but the purpose of their arguments remained the same.

Later realtors could talk about, and ardently believe in, "freedom" in ways that directly contradicted their prior actions—could sanctify owner rights after decades of using racial covenants to limit them—because freedom had never been a core value of realtors to begin with.

The realtor movement, from the beginning, sought to limit personal liberty in real estate for the common good. "The idea that every man's house is his castle is too deep-rooted in our institutions," it was lamented in the *National Real Estate Journal* in 1910. "[W]e have carried this abhorrence of interference with personal liberty to an unwise extreme."[2] Precisely because freedom had not been something realtors had spoken about or defended, Spike Wilson and other 1960s leaders could define freedom in the way that best suited them: not as the individual freedom to do what one wanted, but as the freedom to maintain the social traditions and order that realtors had long established.

At the heart of early realtor values was the fact that early realtors were progressive reformers. Citing Teddy Roosevelt, they ardently applied progressivism to real estate. No one embodied these progressive values more than William May Garland, who helped found the Los Angeles Realty Board, became the only man to serve twice as the realtors' national president, and led realtor efforts for the federal government in World War I. Similarly embodying the idea of private business for the public good, the two leading realtors who created the first racially restricted developments, Duncan McDuffie of Berkeley and J. C. Nichols of Kansas City, were nationally lionized champions of city planning. Civic awards, mountain peaks, and public fountains are still named after these leading realtors. Each sought to limit "selfish individualism" in real estate by restricting the freedom of brokers, owners, and buyers. Organized segregation began not in the name of individual freedom but in the name of civic progress and the good of the community.

1.

Progressive Reformers of Real Estate

In public estimation, the representations of real estate men must be taken as the fisherman. [Given the] misleading advertising of property, one sometimes wonders how the little truth crept in among the untruths.

Speaker at a real estate congress, 1894[1]

If a man under a cloud or down and out cannot go into the real estate business, where in God's name can he go?

U.S. Supreme Court, 1922[2]

What could be done about the lack of trust in real estate and real estate men? This was the problem William May Garland wanted to solve when he invited a handful of Los Angeles's other leading brokers to his downtown office on a spring day in 1903. The gathering in Garland's office that would change the course of real estate in Los Angeles and California was unusual in several respects. These men were rivals, competing head-to-head for clients and properties. They prided themselves on their independence, their freedom to do business as they wanted. Nor was there a deal to discuss. Garland, a famously busy broker and considered "a human dynamo,"[3] did not need any folders on the table.

What Garland wanted to address was the real estate business itself. However honest each of these men strove to be, *real estate man* was a synonym for *shark, shyster, scoundrel*. One need only glance at recent headlines: a broker attempting extortion, another proffering fictitious checks, yet another forging the signature of a federal land agent, others suing each other over disputed commissions. The most glaring involved women and children. On a downtown sidewalk, a respected woman surgeon slapped a broker's face for trying to defraud her of the title to a lot. Another broker fraudulently transferred the property of orphaned children. A third was sentenced to ten years in San Quentin for "cheating a poor woman out of all the money she had."[4] With such stories so commonplace, how could the public trust any real estate man?

The problem of fraud was endemic. The Wild West, realtors later called the real estate business of the early 1900s.[5] In a world of almost perfect freedom, virtually no rules, and unlimited competition, anyone could call himself a broker. No "integrity, capital, experience or education" was required,[6] only a willingness to hustle. Commissions were negotiable, and one dealer often undercut another at the last moment. Brokers did not disclose to their client when they were buying the property for themselves. Many worked on a net basis; the lower the asking price the broker convinced the seller to set, the fatter the broker's commission. On the bustling streets outside Garland's office, salesmen solicited like streetwalkers, asking newcomers and passers-by if they wanted a homesite at a bargain. With little premium on the truth, deception was often the norm.

Nowhere was fraud more widespread than in Los Angeles, the fastest-growing city in the country and one built on growth itself, where real estate hustlers and promoters descended on waves of newcomers "like flies upon a bowl of sugar."[7] Townsites had been marketed as fictitious harbors, and oranges "stuck on Joshua trees in a desert tract advertised as the only region in Southern California in which the orange was indigenous."[8] Subdividers sold staked-out lots with little flags to mark streets that might never materialize. Even the most established subdividers, some of Los Angeles's biggest businessmen, had just opened a Hollywood subdivision complete with hotel, bank, and lavish improvements by planting Sold signs on almost half the lots, none of which had been sold, and dumping building materials to suggest that eager purchasers had already begun construction.[9]

In a business where all these practices were perfectly legal, with no standards, codes of ethics, or fiduciary obligations, brokers, buyers, and sellers could pursue their individual self-interest in almost any way they wanted. The commodity in short supply in real estate at the beginning of the twentieth century was not freedom but trust.

William May Garland

The erosion of public trust affected each of the men Garland had invited, no matter how reputable they were. In fact, the more concerned they were with their reputation and integrity, the more affected they were. "Petty jealousies and cut-throat competition with real estate men in general disrepute abounded," Garland later said. No one was more concerned about his reputation than Garland. He had come to real estate not as a salesman or promoter but as an auditor. The son of a minister from a small island off the coast of Maine, Garland had worked for a bank in Chicago before coming to Los Angeles in 1890 as auditor of an early cable car company. Because such companies made their money less from the fare box than by buying and subdividing the hilltops their cable cars made accessible, Garland became an expert on lot sales. He soon established his own real estate firm, acting as principal sales agent for Henry Huntington's Pacific Electric Railway, which developed streetcar lines and property throughout the city.[10] One of the leading brokers in the city, he knew that his only real asset, the source of all his future business, was his reputation. Yet given the business he operated in, how could he or any other leading brokers protect their reputations?

This issue of trust was more than personal; it went to the public's confidence in real estate itself. Garland was best known to the general public for his red-and-white semaphore advertising signs predicting (accurately, it turned out) Los Angeles's population to triple by the end of the decade, from 100,000 to 300,000.[11] The signs read, "The Lesson: Buy Los Angeles Realty."[12] The climate of fraud and deceit threatened the growth and property sales these men's business depended on.

But how could the men around this table create trust in real estate? "The most dastardly, outrageous frauds were frequently perpetrated, and no effort was made by the better class of real estate men to stop them,"[13] Garland chided. How could they change the real estate business itself?

For if Garland had asked them here together, it was not to share complaints. Practical as well as farsighted, Garland was known for taking on responsibilities. His stately face, hair carefully parted down the middle, and impeccable dress and demeanor belied his energy. At thirty-seven, about the same age as the others, he already displayed the combination of pragmatism and idealistic vision, flair for public relations, organizational talent, and belief in cooperation that would later enable him to lead Los Angeles's successful effort to obtain and conduct the 1932 Olympic Games. Garland was fond of quoting Edmund Burke, British statesman-philosopher and, like Garland, a reformer committed to social stability: "Men cannot act with effect unless they act in concert; they cannot act in concert unless they act with confidence; they cannot act with confidence unless they are bound together by common opinions, common affections and common interests."[14] As Garland put it, "zeal, perseverance, cooperation and optimism," if supported by the pride of community accomplishment, could transform the city.[15]

As the streetcars rattled by down below—the very sound to these men of the city's bustling growth and the opportunities in its real estate—Garland's challenge reverberated in the room. If the most established brokers wanted to turn the public trust to their advantage and to that of the city as a whole, how much were they willing to change the way they worked? In an industry known for fierce competition, could they find an ongoing way to cooperate?

Garland turned to Herbert Burdett, a newcomer to Los Angeles he had invited to the meeting. Burdett had run local newspapers in mining towns in Colorado before becoming a publicist for the real estate board in Denver, one of the first in the country.[16] A dark-haired, mustachioed, sharp-featured, sharp-tongued man who hoped to be, and became, the nascent LA board's secretary, Burdett explained not the details, which board members in each city would need to work out, but the concept of a real estate board.

A local board of any type would require major changes in the way its members practiced real estate. Because all members would have to be governed by the same rules of conduct, they would have to give up something all brokers prized—their independence, their freedom to do business as they pleased. Otherwise, any board would fail. Several early boards elsewhere, Burdett had to admit, had already sputtered and fallen apart.

In the lore of California realtors, the meeting in Garland's office became legendary. The Los Angeles Realty Board (LARB) that these men founded a few weeks later ultimately became the largest in the country. Its founders quickly reached out to organize other boards up and down the state, and moved swiftly to help establish both the state association in 1905 and the national association in 1908. Every five years, into the 1950s, as LARB updated its history for its many new members, its recitation began with this small gathering: the turning point in the practice of real estate in Los Angeles, the state, and to some extent the country.

Garland himself became the best-known realtor in America. Renowned for his public vision and service—as colonel on the staff of a reform Republican governor of California, three-time president of LARB, and honorary president of both the California Real Estate Association (CREA) and the state chamber of commerce—he served as the realtors' national president during World War I, organizing the realtors' pro-bono wartime assistance to the federal government.[17] In their own national promotional materials, in the ways they described themselves for the next sixty years, realtors saw in such careers a model, as Garland described LARB itself, of "honor and integrity."[18]

A BOARD OF THE BEST MEN IN REALTY

The principles of a board were basic, Burdett explained. The board would carefully select its members. Only a small number of the most established and reputable firms would be allowed to join. The board would agree on rules all its members would have to follow. Competition among members would be cooperative: no member would undercut another's fee or disparage a fellow member. "Knocking" or disparaging another member would be eliminated.[19] Taken together, these essential features would separate board members from all other real estate men in the city.

Membership on a board "of the best men in realty"[20] would be a guarantee of honesty and, Burdett emphasized, a powerful marketing tool. Highlighting membership on office signs, advertisements, and stationery would tell potential customers that this was a firm one could trust.[21] By limiting the board's initial size to thirty or forty out of several thousand real estate dealers in Los Angeles, members could distinguish themselves not only from sharks who lied to or stole from their clients but, equally important, from less well established dealers who might be tempted to undercut members' commissions or "butt in at the wrong moment with a wise look."[22] Board members' reputations would be elevated. Like lawyers or doctors, they would become members of a respected profession.

For the men in Garland's office, being able to distinguish themselves from other real estate men was as important to their social status as it was to their business reputations. The two were deeply intertwined. As members of Los Angeles's social elite, these men knew that what they did for a living, and the public image of real estate men, directly affected their own status. Garland and the board's other founding officers— Byron Erckenbrecher, LARB's first president; Robert A. Rowan; John D. Foster; and Frederick Flint Jr.—included members of the Jonathan Club, then and now a venue for the leading men of the city, located downstairs in Garland's building and said to be named for his own father.[23] Rowan served as president of the Los Angeles Athletic Club, a post Garland himself later assumed.[24] Garland and others berthed their yachts at the Catalina Yacht Club. Erckenbrecher, president of the Driving Club, raced his trotters against Garland's champion Sweet Marie and was known in society pages for having "inherited money, likewise a love for horseflesh . . . appreciates both and never lets go."[25] All of these men but Garland had inherited significant wealth. Society pages regularly noted their vacations with their wives to "watering places" back East and their presence at society balls, where Garland was a cotillion leader, an "arbiter elegantarium, an exquisite of the exquisites in society."[26]

Far from populists, the men who founded LARB were thus highly committed to social hierarchy—none more so than Garland himself. In a western city whose rapid growth, fluctuating fortunes, surges of newcomers, and western openness jeopardized class barriers, Garland sought to keep such barriers intact. "Introductions are too easily obtained in Los

Angeles," he told the *Herald*'s society editor. "Society is too willing to accept strangers and . . . introduce them without proper inquiry as to their previous condition of life."[27] A local realty board, limited to men they knew, trusted, and felt comfortable with, offered a way to establish and quietly maintain class distinctions in their real estate work.

Membership on a local real estate board would be like owning a seat on a stock exchange, Burdett explained. The very purpose of a board was to be exclusive. In establishing their initial admission criteria, LARB's founders made this idea of class explicit. They deliberately set dues high in the early years, LARB's internal history explained, to exclude less well established dealers.[28] High financial standing, Garland and the others believed, was a minimum, if not sufficient, condition for high morals. Although LARB ultimately lowered its dues and broadened its class criteria,[29] it continued to limit new members to those its members felt socially comfortable with.

Nothing illustrates this class orientation better than the fact that Garland and LARB never criticized the ruses of such pillars of society as Harry Chandler, publisher of the *Los Angeles Times*; General Moses Sherman, founder of Sherman Oaks; and streetcar tycoon E. P. Clark. These dignitaries faked the Sold signs on the Hollywood subdivision, made profits of 60 percent, and used the same techniques to subdivide forty-seven thousand more acres—seventy-three square miles—around Los Angeles.[30]

Instead, Garland attacked agents at the bottom, those without resources: "Our climate brought many people here with little or no means, who, when everything else fails, turn to real estate." Garland made little distinction between "crooks, confidence men and rascals"[31] and anyone willing to work for lower commissions than established brokers, including the one in twenty working men in Los Angeles who tried dealing in real estate whenever they could find a potential buyer or seller to represent. What especially incensed Garland were "curbstoners" who would waylay potential buyers in front of brokers' offices by offering a lower commission "on the principle that 'half a loaf is better than no bread.'"[32] It was to board members' advantage to lump together all those they condemned, using "sharks" and "curbstoners" interchangeably.[33] It was these ne'er-do-wells who had to be restricted. For Garland and his colleagues who formed the Los Angeles board, the best men in real estate meant, and continued to mean, men like themselves.

The board would provide a clear and simple way for the public to know who was reputable: Was the broker a member of the board or not? The public could count on board members for fair dealing because they had, presumably, been carefully vetted for membership and could be ejected for violating the board's internal rules. After setting themselves up as the arbiters of fairness, Burdett explained, board members were unlikely to violate those rules and "risk killing the bird that lays the golden eggs."[34] A local newspaper noted, perhaps sardonically, how hard LARB's founders sought to change the way they were seen: "Organization Formed to Dignify and Uplift the Hustling Brotherhood."[35]

ROYAL TASTE ASPARAGUS

The men at Garland's office sent invitations to fewer than sixty brokers for a follow-up meeting at the Los Angeles County Chamber of Commerce. The aim: to consider a new organization "open only to approved, established real estate brokers and dealers of the best reputation."[36] LARB, like other boards in the country, started from a very small nucleus, choosing whom to invite; and those invitees, in turn, admitted only those they felt most comfortable with.

Garland chose not to preside at the public meeting because his own reputation had come under attack. The charges made front-page headlines. His former clients, the wealthy Crocker family of San Francisco, dramatically sued Garland over his role in selling their downtown Los Angeles parcel. He conceded that he had not disclosed that the nominal buyer was his distant relative, that the actual money for the purchase was ultimately put up by his own father-in-law, and that, when the property was resold a few months later, it was Garland himself who reaped all the upside.[37] The charge that he had deliberately undervalued his client's property weighed on him. When the case was tried, his attorney swayed hometown jurors against the out-of-town Crockers by explaining, "William Garland is a young, active, resourceful business man. The trouble which threatens him is infinitely more than a mere monetary demand. . . . In signing a verdict against Garland . . . you sign the death warrant of his good name in this or any other country."[38] The jury supported Garland, and although the state supreme court ordered a new trial based on Garland's own admissions, the dispute dragged on for years with no final resolution.

His own close call reinforced for Garland and the others the value of having such disputes quietly adjudicated by a local board's internal arbitration committee. The broader implication of Garland's case was that a field with no clear rules or standards was ripe for fraud and charges of fraud. The men who formed real estate boards could take the moral initiative in restoring public trust. As the reformers, they could define the solution, and what and who constituted the problem.

At the public meeting, some raised doubts. Would a group of real estate men, famously independent, stay "together long enough and agree . . . sufficiently to accomplish any good?" Or, conversely, would the board be too strong and interfere with their way of doing business? Would the dues be too expensive? Nonetheless, a majority of the forty attendees voted to create a board.[39] The newspapers dutifully described it as "embracing all known and reputable dealers and brokers"[40] and, publishing the list of firms, helped board members begin to market themselves as separate and apart from all other brokers in the city.

The board added to its ranks, as a category of associate members, many of the city's largest banks, property owners, and title insurance companies. As a result, LARB became, from its inception, the organized real estate industry of the city. The twelve or fifteen brokers who attended almost every meeting in the early years and served on committees became—for the newspapers, public officials, civic organizations, and major property owners—the voice of the industry,[41] the chamber of commerce of real estate. Indeed, the actual Los Angeles County Chamber of Commerce, which hosted LARB's initial meetings, considered the board its partner in helping create stable growth in the city—a close alliance that would last until disagreeing over Proposition 14 itself.

The new board underscored its respectability at its first annual banquet. Together with guests Senator Thomas Bard, Mayor Snyder—another member of the Jonathan Club—and many other notables, the brokers dined on, among other items, "Eastern Oysters on half shell, Bouillon of Fowl en tasse, Broiled Striped Bass maitre de hotel, Potatoes

Parisienne, Timbales of Sweetbreads aux truffles, Roman punch, Royal taste Asparagus, Shredded Crab en Mayonnaise, Camembert Cheese." "To compute the wealth that was represented in the gathering," the *Herald* reported, "was a task that several diners undertook, but failed to agree [on the] . . . millions that each produced."[42]

PROGRESSIVES

Four values were central to LARB and other real estate boards. First, realtors stressed organized cooperation in place of individual greed. "Who first reached the conclusion that man could do more by cooperation than by individual effort? . . . Who first . . . realized that man was not created for himself alone . . . that out of the earth all that shall come must result from cooperation and service to his fellow man? Do we need to answer," realtors asked rhetorically in their national credo, "that this . . . was the first man who decided to make his career one of devotion to real estate?"[43]

Second, real estate had to be organized for the good of the community. More was at stake, early realtors argued, than their own well-being. Allowing every man to pursue only his own interest undermined the future of the community as a whole. Instead, realtors identified their own interests with those of their customers and the public at large. "Individualism must be tempered with due regard for the general welfare. . . . The purpose of business activity is not profit solely, but a service to society," realtor publications soon proclaimed.[44] This belief contained deep contradictions from the start. In establishing themselves as guardians of the public good—in deciding which actions served the community and which represented selfish individualism—realtors naturally did so in the interests of their own future customers, and thus themselves. In seeing themselves as doing well by doing good, and being constantly reminded of this in their publications, realtors naturally saw what was good for the members of their board as being good for society as a whole.

Third, the key to their own success and that of their customers, community, and society, realtors believed, was stability in real estate. In a complex, rapidly changing urban society, buyers wanted predictability for the neighborhood and the city around them. "First and last is the stability of neighborhood," the leading study of realtor values proclaimed.[45] The highest praise realtors could give a city was that it was "a city of stability."[46] Real estate boards were organized to bring "more stability to the real estate market."[47]

Fourth, the key to "the stability and permanence" of an area,[48] realtors believed, was homogeneity of building uses and residents. Realtors would call this "the law of conformity,"[49] a fundamental principle for organizing cities to achieve "an orderly development that will be best for all."[50] And the key to such stability was a clear social hierarchy. While realtors saw themselves as professionals serving the best interests of society, as if outside and above society, early realtors represented a narrow social elite. They believed as much in the law of conformity among their members as in the organization of cities.

The natural result of these values was a positive view of regulation. Realtors were not alone in this view, but saw themselves carrying out in the realm of real estate the progressive spirit of Theodore Roosevelt.[51] Rejecting caveat emptor, let the buyer beware, which justified both the smallest and largest real estate frauds, they invoked Roosevelt's Square Deal to explain why freedom had to be restricted. "Since civilization dawned there have been those who resented restriction and justified their resentment by crying loudly of personal liberty and the rights of men." But, fortunately, they believed, the average Californian had become "an ardent advocate of the Square Deal."[52] The realtors' principle—that freedom had to be limited to create trust, stability, and order—echoed the president's. Almost to a man, early realtors in California identified as progressive Republicans, including eighty-eight of LARB's one hundred leading officials in its first twenty years.[53]

Realtors firmly believed that private rules were essential to gain the public trust and thus serve the public interest. Even before LARB decided on any particular rules, it announced that its key committee would focus on arbitration and grievances, "to punish or weed out any member who may overstep the bounds."[54] Indeed, the board existed in order to have rules. "What the real estate business of Los Angeles has ever needed," Burdett insisted, was "a regulator by which . . . elements of discord could be . . . controlled or adjusted."[55] By separating "the good from the bad practices," realtors would formulate "socially good practices as a standard of conduct" for all members.[56]

As progressives, early realtors believed just as strongly that private rules must be complemented and supported by government regulation. They saw no contradiction, for both served the same end; the common good of realtors depended on serving the public welfare. It was precisely this belief—"that the best practices from the public point of view are also the best from the private point of view," that "regard for the public welfare is good business practice"[57]—that enabled realtors to call their work a "progressive movement."[58] The history of realtors, from the start, was one of turning to government to enforce realtors' vision of proper real estate practice. LARB fully grasped the need for government regulation if their small group—never more than thirty to forty members in the first few years—was to clean up the field as a whole.

Among LARB's first successes was lobbying the city council to prohibit soliciting real estate deals on city streets, thus putting an end to curbstoners. To help eliminate fraud, LARB appointed a committee to look into significant possible swindles, and brought their dossiers to Los Angeles's prosecuting attorney for action. They then joined with him to seek a state law punishing anyone who sold real estate on false pretenses.[59] When LARB was sued for libel for denouncing in full-page advertisements a forty-thousand-lot scheme in the Mojave desert as "a hopeless, barren, desert spot, with no possible excuse for a city," the judge dismissed the developer's case and proclaimed that LARB deserved "the gratitude of the people" of Los Angeles.[60]

LARB soon turned to the much more fundamental solution of state government licensing of all real estate brokers. A state licensing law could impose board members' own standards on everyone in the real estate business. Realtors would no longer be in competition with dealers whose ethical practices they disagreed with. Such dealers would no longer be in business. This had been the key objective of realtors from the beginning, who had divided real estate men into three types. "Type A" brokers were already members or would be welcomed: well established and financially secure enough not to be tempted to cut corners or act selfishly on the next deal in order to stay in business. At the other extreme were the "Type C" brokers, the sharks, in LARB's view, who had to be driven out. The "Type B" brokers, all the rest, would be forced to abide by the same rules as board members. Over time, the best of such brokers would be invited to join. In this way, brokers who belonged to boards, a tiny fraction of all brokers in 1903, would create a highly successful, trusted field whose practices would be based on their own, and whose sales they would dominate. Only by government regulation could they achieve this.

Nor did realtors look to government only to regulate brokers themselves. They turned almost immediately to the idea of government regulating *property owners* for the good of the community as a whole. Within sixty days of its founding, LARB called for a city ordinance to force property owners to clean up vacant lots. The weeds and trash not only menaced public health but detracted from brokers' efforts to sell nearby properties.[61] Once the ordinance was adopted, newspapers headlined the first arrest. LARB's own president cited a nearby boardinghouse janitor dumping garbage on the president's own lot. "Negro Feels Weight of City Ordinance," the news headline ran, citing LARB's role in fingering this "first culprit."[62] LARB cast itself from the beginning as the source and model of social order.

LARB then proposed, more controversially, that the city restrict what could be *built on private property*. LARB helped lead the initiative for a 1906 charter amendment that limited maximum building heights, and then led the charge for Los Angeles to become, in 1908, the first city in the United States to adopt use zoning for residential areas.[63] This innovative ordinance divided the city between industrial and residential districts, and prohibited business uses in residential districts. This proved a major step in the organization of American cities. As the city's prosecuting attorney explained, Los Angeles had taken the lead in "accomplishing the segregation of industries."

Most lawyers had assumed that state and federal constitutions prevented government from imposing such broad restrictions on private property. But the city wanted to support the "business enterprise of real estate operators" creating beautiful residence districts[64] that attracted future growth to Los Angeles. "Necessity," the city's attorney explained, "became the mother of legal invention."[65] When courts upheld the law, new realty boards helped pass similar ordinances in Oakland, Pasadena,

Sacramento, and many other cities.

Board members' successful argument that the public good of the city required restrictions on the freedom of individual owners soon led to more and more powerful zoning ordinances throughout the country. For zoning reflected one of the key insights that boards brought to real estate and that boards' new appraisal committees instituted in new national appraisal standards. The value of a real estate lot was determined only in part by the site or what was built on it; its real value depended on what was or could be built *around it*, on what the neighbors could do. The key unit and source of value was not the site but the neighborhood. Realtors saw in zoning what they would see in racial restrictions: a way to assure the value of one's own lot by controlling the future decisions of everyone nearby.

LARB's efforts at restricting private property in the interest of the neighbors—described as the public interest—did not stop with these early zoning victories. LARB successfully pushed for Los Angeles's comprehensive zoning ordinance in 1921 and for state subdivision rules and planning codes. Zoning and planning regulations became the key legacy of progressivism in the regulation of American cities.[66] Realtors in California and nationally were intensely proud of their role in the creation of zoning. "We helped think up the idea of zoning ordinances," their national organization proclaimed.[67]

Zoning, as realtors designed and promoted it, incorporated a particular belief about cities and change. Ordinances would protect higher-end districts, "good residence neighborhoods," from encroachment, the realtors' national association declared.[68] Ordinances were based on the idea that predictability and stability of real estate could only be achieved through homogeneity within a district—the same principle that realtors would apply to racial restrictions.

In championing zoning and land use laws, realtors shaped not only cities and public policy but their own role in representing property owners, and thus, they asserted, the community as a whole. Any owner who disagreed with these laws—beginning with the brickyard owner who would be put out of business by Los Angeles's retroactive use zoning law and challenged it all the way to the U.S. Supreme Court—was disparaged as a selfish individual, concerned only about his own interests at the expense of those of the community. Realty boards took up the position they would maintain for generations: they were the one organization that represented the best interest of owners, as realty boards defined that interest.

Realtors thus characterized themselves as experts guiding the creation of beneficial order, in line with leading progressive, and later Supreme Court justice, Louis Brandeis's vision of business professionalism. They described themselves as morally minded civic technocrats, concerned for the future progress of society, with "no special interest to serve, no political bias."[69] More than businessmen concerned with mere profit, they were "leaders of larger affairs," men with "lofty conceptions" bringing "system and progress" to real estate. Such men were allocators of land, creators of future cities. "Cities are no longer to grow helter-skelter but are to be guided in their development for the common good," realtor publications proclaimed.[70] The prosperity of cities, like the practice of real estate as a reputable field, would be the province of this new, elevated real estate profession.

To read the speeches and articles of Garland and others after they established local boards is to see the power and excitement of men who had found a way to link their business practices, the success of their firms, the fellowship and common purpose of like-minded men devoted to a single cause, and an idealistic vision of their role and the purpose of their work. Their publications are dotted with such terms as *progressive*, *organized*, *the common good*, and *the good of the community*. In the first year of the *National Real Estate Journal*, 1910, realtors used *progressive* and *progressivism* more than forty times; invoked the common good, public good, or good of the community another forty times; and spoke about organizing real estate thirty times.

By contrast, early realtors rarely mentioned freedom. In an entire year of their national journal, *freedom* or *liberty* appeared five times. Of those, four were part of arguments that freedom *had to be restricted*: for the sake of fair dealing, public policy, preventing fraud, or limiting "freedom from self-seeking."[71] So proud were realtors of limiting the freedom of owners and brokers that by the early 1920s they touted as their greatest accomplishment having "put the state in Real Estate."[72]

Realtors did not see themselves as opposed to freedom, but to the excesses and abuses justified in the name of individual freedom. For freedom to exist, it had to be limited. Freedom was not the starting point but the result of a stable, well-ordered, responsible society in which men did not take unscrupulous advantage of others—the kind of society realtors would create.

Nor did brokers view their efforts at reform as altruistic. Despite their emphasis on public benefit and the improvement of cities, early realtors assured members that the changes they were proposing would aid their own prosperity. Perhaps "it is not complimentary to civilization that reform movements, to be successful, must march under the banner of the dollar sign," Louis Krepleever of Toledo's board explained in the *National Real Estate Journal*. But because "a reform movement founded upon pure altruism must necessarily be of short duration," realtors should proudly acknowledge that "the ideal reform is one which both reforms and pays the reformer. . . . Real estate and reform! It is a happy, dividend-paying combination."[73]

Here was the formula realtors would strive for: "Be good and you will be prosperous, means being good is synonymous with being a reformer, and . . . being a reformer means being prosperous." This advice was proffered to remind brokers not to forget why reform was personally valuable. While the mission of the real estate board included city growth and prosperity, it was above all "to enhance the welfare of the real estate man." "A board's first business," therefore, was "to provide a profit-getting system for its members."[74]

No element of reform was more essential to establishing a secure "profit-getting system for its members" than controlling who would join real estate boards. Progressive reform in real estate depended, in the view of board members, on being an exclusive private club—one that by benefiting its members would enable them to benefit the city as a whole, and in turn enhance their prestige in the community. This virtuous circle would replace the negative one of distrust that reform was designed to overcome. This was the answer Garland had been seeking at the meeting in his office, the way to transform real estate. Real estate boards across the country adopted this approach. Exclusiveness was the path to success.

2.

The Public Power of a Private Club

> The idea seems to prevail throughout the country that when a commercial body is organized it should be accompanied by a campaign to get the largest possible membership. Now, this idea does not apply to . . . a real estate board.
>
> *National Real Estate Journal*, 1911[1]

> A membership committee, whose proceedings and composition will be secret, will guard this organization from the intrusion of any unworthy dealers.
>
> News article on Los Angeles Realty Board, 1903[2]

Two fundamental facts describe what happened to the small, nascent local realty boards of the early 1900s. The first was highly visible. These reform organizations became extraordinarily powerful, both economically and politically. Within twenty years, half of a real estate man's career, boards came to determine how real estate was bought, sold, and developed throughout the country. Local boards effectively became cartels, able to set the terms of trade and double the commissions owners had to pay. Realtors' influence in public policy increased dramatically as well. Governments came to view realtors as the legitimate voice of property owners and the community in general, and relied on them to define and often implement public policy. Secretary of Commerce Herbert Hoover was not exaggerating in 1922 when he told realtors that it had become their role to "stimulate unity of action in the community to more purpose than any other force in the United States."[3]

Yet while taking on such power and responsibility, realty boards remained exclusive clubs. This fact was designed to be invisible. A board's secret membership committee determined who might or might not join.[4] No reasons for rejection were given. Applicants who were acceptable to the committee could be blackballed by any two (or other small number of) members of the entire board, a system that would last for more than sixty years. Realtors did not drop these vetting systems even after they helped pass state licensing laws to screen out unscrupulous brokers. If anything, their private vetting only became more important. The realtor organizations that came to control much of real estate and shape public policy controlled who could join their ranks as carefully as any Masonic lodge.

Realtors saw this combination of highly public roles and tightly approved membership as naturally linked. Their power and influence, their ability to do good on behalf of the community, depended on their being closed organizations. Controls on membership assured that local boards would be filled with morally like-minded men, with similar outlooks on the role of real estate and what was in the community's interest. As spelled out in LARB's charter, realtors believed that their success in every sphere depended on "united effort and concentrated power,"[5] on concentrated unity of purpose.

The combination of public roles and tightly controlled membership also meant that whenever realtors spoke about the good of the community, their vision was a socially narrow one. Realtors were the first to explain that they could never have effectively created and maintained racial segregation if they admitted any minority members.[6] Their ability to shape the common good in the way they wanted depended as much on their membership procedures as on their economic and political power.

THE MARKET POWER OF ORGANIZED REFORM

There are many ways to gauge the economic power that local real estate boards achieved: the percentage of property owned and developed by their members, their share of real estate sales, and the price-fixing and antitrust lawsuits brought against them by federal and state governments.[7] But the simplest measure of market power was boards' ability to dramatically increase how much their members charged. LARB, for example, doubled the schedule of commissions to 5 percent on all residential properties in July 1911—and had the power "to make it stick." Within ninety days, the board could boast that the new "schedule of commissions has been successfully maintained since adoption . . . and is being used" not only by LARB members themselves but by "practically 90% of the realty dealers throughout California." "If the board had accomplished nothing else this year but this new schedule," LARB explained, "this alone would be easily worth the dues of members."[8]

How were local boards, organized by a small minority of brokers and subject to "cutthroat competition," as Garland put it, able to achieve such success? The answer was a quid pro quo that realtors invented. To create controlled competition that could benefit all realtors and provide surer outcomes for customers, realtors instituted a series of fundamental changes that became industry standards.

Realtors insisted on three key things from every seller, none of which were standard practice at the time. First, the listing agreement must be in writing. Second, the listing must be exclusive, ensuring that a seller or competitor could not go around the realtor during the listing period. If the seller chose to do so anyway, he would still legally be required to pay the listing agent's commission. Third, the commission would be a standard, nonnegotiable, fixed percentage of the sale price so that the realtor could not be undercut.

To make their requirements palatable to sellers, realtors assured each seller the widest range of potential buyers through each local board's multiple listing service. This innovation was the key to realtors' success.[9] "If we can say to owners you must sell through some one man or cannot sell through any of the members of the board, we can make [exclusive agency and fixed commissions] stick," the first secretary of their national organization pointed out.[10] As in a stock exchange, each realtor was required to post his seller listings, initially through card files at the office of the local real estate board, and then with duplicates at all members' offices. Every other realtor was assured that if he brought in a buyer who met the seller's terms, he would receive half the commission.

From the seller's point of view, multiple listing meant his property would be available to all the realtors in the city and all the buyers they represented. Here was a way for every seller to know he was getting the widest exposure, the most competition, and likely the highest price for his property. Similarly, a buyer represented by a realtor had access to far more properties than if he worked through any other broker. As realtors put it, multiple listing means "multiplied effort to dispose of the property. It . . . means co-ordinated effort."[11] Multiple listing would compel the public to accept the "Exclusive Agency Contract—the greatest blessing ever devised for the real estate man."[12]

A multiple listing system therefore created its own market. The local board controlled the system, often through a profitable affiliate. The single local board in each city had the sole right to operate a multiple listing system in that area. The only brokers who could use the system were members of the local board. Multiple listing created an enormous marketing edge over other agents. Members could "dictate favorable terms for their services." Although realtors were a small minority of all agents—less than 2 percent of all California licensees in 1920 and 7 percent in 1927[13]—they controlled over 80 percent of all sales in California.

The objective of boards was straightforward. "The board [a member] belonged to would be able to arrogate to itself the entire control of the real estate market and everything pertaining to it." What did "entire control" mean? Ohio's Krepleever explained: "A model board is champion and warden of the commodity it represents . . . in a position to dictate who should participate in the business which it represents; ample power to enforce honest dealings; command the respect of the honest and fear of the dishonest; lend more efficiency to its members and more stability to the real estate market; and . . . looked up to as one of the solid institutions of its community." This was no idle dream. "Every board in the country can elevate itself to this condition if it can overcome the attitude 'where do I get mine' to see the advantage in cooperating."[14]

Market control was possible only by fully carrying out this principle of organized cooperation on which boards had been based in the first place. "The powers of the board . . . have been surrendered by the individuals for the benefits of the whole," Krepleever spelled out. "The greater its supervisory and inquisitorial powers, the greater . . . its success in bringing about ideal conditions for its members."[15] The unified and concentrated power a local board could exercise on behalf of all its members came from each one giving up doing "things in his own way."

In a business with thousands of other dealers, each looking out only for himself, a board had the adhesiveness, power, and efficiency of an army. The principles of reform, applied systematically, enabled the board in each city to dominate the local brokerage market.

MARKETING TRUST

In seeking market control and dramatically increasing their commissions, board members did not see themselves as opposing the interests of the buyers and sellers they represented, but rather as building trust in a field in which it had been almost entirely lacking. Their insistence on honest dealing enabled them to be successful. They created a market in trust and raised their compensation as the price for such trust.

The first step to achieving trust was each local board's establishing rules of conduct for its members. After significant debate within and among boards, including within LARB itself, over whether net listings should be allowed and whether a broker owed fiduciary duty to his client, a national code of ethics was hammered out and adopted by the national association in 1913.[16] Intended to play a similar role to the one recently adopted by the American Bar Association, this second ethics code in the history of business associations would help define real estate as a profession—and would later play a key role in enforcing residential segregation throughout the country. "It shall be as the Ten Commandments to the real estate fraternity," NAREB's president announced.[17]

The code of ethics focused on the real estate man's duty to his clients and colleagues. "The real estate man should be absolutely honest, truthful, faithful and efficient," the code began. He must treat his client as his employer and give him "his best service . . . his information, time, talent, services, loyalty, confidence and fidelity." The code aligned the broker's interest with that of his client. Early boards had not always taken such an approach. Indeed, LARB devoted its first effort in the state legislature to a bill allowing brokers to sue clients over oral agreements, even though some LARB members had personally opposed such a law. But after long debates, boards decided that they were best served if they adhered to their clients' interests. The 1913 code prohibited net listings and required the broker not to act as a principal unless he disclosed this to his client. (Failing to disclose this was precisely what had gotten Garland himself into such trouble with his own client.) The code further spelled out duties to fellow brokers, including giving an honest opinion on a competitor's proposition, even if that meant losing out on the sale.[18] Boards were designed to create a tightly knit community of colleagues.

The code, like that of the American Bar Association, was instituted as a national guideline, and local boards were encouraged to adopt its provisions as far as possible. Some boards resisted giving up net listings, and only in 1924 would the national association make the code mandatory for all boards, at the same moment that the code first required racial discrimination. But even in its earlier incarnation, "The mere existence of the code, adopted and supported by leading successful real estate men in a community, constituted a check upon . . . conduct," not only of board members but of many other brokers as well.[19]

Branding trust as a unique feature of real estate boards increased the value of membership enormously. Charles Chadbourn, a member of the Minneapolis board, thought of the term "realtor" in 1915 after hearing the cries of a "dirty little newsboy screaming the headlines 'Real estate man swindles a poor widow, read all about it.'" Worried that a member of the board might be involved, he quickly bought a paper and was relieved to see that it concerned "only an obscure shyster." Nonetheless, he realized, "every member of our Board was bespattered."[20] He coined the term *realtor* to distinguish board members subject to codes of ethics from all other real estate men. The national association has fought vigorously over the years to maintain the trademarked term. So valuable did this term become that within a few years, local real estate boards were describing it as "the magic wand of real estate men."[21] No sales tool in real estate had ever been as powerful.

ORGANIZING THE ENTIRE REAL ESTATE INDUSTRY

That the reforms, activity, and economic power of realtors extended well beyond individual home and lot sales would make an enormous difference in the history of segregation. Realtors helped create, set standards for, and dominated the fields of appraisal, subdivision and home building, real estate and apartment management, and real estate education and research, over and apart from brokerage of homes and of commercial and agricultural properties. Local boards organized—and remade— each of these fields.

Within a month of its founding, LARB established a committee of its leading members, including Garland, to provide appraisals at what LARB described as "absurdly low fees." Such a service was of great value to banks, major property owners, and others. The low cost and independent expert opinions strengthened LARB's reputation for honesty. Demands for their appraisals steadily increased.[22] Indeed, the LA committee's approach became the national standard, treating the neighborhood and what happened on surrounding properties as the key source of value. This appraisal approach would be seized on by realtors, starting in the early 1920s, to justify excluding other races from living in surrounding properties.

Board members soon dominated development as well. Many of the most important board members in Los Angeles and other cities became the largest subdividers and developers. The national association's Home Builders and Subdividers division, comprising many of the biggest builders in the country, was spun off in 1942 as the National Homebuilders Association.[23] Although realtors are now thought of as simply sales agents for homes, realty boards initially constituted the entire organized real estate industry.

Board members' power in controlling and reshaping all aspects of real estate, including appraisals, development, and apartment management as well as sales, was not a neutral influence. It would ultimately prove crucial to realtors' ability to organize, justify, and maintain residential segregation.

THE POLITICAL POWER OF ORGANIZED REFORM

From their inception, real estate boards came to wield extraordinary political influence on issues involving real estate practice, the interests of property owners, and the development of land and cities. By the early 1920s, few legislative bodies, mayors, governors, or even presidents could afford to ignore boards' potential power in shaping and carrying out public policy. Secretaries of commerce would open realtors' national conventions by describing realtors' importance to the country as a "great moral as well as business force in the nation" if "our form of government is to stand."[24] Realtor leaders would be invited to their own presidential breakfasts at the White House.[25]

The potential for real estate men to play a central role in public issues had long been present. In 1892, the *Buffalo Real Estate and Financial News* had called real estate men "architects of the fortune of cities," since "the real estate broker points out the opportunity and organizes the forces whereby latent energies . . . are transferred into tangible forms of wealth."[26] But as long as real estate men as a whole were seen as sharks by owners, voters, and legislators, they could hardly play a central role in the public arena. Once this cloud was lifted, and established brokers seen as honest reformers working to clean up real estate and cities, organized real estate men became active public spokesmen not only for themselves but for the property interests they represented and for the broader future of cities.

Realtors' moral legitimacy was thus essential to their political power. The selling of real estate, long a byword for smooth-talking operators, began to be celebrated in the *Saturday Evening Post* and other magazines as an appropriate occupation for earnest, honest, ambitious young men whose success would be based on fair service.[27] Instead of being seen as purely self-interested men, the highly organized fraternity of fellow brokers came to be viewed as both independent experts and advocates for the public good. This transformation in their image allowed boards to successfully campaign for the causes most vital to their own future.

LARB's long and arduous campaign for a California licensing law shows how realtors gained the political power they needed to achieve their key initial objective. Their methods, like the law itself, became a model for realtors around the country. Obtaining a licensing law would be a difficult, multistep process. Recognizing that this would require a statewide lobbying effort, Garland and other officers began visiting brokers in cities throughout California as soon as LARB was founded, to encourage them to establish their own local boards. Within a year, boards copying LARB's documents were organized in San Francisco and other cities across the state.

California State Realty Federation, 1905

LARB then took the lead in organizing the California State Realty Federation in 1905, later renamed the California Real Estate Association (CREA), to represent all these local boards. This new state association, the first in the country, flexed its political muscle from the beginning. Its first president pointedly wrote the governor that this new federation could exert "almost irresistible" pressure "for or against proposed legislation in practically every Senatorial and Assembly District."[28] Brokers in each district could reach out to and mobilize property owners, creating a new political force to be reckoned with. Across the state, boards encouraged their members to run for office themselves, not as politicians, but as antipoliticians, concerned with the broader issues of property and community.

Even with all these efforts, it took years to overcome resistance by legislators, governors, and courts to the idea of state licensing. Independent brokers argued, not unreasonably, that the real object of the law was to create a monopoly for local boards; the law would "cut out . . . small real operators by a license fee large enough to drive them out." Indeed, one of the first headlines about the licensing bill spelled this out: "Urge License System to Cut Out Smaller Dealers."[29] The bill first proposed in 1908 passed the legislature in 1913, but was vetoed by the governor. A new governor signed a similar bill in 1917, but the state supreme court held it unconstitutional on grounds of unequal treatment for exempting insurance brokers. Nonetheless, during its months of operation, thousands of real estate men simply dropped out of the business, concerned that they might not comply. Only in 1919 did a revised law go into effect. This was finally upheld by the U.S. Supreme Court in 1922.

California and national realtors viewed their long battle as a fight well worth winning. All licensees were overseen by California's real estate commissioner, who had been a realtor himself. The commissioner described the new department he operated as "created from the mind of the realtor."[30]

The California battle provided a model not only for licensing struggles in every other state but for virtually all the political efforts realtors would conduct. The organization of boards throughout a state and of a statewide association, mobilization of realtors, publicity campaigns, careful cultivation and lobbying of individual legislators, presentation of realtors as working for the public interest, translation of the trust realtors achieved in their business with clients into a broader public trust—these helped realtors in all the public reforms they sought to undertake. For Californians, who would elect a realtor, C. C. Young, as governor in the 1920s, it was easy to see organized realtors—with their local, state, and national bodies; annual election of leaders; commitment to rooting out corruption; news headlines like that after their first national convention, "Realty men band to kill sharks"[31]; and their commitment to community betterment—as a better version of what government itself should be.

LETTING AND NOT LETTING THE BARS DOWN

At the heart of such economic and political power, real estate boards believed, was their ability to carefully control who became members. "The membership should be confined to only those who will subscribe to a rigid agreement," boards were advised. "For when you enter the contest with the public, with the exclusive contract as the prize, you cannot afford to have a single member who is not absolutely dependable." Having a small membership was not a problem, for "the competition [of] those . . . outside . . . would soon be overcome by the selling machine . . . put in motion" by the multiple listing apparatus of the entire board.[32] But even after exclusive contracts became the norm, boards retained these same filters and controls, limiting who they believed was both professionally and socially worthy of being a realtor.

One way of controlling who could join a board was by limiting the size of its membership. Another was by raising the cost to join. Within a year of its founding, as LARB grew to eighty members, it decided to double its membership fee. After all, the board reasoned, given its high standards, there were only a limited number of other firms who would be eligible, and those who "had omitted to make application for membership ought to be required to pay at least as much as had already been paid by the earlier members who had built up the organization."[33] The aim was to remain small and exclusive, "with quality rather than numbers being . . . the keynote of progress."[34]

By 1910, however, LARB decided it no longer needed to be quite as exclusive. "The schedule of commissions had been established and generally adhered to," LARB concluded. "The curbstoner had vanished. People were actually beginning to talk about the 'profession' of real estate." As a result, "sharp practice had been reduced to such an extent that the bars could be let down" to at least some moderate-size firms. The dues were cut by 80 percent to $10, the board organized deliberate recruiting drives, and membership quintupled.[35] By the end of 1911, there were almost four hundred members. By 1912, LARB had become the largest board in the country, three times the size of the next largest, San Francisco. At the realtors' national convention, LARB was asked to explain to other boards how it had been so fruitful.[36]

But while LARB let down the bars to brokers with less financial net worth and social prominence, deeper social barriers remained. Although LARB reluctantly began to admit a few women after twenty years,[37] at no time from its founding until the 1960s did LARB admit a single nonwhite broker among its thousands of members. The very idea seems never to have been considered in the early years. There were African American brokers who might easily have been invited for membership if they were white. One, Hillard Stricklin, had been so successful that he owned a business block downtown.[38] But in the realtors' fraternal order, where members had to cooperate on listings, met at monthly luncheon banquets, and were encouraged to socialize together, racial homogeneity was a given. The reasons for these barriers were not specific to

Los Angeles. By 1960, out of eighty thousand realtors nationwide, not one was African American, despite repeated attempts to join. Indeed, African American brokers had long had to create their own boards, trademark themselves as Realtists, and form their own national organization.

Asked to explain to the California legislature in 1961 this long history of racial exclusion, a key leader of CREA seemed puzzled by the very question. "No, we're not exclusive," he protested, even after describing how LARB refused to allow local African American boards to merge with it. "I suppose," he conceded, "the natural conclusion to draw is that if over years applications have been made and there are none . . . who are of the Negro race, then there must have been discrimination practiced. I suppose that's the only conclusion."[39] Racial exclusion had been so deeply ingrained for sixty years that no formal policy had ever been necessary.

From the beginning, LARB members had been happy to sell homes to minorities in mixed neighborhoods, but the idea of a minority broker becoming a realtor—of sharing the board's multiple listings, selling homes to their customers, joining the board's monthly luncheons, being part of their exclusive club—had never been discussed.

The nature of real estate boards, as all-white private membership bodies with extraordinary economic power and political legitimacy, enabled realtors to segregate American cities. Boards had not been organized in order to establish segregation; this was not why members joined. Nor was it boards themselves that first instituted segregation. Rather, their organization of the real estate industry—their ability to regulate members; their multiple listing system; their dominance in real estate sales, advertising, development, and appraisals; their quasi-official role in the creation of zoning, planning, and real estate licensing; and their work as spokesmen for city development and community interests—provided the necessary infrastructure by which segregation could become widespread and systematic. Remaining strictly all-white decades after other trade organizations such as the American Bar Association finally began to admit minorities,[40] real estate boards made sure that no minority broker could ever access their multiple listings to sell homes in white neighborhoods to nonwhite buyers. Organized segregation could not have been created until realtors organized the real estate industry itself.

Moreover, the homeowner associations that early realtors established to enforce segregation resembled in all their features—their racial exclusion, membership policies, clearly defined geographic boundaries, and ongoing control over the actions and freedom of their members—local real estate boards themselves. For the same ways of thinking that led to real estate boards—beliefs in organization, racial and social homogeneity, the "law of conformity" in real estate, and sacrificing individual independence for the good of the group—quickly led key board members, innovators who would become widely celebrated and imitated in the industry, to create residential segregation.

3.

It's the Restrictions on Your Neighbors Which Count

> The most comprehensive restrictions of any district in Los Angeles . . . the ONLY ONE where BEAUTY, DISTINCTION AND ORDER can be maintained PERMANENTLY.
>
> Advertisement for Leimert Park, 1920s[1]

> We have been surrounded by invisible walls of steel. The whites surrounded us and made it impossible to go beyond these walls.
>
> An African American in Los Angeles, 1917[2]

Widespread and systematic racial segregation did not exist in Northern cities when realty boards were first organized in the early 1900s. It was the actions of board members that made residential segregation possible. Indeed, the system of segregation that organized brokers created shortly after boards were founded became so ubiquitous that racially divided neighborhoods became taken for granted as if they had always existed.

The reality at the start of the twentieth century in cities like Los Angeles was quite different. A Black real estate agent proudly stated in 1904 that "the Negroes of this city" were not segregated "into any locality but have scattered and purchased homes in sections occupied by wealthy, cultured White people, thus not only securing the best fire, water and police protection but also the benefits that accrue from refined and cultured surroundings." If most African Americans, Japanese, and Mexican Americans lived in the poorer areas of the city, these were racially mixed and dispersed as well.[3] Where one could live depended on where one could afford, not on one's ancestry.

What was true of Los Angeles was true more broadly throughout the country. African Americans lived in many if not most neighborhoods of Northern and Western cities and were rarely more than a third of the population of their immediate area.[4] In border cities, too, with larger African American populations—such as Baltimore, Washington, DC, Louisville, and St. Louis—many blocks were racially mixed. Looking farther south, studies show that, at the beginning of the twentieth century, cities in the South as well as the West were the least geographically segregated in the country.[5] Although, or perhaps because, social barriers in the South were so high, African Americans often lived in the same neighborhoods as whites, in many cases on the same blocks[6] or on side streets or in scattered neighborhoods[7] throughout a city. Nationally, the spatial proximity of the races "most distinguishes" cities in that era from what they became a century later.[8]

The lack of residential segregation did not mean there was no racial prejudice. Job discrimination was common; African Americans typically had to create their own businesses if they were to become other than laborers or domestics. To prevent mixed marriages, California passed a 1907 law denying a license for a white person "with a negro, mulatto or Mongolian."[9] Hostility toward Asians in California was especially intense. News articles expounded against competition by Asian immigrants: "The white man's physical construction will not permit him to be a hunkerer and . . . compete with the laborious, squatting Oriental."[10] Los Angeles's leaders sought white immigration, envisioning Southern California as the ideal home for the white race. Despite California having one of the first laws prohibiting discrimination in restaurants and hotels,[11] in 1912 Los Angeles's city attorney upheld a saloon charging an African American businessman twenty times as much for a beer as his white companion.[12] On occasion, a Black family moving into a white neighborhood in Los Angeles had to fend off an unfriendly group of neighbors by pointing a gun at the crowd.[13] Yet despite such prejudice, African Americans in Los Angeles paid the same prices for housing as whites and participated in the same housing market.

Within a decade and a half of the establishment of realty boards, however, residential racial segregation had become the norm in Los Angeles and cities throughout the country. It did not matter if there were minority buyers and renters who had the money to pay for housing in most neighborhoods. When it came to housing, their money no longer had the same value as whites'—a change that transformed neighborhoods, housing conditions, investment patterns, social lives, and economic opportunities for both white and nonwhite Americans for generations to come. No change in American cities proved more profound or more enduring.

SEGREGATION MYTHS

Many myths have been promulgated about the causes of residential segregation. Real estate boards would claim into the 1960s and long beyond that such segregation was natural. Their argument—that African Americans clustered in preponderantly African American neighborhoods by choice or simply because they could not afford to live elsewhere—disregarded virtually all independent analyses. As Karl and Alma Taeuber, the leading sociologists of residential segregation, described in their detailed 1965 study *Negroes in Cities*:

> Neither free choice nor poverty is a sufficient explanation for the universally high degree of segregation in American cities. Discrimination is the principal cause of Negro residential segregation, and [there is] no basis for anticipating major changes in the segregated character of American cities until patterns of housing discrimination can be altered.[14]

At every income level, African Americans have been half as likely to live in suburbs as white Americans. If income differences did not explain this,[15] neither did individual preferences in an open market. As the U.S. Commission on Civil Rights concluded in 1960: "Segregated housing patterns cannot be explained away by the attitudes and decisions of individual families—of white families who are 'prejudiced' . . . or of black families. . . . [Rather,] powerful institutional forces [were] involved."[16] Nothing dispels the realtors' arguments that segregation was natural as much as the realtors' own extraordinary efforts to maintain it.

The most important myth realtors created was that Americans have always lived in racially exclusive neighborhoods. So pervasive did this idea become that, by 1948, leading housing expert Robert Weaver had to remind fellow African Americans that the past had been very different. "Few Americans realize that widespread, enforced residential segregation is relatively new in the North. . . . Negroes themselves . . . sometimes forget that their ancestors and older friends were not always hemmed into too little space in the North."[17]

But if systematic, widespread racial exclusion was a twentieth-century invention of the realtor movement itself,[18] there is no evidence that realtors were any more—or less—racially prejudiced than other members of their communities.[19] Nor were realtors' exclusionary practices, especially in California, initially established to target or focus on African Americans.[20] LARB did not begin with a plan to deliberately confine minorities to a particular area. Nor was residential segregation first created in response to waves of African Americans moving to Northern cities for the jobs created during World War I. To understand how and why residential segregation began, one needs to look not to grand schemes or sudden upsurges of racial hostility but to a land development dilemma facing innovative early realtors.

UNCERTAINTY IN LAND DEVELOPMENT

No part of the real estate business at the beginning of the twentieth century was more anarchic, unstable, or subject to fraud than land development. A buyer of an existing home could inspect the structure, see how the surroundings had been developed and who the neighbors were, ensure there were utilities and passable streets, and picture how the neighborhood might look in five or ten years. By contrast, a potential buyer of a lot in a newer part of the city knew and could know none of these things. "Until the beginning of the twentieth century," a leading historian of American development explains, "land had simply been carved . . . into building lots and sold for whatever use the new owners intended. Subdividing land exclusively for residential use presupposed a level of planning and control" that rarely existed.[21] The norm was something else entirely.

For both land developers and buyers, subdivisions were often dreams recorded at the county's record of deeds rather than realities. A subdivider in Los Angeles—meaning practically anyone with access to a little capital—would usually purchase a field, divide it into lots, lay out streets, at least on paper, and advertise for buyers. Salesmen would drum up customers on a downtown corner. Buying a lot in such a subdivision was buying a possibility more than an actuality. Typical subdivisions had no streets of completed homes to purchase, nor did the buyer purchase a lot on which the developer would construct a home. Until realtors helped design long-term government-insured financing in the 1930s, there were no large-scale home builders, only contractors who might help put up a few homes a year on customers' own lots. It was up to the purchaser to find a way to buy the lot itself, often with 10 percent down; pay the rest to the subdivider over years; and then find a contractor or build the house himself. Construction would often be done in stages as money allowed, in ways typical of much of the less developed world today. The formerly bucolic setting would often be dotted for years with tents, shacks, or half-completed homes where buyers lived temporarily.

Such a scenario was in fact the best case. Because there were no limits on the subdivision of land, far more lots were laid out than could ever be absorbed. By the 1920s, in Los Angeles with one million people, lots had been laid out for a city of seven million. Subdividers often ran out of the funds to complete the promised streets and infrastructure. Buyers defaulted on their lot installment payments or were left with worthless property. All these problems undermined the value of real estate in neighborhood after neighborhood.

THE VALUE OF CONTROL

To respond to this problem of infrastructure that never got built, real estate boards began pressing for subdivision regulations, performance guarantees, and bonds to ensure provision of infrastructure. At the same time, some of the better-capitalized and most prominent realtors, the ones in the forefront of such planning efforts, saw the value that could be realized if they could create developments that delivered on their marketing promises. They went into the subdivision business themselves, but in a very different way than most land developers, by setting high standards for attractive, beautifully landscaped subdivisions for wealthy buyers. These realtors sought to extend to the development business the reputation for honesty and performance that realtors had begun to earn in sales of existing property.

The most farsighted of these realtor-developers, including Duncan McDuffie (1877–1951) in the Bay Area and J. C. Nichols (1880–1950) in Kansas City, in seeking to create high-end subdivisions, realized there was a still more fundamental problem they needed to solve: how to ensure they would recover the costs of their investment in such expensive infrastructure.

The success of high-end developments depended, in McDuffie's words, on giving "the entire property the appearance of a park or private estate."[22] Such an approach to land development was not only more enlightened but potentially far more profitable. "Ignorance, not avarice, scarred the hills of San Francisco with its gridiron of streets. . . . Contour streets would have produced not only a better plan but a larger profit."[23] Nichols, inspired during a 1901 bicycle trip of Europe by "the stability, beauty, charm and orderliness of the villages and cities as compared with American communities," identified the same profit potential from landscaped, curving streets.[24]

But creating a residence park required far more of an initial outlay than simply recording a subdivision map for a typical development.[25] The only way to ultimately recoup such a major investment—in land assembly, landscape architecture, and infrastructure—was by selling the final lots, years later, at prices that had retained or increased in value. But how could such a developer maintain the quality, reputation, and attractiveness of a subdivision whose lots he had sold off over time?

In a world without zoning or development controls of any type, lot owners might erect an eyesore or a cheap home; build an apartment house or tenement; or open a liquor store, factory, or dyeing works.[26] This was not only possible but commonplace. Go into the part of any city "that was ultra-fashionable a dozen . . . years ago," Nichols warned. "There you will find mansions turned into boarding houses . . . or razed for offices and store(s); . . . their value destroyed by . . . shops, undertaking parlors and the like."[27] The more upscale the development, the greater the opportunity for values to deteriorate. Without any certainty as to what would happen on *the other lots*, the buyer's purchase and the developer's long-term investment in the subdivision as a whole could easily become worthless. The problem McDuffie and Nichols confronted was the problem of control.

For if McDuffie and Nichols were visionaries, they were highly pragmatic ones. On the surface they seemed quite unalike. McDuffie was six-foot-four, a mountaineer, avid hiker, and early leader and for many years president of the Sierra Club and chair of the Save the Redwoods League; his interest in preserving and integrating nature with development in the Berkeley Hills came from six-week outings in the Sierra. Nichols—chain-smoking, gregarious, round-faced with round spectacles—beautified his developments with statues and fountains like those of the Old World cities he loved, and he enjoyed nothing more, on free evenings, than chatting with members of the homeowners' associations he had established. McDuffie was a progressive Republican, while Nichols allied himself with Kansas City's Pendergast Democratic machine.

But their orientation to business and to development planning was very similar. Each recognized that upper-middle-class and upper-class families would pay for future certainty, for knowing that where they built their home would remain, in Nichols's words, "a quiet residential street where children could take their naps in the afternoon" or, as McDuffie put it, for the "happy healthy growth of his children—out of doors! Out of doors!"[28] Two thousand miles apart, each was selling a dream that would last. Nichols called it "planning for permanence." The brilliance of their idea was that buyers would pay up for the same future assurance that would safeguard the developer's own long-term investment. The question was how to achieve—and market—such control.

The answer McDuffie and Nichols each devised in 1905 and that quickly became a national model was to couple high-end land development with restrictive covenants. Covenants were deed restrictions each lot buyer signed to limit what he—or any successor—could do with the property. Covenants primarily focused on building and land use: the minimum cost or square footage of the home the buyer could erect, the required setback from the street, allowable building styles, and prohibitions

Left: Duncan McDuffie of Berkeley *Right:* Advertisement for Claremont Court, Berkeley, 1907

on commercial uses. Both McDuffie and Nichols modeled their covenants on what each saw as the premier subdivision in the country, Roland Park, outside Baltimore. Roland Park had been created in the early 1890s with elaborate landscaping by the Olmstead Brothers, the nation's leading landscape architects.[29] McDuffie and Nichols sought to create the same kind of tree-lined, controlled, park-like setting; they assembled large tracts that could be set off from the rest of the city, consulted with the Olmstead Brothers, and drew on the Maryland subdivision's system of development controls, considered the most extensive in the country.

But to Roland Park's list of covenants, McDuffie and Nichols added one more, as extra assurance for buyers seeking a permanent high-quality exclusive neighborhood. "Only persons of the Caucasian race . . . except servants" could live there. McDuffie began recording such covenants in Claremont Park in Berkeley in 1905[30] and a few years later in St. Francis Wood in San Francisco, soon considered "the most distinguished residential suburb in America."[31] Such restrictions were a crucial "shield," McDuffie explained, "permanently protecting . . . homes and stabilizing and increasing . . . land values. . . . They deny entrance to undesirable neighbors and . . . inharmonious houses."[32] Racial exclusiveness provided a sign of permanence, stability, and harmony. For these same reasons, Nichols began recording racial covenants on Country Club Estates in Kansas City in 1906. Vastly expanding its area, he soon touted the Country Club district as "1000 acres restricted," "the most protected and highest class region" of Kansas City and "the largest high-class restricted residential development under one management in the world."[33]

The key to McDuffie's and Nichols's success was convincing American buyers to accept restrictions on the land they were purchasing. This was not necessarily easy. To many potential buyers, giving other parties the right to control what one could build on one's own lot seemed novel, un-American, and a violation of the very idea of private property. It meant giving up their freedom to use their own land as they wanted. When Roland Park first began selling "restricted land" in the mid-1890s, "salesmen . . . describing the advantages of these restrictions, were met with the comment, 'when I have bought and paid for a lot, I do not understand why you retain such control that I cannot make use of it as I see fit.'"[34] The answer was to market to the buyer's fear of what might happen next door. "The restrictions applying to your own lot mean little to you," Nichols insisted; "it is the restrictions on your neighbor's lot which count."[35] Instead of having difficulty selling property with restrictions, Nichols soon found he could not sell without them. Fear of what a neighbor might do or whom he might sell to trumped restrictions on one's own freedom.

But why did these developers believe racial covenants were essential? McDuffie's were not aimed particularly at African Americans, a tiny minority in the Bay Area at the time, nor at the small number of recent Japanese immigrants. There was little likelihood they could afford these very expensive lots. Rather, restricting such subdivisions to "Caucasians," like setting a minimum building cost, assured each buyer that he was investing in a long-term luxury neighborhood. The wealthy owner, his wife and children would be surrounded only by their own kind. This assurance, backed up in writing, was an extra sales feature that cost the developer nothing.

Crucially, McDuffie and Nichols standardized the mechanisms that made it easy to enforce and perpetuate covenants. Rather than putting the burden on individual owners to have to sue a neighbor, or requiring the developer to remain involved, they created the first homeowners' associations. Collecting fees from all owners, this ongoing organization would act on behalf of the owners as a whole. Because courts might be reluctant to approve perpetual covenants and conditions might change, McDuffie and Nichols made covenants automatically self-renewing after an initial twenty- or thirty-year period—unless the majority of the asso-

Left: Country Club District, Kansas City, 1912 *Right:* J. C. Nichols of Kansas City

ciation voted to terminate them. The developments they created could thus be perpetually racially restricted.

The developers strictly enforced these racial covenants. When two sisters petitioned to teach students in their Claremont home, McDuffie carefully amended their deed, permitting a school on condition that "no children of African, Mongolian or Asiatic descent shall be admitted."[36]

Nor was McDuffie's concern about protecting his subdivisions limited to his own property. To control adjoining neighborhoods, in 1916 he led Berkeley's effort to adopt the first zoning of single-family districts. Expedited to stop a "prominent negro dance hall" from locating in the Elmwood District adjacent to Claremont Park, this ordinance pioneered single-family zoning in the country.[37] The aim was not to zone the entire city but to further protect high-end residential neighborhoods. McDuffie then promoted similar ordinances in San Francisco and nationally. Like homeowners' associations, single-family zoning began as a way to complement racial covenants.

McDuffie and Nichols became two of the most influential, and honored, realtors in the country.[38] The success of Claremont Park and St. Francis Wood helped make Mason-McDuffie the largest real estate sales and development company in Northern California. McDuffie's developments, limited to "persons of pure Caucasian blood," ultimately accommodated one hundred thousand Bay Area residents. In 1935, Berkeley's mayor extolled McDuffie's work as a model for new neighborhoods across America and a testament to "the progressive character of the people of this country."[39] The University of California, Berkeley, gave him an honorary doctorate for his work in residential development. McDuffie was a prominent member of the state's business and government establishment; his close associate and longtime realtor at Mason-McDuffie, C. C. Young, was speaker of the state assembly by 1913, then lieutenant governor and governor. McDuffie chaired Berkeley's first city planning board, led efforts to establish city planning in California and establish the state's park system, and has a thirteen-thousand-foot mountain named after him.[40]

Nichols became a legendary figure for realtors nationally. His 1912 national convention speech detailing his approach to development was a landmark in realtor history; his rules for developing subdivisions became the standard for developers throughout the country and were adopted by the federal government. Seven-time president of the Kansas City Real Estate Board, Nichols served with McDuffie on the realtors' national committee on city planning;[41] chaired the realtors' home builders and subdividers division, now the National Association of Home Builders; and led the realtors' national efforts in World War II. Revered as America's highest-quality developer,[42] he was honored in 2000 by the Urban Land Institute, the leading national organization for public-private development. For the first two decades of the twenty-first century, the institute's highest award was the J. C. Nichols Prize for Visionaries in Urban Development.[43] Only in 2020 was his name removed. Later the same year, the *Kansas City Star*—in its extraordinary front-page apology for having "disenfranchised, ignored and scorned generations of Black Kansas Citians"—singled out its effusive coverage and support for J. C. Nichols.[44]

THE COVENANT SYSTEM

McDuffie's and Nichols's use of racial covenants was nationally touted, and their approach quickly came to serve as the model for high-end developments. Many of these were in Los Angeles, including Beverly Crest, "permanently restricted for particular people"; Beverly Hills; Bel-Air, "the Exclusive Residential Park of the West";[45] and Hillhurst Park, LA's "largest high-class subdivision."[46]

Realtor-developers of middle-class subdivisions almost immediately began to adopt this same approach. Nowhere were racial covenants employed more extensively than in Los Angeles. Harry Culver used them in creating Culver City out of a two-hundred-acre barley field and went on to become president by turns of LARB, CREA, and the national association, NAREB. Guy Rush, celebrated by CREA as "one of the best-known subdivision experts on the Pacific Coast," imposed racial restrictions in Seal Beach and Hawthorne, while Lawrence Burck, vice president of LARB, established permanent "iron-clad race restrictions" south of Exposition Park.[47]

Racial restrictions soon filtered down to working-class subdivisions, too. These tracts established few building restrictions or amenities, but, because nonwhites might have been more likely to purchase here, stressed racial restrictions in their advertisements. Subdivision after subdivision—Eastmont, City Terrace, St. Francis in Highland Park, the new city of Torrance created by LARB leader Thomas Campbell—advertised "moderate building restrictions" and "permanent race restrictions" to protect "the working man."[48] If high-end subdivisions created park-like settings to foster the sense that the buyer was purchasing a private estate otherwise beyond his means,[49] the simpler, purely racial restrictions on lower-end subdivisions fostered the buyer's sense that was he and his family were purchasing not only a plot of land but membership in a permanent all-white club.

Racial covenants reflected a deeper, more fundamental realtor belief. A neighborhood would only be successful in the long run if it was socially homogeneous. Subdivisions were designed to be not only racially exclusive but for a single economic class. Realtors made homogeneity a cardinal principle of real estate for decades to come, and a key justification for racial segregation.

By 1913, racial restrictions on new subdivisions had become so widespread that the Los Angeles Housing Commission lamented that Mexican Americans could secure housing if "restrictions were not placed upon every new tract of land where lots are sold."[50] By the early 1920s, when Los Angeles's greatest building boom took off, adding fourteen hundred subdivisions in two years,[51] racial restrictions were standard. When the 1922 promotional literature for Palos Verdes Estates declared that "there are the usual restrictions prohibiting Negroes, Asiatics and people other than the white or Caucasian race, except in the capacity of domestic servants," the word "usual" was telling.[52] One of the largest subdividers of all, the Janss Company, used racial covenants on over one hundred thousand acres in Southern California for both working-class and middle-class homes.[53] That virtually all new housing, even the lowest cost, was limited to "Caucasians only" had a profound impact on the housing choices, prices, and conditions of everyone who was excluded: Mexican Americans, Asian Americans, African Americans, and many other groups, including Jews, Italians, Greeks, Slavs, and Turks.

As the fastest-growing real estate market in the country, Los Angeles provided a national model. Restricted subdivisions would soon come to dominate the new development market not only in Los Angeles but in cities throughout California[54] and the country. Housing expert Charles Abrams only slightly exaggerated when he wrote that "no subdivision in California is without its covenant barring one race or another."[55] In the burgeoning field of racial covenants, California was the leader. In a 1927 survey, NAREB found that nine out of ten California subdivisions restricted occupancy to Caucasians, compared to only four out of ten subdivisions elsewhere.[56]

Beyond individual new subdivisions, Los Angeles was the leading innovator in imposing racial restrictions on an even broader scale. LARB's members applied covenants both to whole new suburbs and to existing neighborhoods. Together these provided powerful racial controls across much of the metropolitan area.

Major realtor-developers and local officials worked together to ensure that all the subdivisions in entire new cities were covenanted so that no non-Caucasians could ever live in the city at all. A *Los Angeles Times* ad for Eagle Rock, a city near Glendale, boasted in 1925, "Why is EVERYONE talking about Eagle Rock? As you journey about Eagle Rock enjoying . . . the ideal climate that is ours, you will observe that the residents of Eagle Rock are all of the *white* race." How had this been accomplished? Neighborhood associations have "insured the future beauty of our homes and the character of our associates by Building and Race Restrictions."[57] In Glendale in 1914, only one African American owned property, and virtually all properties had covenants.[58] On the opposite side of the metropolitan area, a vast swathe of new suburbs of 650,000 people by 1930 was 0.25 percent African American.[59] "Under the pleasant fiction that" covenants were simply individual "private contracts," an opponent of covenants wrote in 1946, "entire cities can be, and are, closed to Negro use and occupancy."[60]

Effective as suburb-wide exclusion proved to be, the most important use of racial restrictions was in the realtors' approach for existing neighborhoods. The possibility of racial exclusion spread quickly from subdividers to fellow realtors selling homes in older areas. If, as social critic Mike Davis succinctly puts it, neighborhood covenants "were the children of deed restrictions in . . . planned subdivision[s],"[61] they took far more work to give birth to.

Thus, in Pasadena, a city African Americans had lived in since it was founded, realtors sought to limit neighborhoods they could move to. After drafting a covenant limited only to race—since other restrictions could not apply to existing homes—the realty board organized neighborhood associations. Realtors, association members, and ultimately private contractors went door to door, asking owners to voluntarily enter into mutually enforceable race restrictions. These restrictions would go into effect when 75 percent of the owners in the neighborhood had signed. Once the requisite number of covenants had been recorded, if an owner or any subsequent owner ignored the covenant on his own home and sold to a minority—even decades later—any neighbor could sue to evict the new minority owner. This approach, the local realty president acknowledged, was a "laborious method, but it seems to secure the results."[62] Known as the Covenant Plan, Pasadena's approach became standard in neighborhoods throughout the state.

Because of the effort involved, there usually had to be an urgent reason to motivate all the parties. Because minorities, crowded into the few neighborhoods they could still live in, constantly looked for places to move to, realtors explained to white owners that their neighborhoods were vulnerable. To Pasadena owners, they pointed out that almost all the surrounding communities—Glendale, Eagle Rock, South Pasadena, San Marino, and Arcadia—already prevented any African Americans from moving there. "Study Glendale's rules for Negroes," realtors told Pasadena residents; "no Negroes live there."[63] If nearby neighborhoods were restricted, it became even more essential to protect one's own. Moreover, because covenants in existing neighborhoods were generally not self-perpetuating, drives had to be launched to renew them when they expired. In Pasadena, realtors took charge of this effort to prevent "infiltration," collecting funds on a proportionate basis from Bank of America and other banks doing business in the city.[64] The Pasadena Realty Board described its formula to other communities: coordinating its own members, "lenders, the chamber of commerce, the merchants association and planning commission" to designate "certain portions of the community . . . as most suitable for the residence of nonwhites . . . where they and their children would be more . . . happy than in an all-white neighborhood."[65]

African Americans in Pasadena hardly thought this plan was to benefit them. Some had lived in the city for many years, and watched as white newcomers circulated covenant petitions to prevent them from moving nearby. They might have no special ambition to live among whites, they explained to a sociologist studying race relations, but wanted, like anyone else, to be able to choose where to live. A young African American put it bluntly: "Pasadena Whites should awaken to the realization that THEY are creating a minority problem!"[66] Being forced to grimly accept these restrictions was not the same as their being, in one white respondent's words, "happy and satisfied as long as they stay in their place."[67] The purpose of the Covenant Plan was that they have no say in the matter.

The spirit of the Covenant Plan, like that of subdivision restrictions, was to restrict individual freedom—both of white owners and of African American buyers and renters—for an idea of social order. "Can we not bring ourselves to think in terms of the community rather than entirely of individual enterprise," an article in *California Real Estate* magazine urged, "and breathe into the community life the same sense of order . . .?"[68] Realtors had taken on that responsibility and defined who constituted that community.

CREATING THE DEMAND FOR EXCLUSION

What drove the demand for covenants and racial exclusion? In the long battle over segregation and fair housing, realtors consistently argued that prejudice existed in society and that they were simply serving the market as they found it. "Nothing can be done to remove racial prejudice," CREA's magazine advised, "so the realtor should use it as a talking point in his sale because 9 people out of 10 would prefer to be in a neighborhood surrounded by their own race."[69] The history of racial covenants' spread in Los Angeles suggests a more complex reality. The realtors' covenant system required, indeed insisted on, racial prejudice. Every minority person had to be treated by every owner in a neighborhood as racially undesirable. Any owner who did not act in a prejudiced way would be sued by his neighbors. No system could be better designed to constantly stimulate and reinforce prejudice.

Although realtors continually inflamed that prejudice, they were hardly its original source. Covenants, as a tool for marketing lots in a few subdivisions, could only have spread so rapidly because they proved attractive to white buyers and owners. Realtors helped arrange an ever-increasing *supply* of covenanted property, but what drove the *demand* for exclusion, a possibility of urban living that had never previously existed? What made this new idea of living in a racially exclusive area so compelling that, in booming Los Angeles with a total minority population of 4 percent,[70] racial exclusion became first a luxury and then a necessity?

While many of Los Angeles's leaders at the beginning of the 1900s—at newspapers, universities, businesses, and local government—had actively promoted Southern California as an ideal home for the white race, and the chamber of commerce actively promoted white immigration,[71] such white boosterism coexisted with another reality. Japanese and African American immigrants had both found early 1900s Los Angeles an unusually open place to build ordinary and, in many cases, middle-class lives. Black boosters promoted the city with the same enthusiasm as their white counterparts.[72] W.E.B. DuBois, after each of his visits, lauded in NAACP's *The Crisis* how attractive Los Angeles was for African Americans and how they had better housing here than anywhere else.[73] The African American homeownership rate was by far the highest in the nation at 40 percent, and in some areas, such as Santa Monica and Pasadena, approached 90 percent.[74] The spaciousness of Los Angeles and the ease with which minorities could expand with the city itself—rather than being concentrated in a single section known for their living there—initially made it easier for minorities to create a life on their own terms.[75]

But the same features of Los Angeles that made it potentially easier for minorities to be left alone—the city's space, a more relaxed life in a beautiful climate, less competition for industrial jobs—also made racial exclusion more compelling for the white immigrants who were drawn to Los Angeles. White newcomers came, by and large, not from Europe or Eastern cities, but from small towns or rural areas, often from the Midwest, and had adequate means. They were drawn to Southern California, the chamber of commerce learned in having to adjust its early publicity campaigns, not by the prospect of farming in the attractive climate or for economic reasons at all. They were drawn by the idea of "an easier . . . well-rounded life,"[76] a place of attractive streets and residential areas[77]—"a city without tenements, a city without slums," as a popular local minister and booster proclaimed.

Realtors, city officials, promoters, streetcar line operators, and businessmen, recognizing that continued growth depended on the spread-out layout, consciously sought to "ruralize the city; urbanize the country."[78] Realtors had pushed the 1908 use zoning ordinance to assure newcomers that "the city would continue to be a spacious residential paradise of fine homes and quiet, clean surroundings."[79] Los Angeles's design was not the product of economic growth, as in most other major cities, but a way to appeal to newcomers from small towns and rural areas. Its subdivisions were indeed its key marketing feature.

What these white American in-migrants sought in these subdivisions was as much social as physical.[80] These newcomers wanted residential areas that would serve as a sanctuary from "demoralizing metropolitanism,"[81] sift out the undesirable elements of big-city life,[82] and re-create the fellow feeling of the small towns they had left behind.[83] The subdivisions of Los Angeles, in others words, would provide a refuge from the vast, rapidly growing metropolis these in-migrants were quickly creating. Dana Bartlett, social gospel minister and reformer, glorified Los Angeles's subdivisions as "far from the noisy city," a place of "only healthy, happy families."[84]

Racial restrictions reinforced that dream. They promised homogeneity, harmony, and common identity in a city where newcomers lacked shared traditions and ethnic ties; they promised permanence in a city where families changed homes more frequently than anywhere else; they offered a sense of belonging based simply on not being excluded. The first restricted tracts generated demand not only for those particular lots but for exclusion itself. Realtors both tapped a demand for racial exclusion and continually generated one. So rapidly did racial restrictions spread that the African American publisher of the *California Eagle* warned her readers, in a headline on the existence of eighty-one white home improvement and protective associations, "Are You Sleeping?"[85] Almost overnight, it seemed, a new kind of city had been created in which the 2 percent of residents who were African American became people white newcomers were constantly told they had to avoid living next to.

The more Los Angeles grew, as it quintupled in population from 1900 to 1920, and the more tracts developers built, the greater the demand for covenants became. Covenanted subdivisions were marketed as a refuge not only from other races but also from the anonymity and vastness of change that growth itself created. A 1924 advertisement captured this appeal:

> You who have seen the fine residential districts of Los Angeles despoiled by metropolitan development. . . . Protect your family by procuring a home place in the Hills of Hollywoodland— secured by fixed and natural restrictions against the inroads of metropolitanism and yet within 25 minutes of Seventh & Broadway. . . . Are you going to sit idly by and let the March of Progress pass unheeded?[86]

The tract's promoters understood the paradox that drove the city's growth: progress was desirable, and one should be part of its march, while being insulated from its unsettling change.

Thus, the more the city grew, the more desirable it became to avoid the perils of growth. Metropolitanism represented everything native-born white immigrants had chosen to avoid when they moved to Los Angeles rather than Chicago or cities back East: full-throttle commerce, immorality, tenements and slums, minorities of every type. Racial minorities, even if only a small number in Los Angeles, embodied all of this in a city that had few foreign-born European immigrants. The more areas minorities were excluded from, the more that such minorities came to represent what must, at all costs and with realtors' help, be avoided. James Baldwin described what it meant to embody metropolitanism: "What it means to be a Negro in this country is that you represent, you are the receptacle of, you are the vehicle of, all the pain, disaster, sorrow, which white Americans believe they can escape. That is what is . . . really meant by keeping a Negro in his place."[87] Covenants were marketed as a way to escape what racial minorities represented.

Minorities thus had to be excluded from Los Angeles subdivisions not because they would disrupt long-standing community traditions or compete for scarce housing or because great numbers were suddenly arriving in the city—issues that drove segregation in Chicago during and after World War 1. Rather, minorities, however few, would disrupt the citywide ideal of suburban living that Los Angeles pioneered. This ideal, incorporated by realtors into thousands of subdivisions and hundreds of neighborhoods, created places to live defined by who could not live there.

This ideal became so important to realtors not only in Los Angeles but nationally because of what realtors believed they were selling. "We do not sell real estate," a leading California realtor reminded his colleagues.

> A piece of real estate, as a parcel of ground has no particular worth. . . . Real estate has worth only as an IDEA of utility is associated with it. Ideas are mental images. . . . How can you sell a prospect a [house] lot . . . unless you paint it for them. . . . Truly must the salesman be an artist. A creator of pictures.[88]

A neighborhood limited to those like oneself: this was the picture of a future life that realtors could and would now sell white buyers across America.

4.

Implementing Racial Exclusion

No self-respecting Negro could ever sanction segregating the Negro because it would mean a sacrifice of our integrity and threaten the very foundation of our freedom.... It is not for himself but his Race that [Homer Garrott] is so ardently demanding justice.

California Eagle, c. 1917[1]

If marketing racial restrictions in Los Angeles and cities across the country was like running downhill, selling a product that sold itself, realtors soon found that they had done more than create a patchwork of restricted subdivisions and neighborhoods. They had created a new way of dividing American cities. Implementing that racial system, making it work, required transforming the law and the country's free market economy.

ENFORCING COVENANTS

The real worry for realtors as they recorded more and more restrictions was whether courts would enforce them. One concern was property law itself. Restrictions that controlled the decisions of future generations had long raised concerns under the Rule Against Perpetuities going back to the English common law. Realtors alleviated this legal concern by generally setting restrictions for twenty or thirty years, with an ability to extend thereafter. In theory, at least, they were not perpetual. The bigger problem, however, was whether racial restrictions violated the equal protection clause of the Fourteenth Amendment. Indeed, two

California cases in the early 1890s had led the developers of Roland Park to forgo racial rules on the advice of their attorney.[2] Both of these early cases involved Chinese immigrants, and the decisions in these cases worried realtors.

In 1890, San Francisco's board of supervisors—acting under an 1879 state constitutional amendment empowering cities to remove Chinese residents—passed an ordinance requiring all twenty thousand Chinese to move within sixty days to a small geographic area earmarked for slaughtering and tallow-rendering or else face six months in jail.[3] In *re Lee Sing*, a federal court ruled that this ordinance clearly violated the Fourteenth Amendment, prohibiting a state from denying any person equal protection of the law.[4] This view, later endorsed by the U.S. Supreme Court in 1917 in *Buchanan v. Warley*, made clear that racial zoning by a public agency was unconstitutional. Realtors had wanted government to take on the task of segregation; as early as 1912, the St. Louis board had sought zoning ordinances "to keep negroes out of certain sections of the city."[5] But the takeaway from these court decisions was clear: because public agencies could not exclude by race, private restrictive covenants were the only way to do so. This made the racial covenants that realtors were recording far more important; they were the only way to legally limit who could live in a subdivision.

The second early case, from the realtors' point of view, was therefore far more troubling. In 1892, a federal district court held that a private racial covenant prohibiting the purchaser from ever renting "to a Chinaman"—a covenant precisely like that the realtors would later use—was unconstitutional on equal protection grounds. Taking an expansive view of the Fourteenth Amendment, the court concluded that "it would be a very narrow construction . . . to hold that, while state and municipal legislatures are forbidden to discriminate against the Chinese in their legislation, a citizen of the state may lawfully do so by contract, which the courts may enforce. Such a view is, I think, entirely inadmissible."[6]

Upheld by a federal court of appeals, *Gandolfo v. Hartman*[7] was the first case on private racial covenants in the United States and therefore for many years the leading precedent in the country. From 1905 to 1919, California realtors recorded "Caucasian-only" covenants and hoped the courts would ultimately ignore or effectively overturn *Gandolfo*. As early as 1911, title companies urged LARB to "take the matter up and . . . have the question settled for once and all."[8]

The key decision on realtors' racial covenants came from the California Supreme Court in 1919 in a pair of cases that Los Angeles realtors had financed for years.[9] In early 1919, Homer Garrott, an African American police officer, won what seemed to the African American community and the *Los Angeles Eagle* like a clear victory. Covenants, the court ruled, could not limit Garrott's right to buy a home. To do so would be to restrict a key aspect of property ownership itself, going back many centuries in the common law—the right to transfer, or alienate, property itself.[10]

Five months later, however, the same court ruled in *Los Angeles Investment Company v. Gary* that although Alfred Gary could keep his West Side home, he could not live in it.[11] The covenant on Gary's home barred not only sale but *occupancy* by "any persons other than of the Caucasian race." Restraints on who could *use* a property were like building restrictions and perfectly valid since they did not restrict alienation.[12] The chief justice found that it strained credulity that the right to own a home, so fundamental that it could not be limited, did not include the right to rent it to oneself. But his was the lone dissent.

The *Gary* decision, the first upholding racial covenants by any state supreme court outside the South, created a precedent in state and then federal courts around the country. Given its impact, the *Gary* ruling was remarkably brief, only two pages long. In a paragraph, the court dismissed any constitutional concerns about equal protection, saying that the Fourteenth Amendment limits discrimination by states, not individuals. No one had raised the question of whether *court enforcement* of covenants was itself state action; indeed, the justices had "not been favored by either brief or argument" for *Gary*. This hardly mattered, the majority decided. "The correct conclusion in the case seems fairly certain nevertheless."[13]

The impact of these decisions was sweeping. In California, realtors, developers, and owners' associations relied on *Gary* to record and enforce occupancy restrictions for the next thirty years. Los Angeles courts would be filled by minorities being evicted from homes they had purchased, either knowing or not knowing there were covenants. By the time *Gary* was effectively overturned by the U.S. Supreme Court in 1948, California's population and housing stock had tripled, and the vast majority of white Californians lived in neighborhoods whose racial exclusivity they took for granted.

Gary shaped the law nationally as well, becoming the key precedent for almost thirty years.[14] While courts in other states often went further, enforcing covenant provisions against sale as well, the restriction on *who could live* in a neighborhood was crucial for creating segregation.

In addition to receiving carte blanche to continue and expand occupancy covenants just in time for the 1920s building boom, realtors took from these decisions a key lesson that would shape realtor policies from now on. Covenants would do *what zoning could not* in keeping areas permanently all-white. Thus, when the leading zoning administrator in the country, George B. Ford from New York, spoke at NAREB's annual convention in 1921, realtors immediately asked, Can you "eliminate colored people in that zoning plan?" "I wish we could, but every decision of the courts" makes it "extremely dangerous to suggest anything about race . . . in a zoning ordinance." Zoning could help *indirectly*, he explained. Simply creating "certain kinds of residence districts eliminates most of the colored people" by setting requirements that raise prices above what they can afford. Ford knew this from experience; New York City's zoning ordinance, adopted shortly after the one McDuffie promoted in Berkeley, had similarly created exclusive single-family districts. NAREB's meeting chairman then "put the question . . . closer to the point." "Can a realtor restrict" property to prevent its sale "to a colored man under the law?" "That is an entirely different matter," Ford concurred.[15] Private parties could restrict property in any way they want.

The lesson for realtors was clear. Because public agencies could not legally limit where races lived, it was up to *private parties* to do so. If communities were to be racially homogeneous, realtors would have to take the lead. This approach would be the key to the racial system the realtors created.

This racial system, now officially sanctioned by the courts, proved extraordinarily powerful. By the 1920s, 95 percent of Los Angeles's housing stock "was effectively put off limits to Blacks and Asians."[16] The walls established in this early period only grew stronger over the years. By the time of Proposition 14, the divide between African Americans and whites in California was "so complete that it might as well have been decreed by law."[17] Yet precisely because separate housing markets were *not* officially decreed in the law itself, but by the realtors' organized systems, they remained perfectly legal for almost three decades after *Gary*. Given the U.S. Supreme Court's 1917 decision prohibiting racial zoning as state action, only private parties could racially divide America's housing markets.

In practice, realtors and local officials sometimes worked together to skirt the prohibition on racial zoning. A confidential 1920s survey by CREA of realty boards around the state revealed how this was done. In Montebello, two local realtors on the planning commission made sure the city would only approve a subdivision if it had deed restrictions.[18] Glendale remained a "100% All-American City," as city fathers called it, by insisting that all "subdividers put in and enforce race restrictions."[19] Cities did not need to put such policies in writing; they simply made life difficult for any subdivider who would not impose racial restrictions on his own. These were effective end runs around the prohibition on racial zoning.

DIVIDING THE FREE MARKET IN HOUSING

Regardless of method, by recording covenants on new subdivisions and in existing neighborhoods, realtors had created a new economic reality. They had divided the housing market in Los Angeles and metropolitan areas across the country into two markets: a primary market for Caucasian buyers and renters and a residual market for everyone else.

This represented a major economic, as well as physical, change. Prior to the advent of covenants, racial minorities in Los Angeles had been part of a single, common housing market. That is, they generally paid the same prices and rents as white residents and lived in mixed neighborhoods. In 1900, Los Angeles's small African American population, about 2 percent of the total, could "be found in most neighborhoods," "not rigidly confined to one geographic area."[20] In 1907, Japanese Americans, too, were "scattered all over the city," as were Mexican Americans. Although many minorities were priced out of the most expensive areas, what distinguished the Los Angeles of the early 1900s from twenty years later was that families of all races could generally choose where to live, rent, or buy according to their means, not according to who they were.

As covenants spread across the city, however, minority housing conditions soon changed. Charlotta Bass, who managed the *California Eagle* and came to Los Angeles in 1910, sharply observed:

> [By 1924] the time when Negroes could live where they could afford to buy in Los Angeles had . . . come to an end. They were forced to live in despicable hovels with fire hazards, unsanitary conditions, and corroded plumbing. More important . . . although living in such low income areas, they were faced with . . . paying higher rents. . . . What would purchase a cozy nook in Hollywood, would only buy a tumble-down shack on the East Side.[21]

This radical change can be put in economic terms. What covenants had done was not only begin to divide the city physically in racial terms, helping establish areas that would remain all-white, but restrict the market for housing and dramatically increase the prices and rents minorities had to pay.

This same pattern occurred in San Francisco, Oakland,[22] Berkeley, San Diego,[23] Sacramento,[24] and San Jose.[25] Like Los Angeles, each had a very small African American population that grew only gradually until 1940, as did Asian American and Mexican American populations. None of these cities had a sudden influx of minorities during these decades. African Americans' share of the population of Los Angeles remained almost constant from 1900 to 1940. In all these cities, California realtors created separate housing markets not in response to an "invasion" of minorities but long before any change in the racial makeup occurred. Separate markets were fostered by the realtors themselves.

Although what the realtors created is often described as a dual housing market,[26] this gives a misleading impression of both the realtors' intentions and what happened. Realtors systematically organized a *primary housing market* for white individuals and white neighborhoods. They did *not* organize a second market for minorities or mixed neighborhoods. Rather, such a residual, unorganized market was simply what continued to exist outside the primary market.

This distinction is important in two ways. First, what minorities were deprived of was *access*: access to the primary market where new economic investments were being made, new subdivisions built, new cities and employment opportunities created, and homeownership opportunities offered for long-term security and investment. Second, realtors did not have a plan to confine minorities to a small, concentrated ghetto or a specific, limited housing market. Rather, they created a primary market that left behind mixed areas where minorities could live, such as Boyle Heights in Los Angeles with its many ethnic groups. These neighborhoods became more and more heavily African American not by plan but because realtors gradually expanded the definition of who was racially acceptable for the primary market. As Jews, Italians, many Asian Americans, and some Mexican Americans were allowed to enter the primary market in later decades, African Americans could not leave.[27]

If real estate men did not set out to create a separate market for those excluded, they quickly took advantage of it. An early history of the Chicago Real Estate Board laid out how this worked in dollars and cents. "The very tactics of white owners made property especially scarce for the negro and therefore more valuable." As a result, "while organizations of real estate men were trying to present a solid wall to the negro invasion, certain individuals were profiting by their very conservatism. Enterprising . . . agents discovered that negroes often pay more rent than their white predecessors." Such agents and local landlords presented themselves "as the friend of the negro; the negroes have made them rich."[28] These same dynamics played out in every city in the country. Those excluded typically had to pay 20 to 30 percent more for the same quality housing. Limiting supply, limiting where one can live, pushes up what one has to pay. This was an inevitable consequence of divided markets.

Such racially divided markets were something new in real estate and American life. Instead of cities where families of different races often lived in the same neighborhood and participated in the same housing market, a new reality had been created. Realtors had made racially exclusive neighborhoods not only feasible and legal but normal—how Americans were expected to live.

A NEW RACIAL BENEFIT

The result was a new type of property right when it came to housing: the value of being racially acceptable. Many decades later, Cheryl Harris, in the *Harvard Law Review*, would call this "racially contingent form of property and property rights" "whiteness as property."[29] The classic case had been slavery itself. Those not subject to slavery gained a crucial benefit, the right to not be enslaved. This right was "usable property," the material benefit of being legally recognized as white. Until realtors began recording restrictive covenants, there had been no special racial benefit with respect to housing. But once realtors established a primary housing market and limited who could enter it, they created precisely what Harris describes: "an exclusive club whose membership was closely and grudgingly guarded."[30] The essence of this benefit was the right to exclude.

This new type of "property" helps explain what realtors had created. Initially, the first purchasers of racially restricted properties, McDuffie's and Nichols's buyers, had to pay more for this privilege. But as covenants spread neighborhood by neighborhood, the right to live in these restricted neighborhoods became a birthright, a racial right. "Under these conditions," the brief for Homer Plessy had argued with respect to the right to ride in streetcars, in *Plessy v. Ferguson*, the Supreme Court's landmark separate-but-equal decision, "is it possible to conclude that the reputation of being white is not property? Indeed, is it not the most valuable sort of property, being the master-key that unlocks the golden door of opportunity?" Realtors had provided this master-key for white buyers and renters, one they soon took for granted as an unstated benefit of being white. Those who lacked this key were all too aware of what they were excluded from. They and their children and their children's children paid for not being white—in where they could live, what they had to pay, and the housing conditions they had to accept.

This key offered more than a right to be admitted; it offered the right to deny admission. Until the creation of racial covenants, the possibility of living in a neighborhood legally restricted to one race had not existed. Decades later, realtors would defend what they called the "traditional right" of white neighbors not to associate with others, but no such tradition existed until the realtors invented it. Neighbors in American cities had previously neither a right nor an enforceable mechanism to exclude anyone who could afford to live next door. Far from traditional, this possibility of urban life was so radically new that it spread as quickly as the automobile in the first decades of the twentieth century. Racial exclusion offered white Americans a product that had not existed, but whose value—the certainty of knowing that each of one's neighbors, now and in the future, would be white—realtors promoted and helped make essential. They had created a right to exclude.

JUSTIFYING SEGREGATION

Realtors viewed what they were doing in spreading racial covenants as helping their customers and protecting the stability of residential neighborhoods. As with the rest of their progressive philosophy, they saw restrictions on owner freedom—zoning, subdivision regulations, and covenants—as essential to the common good. Covenants subordinated the unlimited freedom of any individual owner to that of the neighborhood as a whole. Any owner or broker who allowed a minority family to move into a white neighborhood, and any minority family who did so, could thus be seen as self-serving, as sacrificing the good of the whole for their own personal interest. In creating their racial system, realtors thus did not see themselves as violating their progressive principles, but as carrying them out. Creating racially separate housing markets reflected not realtors' lack of commitment to the public interest but a narrow view of who the public was. If the ultimate result of their actions was widespread racial segregation, it was because realtors had never considered racial minorities as members or customers to begin with.

No one better exemplified the link between these progressive values and the realtors' racial system than Nathan MacChesney, NAREB's general counsel from 1908 to 1947. A nationally known progressive Republican, MacChesney was long-standing counsel for the National Child Labor Committee and a leader of efforts to reform labor, welfare, criminal justice, and court systems. Applying what he saw as these same progressive principles to real estate, MacChesney drafted NAREB's model broker licensing act, adopted by thirty-two states; the standard text on brokerage law; the realtors' arguments for zoning and planning laws—and the model racial covenant used by realtors throughout the United States.[31] This covenant, which realtors welcomed as "Constitution-proof," classified as Negro "every person having 1/8 or more of negro blood . . . and every person known as a colored person."[32] For MacChesney and the realtors he represented, racial covenants, like realtor licensing, zoning, and city planning, were ways of reforming a disorganized society, of limiting individualism for the common good.

But what realtors did not have by the end of the 1910s, as progressivism began to fade from the country's political and intellectual life, was a standardized justification for excluding minorities—one that could not be attacked as subjective or biased—or even a rationale for whom precisely to keep out. At NAREB's 1917 meeting of high-end residential developers, Nichols himself briefly shared some qualms at least when it came to Jews. That "some fine Jewish families" in Kansas City had complained about the barriers he had set against them was "getting under my skin." "By George, it is so unAmerican, and undemocratic, and so unfair to exclude a man on account of his nationality, regardless of what he is himself." Almost all the other major developers were appalled.[33] Nichols quickly backed off. His developments remained closed to Jews and Catholics for years to come.

Yet the very fact that Nichols himself felt there might be something un-American in what they were doing suggests that realtors needed a stronger justification for racial exclusion. Nichols knew better than anyone that there had been no principle involved in creating restricted neighborhoods, that restriction had simply begun as a sales tool. But, however incrementally created, this racial division of housing markets had now become fundamental to realtors' businesses. What realtors sought going forward was a way to defend racial exclusion, one so objective that it would not be questioned as un-American or unfair and could indeed be adopted by the federal government as its national policy for housing. As the 1920s began, they needed a seemingly scientific rationale for residential segregation. At this, they brilliantly succeeded.

Part Two.

Property Values: Early 1920s–Late 1940s

Starting in about 1920, local real estate boards began to articulate a reason for the racial system they had established, for not selling homes to qualified buyers, whether or not covenants existed. The justification they created seemed both simple and objective. Harry Grant Atkinson, who became the leading appraiser in the country, stated it clearly: "Just as the stockyards or a tannery may pollute the air and give a neighborhood a bad name, so do . . . undesirable human elements work against property values and ruin communities which might prosper."[1] In other words, "Undesirable groups, races and individuals"[2] reduce the value of property. This principle stated as scientific fact—incorporated in all real estate textbooks and appraisal manuals in the country, covered in state real estate licensing examinations, adopted by the federal government—that minorities depreciated property values in white neighborhoods and therefore had to be excluded.

This axiom had many great advantages to realtors. It was based in the one subject—real estate prices and values—on which realtors, land economists, and appraisers were the undisputed experts, and thus seemed incontrovertible. It provided a powerful, easily understandable rationale to convince a client not to sell to a member of a minority group. It made intuitive sense to many white residents. After all, realtors had been marketing the idea that minority neighbors were undesirable ever since 1905. The property-value axiom reflected the impact of that now widespread belief.

Perhaps most important, this axiom allowed realtors, local real estate boards, owners, and public officials to say to themselves and to any individual minority—however qualified, educated, or creditworthy—that their hands were tied, that they had no choice. Thus what became the most notorious statement of this axiom, when publicized by an African American newspaper in 1943, was in fact intended by NAREB to shock those training to be realtors:

> When, for example, in a respectable neighborhood a house is wanted for conversion to an objectionable use, no respectable broker will consent to represent the buyer. The latter might be a bootlegger, a "madam" who had a number of "call girls" on her string, a gangster who wants a screen for his activities by living in a better neighborhood, a colored man of means who was giving his children a college education and thought they were entitled to live among the whites, but no matter what the motive or character of the would-be purchaser, if the deal would instigate a form of blight, then certainly the well-meaning broker must work against its consummation.[3]

This language, from a standard textbook, was meant to impress on realtors that even the most sympathetic and attractive possible minority buyer had to be rejected. Whatever the character or motive, any African American moving into a white neighborhood posed exactly the same threat as an infamous criminal. Indeed, a "colored man of means" was, in real estate terms, a criminal. In seeking to buy a home in a white neighborhood, he was stealing the property value of those who lived there. Therefore, no exceptions could be made.

Realtors used this property-value axiom to institutionalize racially separate housing markets, both through their own actions as racial gatekeepers and ultimately through the federal government's most important housing program, the Federal Housing Administration (FHA). Indeed, it was only by using the realtors' objective-sounding rationale that the federal government could itself discriminate in every real estate market in the country. Mid-twentieth-century America was built and funded on this official belief.

African American housing experts' arguments that this theory was false as well as immoral, that it violated the most basic tenets of economics, were ignored. The presumption that "undesirable human elements work against property values and ruin communities" became such a given, Robert Weaver recognized, that "whether valid or not, its acceptance by a large segment of the American people is important."[4]

By the late 1940s, when empirical studies showed that property values rarely declined and often increased when minorities moved in, realtor organizations, appraisal journals, and FHA began to acknowledge that the axiom had no basis in fact. But learning they had been wrong made no difference to realtors' and FHA's commitment to segregation. Their property-value argument had not been the reason realtors insisted on segregation; it was how they justified that insistence in terms that seemed objective and high minded.

The realtor who did more than any other to promote the property-value axiom, establish FHA, institutionalize segregation, and publish real estate textbooks such as Atkinson and Frailey's shared many traits in common with the most thoughtful and sophisticated opponent of residential segregation. Herbert U. Nelson, NAREB's powerful executive vice president from 1922 to 1955, was a near-contemporary of Charles S. Johnson, the leading sociologist of African American life. Both men, who died within weeks of each other in 1956, were visionaries who helped organize their fields, institution builders, talent scouts, and advisors to government agencies. Both were ardent believers in the power of academic research to shape public policy, even sharing important connections to the same Department of Sociology at the University of Chicago. Yet their most basic views on the nature of research, society, and indeed democracy could not have been more different.

Nelson remade NAREB. A former newsman and brilliant publicist who established one division and institute after another—from the American Institute of Real Estate Appraisers to the Institute of Farm Brokers[5]—he understood that the key to realtors' success and power lay in professionalism and education. He not only helped arrange real estate curricula at hundreds of universities but drew on leading land economists and other experts to publish textbooks that promoted NAREB's vision of social and economic order. Any research that did not support

Left: Herbert U. Nelson, Executive Secretary, National Association of Real Estate Boards *Right:* Charles S. Johnson

NAREB's preset conclusions was swiftly discouraged. These textbooks laid out a seemingly academic, objective, and irrefutable basis for preventing minorities from moving into white neighborhoods. In his frequent articles and radio appearances, Nelson portrayed NAREB as the spokesman and defender of property owners, especially small owners, against the dangers of big government. Privately, he confided his personal philosophy in a letter to an incoming NAREB president: "I do not believe in democracy. I think it stinks."[6]

Charles S. Johnson believed deeply in democracy. "The core of [my] social philosophy" was the conviction that "no man can be justly judged until you've looked at the world through his eyes. It carried over to children classed as delinquents, . . . impoverished tobacco workers, . . . men in prison . . ., humble . . . families of the left side of the tracks."[7] The son of an African American minister from Virginia, Johnson grew up before residential segregation, in a town where "a neat little Negro home might be found nestling in the humble pride between two large and imposing dwellings of upper class whites."[8] He remembered the day when he was seven, when Jim Crow became the law of Virginia and the local drugstore owner told his mother he could no longer serve them at the counter. "The Negroes could not believe their ears, but it was the beginning of a new self-consciousness that burned."[9] Johnson's focus on how people's conditions affected their perceptions led him to study sociology with one of the field's key founders in America, Robert E. Park at the University of Chicago, a white man who had spent seven years working with Booker T. Washington at the Tuskegee Institute.

Johnson directly applied his philosophy of looking through each person's eyes in all his work on race relations, beginning with the Illinois state commission on the 1919 Chicago race riots. The riot, one of the most violent and widespread in American history, lasted for a week as white mobs, often abetted by police, attacked Black residents throughout the South Side. Johnson helped prepare the seven-hundred-page analysis—still considered a landmark today[10]—by personalizing the hopes, economic conditions, community participation, and adjustment to Chicago of a wide range of African Americans who had joined the Great Migration from the South. Johnson, who had himself been shot at during the riots a week after returning as a sergeant-major from World War I, focused on the diversity of their experience: "barber from Mississippi," "railway mail clerk," "factory hand," "baseball 'magnate,'" "physician," "Missouri family," "embalmer," "migrant professional man." Rather than accept abstract myths about whole groups of people, Johnson insisted on the importance of detailed truth, of asking questions he did not know the answers to.

Johnson's deep beliefs in the value of getting people to understand each other and that "while there are inequalities in personal gifts, there is no justification for the inequality in social and economic environment"[11] made him a formidable opponent to those promoting racial myths. Bespectacled, quiet, somewhat aloof, Johnson served as national director of research and investigation for the Urban League, editor of its 1920s *Opportunity: Journal of Negro Life* that actively promoted the Harlem Renaissance, chairman of sociology and later president of Fisk University in Nashville, and founder of its famed race relations institute. He thus brought to his work against housing segregation both formidable research skills and a wealth of experience from both the North and South.

At the 1931 President's Conference on Housing, which helped set the agenda for the New Deal's housing programs, Nelson and Johnson were on opposite sides. Nelson led NAREB's all-out efforts to incorporate the property-value axiom in federal efforts to recover from the Depression. Johnson submitted the extensive *Report of the Committee on Negro Housing* that argued just the opposite, and was almost entirely ignored. Johnson's voice would be a lonely one against Nelson and NAREB in the period between the wars. His research, however, would ultimately influence the U.S. Supreme Court after World War II in dismantling the legal basis for the racial system Nelson helped institutionalize.

5.

Undesirable Human Elements

We are no alley rats or vermin.
An African American doctor in Maywood near Los Angeles, c. 1920s[1]

Like each ideology realtors would use to justify racially separate housing markets, the property-value argument was created to respond to
a new and difficult challenge. By the beginning of the 1920s, realtors
found themselves in a new role. No longer simply subdividers or sales
agents, they had become defenders of racial exclusion. In each city, former, current, and future clients; owners' associations; local officials; and
the white public looked to the local real estate board to permanently
keep neighborhoods white. Boards were expected to be the quasi-official
defenders of residential segregation. A realtor's future business and reputation in the community depended on his commitment to this task.[2]

RACIAL GATEKEEPERS

Realtors thus became seen, and saw themselves, as protectors of what
they designated as white neighborhoods. Realtors' role was sometimes
very quiet: steering minority buyers toward mixed neighborhoods and
away from exclusively white ones. Such racial steering was as powerful
as it was invisible: "real estate salesmen could practically control the
placing of these colored races," by only offering them properties in their
own districts, one California board boasted.[3] Realtors' role as defenders
of homogeneity sometimes became highly public: the real estate board
of Chicago led a massive campaign to exclude African Americans from
entire sections of the city. But whether private or public or often both at

the same time, racial gatekeeping was a role real estate boards took on in each city in the country. For realtors virtually everywhere, "residential segregation is a business necessity and a moral absolute."[4]

Salesmen paid for selling homes took on an additional role: anti-salesmen, preventing minorities from buying homes. Not surprisingly, realtors wished that government would take over this job instead. Boards urged state licensing divisions to revoke the license of any broker who sold or rented to anyone of "African, Mongolian or Japanese blood."[5] But since the Supreme Court banned such state action, maintaining segregation became a prime task of each local real estate board.

To handle this new role, boards appointed special committees to prevent sales to minorities. The charges to such committees could hardly be more explicit. "Immediately attempt to block the deal" "if one of those races" tries to buy. "Restrict all people who are not clearly white." "Confine color to certain districts." "'Clean up' areas by sell[ing] out the undesirable owners and then placing restrictions on the properties." "Eject them from old leases." Make sure the "distinct color line [is] strictly adhered to." Enforce the "'unwritten law' to protect home neighborhoods." "Work . . . for segregation of the undesirable races."[6]

From the beginning of the 1920s, boards sought a nonracial justification for such actions. In 1920, the Portland Realty Board announced that its members would not "under any circumstances directly or indirectly sell to persons of the Negro or Oriental races in districts now inhabited almost exclusively by white persons." Its reason, the board insisted, was "not on account of any prejudice, for it has none, but because it is common knowledge that the residence of Negroes or Orientals in any district greatly depreciates, in the public mind, surrounding property values." Realtors therefore had a moral obligation: "a strict duty to present property owners in these districts not to make such sales, a duty which the board [will] . . . now strictly enforce."[7]

The danger posed by minority buyers became stated as fact by real estate boards throughout the country. The Portland board's qualifier, that a minority presence depreciated values "in the public mind," was rarely repeated. NAREB called depreciation due to minorities a fact of life "more irrevocable than . . . the laws of the Medes and Persians," even though residential segregation had only begun fifteen years before.[8]

Moreover, in the way they framed their statements, both the Portland board and NAREB underscored a deeper point as well. A realtor who recognized that minorities depreciate property values was not himself prejudiced, but simply recognizing the reality of the market. After all, that was his job as a real estate expert. Just as important, when Portland's board stressed that "as to prejudice, it has none," and NAREB said it made no difference if a minority individual was "personally unobjectionable," they were elevating their argument that minorities reduced property values by presenting it as unbiased. The same argument that realtors and planners had made for zoning, that it was a scientific way to maintain the value of property in a city,[9] could now be used to restrict minorities as well.

This high-minded reason for racial exclusion was very much in keeping with the professional style Herbert Nelson brought to NAREB in 1922. His predecessor, Tom Ingersoll, had been more than happy to denigrate other races, and had gone out of his way to do so. Even in an article about outdoor advertising in the official *National Real Estate Journal* in 1918, Ingersoll urged cities to "segregate the unsightly billboards and confine them to certain restricted localities. They contaminate a landscape in about the same degree that a Negro family contaminates a white neighborhood."[10] When Ingersoll decided to move to Los Angeles and become LARB's secretary, Herbert Nelson, a former newsman and secretary of the Minneapolis board, took on the national job and led, indeed dominated, NAREB for the next thirty-three years.

Nelson was very different from the gregarious, informal Ingersoll. A highly effective organizer and publicist, the first to recognize the value of the term *Realtor*, Nelson would ultimately be feared by Congress as the country's most powerful lobbyist. Congressmen who had long opposed his influence were thus delighted when their investigators uncovered Nelson's private letter to a new NAREB president, berating democracy and arguing that "nobody except taxpayers should be allowed to vote . . . [nor] should women be allowed to vote at all," thirty years after women's suffrage. The letter revealed something even more striking: Nelson's discipline in keeping these views out of the public eye for so many years "because I know it would not be acceptable."[11]

Thus, for Nelson and for realtors across the country, the scientific-sounding axiom that minorities reduced property values proved invaluable. It helped them address their three key challenges as racial gatekeepers. It justified whom they had to exclude in each community. It gave them a moral reason for no longer simply selling real estate but preventing its sale. Perhaps most important, it mobilized others to help keep neighborhoods all-white, a task that realtors could not accomplish alone.

WHO HAD TO BE EXCLUDED

If realtors were going to say they were excluding buyers on objective grounds, they needed to legitimate who exactly depreciated property values in each community. As with all questions of racial boundaries, such as the South's one-drop rule for deciding who was Black, this was no easy matter. For who most needed to be excluded, who threatened property values, varied by community. A 1920s "Survey of Race Relations," conducted by CREA at the request of a Stanford economics professor, asked local real estate boards across California which particular races posed an "important problem" in each locality and how "can this important problem be best handled by real estate interests?" The survey form provided boxes to identify concerns and solutions for Chinese, Japanese, Negroes, and Mexicans. The Los Angeles board reported that the "Western Negro is a menace," but Mexicans were not a threat; they were "well-handled and can be quite reliable." For the Hollywood and the Van Nuys boards, however, the problem was Mexicans. In Montebello, Japanese were the only problem; in Pasadena, it was Negroes.

Exclusion went further still. Many respondents identified problems with groups not on the form: "Latin people, Spanish, French, Italian and Grecians" in Santa Monica, or those from the "Turkish Empire, Armenia" or "Mulattoes" or "Filipinos."[12] Many subdivisions excluded Jews and southern and eastern Europeans as being non-Caucasian. A Torrance newspaper in 1921 explained that all the city's subdivisions and therefore all its homes were "restricted against non-Caucasians (negroes), Japanese, Chinamen and for the purpose of this interpretation, Hindoos."[13] The range of people whom realtors sought to exclude in different communities was broad indeed. Additional groups barred explicitly by various racial covenants included Syrians, Persians, Arabians, Poles, Russians, Latin Americans, Hawaiians, Puerto Ricans, Native Americans, and Seventh Day Adventists.[14]

What those to be excluded had in common was how they were perceived. Italian immigrants, excluded from new areas of Eastern cities, were more accepted in San Jose, where the local board was mainly concerned that "Japs are spreading."[15] Historian Robert Fogelson cut to the chase: "What made some people . . . 'undesirable' was that the subdividers branded them undesirable."[16] Conversely, those accepted into a subdivision were thus deemed white, their ethnicity notwithstanding.[17] White and nonwhite meant whom realtors deemed acceptable and not acceptable. Caucasian and non-Caucasian had no intrinsic meaning, but were names for desirable and undesirable. Nothing demonstrated this more graphically than a federal court ruling that an Indian Sikh claiming direct ancestry from the Caucasian region was not Caucasian as socially understood.[18] In places like Glendale—where realtors prided themselves on the "high standard of American citizenship" by having "the smallest percentage of foreign population of any city in the state"[19]—African Americans, citizens for generations, were not considered American.

Any broad, national realtor principle to justify exclusion therefore had to be based on local judgment of who was undesirable. But how could a universal principle be based on particular local biases? Here was NAREB's problem. Local boards dealing with race were asking for clear, consistent national policies, guidelines, and justifications. But what kind of national policy could NAREB offer local boards that were deciding whether and how to discipline members who sold to particular minorities?

NAREB came up with an elegant solution. Under Nelson's leadership, an ethics committee chaired by a Los Angeles realtor added a new Article 34 to the Code of Ethics in 1924: "A realtor should never be instrumental in introducing into a neighborhood a character of property or occupancy, members of any race or nationality, or any individuals whose presence will clearly be detrimental to property values in that neighborhood."[20] These words quickly became famous in the real estate world and infamous for those seeking rights for minorities.

The formula "detrimental to property values" fit the needs of realtors around the country. It was stated in an objective and scientific way based on property values, not the realtor's or anyone else's bias or subjective opinion. The determination depended on the particular neighborhood, the key unit of value from realtors' point of view. Nor did Article 34 ascribe characteristics to any race or nationality, characteristics that could be disputed in any particular case. Rather, a local board need only determine that that buyer was detrimental to property values in a given neighborhood. Since the issue was property values, who could dispute the local board, the experts?

In reality, however, the process of determining who was detrimental to property values was by no means scientific or objective. Local board judgment was inherently subjective. California boards explained that, in deciding who was detrimental to property values, they were simply carrying out "community custom."[21] Since racial covenants had only begun to be used in these communities a decade or two before, such custom of segregating particular areas was one that local realtors themselves had helped create.

Moreover, realtors' own role in protecting white neighborhoods brought their racial feelings to the surface. The San Jose board was irate that a fine residential district had been "spoiled" by the presence of a single Chinese herb doctor. If just one home in a white neighborhood is sold to a "colored person," "to one of them—the community is ruined."[22] Local boards spoke of infiltration, invasion, control, handling, and keeping "them within bounds." Minorities, and their aspirations to improve their lot, were the enemy; the real danger was the "colored wishing to purchase . . . a better class of property."[23] CREA itself made its prejudices clear. Summarizing the results from the survey, CREA lauded realtors for protecting properties "from future depreciation . . . through encroachment of a foreign race. Attention is called to the fact that . . . most of the crime in this country is committed by members of these races."[24] In the case of African Americans, of course, *foreign* did not mean born in another country. It meant a foreign body had invaded the community.

The new Article 34 did more than provide a basis for boards throughout the country to discipline any member who sold to minorities. It declared that the realtor's highest ethical obligation was to the presumed desires of the neighborhood. This obligation was more important than the realtor's fiduciary duty to the client—to the buyer looking for a home or the seller seeking the best price—which the code had been based on. Satisfying the neighbors, and avoiding having neighbors complain about an unwanted newcomer, now became a realtor's highest duty.

Not coincidentally, this official justification reflected realtors' new economic interests. Instead of hustling to undercut other brokers' commissions or horn in on deals, as in the days before real estate boards, realtors with their fixed commissions and multiple listing service now saw the neighbors as their main source of future business. If nearby owners were unhappy with whom a realtor had sold a home to, the realtor's own economic future would dry up all at once. Having marketed the idea that neighborhoods belonged to certain groups, having marketed prejudice, realtors now thought constantly about neighbors' reactions to potential sales. As they revealed in interviews years later, "How do I know where a prospect will fit in? Well, it's no one thing about him. Unless he's a Negro, of course. But leaving them out, there's usually no one thing that you judge him on. . . . But some things are more important than others. . . . It's not that I don't like Jews or Italians . . . but, well, it's just that they don't stand so high."[25] Gatekeeping had become key to realtors' economic livelihood. When it came to what they called "non-Caucasians," the line was absolute indeed.

A MORAL OBLIGATION

Protecting property values made exclusion a noble endeavor, not simply a defense of prejudice or the realtor's livelihood. Berkeley's board proudly proclaimed that no member had ever broken its rule against selling to a non-Caucasian in Caucasian territory.[26] The Santa Barbara board cited its high ethical standards to explain why members "rigidly adhered" to its rule against selling to minorities in all-white neighborhoods.[27] To introduce a minority into an all-white neighborhood, the Martinez board explained, would "injure a white owner's values or home life."[28] It would violate the "unwritten law" to protect home neighborhoods.[29]

Maintaining property values thus translated prejudice and self-interest into moral terms. A Chicago realtor later explained, "I have an absolute responsibility to the people who live in the area where I'm operating to protect and safeguard rather than destroy . . . values."[30] In the words of the Hippocratic Oath that realtors saw as the original model for their code of ethics, first, do no harm. If a realtor personally sympathized with the aspirations of a minority buyer simply trying to find, as in Riverside, "a better class of property,"[31] Article 34 reminded the realtor of his first and highest obligation: do not harm property values.

Nelson, indeed, wanted to showcase the new code of ethics as a model of "social conscience" for American business. A realtor would not turn a quick profit for himself at a cost to the neighborhood: "The purpose of business activity, is not profit solely, but a service to society." Nor could any "instruction from a client abrogate the realtor's obligation to the code." If an owner wanted to sell to a buyer who would harm the neighborhood, the realtor's first commitment was to the public at large. Nelson invoked Garland's argument for creating a board in the first place and for zoning. "Individualism must be tempered with due regard for the general welfare."[32] Selling to minorities was framed as selfishness versus morality. That turning down such sales served the realtor's long-term economic interest and protected and promoted his business was not mentioned.

To underscore that morality was at stake, NAREB inserted the Golden Rule and Article 34 in the same 1924 revision of the code. NAREB was bringing in the big guns. Why did the Golden Rule require restricting minorities? The *Real Estate Journal* explained that the Golden Rule was specific and practical: "Never take a man out and sell him anything that later is liable to prove of less value than the day he bought it."[33] The property-value axiom thus made it immoral to sell to a minority. Discrimination thus did not violate the Golden Rule, but was required by it. Indeed, forgoing a sale to a minority became proof to realtors of their own moral virtue. A Chicago broker put this graphically in an interview years later: "I'm not so anxious to get the . . . yellow metal in my hands. . . . Put yourself in [the neighbors'] position. How would you like it? . . . Some people don't care. They're selfish."[34] The Golden Rule meant treat the neighbors as you would want to be treated yourself. It had nothing to do with treating minority buyers as one would want to be treated oneself. Article 34, the property-value axiom, and the Golden Rule thus worked together to justify segregation.

The new code was meant to ensure a common standard of conduct for realtors throughout the country. NAREB made the code mandatory. For the first time, all boards would need to adhere to it. Just as important or perhaps more important, Nelson emphasized, was its educational role. Its great purpose was to "educate the conscience and quicken the perception of right and wrong." Article 34 was not meant primarily to discipline members but "to make enforcement proceedings unnecessary" by inspiring all those in real estate to live up to and go beyond the code.[35] Preventing sales to minorities thus became more than a requirement. It became a moral crusade. In CREA's annual achievement contests, boards competed by showing who had done the most to protect "districts occupied by the Caucasian race."[36]

PROMOTING THE PROPERTY-VALUE ARGUMENT

But maintaining a rigid color line was not something realtors could do alone. The task was never-ending because it required total compliance to work at all. A neighborhood was either racially homogeneous or not. Residents signed covenants out of a belief that even one non-Caucasian occupant would threaten their status, family life, and property values. This belief created a vicious circle. If a single minority family was allowed to purchase a home, whites would no longer buy, and existing owners would need to sell quickly before property values plummeted. What had once been seen as an ordinary home purchase by a Black doctor or lawyer before there were covenants became a catastrophe. Moreover, the failure of covenants in one neighborhood spurred fear in others, making it even more crucial to enforce restrictions. In many white owners' minds, their own neighborhood might be next. The belief at the heart of racial exclusion—that if just "one of them" moved in, "the community is ruined"[37]—made even a single failure the end of the neighborhood as a desirable place to live.

Yet realtors had limited tools. In many neighborhoods, not all homes were restricted; neighborhood covenants restricted only those properties whose owners originally signed up. Owners of unrestricted properties had to be convinced not to sell to minorities. Even if every realtor refused to sell a home to a minority purchaser, most real estate agents were not realtors. Although realtors controlled approximately 80 percent of all real estate sales, many part-time and full-time brokers were not members of local boards. Minority brokers were automatically excluded; some white brokers did not want to pay the dues; local boards rejected others. "Our (statewide) membership is under 4,000 and there were 55,000 licensed dealers" in California, the San Jose board reminded CREA.[38] The biggest danger to an all-white neighborhood, the Monrovia board reported, was an owner "getting anxious and can't sell the property," who would use a nonrealtor or sell the house himself.[39]

Realtors therefore reminded other brokers and owners that a single sale to a minority would depreciate property values for everyone. That reminder clinched debates. Even if one wanted to be fair to minorities, who could be against maintaining property values? The more widespread the belief that minorities threatened property values, the easier it would be to enlist "property owners [to] bring to bear all possible pressure against" any seller.[40] NAREB made it a top priority to instill and support this belief around the country, to have it accepted by the real estate industry, the courts, media, and the white general public.

Promoting the property-value axiom was easy in some ways. It told many white residents what they wanted to hear, that there was an objective reason for distancing themselves from minorities. Moreover, it seemed intuitively true, precisely because it was a tautology. A nationality or race was undesirable *because* its presence was detrimental to property values. But the only reason people of that race threatened property values was that neighbors did not want them moving in; that is, they thought of them as undesirable. While the tautology did not provide a way to know who was undesirable, that was not its purpose. The property-value argument elevated dislike and prejudice into a collective cause based on a seemingly incontrovertible fact. It helped convince any potentially tolerant owner that he was in danger of harming everyone around him in a real, material way, and enabled anyone opposing a minority buyer to see himself or herself as personally unbiased.

But Nelson did not leave promulgation of the property-value axiom to chance. He wanted to be sure it was seen as an objective, indisputable, economic truth. NAREB hired land economists, appraisers, and other experts on its staff and engaged outside experts to prepare publications and educational programs of all types that supported this axiom. The result was that from 1922 to well into the 1950s, every real estate textbook and guide to appraisals in the country was based on a statement of fact that minorities depreciated property values in white neighborhoods.[41]

Ernest McKinley Fisher, NAREB's director of research, future head of economics at the Federal Housing Administration, and the first professor of real estate at an American university, declared in 1922 that "it is a matter of common observation that the purchase of property by certain racial types is very likely to diminish the value of other property in the section."[42] In 1923, Stanley McMichael, former secretary of the Cleveland Realty Board and a dean of appraisers in the United States, went further. The "increase in colored people . . . naturally has had a decidedly detrimental effect on land values." McMichael spelled out the key implication of the property-value argument: property values could only be protected if no minority could enter. "Property values have been sadly depreciated by having a single colored family settle down on a street occupied exclusively by white residents."[43] The property-value argument made African Americans responsible for the economic harm they caused.

Frederick Babcock's *Appraisal of Real Estate* in 1924 made clear that property value depended on homogeneity. Babcock was a pivotal figure, member of NAREB's Appraisal Division, founding board member of the American Institute of Real Estate Appraisers,[44] and future head of underwriting for the Federal Housing Administration. Babcock explained that land values depend on the race of the inhabitants, that "the habits, character, the race . . . of the people are the ultimate factors of real estate value." Homogeneity was crucial. "Residential values are affected by racial and religious values." Babcock turned this into a utility function. Just as "a barber shop utility seeks location near people . . . with time to be shaved," "a home utility seeks location near people—but always near persons of the same social standing, same races."[45] Race was the ultimate measure of homogeneity. Land economics, Babcock stressed, was driven by a fundamental economic principle: to live only with people like oneself.

Real estate textbooks turned this idea of like-with-like into a fundamental law of real estate, "the law of conformity," as if it were a scientific principle. "Land must be utilized to conform" with the existing standards and the "reflected will of the majority in an area. The danger of economic loss increases in proportion to the degree of variation from those standards."[46] This idea that real estate requires conformity—reflected in zoning, race restrictions, and the property-value ideology—would later shape realtors' vision of freedom as the right to require conformity.

The textbooks did change in one key way from the early 1920s to the early 1930s: experts reinterpreted *who* was a permanent threat to property values. In the anti-immigrant fervor that swept the country in the early 1920s, some real estate experts had focused on the danger from southern and eastern European immigrants as well as African Americans. A neighborhood's real estate "lifeblood," a 1923 textbook concluded, depends "on the character of its citizens, pure and warm if its citizens are 100% American . . . anemic and even diseased if polluted with a large percentage of unassimilated aliens."[47] But after such fervor abated with passage of the 1924 Immigration Act, all real estate texts now focused on African Americans. A 1932 textbook stated the new, standard view: economics dictated that foreigners should be "segregated in sections by themselves for at least one generation," but the only "solution to the negro problem seems to depend upon rigid segregation."[48]

Fourteen of fifteen articles in leading appraisal journals treated the impact of African Americans to property values as a known fact.[49] The lone writer who even slightly questioned the standard view, Elsie Smith Parker in 1943, minimized her own findings. Even if there was no long-term impact on prices per se, she recognized that the presence of large numbers of African Americans destroyed "the acquired benefits and advantages" of all those who already lived in the area, and that as "the lower living standard group moves in . . . the slums creep ever closer like a river in the jungle." This one appraiser—going out on a limb in arguing that African Americans should not have to pay 20 percent more for their housing than whites of similar income—agreed that segregation was nonetheless essential.[50]

The impact of these texts on underwriting and appraisal was immense. Appraisers were consistently admonished to look for "changes in social status due to infiltration of foreign or colored elements in the population,"[51] an admonition that was adopted by federal agencies and dramatically affected the homeownership rates and future lives of white

Americans and African Americans. No economic view was more widely held than the belief that minorities depreciated property values. No government mortgage lending system could have been based on more powerful support from economists.

LOOKING FOR THE EVIDENCE

But, it turned out, not one of these statements on which much of America was built had been based on any evidence. Starting in the late 1940s, the first empirical studies showed that minority entry into white neighborhoods did not typically lower property values. After Luigi Laurenti of the University of California empirically matched twenty pairs of American neighborhoods—and found that in 80 percent of these cases, average property values *increased* when minorities moved in—he asked the writers of the textbooks and appraisal manuals what research they had based their conclusions on.[52] The answer, Laurenti testified before the U.S. Commission on Civil Rights in 1960, was that there was none. "Strangely enough, there is no evidence—at least none that I know of, and I have looked very hard." Why then were these views so widely accepted? "Apparently, the only way this belief continues to be passed along is by word of mouth, that textbooks . . . state this to be true, but present no documentation. And, of course, these textbooks are the means by which people in the real estate industry become educated to practice their profession."[53] The emperor had had no clothes for decades, it turned out.

Laurenti was even more struck by the pattern of statements over time. In the 1920s, textbooks and appraisal articles reported that property values dropped by more than half when minorities moved in. By 1940, "the general opinion had shifted and they were saying that, to be sure, values would be harmed—[but] no such figure as 50% was advanced. Values would be harmed, but there were many instances, it was agreed, where prices would move back again to the original level, perhaps even higher . . . because of the high pressure for housing by nonwhites."[54]

Why had the leading experts been so wrong for so many years? Why, in reality, did prices often go up and rarely fall when minorities entered all-white neighborhoods? And why did these experts insist so strenuously—without ever checking data—that prices would only go down? Why had they ignored the most basic rules of supply and demand?

As Robert Weaver tartly observed in 1948, the most fundamental economic market principles had simply been ignored. "Free enterprise, which so many of the proponents of race restrictive covenants constantly champion, is effectively negated by their efforts." Under free enterprise, "the purchaser is supposed to be guaranteed free access to the supply in the total market . . . [and] the seller . . . assured access to the total demand." The result is supposed to assure the purchaser of the lowest possible price. None "of these processes occurs in the housing market open to colored people."[55]

The natural result of separating markets by race was to establish different pricing systems for those included in the primary market and those excluded from it. For white purchasers, when only a few subdivisions had the new, special feature of restrictive covenants, covenanted property commanded a premium over otherwise similar lots. As more and more covenanted subdivisions were built, buyers came to expect racial covenants as a standard feature that was almost universally offered. The relative premium declined accordingly. In the broad market for white buyers in a city like Los Angeles, the exclusion of 4 percent of potential buyers had little impact on prices paid by whites.

The price effects for minorities were just the reverse. The impact was obvious to ordinary African Americans in Los Angeles as early as 1917. Effectively confined to very limited geographic areas with no new supply, while in-migration increased demand, minorities had to pay more for housing in worse condition. To improve their housing, minority buyers who could somehow purchase a home in an all-white neighborhood would have no option but to pay significantly more for that home than a white buyer. With far fewer choices available to them, minorities often paid top dollar to speculators who frequently pocketed 30 percent differentials. To cover the higher cost, minority buyers often had to bring in roomers.

All of this was entirely predictable under the laws of supply and demand. Artificially divided housing markets, like artificially restricted currency exchanges in the black markets of World War II, created price disparities as a matter of course.

Realtors on the ground knew of these price differentials from practical experience, of course. They knew that the first owners to sell to minorities could make a higher profit. It was up to the realtors to ensure that their clients did not give in to such temptation, did not make economically rational decisions. Realtors also knew that if, despite their best efforts, minorities did enter an all-white neighborhood, prices tended to stabilize over the long run. Realtors in San Francisco candidly admitted this to Laurenti. "If nonwhites, especially Negroes, hit a white district, they depress property values in the eyes of other whites. But nonwhites will pay more than whites. . . . Sellers may not get their price from whites . . . [but] they probably can from nonwhites."[56]

Why had all the experts disregarded the simple economics that would typically prevail? One answer is that NAREB, which commissioned the textbooks and appraisal manuals, created a powerful ideological and economic influence on those it supported. When Nelson had approached Professor Richard Ely, a founder and former president of the American Economics Association and a leading progressive, to help establish NAREB's real estate education program in 1922, he originally had a broader vision in mind. He wanted Ely and his land economics students Ernest McKinley Fisher and Frederick Babcock to establish a research program as well. But when Ely and his students helped establish NAREB's research institutes, they encountered resistance. Realtors, Ely learned to his dismay, "considered land economics an enemy of real estate"; when Ely offered as a model for future research an acclaimed land value study of New York City, realtors were appalled when it did not support the realtors' assumptions. The study seemed "calculated to injure the real estate business." Ely got the message. He deferred land value studies and worked instead on more practical analyses, such as volume of sales.[57] It is not surprising that the books NAREB sponsored by Fisher and Babcock in 1922 through 1924, followed by many others, reflected NAREB's ideology of the impact of race on real estate values. Independent research on this issue was not needed because the answer was already known.

But at a deeper level, what Fisher's and later books described about property values was true—*if one looked only at what white buyers would pay*. If minorities moved into a neighborhood, the price that white buyers would pay for a home did decrease. But, as empirical studies showed, the prices that minorities offered more than offset the reduced prices from white buyers. The experts had ignored these broader economics. They had discounted those outside the primary housing market and considered only the buyers whom realtors saw as their natural customers. This sharply bounded, racialized view of economics reflected the sharply bounded, racialized housing markets that realtors had helped establish.

If we probe still deeper and ask why it was *only* the primary market that realtors cared about, sociologist Rose Helper's later interviews with Chicago brokers suggest the practical reality. "When property is transferred from white to Negro hands," she learned, white brokers viewed it as "lost to the white group forever. Hence the opportunities for future gain that that property might offer to white buyers are lost," together with the broker's own business prospects. Her interviewees were candid. "White people seldom buy and live in property that has been occupied by Negroes. In addition when such property is sold, the broker in charge is usually Negro."[58] Realtors, from McDuffie and Nichols onward, had focused on the customers they wanted. The textbooks, university courses, and appraisal institutes that NAREB sponsored reflected realtors' own business interests and the racially separate market they had chosen to serve.

Stanley McMichael, as one of the country's foremost appraisers, spelled out the implications of these presumably neutral economic analyses for American values. "The colored people certainly have a right to life, liberty and the pursuit of happiness but they must recognize the economic disturbance which their presence in a white neighborhood causes and forego their desire to split off from the established district where the rest of their race lives."[59] Justified as objective economic reality to make it seem inarguable, the realtors' conclusion was clear: the good of the society as a whole required perpetual sacrifices that African Americans needed to accept.

The impact of the realtors' property-value ideology, enshrined in every textbook, used by every real estate board, argued and accepted in courtrooms around the country to justify racial covenants, was powerful indeed. But what magnified its power many times over was its adoption by the federal government in the midst of the Depression.

6.

Shaping Federal Housing Programs

We sat with them for 2 or 3 months to work out a very novel and a very practical idea, called mortgage insurance, and that was how the FHA was born, . . . a joint undertaking by our group, if you wish to put it that way, and the then administration.

Herbert U. Nelson, NAREB, 1950[1]

No agency of the United States government has had a more pervasive and powerful impact on the American people over the past half-century than FHA.

Kenneth Jackson[2]

The telephone call that Herbert Nelson had been hoping for, asking NAREB to play a central role in designing the New Deal's housing programs, came even before Franklin Roosevelt's inauguration. Cordell Hull, a Democratic senator from Tennessee, about to be appointed secretary of state, asked Nelson to take the train in from Chicago and spend three or four weeks working in his office. Nelson, a staunch conservative Republican who liked to say that in his small town in Wisconsin, "We were all baptized into the Lutheran Church and the Republican Party on the same day," was adamantly opposed to expansion of the federal government. But he also knew that, designed in the right way, such federal programs could institutionalize everything realtors had been seeking even long before the Depression. Within a year of Roosevelt taking office— with unemployment at 25 percent; lending, construction, and real estate at a standstill; virtually no new building; three million unemployed construction workers[3]; property sales down by 83 percent, and many of those foreclosures; and realtors surviving by selling more property insurance than real estate[4]—NAREB became the government's partner in establishing and then staffing and operating the Federal Housing Administration (FHA). Realtors were so integral to FHA, they came to view it as their agency of the federal government.

Nelson had good reason to boast that FHA was "the greatest piece of legislation for home ownership ever adopted by any government in any period anywhere."[5] By providing a 100 percent guarantee of home loans it approved, FHA restored the market for homeownership. It provided long-term mortgages for the first time in history. This assured home buyers and banks that loans could be paid off over time, unlike the balloon mortgages that banks had been unable to roll over in the Depression, creating millions of foreclosures. FHA dramatically reduced the down payment a borrower needed. With FHA insurance commitments for all the homes in vast subdivisions, home builders who in the past had often built five or ten homes a year could now access capital to build a thousand or more homes.

FHA insurance transformed homeownership, development, and lending throughout the country. FHA-insured loans financed about one-third of all the mortgages in the United States over the next thirty years. Yet FHA's impact was wider still. The Veterans Administration guaranty loan program, which helped millions of veterans buy homes starting after World War II, was based on FHA's requirements. Federal bank regulators required that federally insured banks and savings and loans—that is, virtually all lenders—use the same types of loan underwriting principles as FHA. NAREB's objective in helping design FHA had been that it "produce far-reaching results in reorganization of the mortgage structure of the country . . . [and] set up a standard for all home mortgages."[6] As the realtors had foreseen, FHA standardized mortgage financing and with it the development and sale of residential real estate.

FHA's underwriting rules from the beginning were based on the realtors' property-value ideology. FHA and the programs based on it, which helped revive and drive the American economy, were designed by realtors to exclude minorities from white neighborhoods. Racial exclusion was essential, realtors and their allied economists claimed, to protect white neighborhoods from depreciation by other races. Only in this way could FHA's loans be safe and sound.[7] Racial discrimination was not an incidental or separate feature of FHA but at the very core of its rules for lenders and developers.

The effect of discrimination in federally backed lending was profound. Of twelve million homes financed with federal guarantees from the 1930s to the early 1960s, less than 2 percent were sold to minorities—and almost all of these were for segregated developments in the South.[8] In 1948, the commissioner of FHA proudly claimed that "FHA has never insured a housing project of mixed occupancy."[9] Indeed, federal discrimination was just as intense after World War II as before it. Of the first sixty-seven thousand VA-guaranteed mortgages in the New York metropolitan area, fewer than one hundred went to minority veterans. On the other side of the country, of two hundred thousand federally financed homes built in the Bay Area during the 1950s, fewer than fifty were available without regard to race.[10] And New York and the Bay Area were two of the places African Americans moved to in order to avoid segregation in the South.

Although the extent of federal housing discrimination has been abundantly documented in recent years,[11] the role of realtors in creating these segregationist policies—in designing and implementing the federal government's racial underwriting requirements—is less well known. What realtors had previously been able to do themselves to segregate American neighborhoods, they now accomplished far more thoroughly through the federal government. Realtors' dream of racial zoning by individual cities had been stymied by the Supreme Court, but the federal government now created a national system for segregating neighborhoods—a system designed, dominated, and controlled by realtors. Nelson was not exaggerating when he described FHA as "a joint undertaking by our group . . . and the . . . administration," nor when he added in 1950 that realtors "had been happy ever since."[12]

The realtors' own national history cites as their three greatest achievements cleaning up fraud in real estate sales, establishing zoning, and creating FHA.[13] These achievements had much in common. Each profoundly transformed American real estate—how it was bought and sold, how it was developed, how it was financed. In each case, the realtors first established standards in their own practice: codes of ethics, building and use covenants, Article 34. Having created an ideology to justify these standards for themselves, other brokers, buyers, and owners, realtors then used that ideology to successfully lobby government to apply these same standards to everyone. And once governments adopted those standards, realtors often served as state real estate commissioners, zoning board members, and FHA staff and consultants to carry them out. In the creation of FHA, NAREB put all these approaches to work, on the largest scale possible.

PARTNERSHIP WITH THE FEDERAL GOVERNMENT

Realtors' ability to influence federal programs under the New Deal did not begin then but with connections, credibility, shared objectives, ideas, and joint initiatives long before. Indeed, what stands out about the relationship between the federal government and NAREB from 1920 on, for the next thirty years, was how closely, collaboratively, and continuously they worked together.

Each needed the other. Presidents and federal officials turned to NAREB for technical expertise and advice, for the unmatched ability of local boards and realtors to market programs in every locality in the country, and for NAREB's lobbying power to mobilize the entire real estate and mortgage lending industries and provide private sector support for government proposals. Realtors, for their part, recognized how dependent their own business was on the national economy, how carrying out government programs could sustain them economically, and how they could effectively shape federal programs to meet their own core objectives. These objectives—expanding homeownership, making real estate financing more available, stabilizing real estate values, and institutionalizing the primary housing market for white Americans— were shared by federal officials.

The partnership between realtors and the federal government began in earnest with William May Garland's World War I role mobilizing realtors to help the government secure and build housing for soldiers and defense workers.[14] Working as a "dollar a year man," Garland not only helped run the Department of Labor's Bureau of Industrial Housing and

Transportation but recruited Duncan McDuffie and scores of others for similar jobs. (So far did the idea of realtor capability extend that McDuffie and a colleague from his firm, as planning experts, oversaw wartime regulation of the nation's wholesale bakeries and bread supplies.)[15] Of more immediate benefit to local realtors, in what would become a model for realtor participation in New Deal programs, Garland designed a key role for real estate boards in performing property assessments and valuations for sites to be purchased by the military.[16] This was financially critical for local realtors because all resources for housing construction had been diverted to supporting the war effort. More significant still in the long run, Garland helped NAREB establish what would become a permanent office in Washington. His own prestige assured a highly privileged, ongoing role for realtor lobbyists in working with the federal government.[17]

Such connections quickly bore fruit in the combined efforts of the federal government and realtors to promote homeownership after World War I. The Department of Labor and NAREB's "Own Your Own Home Committee" launched a joint campaign to encourage demand for new homes to revive the construction industry and national economy. "It is as much a patriotic duty to build [a home] as it was to render service . . . during the war," read a realtor pamphlet distributed by the Labor Department.[18]

In 1921, Herbert Hoover, the new secretary of commerce, worked with the realtors to create "Better Homes for America" as a major marketing campaign that continued through the 1920s.[19] Concerned that the rate of homeownership had slightly dropped since 1910, Hoover feared that America would become a nation of tenants,[20] vulnerable to the appeal of communism and socialism after the 1917 Russian Revolution. "If the proportion of non–home owners becomes so great that legislation is enacted at the behest of a majority of voters, it will be inimical to private property rights. . . . A nation of majority rule should be a nation of majority ownership."[21] Homeownership, Hoover believed, was deeply linked with citizenship, later calling it a "birthright" critical to "the national well-being" and spirit of "enterprise, of independence, and of . . . freedom."[22] Vice President Coolidge similarly declared homeownership a basic right for Americans. "It is of little avail, to assert that there is an inherent right to own property unless there is an open opportunity that this right may be enjoyed to a fair degree by all." Capitalism, he explained, "cannot prevail . . . unless it be of the people."[23] Such beliefs resonated with realtors and were reflected in the preamble added to their Code of Ethics in 1924 that realtors have recited ever since: "Under all is the land. Upon its wise utilization and widely allocated ownership depend the survival and growth of free institutions and of our civilization."[24]

Even as they worked on these joint promotional campaigns, federal officials and realtors both recognized that the great obstacle to expanding American homeownership remained what it had always been: the lack of long-term mortgage financing. Home mortgages in the 1920s, for those able to get them from banks, generally required a 50 percent down payment and had to be paid off or refinanced five years later in a single "balloon" payment. Terms from savings and loan associations were only slightly more liberal.[25] As a result, even in Los Angeles with its vast numbers of single-family homes, the homeownership rate was 35 percent, and less than half of those who were homeowners had mortgages.[26]

The problem was that lenders themselves relied on short-term capital and therefore did not have the financial capacity to make long-term loans. Throughout the 1920s, NAREB proposed a federally assisted system of discount banks to provide such capital, especially for savings and loan associations. Before the Depression, however, the idea of such government intervention in the housing markets fell on deaf ears in Washington. It went beyond the accepted role of government, which Hoover saw as promoting cooperation and voluntary action between government and business. By 1931, however, with banks unable to roll over balloon mortgages or make new loans, millions of homeowners facing foreclosure, and property values down by 50 percent from 1929,[27] it was clear to President Hoover that government had no choice. It would have to play a more expansive role.

A HIGH-STAKES CONFERENCE

In August 1930, Hoover announced an extraordinary national conference on homebuilding and homeownership to be chaired by the secretaries of commerce and the interior and held in Washington in December 1931. The planning was meticulous: fact-finding committees on virtually all aspects of housing, composed of experts around the country, would prepare reports that would then be correlated for a massive four-day conference. Highlighting the conference's significance, Hoover asked one of the committees to advise on the system of home loan banks that NAREB had long proposed; with unanimous support from the thirty-six hundred delegates at the conference, the president announced the Home Loan Bank Act that Congress passed in 1932.[28]

For any group that wanted to shape national housing policy, it was clear that the committees and the conference would be their key opportunity to do so. This proved farsighted. For although Franklin Roosevelt defeated Hoover less than a year later, the conference established many features of what became the New Deal's programs for the private housing market. NAREB saw the conference as crucial to the future of real estate, homeownership, its business, and the economy. It therefore played a central role in staffing many of the twenty-five fact-finding committees and preparing the reports that shaped the conference. For the committee on subdivisions, for example, NAREB provided seven of the sixteen members, including five men who had been or would be NAREB presidents, together with a NAREB research director who chaired the committee.[29]

At the conference, NAREB championed three crucial ideas that became core elements of federal housing programs. First, NAREB proposed the then-revolutionary idea of long-term, fully amortizing mortgages for up to 75 percent of property value.[30] Reducing required down payments from 50 percent before the Depression to 25 percent and ultimately, with NAREB's support, far lower levels, became the central element of FHA lending. No idea proved more crucial for the recovery of housing markets, construction of new homes, lowering of barriers to homeownership, and the dramatic increase in America's homeownership rate from 44 percent in the 1930s to 62 percent by 1960.

Second, NAREB successfully persuaded policymakers to support its ideology of racial homogeneity. The key committee on homeownership financing recommended deed restrictions to prevent "incompatible ownership occupancy," while the subdivision planning committee recommended that all new neighborhoods have "appropriate restrictions."[31]

On this central issue of race restrictions, NAREB had the strong support of the Hoover administration. The director of the president's conference and the chief of the Department of Commerce's housing division recommended that home buyers look for "restricted residential districts . . . as protection against persons with whom your family won't care to associate."[32] Federal loan underwriting and subdivision commitments based on deed restrictions became a fundamental feature of New Deal housing programs.

Not all participants at the conference agreed with NAREB's ideology of racial exclusion. The Committee on Negro Housing, staffed by Charles Johnson, now head of the Department of Sociology at Fisk, strongly disagreed. Johnson's 276-page report sought to dispel what it called the "common belief that . . . deteriorated areas, inherited by the low-income groups of Negroes as a result of their poverty, are alone theirs by right of race; that they are 'happier in their own neighborhoods' . . .; that any attempt on their part to escape this sordidness is prompted by a desire to live socially among white persons."[33] These were precisely the realtors' core tenets when it came to race.

Pointedly, the Committee on Negro Housing showed what the experts' textbooks left out. Johnson, always the expert at marshaling data, cited a study by the Detroit Bureau of Governmental Research that used basic economics to undercut the property-value ideology. "If a neighborhood . . . is 'invaded,'" the bureau concluded, real estate values were, if anything, likely to rise, given pent-up demand from African American buyers.[34] But the committee's argument made little impact, given the expert consensus that realtors had spent years creating. Johnson's voluminous study was reduced to a single short paragraph in the conference's final report, arguing for protection against discrimination.[35] It would be many years before Johnson's perspective would influence federal policy.

Third, NAREB successfully persuaded policymakers that the focus of new lending should be on financing suburban subdivisions that met nationally set standards for layout, infrastructure, zoning, deed restrictions, and market absorption, incorporating everything realtors had stressed since 1903 about proper housing development. New subdivisions would provide permanence, stability, and racial homogeneity for home buyers, NAREB argued. Lending on homes in such subdivisions would therefore be less risky for the federal government than lending on homes in older city areas.

Underlying all three of these ideas—long-term mortgage financing, racial exclusion, and new, carefully planned development—was NAREB's core argument for stability of property values. Such stability would enable the federal government to insure mortgages without losses to federal taxpayers. It would provide for steady recovery of confidence in real estate, make homeownership attractive to an economically battered populace, and realize realtors and federal officials' long-shared vision of the benefits of homeownership on citizenship—at least for the white Americans NAREB was focused on. The key to such stability, NAREB insisted, was racial homogeneity.

DESIGNING FHA

When the new Roosevelt administration came into office, seeking forceful action to stabilize property values and encourage construction, it turned to the ideas NAREB had laid out at Hoover's conference. Most of all, it turned to the realtors themselves. At Hull's invitation, Nelson had helped design the Home Owners' Loan Corporation in 1933, a highly effective emergency mechanism for averting foreclosures by providing longer-term government-backed financing for borrowers in default.

A year later, the administration again asked Nelson to spend several months in Washington, this time to help design the proposed Federal Housing Administration for new lending. Nelson worked with Marriner Eccles, assistant secretary of the Treasury, and soon appointed chair of the Federal Reserve; Frank Walker, one of FDR's closest aides and executive secretary of the National Emergency Council; Lewis Douglas, a conservative Democratic congressman from Arizona who had been named director of the Bureau of the Budget; and Charles Edison, Thomas Edison's heir and chairman of the Edison companies. In such a group, Nelson provided the crucial real estate expertise and industry connections. NAREB then became the major outside group lobbying for the legislation,[36] arguing that FHA was an essential government intervention to support the economy,[37] and playing a key role in the twelve-day conference to develop the detailed work plan for the new agency.[38]

The administration's reliance on the realtors was not surprising. New Deal leaders knew that FHA's very creation and its success would depend on NAREB support, lobbying, expertise, and marketing. Spurring construction of new homes to put people to work, and using federal insurance so that lenders would make loans to home buyers—the two primary purposes for establishing FHA—were both fields in which NAREB was highly involved. NAREB's subdivision committee represented the largest developers and home builders in the country.[39] NAREB's American Institute of Real Estate Appraisers comprised the leading experts on real estate valuation. NAREB's economic and research institute conducted and sponsored the real estate research that FHA would need to use in its risk assessments. NAREB's Mortgage and Finance Division had prepared the National Recovery Act code for the real estate mortgage business jointly with the mortgage brokers. Many NAREB members and associate members were leading mortgage bankers, and realtors had established and controlled many of America's savings and loan associations. And realtors were the salesmen who would have to market FHA programs to their home-buying clients in every city.

NAREB, on its part, saw the creation of FHA as a partnership with the administration. As NAREB's executive secretary proudly put it, "We weren't trying to get any advantage for any individual, or anything of that kind; we were doing what we thought was best for millions of home owners, regardless of party, regardless of politics."[40]

To help ensure that FHA met NAREB's expectations, realtors played key roles in establishing the agency. Fisher, head of research at NAREB, took on that role at FHA, while Babcock became director of underwriting. Babcock's assistant director of underwriting, Ayers Du Bois, had been state director of CREA.[41] Fred Marlow, the Los Angeles subdivider enlisted to run FHA's Southern California district office, touted the program to his former colleagues in *California Real Estate* magazine: "Under this program, realtors have the soundest movement ever initiated in this country for the preservation of property values, and the defense and protection of individual rights in the ownership of residential buildings."[42] Marlow's connections in the industry helped his office lead the nation each year in volume of FHA lending. In the decades ahead, NAREB and the real estate industry would view FHA as "their" separate part of the federal government, largely run by their representatives.[43]

NAREB's close connection with FHA sharply contrasted with its fierce opposition to the New Deal's public housing program. Many inside and outside the administration believed that the solution to the country's most critical housing and employment needs was a massive government-owned housing initiative. NAREB fought this idea relentlessly as a direct threat to the private market and private ownership of housing. NAREB lobbied to lower or eliminate appropriations and restrict public housing. Indeed, when Roosevelt sought appropriations for seven hundred thousand units of defense-worker housing in October 1940, NAREB successfully persuaded Congress to require that every unit be torn down at the end of the war or sold on the private market.[44] For NAREB, the success of FHA was crucial to the country's future as a society of private, not public, ownership. From Roosevelt's point of view, it was important to offset the New Deal's many direct public initiatives—WPA, PWA, and TVA, as well as public housing—with one based on the private market and supported and implemented by private industry. He thus welcomed FHA's close ties to NAREB.

RACIAL EXCLUSION

The realtors' property-value ideology and insistence on neighborhood homogeneity were built into the FHA program from the beginning. They were presented as an essential means of managing risk. The administration had no reason to push back. The property-value ideology had become the consensus not only of the entire real estate industry and the experts but of white Americans generally.[45] If the NAACP and some Jewish groups criticized federal discriminatory practices, their marginal power was limited in a New Deal dependent on support of Southern segregationist senators for all its programs. The courts had accepted racial covenants as protecting property values. Most salient of all, the nation's appraisers, grouped in NAREB's American Institute of Estate Appraisers, who would be asked to carry out the appraisals for government mortgage insurance, insisted on the core economic principle that minorities lowered property values. If the government wanted to manage the loan risks it was taking on, they said, it had no choice but to make race and racial homogeneity a key factor in all its decisions. The realtors' apparently race-neutral, unprejudiced assertion became, without debate, the policy of the federal government.

The 1935 FHA underwriting manual incorporated the property-value ideology directly. The manual's racial policies were highly explicit. "If a neighborhood is to retain stability," the manual stated, "it is necessary that properties shall continue to be occupied by the same social and racial classes. A change in social or racial occupancy generally leads to instability and a reduction in value."[46] The neighborhood thus had to be racially homogeneous at the time the loan was made, and, even more important, the risk evaluator had to determine whether it was likely to remain that way over the life of the loan.

Because FHA loans had a maturity of twenty-five years, long-term protection against minorities ever living in the same neighborhood was the key for loan approval. To make sure the neighborhood would be adequately protected against "adverse influence," especially "infiltration of inharmonious racial or nationality groups," FHA instructed the evaluator to look for racial restrictive covenants on all properties in the neighborhood. But the evaluator had to look *outside* the neighborhood's borders as well. Were there undesirable households—"incompatible racial and social groups"—in nearby areas who might ultimately invade the neighborhood?[47] FHA therefore wanted to know whether there were "natural or artificially established barriers" (such as train tracks and/or race restrictions) to protect the "neighborhood . . . from . . . infiltration of . . . inharmonious racial groups."[48] FHA's decision rule was clear. "Where little or no protection is provided against adverse influences, the valuator must not hesitate to make a reject rating of this feature." Since rejection on this, or any other grounds, meant the loan itself had to be rejected,[49] the realtors' ideology of property values had thus been fully incorporated.

FHA's unequivocality on adverse racial influences was striking, compared to its other underwriting criteria. In its location criteria, for example, FHA told valuators to be extremely cautious in deciding whether to reject mixed land use areas near downtowns of major cities. They urged outlining any areas to be rejected "with the greatest of care in order to save embarrassment to the Insuring Office."[50] In downtown areas, important property owners might object. When it came to race, however, FHA was absolute.

Even more striking was the difference between FHA's racial rules and what it told the public. FHA's racial underwriting rules and redlining maps are well known now, but none of these internal documents were publicly available at the time. Indeed, FHA went to extraordinary lengths to prevent the general public, minority groups, and the NAACP from learning about any of the agency's racial criteria. An owner in a mixed area simply received a form rejection letter stating that the "property does not meet the general requirements of the FHA." It took four years for the NAACP to learn what was going on. "At the outset we felt that perhaps these complaints were merely isolated instances of local prejudice," Roy Wilkins, NAACP's assistant secretary, wrote to FHA. Suspecting that FHA was hiding some type of racial rules, NAACP's counsel and later Supreme Court justice Thurgood Marshall launched multiple inquiries before finally obtaining a copy of the underwriting manuals, guarded so tightly they were "serial numbered and evidently not in use for general distribution."[51]

MAPPING RACIAL UNDESIRABILITY

The same secrecy applied to the redlining maps FHA created to make underwriting decisions. FHA drew up these block-by-block maps for every city in the country, rating the risk level of each neighborhood[52] based on the judgment of leading realtors in each city. To gauge risk not only at the time the loan was made but over its full twenty-five-year term, FHA asked local staff to assemble historical maps for 1935, 1915, and 1900 showing the relative undesirability of each neighborhood at each point in time, as a basis for anticipating its future.

FHA outsourced the preparation of these base maps to the local real estate industry. It instructed the staff in each area office to ask three prominent figures in the local real estate community, all over fifty years old and familiar with local neighborhoods, to prepare maps for each period. These men, inevitably realtors or their close allies in mortgage lending and insurance, were asked to indicate the presence at each date of factors considered unfavorable to underwriting, including "factories, industries, railroad yards . . . and any . . . racial, national or income group that may be considered undesirable if introduced in other parts of the city."[53] This final phrase reflected the realtors' Code of Ethics almost word for word. Respondents were asked to estimate the percentage of "any races other than white" and "any nationalities . . . considered undesirable."[54]

FHA's Residential Security Maps, which institutionalized redlining in America and were compiled from these base maps, thus reflected how each city's realtors assessed racial detrimentality. Recent detailed regression analyses show that the ratings that FHA assigned to neighborhoods had little relationship to land value, which FHA's chief mapper himself had called an accurate index of mortgage risk. Instead, the ratings closely correlated with who lived there. Areas with Mexican Americans and African Americans were inevitably marked in red; FHA and other federally regulated lenders would make no loans there.[55] What the FHA maps showed was the level of realtors' prejudice.

FHA's assumption in looking at cities and creating these maps was ecological: neighborhoods would succumb one by one to the forces of age and succession. The older the district, the more likely that it would be taken over by detrimental influences. Only sound planning and racial restrictions could prevent this decline. This pessimistic view of neighborhood property values, in which neighborhoods can and ultimately must go downhill, also inevitably reflected the reality of the Depression when FHA was created.[56]

Although this succession theory was seemingly objective, it was based on a highly subjective view. It likened neighborhoods' vulnerability to "undesirable" minorities to aging bodies' vulnerability to disease or cancer. "At the period of vigorous youth, the neighborhood has the vitality to fight off the disease of blight. The owners will strenuously resist the encroachment of inharmonious forces because of their pride in their homes and their desire to maintain a favorable environment for their children." Neighborhoods becoming obsolete, however, "do not offer vigorous resistance to the incoming of other racial groups."[57] In FHA's maps, the realtors' image of other races as foreign bodies invading a healthy area became a scientific principle.

Thus FHA's maps graded neighborhoods A to D in terms of their relative vulnerability—based on their age and protections or lack of protection—to the spreading disease represented by "undesirable" groups. Grade A neighborhoods had the greatest protection. Grade D neighborhoods, already overrun, had none. This model of aging translated directly into the maximum term of loans FHA would offer—twenty-five years for A districts, twenty years for B districts, no more than ten years for C districts endangered by undesirable people, and no loans at all for D districts already afflicted with too many undesirable people.

FHA's maps were prophecies. And because FHA itself was the primary source of capital for home mortgages in America, and banks used its maps for their own lending, FHA's prophecies of which neighborhoods would physically deteriorate proved self-fulfilling. The geographic impact of FHA lending rules can be seen on the ground today. A comprehensive 2017 study by the Federal Reserve Bank of Chicago looked at the impacts eighty years later of the lines federal agencies drew in the 1930s in 149 cities. Where ordinary streets had been used to demarcate C or D neighborhoods, there had been little difference at the time in housing prices or conditions in the blocks on either side of these arbitrary boundaries. Eight decades later, the differences in housing prices, conditions, ownership, and who lived in those same blocks were profound.[58] The pattern was the same in cities across the country. The realtors' ideology, applied block by block by FHA to determine where loans could be made, far from explaining property values, helped determine them.

NEW CONSTRUCTION FAR FROM MINORITIES

FHA's view of succession and vulnerability to undesirable racial groups helps explain its extraordinary emphasis on new construction of highly planned subdivisions in outlying areas. FHA's theory that "neighborhoods tend to decline in investment quality" could only be offset by lending in new neighborhoods that are "favorably situated . . . adequately protected from adverse influences and definitely planned in accordance with good housing practice."[59] Equally important, FHA's emphasis on new development enabled it to meet one of its fundamental mandates: to generate construction jobs. Perhaps the most salient argument when FHA was proposed to Congress was that one-third of all American unemployment was related "directly and indirectly with the building trades."[60] Large-scale new development provided a powerful and efficient way for FHA to spur employment.

FHA helped make such development possible on an unprecedented scale. While insisting on planning standards, controls on market absorption, and racial restriction, FHA added a far-reaching innovation that helped radically segregate metropolitan areas: conditional commitments for new subdivisions. If a subdivision plan met all of its requirements, FHA gave the developer's construction lender an advance commitment that FHA would insure the ultimate loans for all the homes. With such preapproval in hand, a developer could obtain financing from banks and insurance companies for 100 percent, or sometimes more, of all the costs, from land acquisition through construction.[61] Ready capital at a time of depressed land prices and chronic cash shortages gave FHA-approved developers an extraordinary ability to acquire larger sites in outlying areas, at the same time that new roads made such land far more accessible. FHA policy did not limit the dollar amount of advance commitments and favored major developers, such as NAREB's leading builders. As Marc Weiss recounts, one only has to look at FHA's subdivision guidelines to see the pattern of America's suburbs.[62] Lending on new homes in such subdivisions, FHA believed, allowed it to meet its mission while minimizing its risks, including the risk of racial change.

EXCLUDING MINORITIES

FHA locational criteria excluded minorities in three key ways. First, the vast majority of FHA's lending was for racially restricted new subdivisions far from any minority groups. FHA effectively assumed the role and perspective of Nichols and McDuffie, even recommending the form of covenant Nichols had created thirty years before. Like Nichols and

McDuffie, FHA was now the party with the single largest long-term financial risk exposure to property values in a subdivision. And like them as well, FHA assumed that racial exclusion was essential both to protect itself and its vision of a successful community. This convergence of the interests of community builders and the federal government was quickly noted by Walter Leimert, a developer who had imposed some of the most stringent racial restrictions in the East Bay.[63] In "Government the Yardstick for Real Estate," Leimert told fellow realtors that "What the government wants . . . makes a very good advertisement for what I have been manufacturing . . . what subdividers have been promising their customers for more than a generation."[64] The result of this alliance of interests between FHA and realtor developers was dramatic. By 1940 in California, with almost one-fifth of all FHA loans in the country,[65] 83 percent of FHA's lending was on newly constructed single-family homes.[66] Virtually none of the loans made on the homes in these communities went to minorities.

Second, FHA would not approve individual loans by minorities seeking to buy homes in white neighborhoods. By FHA's logic, such borrowers would themselves depreciate property values and reduce the collateral value on FHA's other loans in the neighborhood.

Third, the only areas where a minority would not depreciate property values were precisely the mixed neighborhoods that were redlined on FHA's locational maps. Under this triple Catch-22, very few loans were made to minorities anywhere.

Boyle Heights in Los Angeles shows how FHA viewed such mixed neighborhoods and the people who lived there. Just east of downtown, Boyle Heights was marked red for several reasons. Long a working-class, immigrant area with ramshackle houses, it had been zoned for industrial uses in the 1908 realtor-supported zoning ordinance. By the 1930s, the neighborhood was both significantly industrial and populated by many groups—Russians, Jews, Japanese, Armenians, Mexicans, and African Americans—who were excluded from restricted neighborhoods elsewhere in the city. FHA gave Boyle Heights its lowest rating: "This is a 'melting pot' area and is literally honeycombed with diverse and subversive racial elements. It is seriously doubted whether a single block . . . does not contain detrimental racial elements and . . . very few districts which are not hopelessly heterogeneous."[67]

FHA's description of Boyle Heights exemplified the agency's absolute insistence on and belief in homogeneity. An area of diverse ethnicities was, to FHA, the worst of all. Moreover, labeling all these groups "subversive," even in a mixed area like Boyle Heights, shows that FHA viewed these groups as detrimental not only if they infiltrated a white neighborhood—the nominal standard of the realtor Code of Ethics and FHA itself—but detrimental *no matter where they lived*. Underneath the official property-value ideology was simple racial prejudice itself. Because of their race and ethnicity, the people who lived in Boyle Heights should not get FHA loans there or anywhere else.

Boyle Heights also exemplified what happened to inner-city neighborhoods redlined by FHA. For decades to come, it would be difficult for any potential home buyer to get a federally insured loan there. Lack of access to capital meant increased physical deterioration. Then, as members of one European ethnic group after another came to be considered "white" or desirable, its members could get FHA loans to move to white neighborhoods elsewhere. Boyle Heights became Mexican American and cut off from the rest of the city. Parts of the area were demolished and became public housing projects, and the Santa Monica Freeway tore through Boyle Heights in the 1950s.[68]

The process was similar in Watts, which was also redlined by FHA. As late as 1940, the neighborhood was still a mix of Italian Americans, Mexican Americans, Japanese Americans, and, making up approximately 35 percent of the population, African Americans. When African Americans moved to Los Angeles in great numbers during World War II, mixed areas like Watts were the only neighborhoods they were not excluded from. The highly predictable result was extreme overcrowding. As Charlotta Bass of the *California Eagle* described, "It was pathetic. Negro families who came to work in the war industries were forced to live in old garages, broken-down store-fronts, deserted railroad coaches, thatched tents—all without sanitary conveniences."[69] By the late 1940s, Watts and South Central became dense, deteriorated African American ghettos. By 1958, Watts was 95 percent African American.[70]

Although realtors and FHA officials did not plan what would happen in the neighborhoods they redlined,[71] their policies profoundly changed those areas. When FHA made low-cost capital available on favorable terms everywhere else, financed new communities, and made it possible for "desirable human elements" to move away from mixed neighborhoods, these areas became disinvestment zones. They changed socially, physically, and economically. The result was stark. The place where minorities could live became a separate world, economically and physically as well as racially.

By 1947, Charles Johnson with Herman Long showed, in materials for the Supreme Court, how African American residential areas had taken on the same traits in every metropolitan area.

> In every major American city . . . there are certain characteristics almost invariably associated with . . . Negro residence areas. . . . [They are] located in the oldest part of the city [with] the most obsolete dwellings . . . where foreign immigrants usually started who—with improved economic standing and "Americaniza-tion' . . . have been able to move into areas of better housing and greater dispersion. . . . Negroes whose economic status . . . have similarly progressed . . . have been unable to move out in the same way. . . . [These areas] have . . . become the dumping ground. . . . Compared to similar accommodations available to white tenants, the rents are generally high. Most structures are not only old but used for purposes other than those for which they were originally designed.[72]

This happened in so much the same way in Los Angeles, San Diego, San Francisco, the East Bay, Sacramento, Milwaukee, Chicago, and Pitts-burgh, to name only a few, that it is easy to think of the outcome in each of these cities as foreordained. It was not. These patterns occurred in every major city because the same forces had been at work.

The "dumping grounds" that resulted from disinvestment were used to justify the policies that created them. The people unable to leave such ghettos, now almost all African American, were invariably associ-ated with the conditions they were forced to live in. The natural conclu-sion was that the realtors and FHA had been right: African Americans did reduce the value of a neighborhood. They did not deserve to live elsewhere. The longer such discriminatory policies went on, the more such apparent evidence could be counted on to support those policies. Johnson and Long described this dynamic.

> Real estate agents [and] . . . bankers . . . have drawn around the thick and squirming Negro ghettoes a cordon of formal and informal restrictions designed to make it forever impossible for any Negro family to escape this blight. . . . The policy is consciously justified on the grounds of protection of property rights and values that the most gentle and God-fearing Christians can support . . . without moral restraint and leave to time and fate the . . . problems of the Negroes within this invisible wall.[73]

NAREB's own imagery was far more graphic. Its texts warned realtors, and through them their clients, what happened when a white district began "to suffer from the invasion of an undesirable element. Already the invaders have captured the fringe of the district and, like a boa constrictor, are squeezing the inside area. Blight is under way. Property values are definitely going down."[74] The perceived threat from African Americans required, in the eyes of federal agency officials, homeowners, and realtors, the cordon of restrictions that FHA had long institutionalized.

OBJECTIFYING PREJUDICE

FHA insisted it was not prejudiced. It systematically limited access by minorities, but not because the federal government inherently preferred one race over another, which would be unconstitutional. Rather, FHA limited access by minorities because its risk evaluation system treated minorities as unacceptable risks, both for individual loans and because their buying a home would reduce the value of surrounding homes with FHA mortgages. Like the Portland Realty Board in 1920 and NAREB over the years, FHA argued that it was simply dealing with an objective reality in the marketplace: the stability of property values depended on racial homogeneity.

When the NAACP ferreted out and then challenged FHA's policies—

finally obtaining a copy of the closely guarded underwriting manual in 1938 and publicizing FHA's instructions in African American newspapers as the "Jim Crow Housing Policy"—the president defended the agency. The agency's only role was to determine that the loan was "economically sound." "Real estate values are determined by the market which in turn is established by the demands of the buying public. . . . FHA cannot prescribe . . . the market . . . in reverse of public demand. To attempt to do so would cause lenders to lose faith in the stability of FHA and . . . defeat its objectives."[75] FHA would later claim that it had "no responsibility for . . . social policy," that it was solely a "business organization" that only considered "the cold facts and the element of risk." Put simply, "an interracial community was a bad risk."[76]

In reality, there were no cold facts. FHA and its chief underwriter and chief economist, who had written NAREB's textbooks, did not examine actual long-term price trends including prices paid by minorities. Nor did FHA ever provide evidence for its claim that racial heterogeneity lowered property values.[77] Instead, the realtors' property-value ideology, repeated in each successive FHA underwriting manual, became the basis of millions of FHA loan decisions.

Indeed, FHA, real estate experts, and realtors, as in the case of Boyle Heights, hardly distinguished between their axiom that minorities reduced property values and their view that minorities were undesirable wherever they lived. When Babcock wrote that a "neighborhood . . . will not possess maximum desirability unless it provides the right setting for the rearing of children . . . [including] desirable neighbors and their children,"[78] he was less describing market forces of supply and demand than describing what the market should value. When the underwriting manual insisted that "families enjoy social relationships with other families whose education, abilities, mode of living, and racial characteristics are similar to their own,"[79] FHA was giving valuators a moral reason to reject racially incompatible purchasers.

Not surprisingly, when FHA finally conducted its own empirical studies of property values in the late 1940s, it had a hard time accepting the results. FHA acknowledged the facts. "The infiltration of Negro owner-occupants has tended to appreciate property values and neighborhood stability."[80] But what was striking was FHA's terminology. "Infiltration"

—the exact term FHA had long used to describe minority threats to property values[81]—now described minorities' *positive* effects on price and stability. This contorted sentence shows in miniature the pressures that had driven government and experts for so many years. The need for a fiction had been more important than facts.

Looked at as a whole, FHA was among the most effective machines ever created for generating wealth, increasing homeownership, improving housing quality, and providing stakes in democratic capitalism, all while fostering a belief among its beneficiaries that those stakes had been created solely through individual merit and the private market. FHA also institutionalized neighborhood homogeneity and spatial isolation by race. These outcomes were intimately linked. As historian David Freund has put it, the federal programs realtors helped design did not simply "create a new housing market and *then* deny racial minorities access to it. Instead they conceived of the new housing market as exclusively serving white . . . families. [This federal] vision of the free market for homes, and of the citizenry deemed capable of thriving in it, simply had no place for racial minorities."[82]

Robert Weaver summed up how FHA had accomplished the realtors' objectives with respect to race. "What the Supreme Court said was unconstitutional through municipal zoning, what property owners' associations had been able to accomplish only at great expense and imperfectly, FHA encouraged and facilitated. And the people who actually carried out the plans were, in effect, protected against the loss of their investment . . . by Black and white taxpayers alike."[83] Weaver recognized that FHA's racial policies were "probably inevitable once the government turned the agency's operations over to the real estate and home finance boys."[84] In fact, given NAREB's integral involvement in FHA from the beginning, there never was such a transitional moment. There was not, and perhaps could never have been, an FHA that was not, from the start, the real estate boys'.

7.

Reconciling the War against Hitler with a New Racial Entitlement

> If we want to talk about freedom, we must mean freedom for others as well as ourselves, and we must mean freedom for everyone.
>
> Wendell Willkie, 1940[1]

In 1939, when NAREB approved the textbook equating a colored man of means with madams and gangsters, Herbert Nelson in his downtown Chicago office could only assume that the future of residential segregation was secure. With each month that passed, FHA approved new subdivisions permanently protected from racial minorities. All-white real estate boards in every city deterred Black buyers from moving into white neighborhoods by telling them no suitable homes were on the market or that those with a For Sale sign had just been sold. If a rare owner did consider selling to a minority, board members were ready—through what one board called its "meat-axe committee"—to apply "very strenuous measures to prevent unscrupulous sales," exerting every economic and social pressure including buying the property themselves.[2] In covenant cases, board members would testify that, unless the minority occupant was evicted from the home, the value of surrounding homes would drop by half. The property-value axiom was taught at 165 of 165 universities teaching real estate.[3] Perhaps most important of all, it would have been hard to find white owners who did not believe that minorities depreciated property values. Indeed, Black leaders despaired at this idea having become a fixture of American public opinion. All these elements of residential segregation supported each other in a coherent, ever-stronger system.

Yet in less than a decade, residential segregation was under attack at the highest levels of the federal government. FHA and NAREB reluctantly conceded that minority buyers did not reduce prevailing prices and in many cases increased them. And, as constitutional and economic principles that had sustained segregation were invalidated, many white Americans were forced to seriously consider, perhaps for the first time, whether segregation was consistent with fundamental ideals of American freedom.

In responding to such attacks, however, NAREB could draw on the lasting legacy that realtors and FHA had created. Realtors' arguments and FHA lending had changed white Americans' beliefs of what they were entitled to as basic rights. Long after NAREB stopped officially proclaiming that minorities depreciated property values, it could appeal to these deep beliefs to continue segregation.

THE ATTACK ON SEGREGATION

The decisions that began to shake the segregated system realtors had created were made not in Washington or even the United States but in Berlin and Tokyo. The racist imperialism of Hitler and the Japanese leadership began to jeopardize the broad consensus that realtors had established in the United States. To the dismay of realtors as well as Southern segregationists, the rhetoric of race from America's enemies threatened to discredit the most fundamental premises of racial systems at home.

With government, media, and virtually every organization urging unity and sacrifice for a common national cause, President Roosevelt called being an American "a matter of mind and heart, never a matter of race and ancestry." The secretary of state proclaimed that "all peoples, without distinction of race, color or religion, who are prepared and willing to accept the responsibilities of liberty are entitled to its enjoyment."[4] That this ignored the incarceration of Japanese Americans did not diminish the sweep of the rhetoric. Speaking in Los Angeles, Wendell Willkie, who had been Roosevelt's Republican opponent in 1940, made racial bias a wartime issue. "The attitude of the white citizens of this country toward the Negroes has . . . had some of the . . . tragic characteristics of an alien imperialism—a smug racial superiority, a willingness to exploit an unprotected people."[5]

In the climate of the war, racial discrimination became a national issue. Despite Southern opposition, a modest federal employment discrimination law passed Congress. The Carnegie Corporation engaged Gunnar Myrdal to write his path-breaking *An American Dilemma: The Negro Problem and American Democracy*. Myrdal, drawing in part on extensive research from Charles Johnson, highlighted residential segregation as a betrayal of American freedom.

For those committed to segregation, this emphasis on freedom as an end to discrimination was threatening indeed. A constitutional lawyer from Alabama, Charles Wallace Collins, who would play an important postwar role in shifting Southerners away from the national Democratic Party, recognized the threat posed by these wartime values. Shortly after the war's end, Collins warned of the "refrain" throughout *An American Dilemma* "which represents a new propaganda for Negro advancement . . . [that] America is a 'democracy' and the Negro should demand equal rights under it. 'The Four Freedoms,' for which they assert we were at war, should be won for the Negroes at home."[6] Such war aims were dangerous, Collins insisted, because civil rights advocates were using them to challenge all forms of segregation.

Indeed, civil rights lawyers began using the country's war aims and opposition to Nazi racism to attack racial covenants. They pointed out that "happily enough" in the ghettos where "Negroes and non-Caucasians are forced to live separate and apart from other Americans by force of law," they "are not required to carry a yellow card."[7] In Orange County, California, attorneys for a Mexican American family not only challenged realtors' rote claims "that having Mexicans live in a neighborhood brought down property values by at least half" but also argued that the neighbors' effort to evict the Bernals "was taken from Hitler's *Mein Kampf.*" Skeptical of the realtors' property-value claims, the judge wrote that he would rather "have people of the type of the Bernals living next door to me than . . . the paranoid type now living in Germany."[8] International racial issues began to play in American courtrooms.

By 1945, a local judge in Los Angeles, for the first time anywhere in the country, dismissed a racial covenant case on constitutional grounds.

The "Sugar Hill" case was covered in *Time* magazine because it sought to evict famous Black actresses—Ethel Waters; Hattie McDaniel, who had played the maid in *Gone with the Wind*; and Louise Beavers—from their homes near Hollywood. "It is time," Judge Thurmond Clarke wrote, that "members of the Negro race are accorded, without reservations or evasions, the full rights guaranteed them under the 14th Amendment. . . . Judges have been avoiding the real issue too long. Certainly there was no discrimination against the Negro race when it came to calling upon its members to die on the battlefields in defense of this country."[9] The Los Angeles NAACP lawyer who brought the case, Loren Miller, would play a major role in opposing realtors nationally.

Two years later, a second judge in Los Angeles, in another Miller case, stressed these same wartime values in holding covenants unconstitutional. Noting that one of the defendants was a Purple Heart veteran who had served in both world wars, Judge Stanley Mosk was scathing: "There is no more reprehensible un-American activity than depriving people of their own homes on a 'master race' theory. . . . Our nation just fought against the Nazi race superiority doctrines. This court would indeed be callous to constitutional rights if it were to permit [him] to be ousted from his own home by using 'race' as the measure of his worth as a citizen and neighbor."[10]

Such judges might have been unusually racially liberal; indeed, later as state attorney general and state supreme court justice, Mosk became a leading opponent of Proposition 14. But realtors understood that they would need to counter such views in the press, in the courts, and in public meetings with arguments that would resonate with the country's wartime values. They could no longer simply appeal to property values or prejudice.

Indeed, in the midst of World War II, when the *Pittsburgh Courier* issued a front-page expose of the NAREB textbook passage on call girls and colored men of means, saying it ran on "parallel lines" to "the Hitlerian philosophy of 'ghettoes for the Jewish people,'" NAREB, for once, backpedaled. Acknowledging that it had reviewed and approved the text, it called the wording "most regrettable" and denied that it represented the "official attitude" of the association.[11] That NAREB felt it necessary to apologize was remarkable in itself, even if it was only to fend off any changes to realtor policies.

Charles Abrams, a leading opponent of housing discrimination, similarly used the example of Nazi Germany to launch a telling attack on FHA's lending policies. Abrams, a white New York urbanist and lawyer who would figure importantly in the fair housing movement, famously coined the term "socialism for the rich and capitalism for the poor." Describing himself as "a practical planner who becomes a propagandist when necessary,"[12] Abrams took on this almost universally lauded agency in terms of what America had fought the war against. In barring "inharmonious groups from new neighborhoods," Abrams said, "FHA adopted a racial policy that could well have been culled from the Nuremberg Laws."[13]

The Four Freedoms, Hitlerian philosophy, *Mein Kampf*, Nazi race superiority, Nuremberg Laws—realtors and FHA were not used to responding to such critiques. Racial covenants and government policies that realtors had promoted for decades, whose popular appeal they had taken for granted, were now portrayed as threats to American freedom.

Not surprisingly, the discrediting of the property-value ideology began during the war. The first appraisal journal article to question the realtors' orthodoxy, Elsie Smith Parker's in 1943, cautious as it was in its conclusions, raised a question that had not been asked in such publications: "We hear much of the equality of man these days. We are fighting a war to prove it. Can anyone deny that the Negro should be given the opportunity to earn for himself adequate housing?"[14]

Within months, Frank Horne, head of FHA's Office of Race Relations, recognized what a flood of such articles could do. Consistently frustrated in his efforts to change the agency's racial policies, Horne wrote to Walter White, head of the NAACP and active in its Double V campaign for victory for African Americans fighting for freedom overseas and at home. "What happens to the 'values' of these respective properties?" Horne asked. "Who determines the 'loss of value' of properties in neighborhoods recently opened to Negroes? These . . . questions have apparently never been thoroughly explored. The concepts . . . have not been seriously challenged."[15] Empirical studies, Horne realized, could help bring down the house of cards. By "reducing superstition and hearsay with facts in regard to the effect of Negro occupancy upon real property values," such studies might have a powerful impact. FHA and realtors would "lose their main justification for covenants and other restrictive practices." Here was a crucial topic the NAACP and its allies should encourage researchers to focus on. As detailed studies began to show that there was no adverse impact on prices from minorities moving into white neighborhoods, civil rights organizations reprinted and publicized them. Abrams compiled these new findings and summed them up in a coup-de-grâce article in the *Appraisal Journal* in 1951.[16]

Together, the discrediting of the property-value axiom and the wartime ideal of freedom placed realtors on the defensive. NAREB and FHA both toned down some of their rhetoric, with FHA removing explicit racial references from its underwriting manual by 1947.[17] But realtors did not change their objective of maintaining all-white neighborhoods. What they needed was a new way to defend segregation in a postwar America where freedom was increasingly being used to mean equal freedom.

ENTITLEMENT

Yet even while these changes were occurring, a different reality had also been created. The all-white neighborhoods that had been built, FHA's economic and other impacts, and the realtors' arguments had an important and lasting effect. They changed what many Americans believed they were entitled to.

Part of such entitlement was economic. James Moffett, FHA's first administrator, promised that there were "billions and billions" to be made using FHA, at a time when the average cost of a new home was $6,000 and an average wage was $1,600 per year. "No such market has ever before in all history been offered [to] industry," Moffett asserted. He was not exaggerating.[18] The government's reduction of private market risk allowed wealth to be generated for developers, lenders, real estate agents, construction workers, architects, engineers, title companies, and, most of all, tens of millions of home buyers who could afford homes for the first time.

The cost of ownership, thanks to the low interest rate on government-insured mortgages and to tax deductions, was often less than that of renting. Because eligible borrowers could buy homes at much younger ages without needing to have saved up as much capital, they had a longer period for homes to appreciate.[19] This allowed them to significantly increase equity for themselves and their descendants. African Americans were largely excluded from these increased opportunities. As a result, the differential between the white and African American homeownership rate widened significantly.[20] The possibility of buying and owning a home more easily and affordably than ever before became a more common expectation, a birthright, for white Americans.

Widespread homeownership, as Coolidge and Hoover had hoped, gave a much larger share of American households a stake in America's capitalist system and helped create political stability. Millions of new home buyers found the realtors' argument about property values especially compelling; it conveyed their right to protect what they now owned. They became far more concerned about private property rights and saw homeownership as a fundamental mark of full citizenship.[21] Moreover, as David Freund has argued, FHA borrowers came to see their home and the security and status it provided as due not to government assistance but solely to their own hard work, savings, and individual merit, as recognized through the private market system. FHA's public relations strategy to support this narrative had paid off.[22]

The racial homogeneity of the neighborhood became part of the natural bundle of rights a homeowner had purchased with his or her home—something that the government, along with the developer and the realtor, helped assure. The insistence on homogeneity was not merely a function of individual prejudice, FHA implied, but an objective requirement of the free market itself—the market through which the white homeowner had earned and deserved his home. Further, racial homogeneity became, as a realtor had described it years before, an essential part "of the enjoyment of the constitutional provision of the protection of the home."[23] The right to racial homogeneity was thus, in some sense, a component of full citizenship, a right on which the federal government itself had sealed its stamp of approval.[24] When a buyer bought a new home in an FHA subdivision, the deed restriction often began by reciting that FHA was "one of the reasons for the restrictions imposed."[25] To millions of white homeowners, it was not only the developer, the market, and the economic laws of property values that sanctioned their living in an all-white community but the government itself.

These beliefs about rights would long outlast FHA's and the realtors' official use of the property-value ideology that had justified racial discrimination to begin with. As NAACP lawyer Loren Miller explained, "Americans of all walks of life have accommodated themselves to the hard fact of residential segregation. That accommodation shapes their thinking and their actions." "It seems to justify the commonly held belief that a particular section of the city 'belongs' to members of the group who live there and that they are justified in trying to exclude members of other groups."[26] That one could and should live in an all-white community, a right that depended precisely on minorities not having such a right, became part of what white Americans expected. This was the key belief realtors could draw on and find ways to articulate.

THEFT

The property-value ideology triggered a second set of beliefs that would prove equally enduring. That minorities depreciated property values—a fundamental truth Americans heard from realtors, owners' associations, the federal government, and the media for decades—created for many white owners a powerful and lasting image of minorities. The message was inescapable. A minority family buying a home in a white neighborhood *at or above the asking price* was stealing something from the neighbors, something he or she was not entitled to.[27]

This idea of theft had deep resonance both for white owners and for courts dealing with racial covenants.[28] To be "undesirable" meant that one's very presence subtracted from what white owners were entitled to. Judicial enforcement of covenants relied on this idea of theft. In 1945, a federal court enforced a racial restriction in the nation's capital because, it found, occupancy by Negroes "will be injurious, depreciative and absolutely ruinous of the real estate . . . and harmful, detrimental, subversive of the peace of mind, comfort and property rights . . . of other . . . owners. . . . [Thus] occupancy . . . by any persons of the Negro race or blood will constitute a continuing wrong and injury."[29]

Seeing minorities as taking away what did not belong to them made their very desire to move into a white neighborhood illegitimate. In this view, members of minority groups could not have a valid, economic reason to move in, because they would be reducing prices for everyone, including themselves. What a minority buyer must really want, in this view, was the social status of living with whites. Here, too, he would destroy what he was seeking, because whites would move away. The idea that minorities wanted white social acceptance denied that minorities might want or be entitled to the same freedom to choose where to live as everyone else. As Byron Rumford would later put it in sponsoring California's fair housing law: for African Americans, as with all Americans, "there is a natural tendency to break out of" limited areas, "based upon the principle in America that an individual can go as far as his ability and economic condition will allow him." "It isn't that we want to live next door to a Caucasian. I see nothing uplifting or degrading, really, about wanting to live next door to one. They are people and if they are decent people, we like to live next door to a decent neighbor."[30] Framing minority aspirations, instead, as wanting white social acceptance illegitimized those aspirations as wanting to steal something from whites. This view proved so long lasting because it expressed in the most commonsense terms the differential racial entitlement realtors had worked so hard to create.

Not surprisingly, when *Fortune* conducted a national poll in 1939, only 15 percent of white Americans outside the South believed that African Americans should be allowed "to live wherever they wanted to live."[31] Thirty-five years earlier, there had not been limits on where African Americans were allowed to live; by 1939, the vast majority of white Americans believed such limits were necessary. Such views, once established, tended to be enduring, and changed more slowly than those on school integration.[32]

As realtors struggled to find a new ideology to defend segregation against World War II–inspired views of freedom, they could appeal to the rights that owners now believed they were entitled to. The question for realtors was how to describe such racial rights in the language of equal freedom that World War II had popularized. How could they formulate such an appeal as millions of veterans of all races returned from overseas?

Part Three.
Freedom of Association: Late 1940s–Late 1950s

In September 1947, when Charles B. Shattuck, a key realtor leader, urged a mass meeting of four hundred white homeowners to resist non-Caucasians moving into Los Angeles's West Side, he made a new argument for racially separate markets. For a quarter century, realtors had been defending racial separation by claiming that "undesirables," non-Caucasians, threatened property values. Now, however, Shattuck did not talk about property values. Instead he invoked the Constitution. At the heart of American rights, he claimed, was the right of neighbors to exclude those of other races from their neighborhood. It was this right that non-Caucasians threatened when they moved into all-white neighborhoods. Shattuck's argument would become the mainstay of realtor ideology for the next decade and a half. Realtors would describe this right as "freedom of association," the right to associate and thus live only with others like oneself. It would become realtors' key justification for racial segregation as they helped the nation build its postwar white suburbs.

Shattuck's argument to these homeowners was not about property values. Few people knew more about such values than Shattuck himself. He had been chief state appraiser for the federal Home Owners' Loan Corporation during the Depression and one of the first five Californians inducted in the American Institute of Real Estate Appraisers; its national award for advancement of appraisal knowledge is named for him to this day. As a national expert, he knew that recent empirical studies had largely discredited the claim realtors had long been making.

More important, Shattuck knew that in the context of World War II and the beginning of the Cold War, he needed a more idealistic, patriotic argument than property values. A blunt New Dealer and lifelong Democrat who liked to appeal to the common man (unlike his brother, who was head of the California Republican Party), Shattuck understood the problem he faced in the room this night. He was urging homeowners whose family members had fought in the war to sign petitions and raise funds to prevent recently returned veterans from moving into their own homes—men like Tommy Amer, a Chinese American who had received a Purple Heart and numerous other medals, and Yin Kim, a Korean American dentist and decorated Army captain.[1] In a country with thirteen million returning GI's of all races, some white owners were reluctant to force former soldiers out of the homes they had purchased. "They just won't sign," owners' association organizers had warned Shattuck before the meeting. Shattuck therefore spoke forthrightly to the crowd. "We can't let the bars down to anyone," he declared. No exceptions could be made. Racial covenants depended on excluding entire groups, on not treating any minority as an individual. The situation was unfortunate, Shattuck conceded, that a "white [homeowners'] association" had to work against men who had fought for them in the war.[2]

Shattuck spoke, therefore, of wartime values—freedom, citizenship, patriotic duty, equality—to make his case for why discrimination should continue. "According to the Constitution, we are all equal before the law. Non-Caucasians can buy anywhere, the same as whites can. But it is also Constitutional for any group to band together and agree that no member of any other group should live there. Koreans may utilize this. Chinese. Negroes. And so may pure Caucasians." Exclusion was not a special privilege for whites but part of every American's freedom. Shattuck turned this right to exclude other races into a responsibility: "I could sell out and buy a home somewhere else. . . . But I wouldn't be doing my duty as a patriotic citizen."

Shattuck understood that more was at stake than these specific West Side homes. Tommy Amer and Yin Kim were not exceptions. Many covenant lawsuits involved former soldiers and officers. In Watts, an African American woman whose husband had been wounded at Pearl Harbor and returned to the war had been sued to leave a covenanted home.[3] A month before Shattuck's speech, Kakuo Terao—who had lost an arm and the use of both legs while serving in the 442nd infantry, the most decorated army unit of the war—was prevented from buying a home in the San Fernando Valley.[4] It would be hard to call returning soldiers, at least in public, "undesirable human elements."

By making freedom the central reason that white Americans were entitled to live in all-white neighborhoods, Shattuck drew on the power of America's almost sacred postwar ideal. He did so for a specific reason: to contest any claim that American freedom required an end to racial restrictions. Shattuck personified the realtors' efforts. One of the most widely respected realtors in the country, often referred to as "Mr. Real Estate," Shattuck had served as president of both the Los Angeles Real Estate Board and CREA. He would become president of NAREB and a key spokesperson in California realtors' opposition to fair housing.[5] To justify racially separate housing markets, realtors like Shattuck had to portray American freedom as racially separate too.

If Shattuck came across as direct and plainspoken, at times too much so for his real estate allies,[6] his key opponent on racial covenants in Los Angeles, and the realtors' nemesis in California and nationally for the next two decades, could hardly have been more different. Shattuck had been in real estate all his adult life, a career businessman whose speeches

Charles B. Shattuck in 1946   Loren Miller in the 1930s

often cut to the chase. The ironic, witty Loren Miller, lead attorney for the Los Angeles NAACP, had led a mercurial life.

The son of a formerly enslaved man and a white Midwesterner, the slight, wiry Miller, known as "Lemon" in the family for being "always sour" and serious, grew up in a tiny, almost all-white town in Nebraska. An outstanding student, he had a hard time settling on a profession. Although inspired by the example of his granduncle Bird Gee, whose fight against discrimination led to the Civil Rights Cases in the Supreme Court in the 1880s, Miller hesitated about becoming a lawyer.[7] Passionate about writing and poetry, a radical and a close friend of Langston Hughes, Miller chose law reluctantly, as a way to pay the bills. As he put it in a bitter poem, "I took a page from you and murdered / Dreams before my Dream had become / Executioner."[8]

Even after moving to Los Angeles in 1930, he postponed taking the bar. Miller wrote features and political articles for African American newspapers, moved briefly to New York as an editor of the Communist Party's *New Masses* magazine, and worked on a film in the Soviet Union with Hughes, which disillusioned him about communism. Only in the late 1930s did he begin taking on ordinary divorce and probate cases. A well-known figure in African American society in Los Angeles, with his shiny straight black hair, dapper mustache, and often stinging editorials, Miller soon found himself handling racial covenant cases and working with the ACLU against Japanese American registration and internment. Winning the celebrated Sugar Hill covenant case in 1945 had brought Miller to the attention of Thurgood Marshall, who viewed him as "the best civil rights lawyer on the West Coast."[9]

Only now, in scores of covenant cases in postwar Los Angeles, taking on the "hucksters of prejudice" as Miller called men like Shattuck,[10] analyzing constitutional claims, giving speeches and writing articles, did Miller come into his own. While Shattuck was speaking to West Side homeowners, Miller was meeting with Thurgood Marshall and other attorneys in New York to plot the legal strategy for asking the Supreme Court to end racial covenants.

But Miller also understood that victories in the courts on such high-profile cases depended on shaping public opinion as much as on identifying legal vulnerabilities. Editor and then owner of the African

American newspaper that alone covered Shattuck's speech, he urged the NAACP "to make every effort to arouse the press of the country, we need some 'popular' articles on the matter."[11] As Miller would later put it in his book about Supreme Court decisions on race: "Part of the genius of the NAACP lawyers lay in the acute perception of the depth and direction of these changes [in Supreme Court personnel and attitude] on social issues and their ability to take them at their flood and translate them into constitutional concepts palatable to supreme court justices, who were at once propelled in new directions by social change and architects of that change."[12] Miller saw the constitutional arguments he formulated as a tool, one that could allow new beliefs shaped by the war effort to be expressed.

Just as Charles Shattuck had turned to patriotic arguments about freedom to defend residential segregation, Miller seized on America's wartime values to challenge segregation itself. "One of the first laws imposed by the United Nations when their armies marched into Berlin," Miller pointed out, "was a directive abolishing the ghettos imposed by Hitler's decrees. Can we pretend that ghettos established by judicial decree are any whit less reprehensive than those imposed by the decree of dictators?"[13] The conflict between these different lessons from the war would play out at the highest levels and for the highest stakes.

8.

Defending Racial Covenants

> The rigid separation of urban areas into white neighborhoods
> and Negro neighborhoods sets in motion a vicious circle. Whites
> must stand guard to keep Negroes out and must invent ever new
> reasons . . . for their exclusionary practices.
>
> Loren Miller, 1946[1]

In 1947 and 1948, as realtors such as Shattuck faced increasing political
and legal challenges to racial covenants, they heard the same argument
again and again. Whether from minority veterans, the NAACP, other
advocacy groups, or, ultimately, the president of the United States, the
claim was the same: racially and religiously restricting where people
could live violated American freedom. "Ours is the only nation in the
western world where a person can be deprived of the right to own or
occupy a home solely on the basis of race or color," Miller argued.[2] To
defend racial covenants, realtors needed to show that, far from violating
freedom, such covenants precisely expressed a basic American freedom:
the freedom not to associate with others.

In appealing to freedom of association, however, realtors were
appealing to a novel and unusual meaning of freedom in 1947. In describing it as a constitutional right, they were making more of a rhetorical
argument than a legal one. Freedom of association was not in the Constitution, the Bill of Rights, or English common law; it had first been
included in federal law in 1937 in the context of labor unions. No law
referred to such freedom with respect to neighborhoods, housing, or discrimination.

To the extent that freedom of association had been discussed, there had been three general meanings. The first, which seemed closest to the Bill of Rights, was political: a positive right to join with others in activities protected by freedom of speech and freedom of assembly, such as in a political party. Freedom of association in this sense was not a legal right in itself, but a way of protecting other rights,[3] especially the right to dissent. One of the first American references came from William Lloyd Garrison, fighting attempts to ban abolitionist meetings: "Abolitionists, of all men, believe in freedom of association."[4] American liberals in the 1930s decried the Nazi ban on opposition parties as violating freedom of association, and freedom of association would be incorporated in the United Nations' Universal Declaration of Human Rights in 1948. This right to join with others politically had not been used to support racial discrimination; to the contrary, the Supreme Court ruled in 1944 that political parties in the South could not exclude African Americans.[5] Indeed, the Supreme Court had mentioned freedom of association only once, denying that an individual had an absolute right to join California's Communist Labor Party after World War I.[6] The court thus undermined the realtors' claim that there was any absolute right to freedom of association.

A second meaning involved labor unions, but here, too, federal law pointed in a direction opposed to that of the realtors. Federal law cited freedom of association in protecting the right to join a labor union and then, in the 1947 Taft-Hartley law, to choose not to join one. But even Taft-Hartley asserted an *individual's* right to choose whether to join an organization—not, as the realtors claimed, a *group's* right to exclude others, especially on racial grounds.[7]

What realtors meant by freedom of association was racial: whites should have the right, recorded in every racial covenant in the country, not to associate with anyone of another race. Such a freedom *not* to associate had never been formally stated as a legal or constitutional right, even when the Supreme Court had limited the impact of the Fourteenth Amendment in *Plessy v. Ferguson* in 1896. The court had held that the Fourteenth Amendment "could not have been intended to . . . enforce social, as distinguished from political," equality.[8] When Shattuck and other realtors spoke about freedom of association, they were turning a negative finding—that the Supreme Court had not invoked the

Fourteenth Amendment to ban racial covenants—into a positive statement, indeed a rallying cry for white owners. Realtors were taking the implicit principle of racial covenants—neighbors' deciding which races can live next to them—and describing it as a fundamental American freedom.

Nor were realtors alone in turning to freedom of association in defense of segregation. Less than a year after Shattuck's speech, the new States' Rights Party of Southern "Dixiecrats" campaigned against President Truman's integrating the armed forces by calling for "the constitutional right to choose one's associates."[9] Freedom of association's great power for both realtors and Southern segregationists was less as a legal argument than as a way to mobilize themselves and those they were appealing to. It recast their cause not merely as self-interest but as rooted in fundamental rights.

Realtors needed such an ideology to deal with three tectonic changes—in minorities' postwar demands for freedom, in the views of the president of the United States, and in those of the Supreme Court—that threatened the very system of racial covenants that realtors relied on.

POSTWAR MINORITY DEMANDS FOR FREEDOM

The first major challenge to postwar racial discrimination came from the increased demand for freedom that World War II generated among minorities. The highest-priority issue for minorities was employment, and their aim was fair employment laws that prohibited employers from hiring, firing, or compensating employees based on their race or religion. After Southern Democrats and Northern probusiness Republicans killed any extension of the wartime federal fair employment practices law, minority advocates pushed for state fair employment commissions across the country.

When their bill in the California legislature stalled, activists circulated petitions for a fair employment initiative on the 1946 ballot. The initiative process had been established under a progressive governor in 1911 as a direct democracy reform to circumvent the enormous lobbying power of the Southern Pacific Railroad in the state legislature. Under this reform, initiatives for new laws and state constitutional amendments, referenda to overturn new legislation, and recalls of state elected officials could all be put directly to the voters. California quickly became the leader in initiative campaigns. No other large state has had as many ballot initiatives as California. Although 90 percent of petitions never receive enough signatures and two-thirds of qualifying initiatives have failed, the possibility of popular campaigns, often "public spectacles" in which both sides seek to claim the public good, has been a defining feature of the state's politics.[10]

Although some civil right leaders were apprehensive about putting a minority-rights issue up to the voters, others were confident that their message would resonate after the war. Their campaign ad featured a GI looking out from under his helmet: "DON'T MESS IT UP NOW, BUDDY! Be sure that Home-Front Jobs Are Open to ALL Americans!"[11] Here was the unifying message of World War II—that all Americans deserved the same kind of opportunities. With support from labor unions and the state's attorney general, in a cause of fairness and democracy for all, advocates believed they would triumph over the narrow "special interest cliques" of big business and agribusiness.[12]

The opposition campaign was led by the Los Angeles County Chamber of Commerce and its former president Frank Doherty. Realtors, under Shattuck's leadership, joined with the chamber in this effort and saw at close range how an effectively managed and messaged campaign could turn voters against an initially popular antidiscrimination measure.[13] The campaign would provide a model for Proposition 14.

Recognizing that many voters might support fair employment because of the wartime emphasis on American racial and religious tolerance in the fight with Nazism, the chamber and its allies described *themselves* as those in favor of tolerance. Calling themselves "The Committee for Tolerance,"[14] they put that name on all their literature.

"Racial and religious tolerance are highly desirable," the chamber insisted. "Tolerance, however, by its very definition is something which cannot be forced by law. It is a matter of individual conscience and private judgment." By defining tolerance in this way, the chamber could convincingly argue that it was impossible "to legislate prejudice and intolerance out of people." A government commission would only arouse racial animosity. "*It would inflame hatreds and work to the disadvantage of every minority.*"[15] The *San Francisco Chronicle* agreed. "No one can quarrel with the spirit of Fair Employment Practices without refuting the principles underlying American democracy," but a compulsory law would do more harm than good.

When it came to describing rights and freedom, the chamber claimed that fair employment would "lead to the destruction of certain Constitutional rights," and was "the most dangerous threat to individual rights . . . basic in the structure of the American system."[16] Although the chamber did not indicate any specific provision of the Constitution that fair employment would violate, it suggested that two kinds of rights were at stake. The first would become the realtors' central message: the right not to have to associate with a minority. The chamber put this viscerally: a state commission could require that "you, your wife, your daughter or your sister must work with anyone the commission directs, regardless of color or race."[17] Using the classic racist threat of miscegenation, the chamber suggested, as Shattuck had, that what minorities really wanted was not freedom to buy a home or have a job, but a social privilege they had no legal or moral right to: being able to associate with whites. The chamber urged against passing laws that "enforce on everybody the obligation to accept anyone as social equals."[18]

The second right the chamber emphasized was the right to discriminate. "The careful selection of employees necessarily entailed discrimination, which should be regarded as a virtue not a vice." Antidiscrimination laws would destroy the "precious" tradition that permits employers to hire, promote, and fire whomever they pleased.[19] Because business owners alone could hardly defeat a statewide proposition, the chamber stressed the broad group and racial identity of those whom a fair employment commission would supposedly discriminate *against*. These were the ordinary, hard-working American taxpayers too decent to claim "special privileges": the quiet majority, soldiering on, "too busy doing their jobs."[20] They were, in short, the civilian image of America's GI's. These average Americans were, by definition, white, because the chamber emphasized that it was only minorities who would file complaints with a fair employment commission.

The chamber's campaign provided a way for white voters to maintain an existing discriminatory system while seeing themselves as tolerant and in favor of American freedom. The fair employment initiative was defeated overwhelmingly, 70%–30%.

This stunning defeat did not end the battle for fair employment. Minority advocates, liberals, and labor unions concluded, however, that no matter how difficult it was to get antidiscrimination bills through the legislature, future referenda would only further set back their cause. Indeed, C. L. Dellums of the Brotherhood of Sleeping Car Porters recognized, in words that would echo in Proposition 14, "we should never set a precedent that we recognize that people have a right to vote on . . . civil rights. . . . Even if we won we would have lost."[21] Having seen how effectively the chamber mobilized public opinion, the NAACP therefore rejected the idea of future statewide referenda, since discrimination "would become submerged, distorted and perverted in the slogans and propaganda" that would be launched against rights for minorities.[22] Civil rights advocates therefore focused solely on legislation, both for fair employment, finally passed in California in 1959, and then for a fair housing bill that would utilize the state's new fair employment practices commission.

The realtors, by contrast, learned how effectively public opinion could be mobilized by redefining key terms—tolerance, freedom, discrimination—against those seeking civil rights laws. The Los Angeles Realty Board gave its William May Garland trophy, the award for the citizen who had performed the most valuable service to Los Angeles, in turn to Charles Shattuck, who led the realtors' effort on behalf of the campaign, and then to the campaign's architect, Frank Doherty.[23] The realtors and Doherty would work closely together on state and city ballot campaigns against public housing over the next six years, and in 1966, Doherty, then in his eighties, would be brought back from retirement to help the realtors defend Proposition 14.

***

Postwar minority demands for freedom proved just as intense when it came to housing as to jobs. The extraordinary competition for postwar housing in Los Angeles and cities across the country affected everyone, but the problems for minorities were far worse because the realtors' racial system so limited where they could hope to live.

The boom in wartime defense employment had brought millions to cities like Los Angeles. As the war ended, few wanted to move back to the places they had come from; 85 percent of 750,000 Los Angeles defense workers chose to stay.[24] Veterans and Japanese internees returned, and with no new homes having been built for years, the marriage rate outpaced even record new home production. Overcrowding was commonplace. People lived in garages, doubled up in apartments, put cots in kitchens, slept on tables, took shifts in beds. Indeed, overcrowding was so widespread in cities across the country, housing became a central issue in the 1948 presidential election. With realtors and Republicans delaying any postwar federal housing program that included public housing, Truman mocked that his opponent's true slogan was "two families in every garage."

But while white families could begin to move to new FHA and VA subdivisions, members of rapidly growing racial minority populations remained confined to just a few small areas in each city. Los Angeles's African American population quadrupled during the war, but there was nowhere else they were allowed to move.[25] Nationally, minority families were three times as likely to be overcrowded as American families as a whole.[26]

That they could afford to move to new homes only intensified minorities' frustrations. Wartime jobs or service had given many African Americans more financial resources than before the war, and thousands of new homes were being built that they could afford.[27] But instead of being able to buy such homes, they had to pay inflated prices for dilapidated ghetto housing. Where they could find homes in white areas, often through speculators, they typically had to pay 20 to 30 percent more than white Americans for the same units.[28] Minority members therefore became increasingly willing to contest racial covenants and to appeal orders evicting them from homes they had bought.

Minorities whose families had fought in the war kept asking the same question, one echoed by the *California Eagle*: "What is the right of this government to compel men to risk and lose their lives fighting to preserve . . . a way of life . . . that refuses them the right to live in the homes they buy with hard-earned cash?"[29] Henry Laws, an African American, was jailed with his wife for refusing to leave the covenanted home they owned in Watts. "Why should I move? I bought this property 13 years ago and I built this house. . . . My sons are fighting . . . in the South Pacific. I buy war bonds. I am working for a defense plant, and so is the rest of my family."[30] A month before Shattuck's speech, John L. Alexander, a glazer and Navy veteran who had fought against the Nazis, put this question desperately. Hearing radio spots for "Homes for GI's" at new developments, and anxious to buy a home for his wife and their three-year-old girl and ten-month-old boy, he went to two different new tracts. Told that homes for GI's meant homes for white GI's only, he could not understand how such discrimination could be permitted under the Constitution.[31]

Realtors and their allies found themselves challenged even more broadly when the question of unfair treatment was raised about the vast new suburban communities under way. When secretaries of chambers of commerce across San Fernando Valley met in June 1947 to design racial restrictions, Loren Miller's *Los Angeles Sentinel* asked about World War II and the new Cold War.

> While the rest of the country was worrying about democracy or about the danger of war and about how Americans can work together to preserve the peace and meet the common danger, these secretaries were . . . warning "that the need for racial restriction is serious." They couldn't be expected to remember the dark days after Pearl Harbor or the fact that the anti-aircraft unit that was stationed there to protect them and their . . . homes was a Negro unit. Of course, they've forgotten the bravery exhibited by the Nisei units in Italy. . . . Are the . . . city's leading citizens [who] make the San Fernando Valley their home . . . [and] constantly adjured the rest of us to work for and support democracy . . . going to stand around and see American citizens, many of whom fought for democracy in WWI and WWII, deprived of their right to live where they choose?[32]

This argument created sufficient publicity that the local chambers of commerce denied that the purpose of their meeting had been to exclude African Americans. Rather it was to "see if we couldn't settle this issue once and for all on an amicable basis." One answer, they explained, would be to "set aside an area in the valley . . . where you people could come in and have nice homes. . . . No, not exactly a segregated community." Representatives of the all-white chambers of commerce recycled old slogans. "Most Negro people wouldn't be happy if they lived in an area that was all white. They would probably be a little uncomfortable."[33]

It said much about the racial climate in the country that the covenant cases that aroused the most publicity and most sympathy for those excluded did not involve African Americans. It made the national news when Isabel Crocker, a three-quarter Seneca Indian, was evicted along with her children from their West Hollywood home while the French-Canadian husband and father could remain. The publicity was even greater in October 1947, when nine neighbors in the Washington, DC, suburbs sued the Christian wife of Aaron Tushin, a Jewish government patent attorney, to force her to oust him from their family home. These cases "shocked the conscience of the nation," while there had been little "outcry over Negroes being ousted," an African American newspaper noted. But whatever called into question the fundamental basis of covenants themselves was still helpful in the fight to end them, it went on. "No American is secure in any of his constitutional rights as long as any other American is denied the full measure of his democratic rights and privileges."[34]

Finally, and most momentous both for realtors and minorities, was the joint effort of the NAACP, American Jewish Committee, Japanese American Citizens League, American Indian Association, Anti-Nazi League, and a host of other organizations to challenge restrictive covenants in the Supreme Court. While Charles Shattuck was haranguing West Side homeowners, Loren Miller and his colleagues were immersed in their strategy session in New York. As they laid out a range of arguments based on public policy, sociology, economics, and race relations, including new studies by Charles Johnson, the attorneys focused on a new legal insight from a law school professor at the University of California.

Reanalyzing the Supreme Court's 1926 *Corrigan v. Buckley* decision that had upheld restrictive covenants, D. O. McGovney perceived a legal window. The court had ruled that the Fourteenth Amendment did not bar covenants themselves because the amendment only restricted *state* action, not private discrimination. But, McGovney argued, *judicial enforcement* of a private contract was state action. No court had ruled on this. It had not been effectively raised or resolved in *Corrigan*, nor in California's *Gary* case. Here was the lever the attorneys were seeking. Here was the tool, as Miller put it, for the court to end racial covenants if it wanted, without having to overrule its own precedent.[35]

McGovney's theory was audacious. For the Supreme Court to hold that judicial enforcement of a contract was state action could mean that every possible type of contract—wills, business agreements, and employment contracts, all of which ultimately depended on court enforcement—was subject to the equal protection clause of the Fourteenth Amendment. The attorneys hoped that the sociological and public policy arguments would make the court willing to take such a step at least with respect to racial covenants. Here a second tectonic shift proved crucial, one involving the president of the United States.

A BILL OF RIGHTS IN FACT, NOT JUST IN NAME

The second major postwar challenge to racially separate housing markets came from a change in the views of President Truman and was in many ways the most disturbing for realtors. Realtors had long been able to rely on the support of government at all levels for racially separate housing markets. FHA carried out and institutionalized the realtors' ideology on a vast scale. Local governments used zoning to the extent legally possible to try to effectively keep districts or entire suburbs all-white; in some cases, cities only approved subdivisions with restrictive covenants. No government regulation or law had ever challenged the idea of residential racial segregation. It was therefore a watershed moment when President Truman, after many months of work by his President's Committee on Civil Rights during 1947, strongly endorsed the committee's central principle: the federal government should play the leading role in "the elimination of segregation based on race, color, creed or national origin, from American life."[36]

The event that precipitated Truman's establishing the first presidential committee on civil rights in American history occurred on a bus in South Carolina in February 1946. Isaac Woodard, a returning African American army sergeant, had spoken back to a Greyhound bus driver and been beaten and blinded by police. When NAACP leaders described this in a meeting with Truman, he wrote the next day to his attorney general, Tom Clark. Members of the NAACP, Truman recounted, "told me about an incident in South Carolina where a negro Sergeant who had been discharged from the Army just three hours, was taken off the bus and not only seriously beaten but his eyes deliberately put out, and that the Mayor . . . bragged about committing this outrage." Truman went on to consider what needed to be done, for there had been attacks on returning veterans in several states. Although Truman had never been seen as sympathetic toward African Americans, these events particularly offended his sense of what soldiers deserved, and roused memories of Ku Klux Klan attacks on World War I veterans. "I know you have been looking into the Tennessee and Georgia lynchings . . . but it is going to take something more than the handling of each individual case after it happens. It is going to require the inauguration of some sort of policy."

Truman outlined the idea of a high-level committee on civil rights, something that had never existed. "I have been very alarmed at the increased racial feeling all over the country and I am wondering if it wouldn't be well to appoint a commission to analyze the situation and have a remedy to present to the next session of Congress."[37] Truman appointed the committee three months later, after a federal investigation he personally requested into the blinding led to an almost instantaneous not-guilty verdict by an all-white jury.[38]

Truman had weighed the political ramifications of elevating civil rights. He knew that Thomas Dewey, his likely opponent in 1948, was taking credit for New York State's fair employment law and might claim the swing African American vote in key big cities. Truman recognized, as well, that his ability to implement recommendations would be limited to executive orders; Southern Democrats would filibuster any legislation. But the committee would allow him to take a stand on civil rights.

How far Truman wanted the committee to go was not clear, perhaps even to himself. Truman's charge to the committee went beyond what any president since Lincoln had ever said: "I want our Bill of Rights implemented in fact. We have been trying to do this for 150 years. We are making progress, but we are not making progress fast enough."[39] Truman recognized federal responsibility. "The Constitutional guarantees of individual liberties . . . place on the Federal government the duty to act when state or local authorities abridge or fail to protect these Constitutional rights."[40] Yet, as the committee began its work, Truman was unwilling to publicly challenge segregation. He cautioned that his "appeal for equal economic and political rights for every American citizen had nothing at all to do with the personal or social relationships of individuals or the right of every person to choose his own associates."[41] But despite Truman's disclaimer about freedom of association, the committee would provide a report that took on this very principle.

If Truman's charge to the committee—to implement the Bill of Rights in fact and not just in words—had been general and somewhat ambiguous, what the committee brought back after months of hearings around the country was, in one scholar's words, "dynamite."[42] The committee, chaired by the president of General Electric, with top executives from business, unions, and universities, looked at the North as well as the South. Its recommendations, indeed its entire conception of freedom, challenged virtually everything realtors had sought to achieve in creating racially separate housing markets. The committee called for the elimination of segregation, including residential segregation, throughout the United States.[43] By titling its report *To Secure These Rights*, the purpose given to government in the Declaration of Independence, the committee emphasized that, in its view, ending segregation was no general hope but the active responsibility of the federal government.

The committee focused much of its attention on discrimination in housing as one of the fundamental impediments to freedom. It recommended two actions. One was a general recommendation: "enactment by the states of laws outlawing restrictive covenants."[44] The other, of immediate moment given the pending Supreme Court covenant case, involved executive action: "intervention by the Department of Justice upon restrictive covenants."[45] The committee was asking the administration to take sides in a lawsuit between private parties, something the federal government had never done.

To make the case for its recommendations, the committee sought to provide the most compelling and comprehensive vision of freedom possible, arguing that segregation was in fact the single greatest threat to American freedom. The report invoked the national purpose of World War II: "We abhor the totalitarian arrogance which makes one man say he will respect another man as his equal only if he has 'my race, my religion . . . my social position.'"[46] The committee then spelled out essential features of freedom that directly opposed the realtors' arguments for freedom of association. Because fair housing advocates would largely echo the committee's view of freedom, these issues would come up repeatedly as fundamental differences between the realtors' view of freedom and that of their opponents.

Rights belong only to individuals as individuals and not as members of a race or other group, the committee insisted. This attacked Shattuck's claim that restrictive covenants were fair because minority groups had the same right to exclude whites as whites had to exclude minorities. Groups had no rights, the committee argued. It made no difference to a minority individual that other members of his race could hypothetically exclude members of other races. Freedom meant precisely being treated as an individual, not as a member of a group. Indeed, the committee argued that assuring the freedom of each individual—the right to be treated as an *individual*—was the very purpose of American society. "We can tolerate no restrictions upon the individual which depend upon irrelevant factors such as his race, his color, his religion."[47] Society and government therefore had to be based on this idea of individual freedom.

Realtors, by contrast, in their support for zoning, subdivision regulations, and restrictive covenants, had always viewed freedom not as the way to organize either real estate or society but as *a result* of how society was organized, of the American way of life they had been helping create. "Believing that home owners are the nation's best citizens and that widespread ownership of real property is the foundation of civil and religious liberties," NAREB declared in December 1947, "when a broker assists an American family to become a home owner he has made an effective contribution toward the American way of life."[48] Stable neighborhoods for such homeowners were the basis for American freedom. In such neighborhoods, families would raise children who believed in the sanctity of private property, social stability, and free enterprise. Not only was discrimination acceptable; it bound social groups together and sustained their communities. Overriding the neighbors' right to determine who lived next to them would violate their freedom. If this view was partial and narrow—if it reflected the realtors' own clientele, and if their belief that "home owners are the nation's best citizens" did not require allowing minorities to become homeowners—what the realtors meant by freedom was the right to maintain this existing way of life, the right to maintain segregation.

The committee dismissed the distinction realtors drew between a racial minority's theoretical legal right to buy a home and the "social privilege," determined by his neighbors, of whether he could live in that home. Without equality of opportunity, "freedom becomes an illusion."[49] One was either free to live where one chose or one was not. For the committee, it made no difference *who* imposed restrictions, whether it was the law or government or homeowner associations or real estate brokers. A country in which millions could not choose where to live because of their skin color or creed was not, in the eyes of the committee, a free country. For the realtors, by contrast, it was essential to insist on the distinction between freedom and social privilege. Only by narrowly defining freedom as the potential legal right to buy property in general, and ignoring the actual limits placed on that right, could realtors claim that minorities were equally as free as Caucasians.

The committee further recognized that residential segregation was not simply a matter of individual discrimination. Its report laid out, based on its hearings, the role that realtors played:

> Discrimination in housing results primarily from business practices. These practices may arise from special interests of business groups, such as the profits to be derived from confining minorities to slum areas, or they may reflect community prejudice. One of the most common practices is the policy of landlords and real estate agents to prevent Negroes from renting outside of designated areas. Again, it is "good business" to develop exclusive "restricted" suburban developments which are barred to all but white gentiles.[50]

It was precisely because discrimination was systemic, organized, and widespread that government needed to play an active role in preventing it. No right or freedom is absolute, the committee declared, thus challenging the idea that private parties can discriminate against minorities as they please. Government "must referee the clashes which arise among the freedoms of citizens and protect each citizen in the enjoyment of the maximum freedom to which he is entitled."[51] Government had a right, indeed a duty, to stop such discrimination.

The committee directly challenged the real estate industry and the chamber of commerce, as well as Southern segregationists, all of whom believed that government had no such right to interfere on behalf of minorities. Realtors, of course, believed that government had a right, indeed a duty, to enforce property rights. And they had long supported government efforts to regulate the market with regard to state licensing, subdivision regulations, and zoning, and to provide credit, in the case of FHA. But in all these cases, government was supporting or enhancing interests of property owners, at least generally—including their right to discriminate and to enforce covenants even against other owners. Government limiting private discrimination, realtors argued, would restrict owners' rights.

All the clashes that were to come over the next decades, between fair housing advocates and the realtors, were thus set out in the committee's report. The report provided in many ways the agenda and the view of freedom that the civil rights movement would seek to carry out.

The committee's two highest-priority recommendations—actions the president could take without needing Congress's or anyone else's support—were desegregation of the armed forces and the attorney general's intervention in the challenge to racial covenants. Truman called the report "an American charter of human freedom," and, on the day after the report was released, October 30, 1947, the Department of Justice announced it would file a friend-of-the-court brief in the covenant cases.[52] In supporting the NAACP in the first major covenant case in decades, the government of the United States would go on record, as a matter of public policy, in opposition to residential segregation.

SHELLEY V. KRAEMER

The third great postwar challenge that the realtors faced in maintaining racially separate markets was the May 1948 Supreme Court decision in *Shelley v. Kraemer*.[53] *Shelley* consolidated a set of cases from several states and the District of Columbia. Given the potential implications for neighborhoods in every city in the country, it attracted "as much public attention and interest as any [litigation] in our history."[54]

The NAACP argued that judicial enforcement of racial covenants constituted state action and thus violated the equal protection clause of the Fourteenth Amendment. Three of the justices recused themselves, presumably because they lived in covenanted communities themselves. In what would become a landmark decision, the remaining six voted unanimously in favor of the NAACP.

The court rejected or ignored each of the claims that NAREB made in its brief. The realtors' long-standing claim that minorities have equal rights because they too can establish restrictive covenants was dismissed out of hand. "This contention does not bear scrutiny. The rights created by the . . . Fourteenth Amendment are . . . guaranteed to the individual. The rights established are personal rights. It is no answer to these petitioners to say that the courts may also . . . deny white persons rights of ownership and occupancy . . . . Equal protection of the laws is not achieved through indiscriminate imposition of inequalities."[55]

The realtors argued strenuously that the right to equal protection and due process under the Fourteenth Amendment was extremely narrow. Indeed, in its brief, NAREB dismissed almost sarcastically any right of minority families to live in homes they had bought: "Petitioners have not shown in what respect they have been deprived of life, liberty or property. They are alive, and have not, as far as the record indicates, been restrained." NAREB thus defined liberty as not being in jail. Nor had the families been deprived of property, as, "according to the law of real property"—that is, the recorded covenants—they "had no . . . right to occupy" their homes.[56] The Supreme Court, like the president's Committee on Civil Rights, sharply disagreed. "It cannot be doubted that among the civil rights . . . [under] the Fourteenth Amendment are the rights to acquire, enjoy, own and dispose of property. . . . Equality in the enjoyment of property rights was regarded by the framers of [the Fourteenth] Amendment as an essential pre-condition to the realization of other basic civil rights and liberties."[57] Freedom, at its heart, included the freedom to buy and live in one's property.

NAREB and the neighbors' attorneys brought up freedom of association: "The right to discriminate is a precious privilege. Forced social equality is tyranny." Indeed, what turned out to be the key exchange in the oral argument concerned freedom of association. Making what he believed was a critical point, the homeowners' association attorney argued that "all that was involved was the right of people to choose their associates by making private contracts." Therefore, in enforcing the covenant, "the state court was not enforcing discrimination but . . . the private rights of citizens." Justice Frankfurter leaned in: these private citizens "[needed] the full strength of the state's judicial power, to enforce something which the state could not itself declare as state policy"? This, the attorney had to concede.[58]

When Chief Justice Vinson gathered views among the justices, he commented later, they "found the cases rather easy."[59] The chief justice focused his opinion almost exclusively on the point Frankfurter had made: "These are not cases . . . in which the States have merely abstained from action, leaving private individuals to impose such discriminations as they see fit. Rather . . . the States have made available to such individuals the coercive power of the government to deny to petitioners rights which the States could not take away by legislation."[60]

McGovney's approach had prevailed in a landmark decision that would pave the way for *Brown v. Board of Education*. Thurgood Marshall immediately grasped how powerful this Fourteenth Amendment precedent would be: "This blow to racial segregation in . . . housing . . . opens up the pending fight . . . in education which . . . must be carried on with renewed vigor."[61] His cocounsel Loren Miller recognized how *ordinary* the right upheld by the Supreme Court should have been: "What the court did . . . was reaffirm the historic right of an American citizen to own, use and occupy property in accordance with his ability to do so. There's nothing revolutionary about that; it's a pretty well accepted tenet of a private property economy."[62] It had been the ordinariness of this

Ethel Shelley of St. Louis reads about Supreme Court decision, 1948

right that freedom of association had been invoked to oppose.

The reaction in African American newspapers around the country was joyous. "Negroes Can Now Live Anywhere, Says High Court." "All We Wanted Was a Decent Place to Rear the Children." Stories showed attractive homes, such as those in Los Angeles's Sugar Hill, that had figured in prominent cases. "Homes Like These No Longer 'Out of Bounds.'"[63]

Such optimism was natural after forty years of racial covenants. But it would count for little as realtors decided how to maintain segregation after *Shelley*. Judicial enforcement of racial covenants might have ended, but this did not diminish the realtors' commitment to segregation. Realtors would instead only intensify their efforts.

9.

Recommitting to Segregation after *Shelley*

> The magnitude of the economic and social loss with which we are confronted is appalling. . . . The insistence of some Negroes upon moving into areas previously restricted exclusively to the occupancy of Caucasians will necessarily create racial tensions . . . and do much harm to our national social structure.
>
> Los Angeles Realty Board to NAREB, August 1948[1]

If minority families and civil rights advocates were jubilant in the immediate wake of *Shelley*, realtors and many white owners were stunned. Court enforcement of racial covenants had been the central tool for maintaining housing segregation. For all the limitations of covenants—the need to renew them before they expired, the need to file lawsuits, that many properties were not or were only imperfectly covered—the real estate industry had relied on them to create an entire racial system. Developers had used them to assure that projects remained all-white, realtors to persuade buyers, and FHA to underwrite new communities. Perhaps above all, the court enforcement of covenants for thirty years had told all these parties that what they were doing was right, was officially sanctioned, was how America should be.

Thus, although the *Shelley* decision was itself narrow, realtors' immediate reaction was a feeling of betrayal. *Shelley* resolved a single issue: courts could not enforce covenants against those racially excluded. Minorities who already owned or lived in covenanted properties were now protected; lawsuits by homeowners' associations and neighbors against Tommy Amer, Yin Kim, and thousands of other families were dropped. This removed a cloud of uncertainty over many minority owners;

Loren Miller estimated that the vast majority of African Americans in Los Angeles lived in areas where the covenants had not yet expired, and could in theory have been enforced against them.[2] Nor would courts enforce covenants against new minority buyers, *if* owners would sell homes to them.

But the Supreme Court ruling was limited. The court did not say that covenants were illegal or invalid, only that courts could not enforce them against minorities. Further, *Shelley* did not limit discrimination by developers. Although it made clear that government could not discriminate, the decision did not deal directly with FHA. Moreover, *Shelley* did not prevent the most widespread discrimination of all—namely, sellers and realtors selling homes only to whites. But if there were limitations, it quickly struck realtors that *Shelley* had taken away what they had counted on for thirty years: courts enforcing racial covenants. The question for boards around the country was not whether to continue segregation but how to do so.

TRYING TO ENSHRINE FREEDOM OF ASSOCIATION IN THE U.S. CONSTITUTION

California realtor organizations initially reacted in apocalyptic tones. The Los Angeles Realty Board proposed an amendment to the U.S. Constitution to overturn *Shelley*. The amendment would "validate, and render enforceable, restrictions against the ownership or occupancy of real property by Negroes or Caucasians respectively." Separate districts would be created for African Americans, presumably by local governments.[3] The board's proposal was quickly circulated to and endorsed by CREA and numerous boards around the country.[4]

While still mentioning the realtors' old argument about property values, LARB made explicit the social issues that property values had long been used to represent. The board focused on the "social loss," on "conditions that menace the family life of the nation as we have enjoyed it." LARB's amendment targeted African Americans specifically. "The problem arises from the purchase and occupancy of property by Negroes." Repeating a long-standing realtor theme from the 1927 Survey of Race Relations, the president of LARB charged that "as no other group, Negroes were continually . . . trying to live where they were not wanted" and "suggested they take a hint from the Japanese, Mexicans and other groups."[5] Unless the Constitution was amended, those who will "suffer most are owners of comparatively modest homes" with prices "well within the purchasing power of vast numbers of Negroes." By *suffer*, the board meant that such owners might have to live in the same neighborhood as African Americans.

The proposed amendment would enshrine the concept of separate but equal in the Constitution. "In the interests of fairness," it would be drafted so as to "assure Negroes of the enjoyment of areas restricted to the occupancy of their race."[6] In those areas, African Americans would be free to exclude whites. The board's lawyer explained that "Negroes should enjoy first class citizenship but on a separate but equal basis."[7] By drafting the amendment so that it would "leave no room for construction by the courts,"[8] the LA realtors were seeking to effectively repeal the Fourteenth Amendment with regard to housing. This would undo not only *Shelley* but the Supreme Court's unanimous 1917 decision against racial zoning. A UCLA professor from South Africa would be struck by the parallels between realtors' 1948 efforts to separate races and the simultaneous establishment of apartheid in his home country.[9]

Regardless of whether such a constitutional amendment would ultimately be adopted, LARB wanted its proposal to have an immediate, chilling effect on purchases by African Americans in white neighborhoods. The amendment would be retroactive, to "act as a deterrent on the acquisition and occupancy of such restricted properties by Negroes. The threat of forfeiture of title and possible loss of purchase money . . . may well cause many to hesitate who would otherwise acquire and occupy such restricted properties." If not retroactive, the amendment might simply encourage African Americans to buy homes before it could be adopted.[10] Realtors wanted to stop *Shelley* from ever having any effect. At a minimum, the proposal would give realtors time to figure how to maintain segregation most effectively. This idea of a constitutional amendment provided a model that California realtors would use to respond to future adverse court decisions and legislation, including a successful 1950 state constitutional amendment against public housing, as well as Proposition 14.

QUIETER WAYS TO USE FREEDOM OF ASSOCIATION

What proved most significant about the 1948 proposal was that realtors let it quietly drop. NAREB did not endorse the amendment and, after a glowing article in *California Real Estate* magazine, the amendment was never mentioned again there or in mass media. Rather than attack *Shelley* directly, counsel for CREA suggested techniques that could comply with the court decision *but* effectively maintain segregation. In contrast with the proposed amendment, these techniques depended on *not* being racially obvious in motivation.

How could this be done? H. L. Breed, CREA's counsel, outlined several methods in *California Real Estate* magazine under the title "Racial Restrictions—Brokers' Rights under Supreme Court Decisions." In giving legal advice on how to comply with *Shelley*, he suggested three specific tools. All were based on freedom of association and all would allow neighbors to control who lived next to them, as before *Shelley*. They would not, however, officially make race a criterion.

First, a homeowners' association could require a discretionary occupancy permit for all homes. Such permits would make "no reference to race or color, but [require] personal qualifications as a good neighbor, or in other words, cultural status." An advantage of this approach was that it "will permit exclusion of undesirable whites. If fairly administered so as to exclude undesirable persons irrespective of race or color," CREA's attorney advised, "no difficulty should be encountered." Many owners' associations took up this presumably color-blind approach, using approval rights, occupancy standards, and other types of measures to decide who was undesirable.[11]

Second, Breed advised, the actual title to properties in a subdivision could be vested in a corporation owned by the residents. This would be somewhat similar to a cooperative. The advantage was that no court enforcement, and thus no state action, would ever be needed. Third, a subdivision could require that all owners post a cash bond that would be forfeited if the home were "occupied by some not approved by the association." Breed also suggested revisions to realtors' listing contracts so that they did not have to report an offer "from a non-Caucasian."[12] The realtor could just throw the offer away. CREA's counsel was telling realtors exactly how to racially steer customers without violating the Supreme Court decision.

National experts for NAREB also quickly offered advice on continuing segregation without violating *Shelley*. Stanley McMichael's major textbook *Real Estate Subdivisions* suggested that developers retain a right of first refusal before a property could be resold, to help make certain it was not resold to a minority.[13]

Further study of *Shelley* offered other approaches that were used far more widely. The court did not say covenants were illegal or invalid, only that courts could not enforce them against minorities. Therefore, racial covenants remained in place as recorded documents, and developers recorded hundreds of thousands of new ones. Such covenants sent a clear signal to any potential buyers that minorities were not wanted.[14] To prevent minorities from buying in the vast new suburb of Lakewood near Los Angeles—seven years after *Shelley*—realtors would warn them about the covenants. If asked, "But how can you enforce the covenant when it isn't legal?" realtors would insist that "It is valid for fifty years" or explain, "It is my opinion that an insured title would not be granted if restrictions are listed on the original subdivision. To my knowledge this has never been tested."[15] Realtors made the existence of covenants as ominous as possible.

Moreover, because *Shelley* only outlawed lawsuits against minorities themselves, it did not prevent lawsuits by neighbors or a homeowners' association against the *white* sellers of restricted homes. Thus covenants could require that the white owner pay a fine—an enormous cash penalty—to surrounding neighbors if the home was rented or sold to a non-Caucasian. The covenant would not be enforced against a minority; rather it would be used to prevent any white person from selling them a home in the first place. This idea was quickly instituted by Henry Doelger in the Westlake development of Daly City, covering 6,100 homes, with the largest homeowners' association in California. If a white owner sold her home to a non-Caucasian, she was required to pay a fine to each of the nearest eight neighbors—a total penalty worth more than the sale price of the home.[16] Realtors and homeowners' associations throughout California and nationally fought vigorously for court enforcement of such covenant penalties. In Los Angeles, thirteen associations pursued such actions; an owner who had simply shown a house to a Filipino family was threatened with a $10,000 lawsuit.[17] Just as important, realtors and associations widely publicized such suits to discourage any other owners from even considering selling to minorities.[18] For five years after *Shelley*, this new type of lawsuit took the place of those the Supreme Court had ended.

Such penalties against white sellers remained enforceable until Loren Miller brought a Los Angeles case, *Barrows v. Jackson*, to the Supreme Court in 1953. He realized that the case itself and his argument would have to be subtler than *Shelley*; no one was suing an African American buyer because of her race. How could Mrs. Jackson, a white seller, claim discrimination? Even Chief Justice Vinson felt this was going too far. But Miller convinced the other eight justices that in enforcing damages against her, the state would be coercing her into using her property in a discriminatory manner.[19] He designed his argument, as he would later against Proposition 14, to look past realtors' neat framing of the situation. Was there state action, he asked, and was that state action supporting discrimination?

Westlake Improvement Association, Daly City, California, 1950s

When it came to new homes, the easiest way to continue discrimination was for the developer to limit whom he sold to. *Shelley* did not limit discrimination by developers or other private owners. Developers took every advantage of this. An African American veteran visiting a new subdivision in Van Nuys was handed a sheet: "No person whose blood is not entirely that of the Caucasian race . . . shall at any time live upon any of the lots in said tract."[20] Of the new homes built in Los Angeles from 1950 to 1960, less than 1 percent were occupied by non-Caucasians, and most of those were in segregated subdivisions built exclusively for African Americans.[21]

Shelley did not deal directly with FHA. Although the ruling implied that the federal government itself could no longer *require* restrictive covenants, it did not prevent developers using FHA insurance from discriminating. Such discrimination would continue until the early 1960s. In Lakewood, built from 1949 to 1953 with FHA financing, out of sixty-seven thousand residents in 1960, there were seven African Americans.[22] Lakewood illustrated, too, many of the features of these post-*Shelley*, large-scale, racially segregated, FHA-financed starter-home developments around the country. "When any salesman sold a Lakewood . . . home, he also sold the idea of Lakewood as a community . . . of community pride in Lakewood." Racial exclusion was an essential attraction of such a community; the *Los Angeles Times* identified such tracts for potential buyers as "the white spots" of development. Racial restrictions were written into every deed. Lakewood too, like the Levittowns in the Northeast, was developed by—and many of the homes sold to—white ethnic minorities, including Jews, who would themselves have previously been excluded from many covenanted developments. Lakewood created a new model of local government as well; to retain local control without having to provide its own services or staff, the new city of Lakewood contracted for services with the county—a model that quickly spread throughout, and has helped fragment, California and other states.[23] These new, FHA-financed, intentionally segregated cities became key features of our social, economic, and political landscape.

The simplest way for realty boards to maintain segregation, as McMichael's textbook reminded them, was strict "ethical control" under Article 34: discipline any realtor who introduced undesirable persons.

To ensure the widest reach of Article 34, CREA stressed including other brokers under its umbrella: "It [is] all the more necessary that every ethical person in the real estate business belongs to a real estate board and to state and national associations."[24] It went without saying that every such ethical person would have to be white. Such new members would thus be subject to boycott, sanction, and expulsion if they introduced non-Caucasians into white neighborhoods.[25]

NAREB thus made a crucial decision in responding to *Shelley*. Rather than embark on an explicit constitutional campaign to officially segregate African Americans, NAREB chose quieter approaches. These approaches had three things in common. First, they did not require public approvals or political debates and—realtors presumed—were permitted within their own, narrow interpretation of *Shelley*. Second, NAREB could portray these methods not as based on *realtors'* racial animosity against a particular group but as a reflection of owners' wishes; a realtor-led campaign for a constitutional amendment aimed at African Americans would have jeopardized such a seemingly unprejudiced stance. Finally, each approach was based on the same principle Charles Shattuck had invoked to appeal to West Side homeowners a few months before *Shelley*: neighbors had a basic right to control who lives next to them. That the Supreme Court had rejected freedom of association as a reason for courts to enforce racial covenants only made it more attractive as a popular argument. Americans were entitled to freedom of association, and it was under attack.

So appealing was freedom of association as a theme for realtors to seek public support, CREA quickly used it as the centerpiece of two statewide ballot campaigns. When liberals and progressives put a bond issue on the November 1948 ballot for a state public housing program that would make units available to all races, realtors ran the No campaign as a referendum on freedom of association. As they would with Proposition 14, realtors titled their campaign organization the Committee for Home Protection and called their effort "not a campaign but a crusade."[26] They saw their successful campaign against integrated state public housing as central to, not a diversion from, their efforts to maintain racial segregation in private housing.

Buoyed by their success in stopping state-built public housing,

CREA then took the initiative. It put a state constitutional amendment on the 1950 ballot that would require a local popular vote before any publicly funded housing could proceed. The aim was to prevent federal public housing from being built in California. As later with Proposition 14, CREA called their effort a campaign to "restore American freedom." Although local referenda had never been required on past public housing or on any other local actions except general obligation bond issues, the realtors nonetheless claimed that their proposition *would give back* to the people a right that had been "taken away" from them. The theme of the realtors' successful campaign—that the people in each locality had the right "to decide whether public housing is needed or wanted in each locality"[27]—was the same as their argument for freedom of association: neighbors have a basic right to decide who will live next to them. Charles Shattuck, leading CREA's efforts, spelled this out: "If you hold liberty dear," he said, "if you love this land of the free and the home of the brave," the right to vote against public housing being built nearby would be "the one and only means by which our great Republic will be preserved and improved." Race was at the heart of the battle, with realtors' advertisements claiming that "minority pressure groups" were the ones behind public housing.[28]

This provision of the Constitution of California, drafted by the realtors in 1950 and passed by a margin of fewer than fifty thousand votes, remains in force today. Written broadly, it applies to more than the public housing projects it was designed to stop. Local referendum authority is required for any affordable development financed in whole or in part by the federal government, the state, or any city. Three attempts have been made to repeal the amendment, including in 1993 with the support of the California Association of Realtors.[29] All sorts of means are devised to build affordable housing without violating the rule, including local votes authorizing a set number of units and the use of tax credits rather than direct public funds. That California's constitution still requires local public votes for affordable housing—but not for roads, schools, prisons, nuclear power plants, or junkyards—is a testament to the realtors' argument for freedom of association more than seventy years ago.

Being on the side of freedom, and making clear that such freedom was necessary to maintain all-white neighborhoods, helped postwar realtors change their public image. Previously their longtime support of business interests, their delaying any postwar housing bill for four years because it included public housing, and their elitist statements had made realtors seem uninterested in the plight of ordinary citizens. California realtors had defiantly published a 1948 editorial of aphorisms against the common man: "The weak cannot be strengthened by weakening the strong. Small men cannot be made into big men by reducing men who have become big. . . . The wage-earner cannot be lifted up by pressing down the wage payer."[30] Herbert Nelson told a national columnist with respect to rent controls: "We've got a gang in power who thinks solely of the consumer, and usually in terms of protecting him."[31] Now, by portraying themselves as defending freedom, realtors used populist imagery to show that they were, in fact, concerned about the majority of white Americans. This had been Shattuck's precise objective when he appealed to American freedom to continue segregation.

Paradoxically, the realtors gained something from their defeat in *Shelley*. No longer would there be highly public cases of courts ousting individual veterans from their own homes or putting them in jail for contempt. Minorities would now be excluded in more general and less public ways, without the heavy hand of government. Realtors could argue that the continuation of all-white neighborhoods and minority ghettos was natural; it showed that "birds of a feather flock together." The continuation of racial patterns first established by court-enforced covenants and FHA underwriting rules now reflected market forces and voluntary choices.[32] In this new vocabulary, all-white neighborhoods simply reflected freedom of association; how they had become all-white in the first place, why only whites had been able to live there, was never mentioned.

Freedom of association did not require government action; the government simply had to get out of the way. Without court orders to evict minorities, the future of residential segregation would be up to realtors and the allies they enlisted under the banner of freedom. As their lawyers had advised them, if realtors wanted to continue segregation without government backing, they would need to step up their own efforts. This they were more than prepared to do.

10.

Using Freedom of Association to Intensify Segregation

> I firmly believe in the Constitution and . . . the freedoms that our ancestors came here to enjoy and among those . . . [is] the right to choose your neighbors.
>
> Chicago real estate broker, 1955[1]

In the Buffalo suburbs in 1963—some fifteen years after *Shelley* led African Americans to hope that they might be able to buy homes on the same terms as white Americans—Joanne Champion knocked on the door of a house with a For Sale sign. Champion was a chemistry teacher at a prestigious Catholic girls' school, a Wellesley graduate with a master's from the University of Michigan, the wife of a doctor, mother of three, and member of the women's committee at the art museum. To see the house, Champion was told, she must first have the majority of the neighbors sign a petition. If she had been white, she reflected, the story would have been different: "You don't need to have anything but money. Your future neighbors don't investigate you before they let you buy a house. But if you are a Negro you face discrimination no matter . . . what you have achieved."[2] To the Champions and millions of others, the systemic denial by realtors, owners, and developers of their ability to find a place to live was a fundamental violation of American freedom. From the realtors' perspective, Champion's experience was freedom of association in practice.

A SLOGAN TO MOBILIZE NEIGHBORHOODS

No longer able to rely on court enforcement of covenants, realtors invoked freedom of association to mobilize neighbors to prevent sales to minorities. In San Jose, neighbors circulated petitions: "Not because of any feeling of discrimination for people other than the white Caucasian race, but rather under the laws of our country that a man has a right to protect his property and his home, we . . . protest the selling of the home on Thornton Way to anyone who is not a member of the white Caucasian race."[3]

Freedom of association gave realtors themselves an idealistic way to justify discrimination; sociologist Rose Helper's in-depth interviews of Chicago brokers in the mid-1950s showed how powerful this idea proved. "If the majority in a neighborhood does not want Negroes to enter, the real estate man, as a good American, is bound to respect their wishes," one broker explained, as if elections were held, when it was actually the broker himself who made the decisions on their behalf. Broker after broker talked about the Constitution ensuring "the right to choose [one's] neighbors," as if everyone knew this.[4] No longer having to cite property values for excluding minorities, brokers could simply cite American freedom. By the mid-1950s, this belief in freedom of association as a constitutional right had become part of the basic ideology of real estate throughout the country.

Only one of the brokers Helper interviewed suggested that an African American too might have a right to choose his neighbor and neighborhood.[5] Although Shattuck had called freedom of association an equal right of all Americans, in the world of real estate it meant the right of whites to exclude minorities. This was hardly surprising, considering that virtually no real estate board from the early 1900s into the early 1960s had a single nonwhite member. Not one of Los Angeles's two thousand members in 1960 was African American.[6] Indeed, the right to limit who could join, which prevented minorities accessing the multiple listing service, was the organizing principle of real estate boards themselves.

Beneath these justifications lay a system of intense pressures on brokers not to sell to minorities. If a realtor dared to do so, the local board took disciplinary action. But while boards expelled members in city after city,[7] such formal actions were rarely necessary.[8] When a Los Angeles realtor sold two homes in white neighborhoods to African Americans, his referrals from other realtors dropped so drastically he had to quit real estate entirely. When composer-conductor Benny Carter sought a house in Beverly Hills in 1962, a real estate agent told him she could not show him a home. "I would be blackballed by the . . . Realty Board. I would never work as a realtor again."[9]

Similar economic pressures affected all brokers, whether members of boards or not. In a Los Angeles area with twelve thousand new homes, not one broker surveyed would sell to African Americans. "Eventually there will be integration, but I don't have the courage to sell to a Negro," one admitted.[10] "Selling to a Negro," another explained, "would be . . . putting myself out of business as well as ostracizing me."[11] Across the country, an East Coast broker with an offer in hand from an African American buyer received a call from a city councilman. "Now, we don't want to pressure *you* but just let's be sensible. . . . One sale doesn't mean very much to you and you can sell it to somebody else. You've got a nice business there and you wouldn't to see it go downhill." "What the hell do you think I did?" the broker asked an interviewer. "I told the N----- I couldn't sell it to him. I sold it later to a white family for three thousand less than I'd have got from the N-----."[12] In avoiding selling to minorities, brokers were thus serving neither the owner nor the buyer, the client they owed a fiduciary duty to, but protecting themselves. "If I didn't steer people around and match them up with a neighborhood where they'd fit in, I'd be out of business so fast my kids would starve to death," one broker explained. "When I sell a house, I make damn sure there aren't going to be any repercussions in the neighborhood."[13]

Brokers went to whatever length was necessary to avoid selling to minorities:

I told [an African American customer] I was awfully sorry but I had forgotten the key . . . but would he call me and make another appointment? He was a perfect gentleman and he said he would be glad to call me the next day. . . . I drove off thanking my stars I had thought quickly enough. . . . If I'd ever shown that man through that home—and the neighbors—well, you can imagine.

. . . I told my secretary that no matter when that man called to say I was out and she was not allowed to make appointments. I was afraid to answer the 'phone myself for the next 3 days.[14]

The result was that any owner who was in fact willing to sell to a minority had a hard time finding an agent. Of brokers in San Francisco in 1955, realtors and nonrealtors alike, 85 percent said they would not handle such a sale.[15] Of six hundred brokers in the Palo Alto area in 1961, one-half of one percent would consider showing property on a nondiscriminatory basis.[16] A San Francisco broker told a white homeowner that "she must be psychotic for even thinking of selling to a nonwhite family."[17]

Even when state laws changed to end discrimination by brokers, the pressures within brokers' offices prevented such sales. After California passed a 1959 law making it illegal for all businesses, including real estate brokers, to discriminate on racial or religious grounds, Black couples and white couples tested compliance. In the San Fernando Valley, a white tester asked about the Black testers who were waiting nearby. "How selective are you?" "You don't have to worry," the agent explained. The state sent "notices to all real estate brokers to give equal treatment. . . . We show them the homes and give them information. . . . We refer them to Mr. More. Only if Mr. More sends them back do we have to consider them. But there are always ways to get around them. . . . We can always tell them 'I don't think you will qualify.'"[18] Variations of Mr. More were the way realtors resisted efforts to end segregation throughout the country.

DEFENDING THE COLOR LINE

This combination of belief in the rightness of what they were doing and fear of doing anything else—of the conformity imposed by freedom of association—enabled realtors to not only continue segregation after *Shelley* but intensify it. From 1950 to 1960, San Fernando Valley's fair housing council learned of one African American family able to find a house in an area of 750,000 people. Education, income, occupation made no difference. A missile engineer, hired by one of the Valley's booming aerospace firms, tried six times to find a broker before giving up. By 1963, outside the segregated community of Pacoima, African Americans constituted 0.0015 percent of the Valley's population.[19] Indeed, in all of Los Angeles County, fewer than 1 percent of African Americans lived in areas that were not majority Black. The U.S. Commission on Civil Rights found the same pattern virtually everywhere.[20] Nationally, for the ten largest metropolitan areas in the country, thirty times as many white Americans as African Americans moved to the suburbs from 1930 to 1960.[21]

When minorities did manage to buy homes in a neighborhood, this only stiffened resistance in the neighborhoods whites fled to. In areas with older homes on the edges of a Black ghetto such as Compton, where economic and social pressures to sell proved overwhelming, white residents eventually moved out en masse. Such white flight was only possible because there were other all-white neighborhoods farther away and better protected where residents could easily move. These included tens of thousands of units in new FHA- and VA-financed subdivisions sold only to white buyers. The color line shifted geographically, but was only reinforced.

What did change during the 1950s was that the color line began to soften slightly against Asian Americans and some Mexican Americans, further isolating African Americans as the one group realtors excluded from "white" neighborhoods everywhere. The children of eastern and southern European immigrants had gradually begun to be viewed as individuals after the war, but it often took battles for Asian Americans and Mexican Americans to be treated this way.

The key case for Asian Americans drew national attention and tested whether freedom of association was the same as American patriotism. In 1952, Sing Sheng, a Chinese American aircraft mechanic tried to buy a home in the Southwood tract of South San Francisco. In response to threats from potential neighbors, he decided to test the idea of neighbors voting on whether he could live there. Offering to abide by a vote of neighborhood residents, Sheng hoped the results would reflect the "democratic principles" American soldiers were fighting for in the Korean War. "I was sure everybody really believed in democracy," Sheng explained to a reporter. "If the votes are not in my favor, it is a good indication that this war is being fought in vain." When the Shengs lost 174

to 28, the story became national news.[22] The neighbors, to their aston-
ishment, were widely condemned as aiding the Communist cause. The
San Francisco Chronicle wrote that "Southwood has undone . . . the work
of the Voice of America, of Radio Free Asia, and . . . of American men . . .
fighting in Korea." Governor Earl Warren apologized to Sheng: "I agree
with you that it is just such things that the Communists make much of
in their efforts to discredit our system." The Shengs received numerous
house offers in other white neighborhoods.[23]

As a result of Sheng's case, the San Jose neighbors petitioning
against a non-Caucasian buyer by invoking "the laws of our country"
found themselves forced to recant; newspapers publicized that the buyer
was a Japanese American disabled veteran. When sales agents in Garden
Grove rejected former army major and Olympic gold medalist Sammy
Lee, newspapers weighed in again. Noting that Lee had toured Asia for
the State Department promoting democracy, the *San Francisco Chronicle*
warned that "Rejecting him will embarrass our country in the eyes of
the world." Vice President Nixon quickly condemned the discrimination,

Sing Sheng and family,
seeking to buy a home
in South San Francisco,
1952

the governor urged Garden Grove to "uphold the finest traditions of Americanism and freedom," FHA started an investigation, and the tract's developers quickly changed their minds.[24]

But if freedom of association could be trumped by a larger notion of American democracy and patriotism in the case of some Asian Americans, this did not prove true for African Americans. As soon as the FHA commissioner and Nixon condemned discrimination against Sammy Lee, Loren Miller telegrammed them informing them of fifty other tracts, all of whose discriminatory policies FHA had long known about, that refused to sell to African American veterans. No investigation was ever held.[25] When neighbors prevented a sale to a Black air force lieutenant in the same neighborhood as Sammy Lee, neither the vice president, the governor, nor FHA said anything. When a Black teacher's home was fire-bombed in Los Angeles, the state assembly tabled a resolution that "such incidents are not in keeping with the American tradition . . . and furnish . . . propaganda [for] the Communists." When three hundred neighbors organized to prevent a Black family from buying a home in South San Francisco a year after Sing Sheng, no public officials or newspapers condemned them. The Southwood neighbors complained that they had been singled out for criticism. "Aren't there other neighborhoods where Chinese, Negroes, and minorities are excluded?" "Of course there are," a neighbor angrily chimed in.[26] But by the early 1960s, if Asian Americans might be accepted in some of those neighborhoods, that was not true of African Americans. One in ten San Francisco brokers was willing to make the first sale in a neighborhood to an Asian American; not one would sell to an African American.[27]

This pattern of grudging acceptance also began to apply to some Mexican Americans. By 1960, the working-class suburbs around Los Angeles's South Central ghetto—cities like South Gate where racial segregation had been particularly intense—were home to nine thousand Mexican Americans but fewer than seventy African Americans. This relative acceptance was true in the outer suburbs of Los Angeles and in San Diego as well.[28] By 1960, the U.S. Commission on Civil Rights concluded unanimously that housing discrimination in California was "largely a Negro problem" rather than one affecting Asian and Mexican Americans.[29] A sales agent near Los Angeles thus spoke for many when he refused to take an application from an African American: "We've taken in Japanese and Mexicans in this development, but . . . Negroes would be going too far."[30] That there had to be a group it would be going too far to admit, was, for brokers, a basic fact of real estate, an elementary truth. The freedom to not associate required a group to exclude.

It was African Americans who remained intensely segregated. Their numbers in Los Angeles County more than doubled in the 1950s, but this only increased their racial isolation. The probability that an African American in Los Angeles County would have a white neighbor dropped by a third from 1950 to 1960.[31] Formerly mixed neighborhoods became almost entirely African American as members of other groups were accepted as "white" and moved to the suburbs. A decade after *Shelley*, Loren Miller summarized the results. "Residential segregation in Los Angeles . . . is as great in degree, and is greater in extent today than when *Shelley* was decided."[32]

NAREB AND FHA

But while realtors took the initiative throughout the country in defending segregation in the name of freedom of association, both NAREB and FHA in the aftermath of *Shelley* sought to remain out of the limelight, in part to avoid Justice Department scrutiny. Both NAREB and FHA suggested that discrimination had nothing to do with the systems they had created, but was a matter of the rights of those in each area not to associate with minorities—and thus nothing could be done about it.

NAREB—which had established Article 34 of the Code of Ethics against introducing undesirable races and nationalities, had provided a standard-form racial covenant across the country, and prominently defended racial covenants in *Shelley v. Kraemer*—was steadfastly silent after the court's decision. In fact, while local boards continued to cite Article 34 as their fundamental principle for racial exclusion, NAREB changed its wording so quietly that almost no one noticed. When the Louisville board asked NAREB in 1949 how *Shelley* affected the Code of Ethics, NAREB replied briefly that it doubted whether the ruling would affect the prohibition on realtors introducing undesirable residents.[33]

The next year, however, NAREB altered the language of the code. Realtor publications buried the change, simply noting that two revisions had been approved, one "about charging of fees" and the other, without any comment, a revised text of Article 34.

The difference was so subtle that it was hard to know anything had changed. "A realtor should not be instrumental in introducing into a neighborhood a character of property or use which will clearly be detrimental to property values in that neighborhood," the new code read. The message seemed the same as the old: "A realtor should never be instrumental in introducing into a neighborhood a character of property or occupancy, members of any race or nationality, or any individuals whose presence will clearly be detrimental to property values in that neighborhood." So little attention was paid to this change, so easy was it to assume that "character of property or use" referred to occupancy, that separate in-depth studies of realtors years later found that brokers in Chicago, New Haven, San Francisco, and San Jose all thought the new Article 34 had *exactly the same meaning as the old one*.[34] As a result, boards around the country continued to sanction members who introduced non-Caucasians.[35] Not a single board announced "that introduction of a minority buyer into a white neighborhood was permissible."[36]

In other contexts, too, NAREB did its best to avoid speaking about race throughout the 1950s. While the realtors' national organization took forceful, widely publicized stands on public housing, local rent control, government spending, taxation, and mortgage financing, it said nothing about discrimination, segregation, integration, or the rights of neighbors. When Miller helped bring a Sacramento lawsuit challenging discrimination on FHA projects, NAREB advised the local board to settle quietly out of court.[37] When a 1959 national Commission on Race and Housing, headed by corporate and university leaders, found that "it is the real estate brokers . . . which translate prejudice into discriminatory action,"[38] NAREB responded only that it "has no policy on minority housing." Asked about the organization's position on racial issues, NAREB explained that "in regard to segregation, we don't interfere with the local situation."[39] Even as battles over fair housing heated up in the late 1950s, NAREB said nothing on the subject.

What led to NAREB's silence? The national organization had

positioned itself so that no attorney general, court, or critic could say that the new Article 34 excluded minorities. This was left to local boards for "determination in accordance with local practice."[40] The message was simple: NAREB's hands were tied. Such distancing could be highly useful.

For if NAREB was vulnerable as an organization, it was to potential antitrust litigation. The entire structure of NAREB and local boards could be viewed as an attempt to restrain competition. This was no idle possibility. The Department of Justice had sued NAREB and the Washington, DC, board in 1947 on antitrust grounds for price-fixing of commissions. Although the Supreme Court only found sufficient evidence against the local board, it went out of its way to warn NAREB that it would be liable if any evidence showed that it was engaged in interstate conspiracies with local boards.[41] Even while the price-fixing case was pending, and equally crucial to their economic power, the realtors were finally hoping to win trademark office approval for the word *Realtor*. Meanwhile, NAREB and Nelson were at the center of harsh congressional investigations of their lobbying power.

At this critical moment, when NAREB's cartel-like control of real estate sale was most at stake, civil rights advocates suggested that realtors "clubb[ing] together to limit the right of Negroes to purchase and occupy homes," causing "Negroes [to] pay more in purchase prices and rentals," was an equally "monopolistic practice" that should be investigated next by the grand jury.[42] This idea was amplified in 1951 by a University of Chicago law review article showing how the attorney general could bring antitrust charges against NAREB and local boards for limiting sales to minorities and excluding minority brokers, now that *Shelley* held such restrictions to be against national policy.[43] In particular, antitrust laws "may properly be applied to the realtors' Code of Ethics." NAREB had thus been one step ahead in quietly changing its code. The less NAREB itself said about race, the safer it was.

FHA, too, had been deeply concerned about the impact of *Shelley*. Although *Shelley* effectively prohibited the government from denying "rights of property" because of race or color,[44] FHA tried to avoid making any changes to its program. In an internal memo two weeks after the decision, FHA's commissioner determined that "the Supreme Court decision will in no way . . . [restrict] the operation of the programs."

FHA claimed, like NAREB, that it did not have a racial policy, as it had recently removed the explicit references to race in its underwriting manual. Deciding on racial restrictions, it now said, was up to the developer.[45] Therefore, it announced, FHA would not in any way prevent developers using 100 percent FHA mortgage insurance from limiting their properties to white buyers or tenants.[46]

Indeed, the same agency that had for years *required* protection against undesirable races now claimed it *did not* have legal authority *to refuse* to insure mortgages to developers who racially discriminated.[47] Like NAREB, it claimed its hands were tied. The federal government that made such housing tracts possible—insuring 100 percent of the risk on loans and enabling developers to obtain construction financing for virtually all the development costs[48]—would not interfere with freedom of association. As a result, massive developments such as Westlake in Daly City, Panorama City in the San Fernando Valley, and Lakewood and Westchester south of Los Angeles were limited solely to whites.[49] With FHA's hands-off approach, fewer than fifty homes built in the Bay Area in the 1950s with FHA financing were available for open occupancy by African Americans.[50]

FHA's explanation for its policy was simple. "Federal intervention is incompatible with our ideas of political and economic freedom," Eisenhower's FHA administrator Albert Cole announced in 1956. "The role of the Federal government is . . . never to stifle the proper exercise of private and local responsibilities."[51] To Loren Miller, "this means the government regarded wholesale discrimination as a proper exercise of private and local responsibilities."[52] Indeed, in May 1958, in *Ming v. Horgan*, Miller would eventually convince a judge in Sacramento that a developer using FHA insurance was in fact *being vested with federal power* and so could not discriminate.[53]

In a November 1958 speech to a national realtor meeting, FHA administrator Cole pushed back against any implication that the government had any responsibility for limiting discrimination on projects it financed. After all, he asserted, "Neither the Government nor the private real estate industry had caused segregation in housing."[54] But if neither FHA, who helped finance these all-white developments, nor the developers who built and sold them, caused segregation, what was its source?

The answer, FHA explained, was not "discriminatory operation of the National Housing Act [but] . . . market attitudes"[55]—in other words, the desire of whites to exclude African Americans. Both the agency and the developers had simply been reflecting that desire. Even though FHA was financing new communities that did not yet exist, where no neighbors yet lived, the right of future residents not to associate with others was already built in.

Local real estate boards, NAREB, and FHA thus all used the language of freedom of association to continue and increase segregation. They did this so successfully that by the late 1950s, civil rights advocates sought laws that would directly put an end to residential segregation, based on a very different view of American freedom. Such freedom did not refer to the neighbors' right to exclude Joanne Champion because of her race but to *her* right *not* to be excluded. This new view would necessarily threaten freedom of association. As this battle escalated, realtors would find themselves on the defensive in the North and West. For during the exact same postwar years that realtors had been invoking freedom of association, other groups had turned to the same idea, especially those committed to white supremacy in the South.

11.

The Idea of a National Conservative Party

> No decent and self-respecting Negro would ask for a law to force
> people to accept him where he is not wanted. They themselves
> do not want social intermingling. They are entitled to equality
> of opportunity, and they will get it through our efforts. But all
> the laws of Washington, and all the bayonets of the Army, can-
> not force the Negro into our homes, our schools, our churches,
> and our places of recreation.
>
> Strom Thurmond, 1948[1]

Freedom of association became a rallying cry not only for realtors from
the late 1940s to the 1960s but for conservatives far more broadly. Step-
ping back briefly from the realtors lets us see how other invocations of
freedom of association cast a shadow on the realtors' own and ultimately
led them to develop another vision of American freedom to defend housing discrimination. It also shows how the plan for a majority conservative
party—the party that adopted the realtors' vision of color-blind freedom
after Proposition 14—began as a way to protect Jim Crow in the South.

AN IDEOLOGY OF RESISTANCE

White Southern leaders began using the right to select one's associates to
oppose school integration and maintain official discrimination. *National
Review* intellectuals, taking up the Southerners' cause, argued that the
right not to associate with others was an essential part of American freedom. In California and thirteen other states, a small group of extreme
right-wing conservatives tried to build a political movement in the early

1950s around the right of neighbors to exclude other races. In failing, they created cautionary lessons for California realtors that would affect Proposition 14. In a nonracial context too, the right not to associate with others became part of the country's political vocabulary. Business groups and politicians across the country appealed to the right not to associate in order to weaken labor unions. Under state "right to work" laws, workers in companies or industries represented by a union would not have to join the union or pay dues.

Although the realtors and other groups who insisted on freedom of association had different goals in mind, they each employed the term in the same way. Each defined freedom of association not as the positive right *to join a group* but as the right *to avoid dealing with others*. Instead of protecting Communist party members or the NAACP from government restrictions, this right *not to associate* was used to oppose postwar changes in American society—minorities moving into white neighborhoods, school integration, and the rise of labor unions—that threatened traditional social hierarchies. Because these postwar changes were connected to government actions, Supreme Court decisions, and new liberal orthodoxies, this right not to associate became an ideology of resistance. It stood for not having to change.

For homeowners and realtors who advocated all-white neighborhoods, for white Southerners who believed in Jim Crow, and for businessmen who viewed labor unions as an economic or political threat, freedom of association gave their cause a nobler meaning. It provided another, elevated reason to insist on the rightness of what they already believed in. That this claim was not recognized by the courts as part of the Constitution only added to their sense of righteous grievance.

But while freedom of association mobilized those who already believed in the underlying cause, justifying their anger and intensifying their commitment, it did not broaden the base of support. As with "states' rights," "the lost cause," "Southern pride," "anti-imperialism," "pro-life," and "restore religious freedom," one had to be passionately committed to begin with. Partly this was because this use of freedom of association was new. Its meaning was counterintuitive: not a freedom to do something, but to avoid or prevent something. It was transparently invented by current advocates; it was not a long-held fundamental value like freedom of speech or democracy. America had not fought its wars for freedom of association.

Each of the uses of freedom of association was therefore provocative; indeed, freedom of association was meant to be provocative, to say here is a right that has been overlooked, has been trampled on. Inevitably, therefore, its use in each of these controversies bled into the others. When realtors invoked this ideology, they inevitably evoked the other battles in which it was being used. These controversial connotations only increased over time. In states like California, candidates who argued for freedom of association in the late 1950s and early 1960s received about 40 percent of the vote. Partly this was because freedom of association had come to be connected to being antiunion. But it was also because, no matter how realtors sought to avoid the connection, the use of freedom of association to defend white supremacy in the South increasingly cast a shadow over its use in the North.

Realtors sought to present themselves as reasonable businessmen, simply and benignly providing what neighbors wanted. They were not "anti-Negro"; they were not seeking to take anything away from other races. Realtor organizations were not against African Americans being able to vote or sit where they wanted on a bus or have the same legal rights as anyone else. Private discrimination was legal and permitted under the Fourteenth Amendment, and having lost in *Shelley*, realtors were not asking government to enforce such discrimination. Yet the same idea of freedom of association that realtors were using to justify quiet, private discrimination had become the white South's rallying cry for denying legal rights to American citizens.

The right not to associate became the central argument of Southern massive resistance to school integration. James Eastland of Mississippi proclaimed on the Senate floor ten days after *Brown v. Board of Education*, "All free men have the right to associate exclusively with members of their own race, free from governmental interference" since "it is the law of nature, it is the law of God, that every race has both the right and the duty to perpetuate itself." Sam Ervin of North Carolina similarly argued that school integration violated "a fundamental American freedom—the freedom to select one's own associates. [This is] virtually always . . . within their race." Ervin cited the same rationale realtors had for years in their property-value ideology: "a basic law of nature—the law that like seeks like."[2] The more combatively Southerners claimed freedom of association to oppose school integration and civil rights, the more difficult it became for California realtors to invoke the right to select one's neighbors without triggering images of angry white mobs in Little Rock taunting schoolchildren and defying the National Guard.

From the late 1950s on, throughout their entire war against fair housing, realtors therefore tried to justify residential segregation while distinguishing themselves from Southern segregationists. This became their key political challenge. Ever since Truman appointed his President's Committee on Civil Rights in 1947, both realtors and Southern segregationists had found themselves, if not on the same side, under attack by the same ideological enemy. Each group had turned to freedom of association in 1947 and 1948 for the same reason: to argue for racial separation in the name of American freedom. The practices they were defending were different, but their need to describe them in the language of freedom was the same.

In their far more visceral battle against the federal government, Southern segregationists conceived of a majority conservative political party even before Truman's committee completed its report. Their explicit aim was protecting white supremacy. By the time such a national party could be realized in the late 1960s, it needed a racially neutral-sounding ideology to be politically acceptable across the country. The party proposed by an unapologetic Southern racist in 1947 eventually adopted the realtors' vision of individual freedom—a vision realtors created precisely in order to sound less racist than Southern segregationists. The parallel efforts by realtors and Southern segregationists to oppose the ideal of equal freedom ultimately converged in what became a highly successful national conservative party.

A GRAND ALLIANCE

The plan for such a party—laid out in detail by an influential lawyer and native Alabaman named Charles Wallace Collins, in his 1947 book *Whither Solid South?*—reads as though it could have been written today.[3]

Charles Wallace Collins

Strom Thurmond at Democratic National Convention, 1948

Its proposed political strategy became a blueprint of today's Republican party: an alliance of "the men of affairs" across the country, white voters from "all the states below the Mason Dixon line," and voters believing in the values of "the rural sections of the Middle West." As Collins predicted, such an alliance would be "be the strongest in the country" and therefore unconcerned over its "failure to attract Negro votes."[4] It was an alliance neither Democrats nor Republicans imagined at the time.

Collins outlined the public values of this national conservative party: "private capital in the hands of free individuals," "restriction of the Federal Government," and protection of discrimination. Rather than equal rights, the party's central theme would be freedom from government intervention. Collins proposed this at a time when the solid Democratic South provided the strongest electoral support for continuing the New Deal.

But Collins's own argument for the plan could hardly win national elections today (or indeed in the 1950s or 1960s). Collins focused on "the overweening ambition of the Negro race in America to . . . force its way into the inner sanctuary of the white man's daily life, to work with him, to play with him, to eat with him, to be educated with him and to worship with him—with the white man and the white woman."[5] Collins's plan justified white racial prejudice as a good thing, as the "pride of blood in the white man."[6] To put this plan into effect, to create a party that could win in both the North and South, would ultimately require the racially neutral language of freedom that realtors would perfect in the 1960s—not the racist language Collins used.

Collins was both a brilliant banking lawyer and an ardent Southerner. Born in Gallion, Alabama, three years after the end of Reconstruction, he became a Coolidge administration official as counsel for the Bureau of the Budget and deputy comptroller of the currency. From 1928 almost until his death in 1964, he served as senior counsel to many of the country's largest banks, including Bank of America. As early as 1912, he had written a book urging the repeal of the Fourteenth Amendment, since it had been abused by corporations and was "of no practical benefit to the Negro race."[7] In 1947, semiretired, living on a historic estate he had restored outside Washington, DC, Collins realized, as soon as Truman appointed a civil rights committee, that the Southern way of life was doomed if the region remained loyal to the Democratic Party.

As long as the South was taken for granted, Collins argued, Republicans and Democrats would compete for the votes of big-city liberals and minorities in the Northeast and Midwest; indeed, Republican New York governor Thomas Dewey and Truman were seeking to outdo each other in support for fair employment. Although the seniority system and Senate filibusters had protected the South so far, the Southern bloc in Congress would eventually lose its effective veto over federal legislation on racial issues. "The South," Collins warned, "cannot in safety remain inactive in the face of the forces arrayed against her lest political and social erosion gradually carry away the last means of resistance."[8] The issue, as he saw it, was urgent.

To forestall such a transformation, the South needed to convert a "Republican–Southern Democratic coalition into a new conservative political party," united by opposition to federal power.[9] Southerners would abandon support for New Deal policies while conservative Republicans would abandon any support for equal rights, in a common ideology of freedom from the federal government. Such a party would dominate American politics, since "failure to attract Negro votes in the North would be as nothing in comparison with the strength that the South would bring." In the same way that Northern Republicans and

Southern Democrats had ended Reconstruction in 1878, a new "North–South coalition . . . would save the United States from stateism."[10]

Such a party would need to confront what Collins, like the realtors of the time, saw as the great ideological danger. For Collins, the wartime ideal of shared freedom and "all men are created equal" would be used to justify government encroachment in all areas of people's lives, regardless of constitutional limitations and long-standing traditions. Collins took on this ideal directly. Any claim that the aims and sacrifices of World War II justified an end to discrimination was insidious, he argued. Northern liberals had used the rationalization "of the Negro as a citizen of the United States in time of war" to bring "every aspect of Negro life . . . under review de novo as though the Negro had just landed on these shores and had been declared a citizen of the United States with all of the constitutional rights of the white man." The claim that Negroes, having fought abroad for democracy, were therefore entitled to it at home was an "over-simplification. . . . 'Democracy' is undefined and what our war aims really were may remain a question for many years."[11] Yet the "slogan of . . . 'democracy'" was being used to condemn "the whole Southern system,"[12] using a "gross misapprehension of what equality, freedom, democracy, human rights have meant."[13]

This misuse of "freedom" and "democracy," Collins argued, would do away with traditional American freedom. To describe such freedom, Collins looked to the rights that had existed *before* the Constitution, in language almost identical to what realtors would use in Proposition 14. "Back behind his long struggle throughout the centuries to gain the Rule of Law there shine . . . the Magna Carta . . . the common law of England . . . the Petition of Rights from Charles I, . . . the Declaration of Rights from William and Mary."[14] For Collins, it was not merely these long-standing principles that mattered, but that white men had created and deserved to benefit from them: "The great moral values held by the words 'equal protection of the laws,' 'due process of law' and 'the right of suffrage' were given to [Negroes] by the white man's long travail. . . . They are the heritage of the civilization which he built."[15] Those demanding civil rights for Negroes were "pushing aside history, tradition, custom and manners of generations. . . . Having seen themselves as black white men under a new orientation of the Fourteenth and Fifteenth Amendment . . . the old way of life for black and white together in the South seems to have been altogether lost."[16]

The most dangerous, politically seductive idea that the South had to resist, Collins argued, was voiced by New Deal administrator David Lilienthal: "that all government and private institutions must be designed to . . . defend the integrity and the dignity of the individual. That that is the essential meaning of the Constitution and the Bill of Rights." This argument was particularly insidious, Collins warned. Government's belief in protecting such dignity would lead to the destruction of all freedom. Lilienthal's "basic tenet that the . . . Federal Government must be used as a means to the realization of 'democracy,' makes his theory one of stateism, no different in principle from any other form of totalitarianism."[17]

Collins's aim was twofold. First, by reminding white Southerners what was at stake, he showed why the "Solid South" had to abandon the national Democratic party. "All of the ancient mores . . . of the South" were under attack, including "compulsory segregation of Negroes, their exclusion from the polls."[18] The result, Collins asserted, would be destruction: "The Southern negro would be irresponsible as a voter and as an office holder. He can be aroused to frantic hysteria and superstition. In his heart there still lurks dark and mysterious murmurings brought over from Africa. They still practice voodoo."[19]

Second, Collins sought to lay out the very different, freedom-based messages that Southerners needed so as to attract Northern support. The issue to talk about was centralized government. In words that anticipated the realtors' argument against fair housing, Collins foresaw a "reign of terror of a centralized national police state with a vast secret service to track down individuals who have been charged with the violation of the rights of other individuals." Thus, he argued, "the whole Negro program is infected with the deadly virus of stateism."

A permanent national conservative party would oppose such "stateism," defend private enterprise, and insist that men should not be "merged without distinction,"[20] an idea Barry Goldwater would later reiterate when he wrote, "To regard man as part of an undifferentiated mass is to consign him to ultimate slavery."[21] The Solid South "would naturally fall in with" this conservative party, Collins argued, on one key condition. "The issue of Negro equality" would be left to the remaining Northern Democratic party.[22] Here then was Collins's formula for a national conservative party that would oppose federal power, protect discrimination, and be able to dominate American politics.

Collins understated the obstacles to creating such an alliance. There were two great difficulties in linking Southern Democrats and conservative Republicans. The first was a difference in rhetoric and beliefs. Even in working together to defeat fair employment in Congress in the 1940s, Southern Democrats and Northern Republicans used far different language. Southerners' arguments almost invariably devolved into attacks on other races. Senator Richard Russell of Georgia, in the *Southern Review*, wrote that fair employment would "result in discrimination in favor of aliens and other minority groups."[23] Southern congressmen warned that fair employment forced "every enterprise to employ Negroes, Japs or members of any other race, whether they were wanted to or not," was "fomented and practiced against Caucasians—native-born American citizens," and would "ignore the rights of solid white Americans."[24] By contrast, Northern congressmen who opposed fair employment generally used race-neutral language, as the realtors would do, to argue against special privileges of protection against discrimination for minorities. "We are all Americans and should be treated equally," an Illinois business lobbyist proclaimed, "and should not ask for special privilege because we are representatives of any . . . class, religion, creed, race or color."[25] The conservative *Los Angeles Times* argued that fair employment would in fact lead to "promotion of race prejudice."[26]

The second difficulty in forging a common party was a difference in political necessity. Southern Democrats were facing far-reaching attacks by their own national party on the Southern way of life. Conservative Republicans, however, had major influence within their party and felt no necessity in the late 1940s to either split from their party or narrow it ideologically to embrace Collins's vision. Their leading figures, such as Senator Robert Taft, disdained Southern segregationist arguments and in 1947 refused to seat Theodore Bilbo of Mississippi because of his intimidation of Black voters.[27] As late as the end of 1962, Americans viewed the national Republican and Democratic parties as having similar positions on civil rights. Only with Goldwater's candidacy in 1964 did divisions between conservative and liberal Republicans so deepen that it seemed more promising for a Republican presidential candidate to seek votes and support from Southern Democrats than liberal Republicans.

Although these two difficulties pushed back Collins's idea of a national conservative party, his interim plan of withholding Southern electoral votes from the national Democratic ticket was quickly implemented. Collins's book had hardly been published when Truman's President's Committee on Civil Rights recommended an end to racial covenants and segregation in the armed forces. By July 1948—as Los Angeles realtors drafted their constitutional amendment to overturn *Shelley* and officially restrict where African Americans could live— Southern politicians met in crisis mode. Stung by the civil rights plank of the Democratic National Convention and Truman's integration of the armed forces, they organized around Collins's proposal. Collins met with governors and senators. Mississippi's governor and senator sent his book to key leaders throughout the South. What had seemed like a general plan was now urgent business.

Meeting in Birmingham, a group of Southern governors and legislators accepted Strom Thurmond's resolution not to "stand idle and let all of this happen." Embracing the Constitution as "the greatest charter in human liberty," they created a States' Rights Democratic Party, nominated Thurmond as the presidential candidate, and adopted a platform opposed to "the elimination of segregation, repeal of miscegenation statutes [and] control of private employment by federal bureaucrats."[28] Using Collins's approach of making the Southern case as national as possible, Thurmond focused his campaign on freedom from federal oppression: "We oppose the totalitarian, centralized, bureaucratic government and the police state called for by the platform adopted by the Democratic and Republican conventions."[29] The media's nicknaming the new party the Dixiecrats infuriated Thurmond, precisely because it undermined his and Collins's national claims.

After the 1948 election, Southern leaders therefore followed Collins's advice "to educate the North." States' rights and opposition to civil rights were not regional issues, they explained, but part of a national conservative agenda to protect the Constitution by limiting the federal government. They established a new nonprofit institute in Washington, one that proposed constitutional amendments and legislation opposing "nationalization of labor, business, industry or the professions," requiring that "proceeds of all taxes not spent on the armed forces . . . be returned to the states," prohibiting "deficit spending except in war," and prohibiting Congress from enacting any law that "conflicts with a state law pertaining to education, elections, . . . civil rights of individuals, racial relations, labor, zoning [and] transfer and ownership of property."[30] This comprehensive agenda was intended to appeal to free-market advocates, opponents of federal spending and regulation, and supporters of states' rights. Arguing for a broad alliance to support such causes, Collins declared that "I . . . classify everyone a conservative who fights on our side to conserve those basic principles of government upon which the Republic is founded."[31]

During the late 1940s and 1950s, the Southern call for a joint party made little headway in shifting the views of the Republican Party. Efforts of Southern congressmen to oppose integration of the armed forces received little support from Republicans. Eisenhower and Senate Republicans supported a stronger civil rights act than was ultimately passed in 1957, the first since Reconstruction. Although Eisenhower's silence on *Brown v. Board of Education* may have encouraged Southern resistance, he nonetheless federalized the Arkansas National Guard in Little Rock; on national television, he warned that violent resistance to desegregation hurt American prestige and let Communists "misrepresent our whole nation."[32]

Nor did the Southern argument gain much traction in the North. As freedom of association along with states' rights became the mainstay of Southern massive resistance to school desegregation, realtors in California and elsewhere had no desire to have their cause viewed as part of Southern efforts. For realtors found themselves facing the greatest challenge to racially separate real estate markets yet, a challenge that took them by surprise, grew to encompass cities and states across the country, and would require all their ideological creativity to combat. This challenge came from an organization so small it hardly seemed worth paying attention to.

Part Four.
Freedom of Choice: Late 1950s–June 1963

A single office the size of a bedroom, 150 square feet. After ten years, a professional staff of two, plus a secretary. The National Committee Against Discrimination in Housing (NCDH), which led the fight to end private discrimination in the late 1950s and 1960s, likened itself, in taking on NAREB, the real estate industry, and FHA, to "fleas on a tiger."[1] The struggle that NCDH spurred on would divide city councils, state legislatures, Congress, and high courts; torment presidents; and force realtors to mobilize all their resources and redefine American freedom to try to sway public opinion.

NCDH had been founded as a tiny nonprofit research organization by the groups that had striven so hard for *Shelley*. In 1950, a coalition of such groups—the NAACP, American Civil Liberties Union, Anti-Defamation League of B'nai Brith, Congress of Racial Equality, National Urban League, Brotherhood of Sleeping Car Porters, United Auto Workers, and American Friends Service Committee—agreed to provide modest funding.[2] These activists had few illusions about the power of their adversaries or the scale of their task when, in 1956, NCDH began to go beyond research and publish a national newsletter to lobby for change.

NCDH was driven by the fact that segregation had only increased since *Shelley*. Without needing LARB's proposed constitutional amendment to create separate Negro districts, realtors had perfected other ways to exclude African Americans so effectively that white Americans were hardly aware of these methods.[3] The results of segregation were evident to everyone, but realtors worked hard to represent segregation itself—so embedded in real estate practice, so pervasively enforced—as a normal, inevitable phenomenon, rooted in human nature and outside the power of anyone to change. But as so often happened in the long, bitter struggle over residential segregation, one side's achievements inspired renewed efforts by the other, and the very success of realtors' efforts in the 1950s spurred civil rights advocates to find new, more powerful legal tools.

NCDH established two specific lobbying goals. One was a presidential executive order to ban discrimination in federal housing programs, including FHA and VA. By 1960, NCDH convinced both Republican and Democratic parties to include the proposal in their platforms. After John F. Kennedy was elected and waffled on his campaign pledge to end housing discrimination in federally funded programs with "the stroke of a pen," NCDH flooded the White House with pens, urging the president to do what he had promised.[4]

The second lobbying goal directly threatened realtors' racial practices. NCDH used its national newsletter and model statutory language to push state legislatures and city councils to ban private housing discrimination. Since the Fourteenth Amendment did not prohibit private discrimination, the only way it seemed possible to do so was for government to use the same police powers employed in zoning and other restrictions on private property. Because the Constitution reserved such police powers for state and local governments, advocates would need to bring this battle to statehouses and city councils across the country.

NCDH therefore drafted fair housing ordinances that were then promoted by local "open occupancy" committees around the country.[5] These committees focused public attention on housing discrimination, conducting surveys that showed the role of local realtors, builders, and apartment owners, and reaching out to church, labor, and other groups. Most important, they pushed legislators to sponsor "fair housing" or "open occupancy" laws in state after state. NCDH thus hoped to create legal precedents and momentum that would spread from one jurisdiction to the next. By 1957, eleven states were considering such legislation. New York City adopted an ordinance that went into effect on January 1, 1958. Colorado adopted the first such state law in 1959. Realtors now found themselves on the defensive, trying to stop such bills wherever they appeared.

In fighting back, realtors found that growing support for civil rights had shifted the ideological ground under their feet. Their freedom of association argument, so effective in rallying owners and neighbors to stop individual home sales, did not always work as well in public debates. Opponents portrayed the argument that realtors had long relied on as racially biased and a distortion of American freedom.

Realtors believed that their problem was largely one of mobilizing those who already agreed with them. They knew their customer base and that most whites did not want to live near African Americans. As LARB's attorney Byron Hanna had said after *Shelley,* "Eight out of ten whites do not wish to live in mixed neighborhoods."[6] But the number of white Americans willing to say so publicly was dropping.[7] How could realtors openly appeal to such sentiments in the changing political and social climate of the 1950s and early 1960s? In states like California, realtors could no longer say in public, after *Brown v. Board of Education* in 1954, what Hanna had said in 1948: "Negroes should enjoy first class citizenship but on a separate but equal basis."[8] To retain racially separate housing markets against the challenge of fair housing, realtors sought a new way to talk about American freedom that justified discrimination.

Each local board was largely on its own in figuring out how to achieve this objective. Realtors had no common script to make their case. Indeed, when an open housing committee began to mobilize in a community, the local real estate industry often found itself the sole or leading opponent of fair housing. Boards often had to improvise. The realtors' ideological response that culminated in Proposition 14 did not emerge all at once.

Through 1961, realtors created freedom-based arguments on a largely local level, as boards and state associations rushed to fend off particular threats of fair housing. The points that realtors made in different states were often similar. But the style and relative emphasis of these arguments varied, depending on the personalities, beliefs, and natural instincts of key local realtor officials, and the specific fair housing proposal and political situation they had to deal with.

In 1962 and early 1963, NAREB began to coordinate, deepen, and standardize the freedom-based arguments of local boards, offering a common set of ideological tools for boards throughout the country. CREA developed one of the most important of these resources, the

"Property Owners' Bill of Rights," and persuaded NAREB to adopt and disseminate it to realtors opposing fair housing everywhere. Framed in the vocabulary of America's founding and the original Bill of Rights, this Property Owners' Bill of Rights created a positive and egalitarian-sounding defense for continuing organized racial discrimination.

This new vocabulary was the work of a new realtor leader, Spike Wilson from Fresno, whose style could not have been more different from that of Charles Shattuck. Unlike Shattuck, an appraiser more comfortable with unvarnished conclusions than sales talk, Wilson had begun his career as city editor of the *Sacramento Union* and believed in salesmanship itself, in selling as a fundamental value. Wilson's life-changing experience, he would explain, took place one night during the Depression when he went to report on a real estate board meeting.[9] At a time when most men were abandoning real estate work, he was inspired by the stories these remaining members told, by their powerful belief that selling itself would lift America out of the Depression. Wilson, transformed, decided that this was the work he wanted to do, and the group he wanted to be part of.

Wilson's belief in the absolute rightness of what he was promoting distinguished him from other realtor leaders opposing fair housing. In California and across the country, most realtor leaders found themselves on the defensive in this new era of civil rights. They justified past practices as the way they had always done business, or deployed racist stereotypes, or argued that integration was impractical because white homeowners would simply move away from Black newcomers. By contrast, newly installed as president of CREA in late 1962, Wilson responded to President Kennedy's executive order on discrimination in federal housing programs by spelling out a new set of owners' rights. Here were clear principles that he could announce to meetings of thousands of California realtors, who would unanimously stand up and applaud. Here was a cause they could believe in. Realtors who had spent years dissembling to minority customers—having to pretend to have forgotten the key, that homes had already been sold, that their secretary could not reach them,[10] or telling the customer he would have to talk to Mr. More—could be proud of these ideals. That these beliefs were stated as absolutes, and such owner rights as inviolable, only enhanced the power and appeal of the principles Wilson proclaimed. By ignoring buyers and tenants, the other half of real estate, Wilson could proudly assert that his ideals were for all Americans.

12.

Struggling for an Ideology to Defend against Fair Housing

We are not going to be a party to the salt and peppering of the whole community.

Charles Shattuck, 1961[1]

As NCDH began its lobbying efforts around the country, starting with its home in New York, drafting state and local ordinances and inspiring establishment of local "open occupancy" committees in city after city, local real estate boards found themselves unprepared. Accustomed as the boards were to insider lobbying of councils and legislatures, these new public debates about fair housing and civil rights took them by surprise.

For decades, boards around the country had looked to NAREB for national leadership in establishing positions and making their case. But NAREB had systematically avoided saying anything about race since *Shelley*. Herbert Nelson retired in 1955 and died months later, and his successor, CREA's executive secretary Eugene Conser, was more reserved and less of a public figure or national lobbyist. Even if NAREB was willing to take a position on fair housing, its staff seemed more interested in supporting local boards than asserting public leadership.

Left to their own devices, most local boards used apocalyptic tones to describe what would happen if discrimination were prohibited. In its final appeal to Mayor Wagner of New York, the city's real estate board warned that the law "would be one of the gravest errors . . . in the 350 year history of the City of New York. . . . Those responsible for it will live to rue the day they brought it into being."[2] Jeremiads of impending catastrophe characterized realtor responses to fair housing almost everywhere.

When local ordinances were proposed the following year in Pittsburgh and Philadelphia, Pennsylvania's realtors appealed forthrightly to freedom of association. At a massive public hearing, Pittsburgh realtors claimed that most of the three hundred white attendees supporting the law "had been duped by Negroes." Instead, the realtors insisted that they were the ones speaking in "defense of the white majority against whom the colored is pressing this legislation to have all housing made available for itself."[3] *Available for itself*, in this language, meant to be able to choose to live there. Philadelphia's realtors similarly argued that "it is impossible to force neighbors on people who do not want them."[4] Pittsburgh passed its ordinance, while Philadelphia's realtors were able to delay fair housing there for four years.

Just as the proposals differed among jurisdictions, realtors did not all agree on how to respond to fair housing bills. In Massachusetts, after polling members and doing some soul-searching, the state realtors association agreed to support their state's bill. When NAREB later urged Massachusetts realtors to change their position, fight this "odious law"[5]—a phrase harking back to the Stamp Act—and recognize that racial issues in housing could not be solved by legislation but only when whites were willing to accept Blacks, the Greater Boston Real Estate Board responded simply, "We have turned a deaf ear to that kind of reasoning a long time ago."[6] There would later be disagreements among realtors in other states, including in California, where a small minority, perhaps 5 percent of realtors, spoke out against Proposition 14.[7]

That some individual realtors, local boards, and even state associations accepted and indeed supported fair housing shows that realtor opposition to fair housing was not foreordained. Realtors made a choice. CREA, like realtor associations in almost all states, fiercely opposed fair housing, devoted their resources to fighting or rolling back such laws, and launched crusades for freedom to support discrimination. But CREA's was not the only possible response.

In their initial reactions to fair housing, even some CREA leaders expressed mixed feelings. In a 1960 column for the association's magazine, Edgar Stewart, CREA's general counsel, described how realtors could still discriminate despite new legislation, but he also recognized the impact of "civil rights principles upon public policy." "We must all accept the increasing transcendency of these personal civil rights and must gear our own thoughts and actions to these principles." He then noted that in battling fair housing, CREA had had to turn its definition of freedom almost upside down: "Now, it seems, police power, once [regarded by CREA as] good, is bad. Restraints upon [the owner's] absolute discretion such as restrictive covenants were once fully supported, now the owner himself emerges supreme."[8] Such doubts did not prevail within CREA. Stewart's column would be his last. But his comments did reflect the new, defensive position CREA found itself in. When fair housing was raised as a statewide issue in California in 1959, CREA, accustomed to governors and legislatures who had longed accepted the association's views, found itself in a position it had never anticipated. Its ability to control real estate legislation in the capitol, unchallenged for decades, was suddenly in question.

THE BIG SWITCH

Fair housing became part of the legislative agenda in California because of a remarkable personal decision that had unintended but powerful impacts on the state's, and even the nation's, politics. William Knowland —Republican Senate minority leader, successor to Robert Taft as Mr. Conservative and *National Review*'s favored candidate for president[9]— decided that instead of almost certain reelection to the Senate in 1958, he would enhance his presidential prospects if he first became governor of California. Knowland's decision astounded almost everyone, as he had previously been reelected with 85 percent of the vote and would likely face no serious opposition—and there was already a Republican governor of California. Many said publicly and more politely what Eisenhower had confided to his diary about Knowland: "In his case there seems to be no final answer to the question 'How stupid can you get?'"[10] Most of all, his decision astounded moderate Republican governor Goodwin Knight, who had seemed a safe bet for reelection himself. Knowland effectively forced Knight to run for his own Senate seat, which quickly became labeled "the booby prize."[11] This "Big Switch" alienated voters, galvanized Democrats who had long been out of power, and drew in the lone statewide Democratic office holder, Attorney General Pat Brown, to run against Knowland.

Two issues dominated Knowland's campaign and would affect CREA's ultimate arguments against fair housing. Knowland endorsed a "Right to Work" initiative that was on the ballot. If workers have a right to associate in a union, he contended, they must have an equal right not to associate: "Free men and women" should have the "basic civil right" of deciding for themselves whether or not to join a union.[12] Such right to work laws were deeply unpopular in heavily unionized California, however, and CREA learned of the unpopularity of this freedom of association argument firsthand. It prominently backed the 1958 initiative and conducted "a vigorous campaign throughout the state, with the cooperation of its 155 real estate boards,"[13] based on freedom of association.

Knowland's second, broader theme, the one he wanted the election to turn on, was "freedom versus tyranny."[14] Knowland employed *freedom* not as a unifying term for Americans together in World War II or the Cold War but as an angry protest against government involvement, control, and interference. In an open letter to Eisenhower, Knowland proclaimed, "We shall not stand idly by while freedom is being nibbled

U.S. Senator William F. Knowland

California Governor Edmund G. "Pat" Brown

away bit by bit."[15] Knowland's campaign—with his criticism of Eisenhower as too moderate, attacks on big government, and refusal to turn against Senator Joseph McCarthy—galvanized right-wing conservatives, especially in Southern California. Knowland called himself a crusader for freedom, and his campaign was "the first true conservative crusade in California of the post–World War II era."[16]

Knowland's crusade, however, like the Right to Work initiative, ended in overwhelming defeat. Each received barely 40 percent of the vote. Goodwin Knight, for good measure, lost the Senate race.

Most significant for realtors, Brown's landslide victory swept Democrats to majorities in both houses of the legislature. Democrats now controlled California's government for the first time in one hundred years. Brown's highest campaign priorities had been fair employment and anti-business discrimination laws, both of which passed in 1959. With strong support from emboldened liberals, union leaders, and minorities—FDR's New Deal coalition—Brown made fair housing his next priority. From the moment of Brown's first victory, realtors were on the defensive.

But Knowland's loss not only put fair housing on the table but also transformed the state's political landscape in ways that would, in fact, provide opportunities for CREA. Many Knowland supporters, after working together for a cause they deeply believed in, became the most active California Republicans.[17] They volunteered in local races, fighting to make sure the Republican party reflected their ideas. Meanwhile, many moderate and liberal Republicans, who had long supported Knight and Earl Warren, abandoned the party or became less involved. The Republican party, those who would work hardest for its future, shifted to the right. In 1959, the Democratic legislature's end of cross-filing in California primaries sealed this change. Candidates would now be chosen only by each party's own voters. California Republicans became far more ideologically conservative (and California Democrats more liberal). This more conservative party became the natural home for "suburban warriors," homeowners concerned about their rights, low taxes, and all-white neighborhoods.[18] Many of these conservative activists took over and dominated volunteer groups, such as the California Republican Assembly, who would vigorously support Proposition 14.

If the realtors could attract such right-wing Republicans and racially conservative Democrats, they could create a broad majority of Californians against fair housing. But to build such a coalition and achieve more than the 40 percent support for Right to Work and Knowland himself,[19] they would have to avoid alienating the white union voters who had long been and still saw themselves as Democrats on social security and economic issues.

Freedom of association, which had been used so directly against union voters, was hardly the best argument. Indeed, CREA's 1958 anti-union position would be turned against it in Proposition 14, with the AFL-CIO pointedly reminding its members of CREA's attack on unions.[20] Getting beyond this feature of Knowland's campaign would be crucial.

By contrast, Knowland's broader theme of "freedom against tyranny" could help forge a broad coalition against fair housing. *Tyranny*, in this conservative vocabulary, always referred to government coercion. Because fair housing required the power of government to prohibit discrimination, realtors could depict it as a form of tyranny taking away the rights of property owners. Such an argument could appeal to anyone who might oppose fair housing: right-wing conservatives, racially conservative union members, and any homeowners who could be persuaded that their rights were at risk.

But in the immediate aftermath of the 1958 election, neither liberal nor conservative observers recognized that Knowland's loss created the chance to shape a new and far more broad-based conservative coalition. What realtors focused on were the visible and, to them, highly dangerous consequences of the election. Brown's overwhelming victory suddenly made California a battleground for fair housing, one that quickly became the most prominent in the country. California's home sales dwarfed those of any other state. Half the nation's realtors worked in California. The vast, racially separate housing markets they had helped create in Los Angeles, the Bay Area, San Diego, Sacramento, and every other city in the state were now at risk.

FAIR HOUSING IN CALIFORNIA

Brown's opening message to the 1959 legislature emphasized what he called responsible liberalism and racial equality. "Offered reaction by the radical right," he declared, "the voters emphatically declined. Offered government by retreat, the people preferred progress. Clearly, then, our duty is to bring to California the forward force of responsible liberalism." The new governor then called "the essence of liberalism" a "genuine concern and deep respect for . . . not one race, or . . . creed . . . or nationality but all the people." He laid out the meaning of freedom that Truman's President's Committee on Civil Rights had described a dozen years before: "Conduct which degrades any member of society, degrades society as a whole. Every man must finally see the necessity of protecting the rights of others as the most effective security of his own."[21] The realtors, who had relied on California government to support and protect their position since they first introduced state licensing laws in 1908, would be politically tested as never before.

The 1959 legislature passed three bills that proved important to the fight for fair housing. It approved Brown's highest priority, creation of a state Fair Employment Practices Commission. Byron Rumford, an African American assemblyman and pharmacist from Berkeley, and Gus Hawkins, the longest-serving African American assemblyman, from Los Angeles, had been sponsoring such legislation ever since the chamber of commerce, with realtor support, had overwhelmingly defeated the 1946 ballot initiative for fair employment. Finally, such a commission had been created.

With respect to housing, the legislature passed the Hawkins Act prohibiting discrimination by developers of FHA- and VA-assisted projects. This made little immediate difference, as Loren Miller had won the 1958 court decision in Sacramento effectively prohibiting such discrimination in California. Moreover, the realtors fought off any administrative enforcement mechanism for the Hawkins Act. Minority buyers who believed they had been discriminated against would have to engage lawyers and sue, one at a time, in state court. The advocates' victory on this bill was thus largely symbolic. Hawkins himself noted that, with CREA opposing any bill, he had had to settle for "half a loaf rather than lose everything."[22]

Finally, the legislature passed a general antidiscrimination law, the Unruh Act,[23] which applied to all businesses. Members of all races were now "entitled to the full and equal accommodations, advantages, facilities, privileges or services in all business establishments of any kind whatsoever,"[24] including apartment house managers, developers, builders, and brokers themselves. But what would the Unruh Act actually mean for realtors? CREA's attorney provided careful advice to its members. True, a realtor could no longer simply tell minority buyers he would not serve them. But a realtor had other tools available. To avoid assisting in sales to minorities in white neighborhoods, he could "suggest or insist upon a discriminatory restriction" in each seller's listing. After all, CREA's counsel reasoned, the realtor "is not required to accept the listing at all, and certainly at the time he does accept it he is making no discrimination against any individual. It is true, of course, that he is . . . insisting that the owner discriminate, but the owner . . . is not a person prohibited from discriminating."[25] Realtors could thus effectively discriminate by simply making sure the seller did.

By July 1959, when the legislature adjourned, CREA's Legislative Committee called it "the toughest legislative session in the history of the State of California"—that is, the most difficult for business organizations and the real estate industry. Fair housing advocates, by contrast, vowed that when the legislature met in its next biennial session in 1961, they would push for new housing legislation that would cover homeowners and give the new state Fair Employment Practices Commission the power to enforce such a law. The new law would "have teeth."[26] Brown and Hawkins wanted "the whole loaf."[27]

"MINORITY GROUPS ARE NOT DISCRIMINATED AGAINST"

The key to victory in the next legislative session, fair housing advocates believed, would be establishing overwhelming proof of the extent of housing discrimination in California. They therefore marshaled testimony and evidence for four days of hearings before the U.S. Commission on Civil Rights in Los Angeles and San Francisco in January 1960. They could then point to the commission's records and conclusions to legitimate their claims.[28]

But while civil rights organizations prepared detailed documentation for the commission, the realtors took a very different approach.

They sought to rebut allegations of discrimination not with evidence but with philosophy, anecdotes, and general arguments. Having to explain that all the senior realtor officials were at a national meeting, Betty Elliot Davis, an assistant secretary of the Los Angeles board, offered up the gamut of arguments realtors had so far relied on. Racial discrimination was a myth, Davis explained: "Minority groups in Los Angeles are not discriminated against. . . . We have cases of minority groups living in practically every section and area of the city." She similarly claimed that "mortgage financing is available to all groups . . . on equal terms."[29] This blanket discounting of discrimination would become a standard feature of realtor rhetoric throughout the war against fair housing.

How was it possible for Davis and realtors to claim that housing discrimination did not exist, given the overwhelming statistical and survey evidence to the contrary? One reason was that most whites did not perceive discrimination because they were not directly affected. Frank Quinn of the Council for Civic Unity in San Francisco explained to the U.S. Commission on Civil Rights how this worked. "Awareness [of discrimination] is not widely shared . . . except [by] those who have had the experience themselves of . . . being turned [down]."[30] In a wide range of national surveys, from the mid-1950s to the mid-1960s, and despite growing awareness of the civil rights movement, 70 percent "of white Americans do not perceive the existence of discrimination against the Negro."[31] This was especially true of housing discrimination in the North, because unlike discrimination in restaurants, theaters, public accommodations, and transportation, it did not occur publicly but rather in the quiet of real estate offices, in the homes not shown and the phone calls not returned. Even the general recognition that there were no African Americans in one's own neighborhood did not make whites think about the consequences. It was easy to assume, "They can always live somewhere else, can't they?"[32]

Not perceiving discrimination had powerful consequences. "The citizen who perceives discrimination is likely to view civil rights activity as a legitimate pursuit," a survey showed during the Proposition 14 campaign a few years later. "Those who do not perceive discrimination, in contrast, reject the basic premise of much civil rights activity" and see it "as besmirching the community's reputation." Those wanting to continue the status quo discounted information that African Americans were widely discriminated against.[33]

To those who believed, like 70 percent of white Americans, that "Negroes are treated the 'same as whites in this community,'" Davis's anecdotal assurance that discrimination did not exist because "we have cases of minority groups" living in practically every section confirmed their views. What she meant was that one Black resident in Burbank, a city of ninety thousand,[34] and seventy Black residents across seven suburbs[35] proved there was no discrimination.

More important, Davis redefined discrimination so that inability to buy a home because of one's race was not discrimination. "Each of us . . . would live in a mansion . . . if we could," she said, "but, as a practical matter, . . . the people with whom we are able to associate . . . limits [where] each of us may find our homes and live in peace and security." "The inability of one to fulfill a desire is not discrimination—it is frustration which only the individual can overcome by personal improvement in his financial and social position."[36] Being able to buy a house, in other words, should and must depend on whether one would be socially accepted. Since one had no right to social acceptance, rejection because of one's race was not discrimination. Having spent almost sixty years making certain that African Americans were not viewed as individuals in buying homes in Los Angeles, LARB now blamed the individual buyer for being socially rejected. It was up to him to improve his social position. That there was no way to do so without changing the color of his skin did not change the situation.

Indeed, Davis emphasized that realtors were absolutely committed to freedom and equal rights, as they defined them: "LARB holds that civil rights are secured by the 13th and 14th amendments . . . that all persons, regardless of race, color, creed or national origin, are entitled to . . . equal protection of the laws under the Constitution." Since the Fourteenth Amendment only restricted government discrimination and not discrimination by private parties, realtors could easily assert this. They then made clear what could not be sacrificed in any discussion of housing discrimination: "The most precious right each American has is civil liberty which guarantees exemption from arbitrary governmental interference with person, opinion, or property."[37] Davis stated the realtors' case: individuals already had property rights; these were sacred; no one had a right to buy a home who was not socially accepted; and government must not interfere with property rights to help minorities achieve social acceptance.

The most important message LARB wanted to leave with the U.S. Commission on Civil Rights was simple: there was no racial problem with respect to housing. Asked if "the subject of minority groups not being able to obtain housing because of their [race has ever] been discussed in realty board meetings," Davis, who had worked for LARB for twenty-seven years, said "I am not familiar with any discussion like that." Asked if LARB was "cognizant of the problem" about which commissioners had just listened to days of testimony, if the board had "indicated an awareness of this problem," she simply responded no.[38] Realtors were not aware of any problem that needed to be solved, any problem that minorities might have in finding a place to live because of their race. What realtors were very much aware of, and disturbed by, were government attempts to restrict housing discrimination.

FORCED INTEGRATION

While the realtors fought back against any new legislation, Governor Brown and Assemblyman Hawkins renewed their commitment to ending segregation. Government can no longer "hide behind the reactionary and discredited folk tale that segregation and discrimination are natural and tolerable because minorities prefer to be restricted in the ghetto," Brown told the commission.[39] With the new Kennedy administration in Washington cautiously echoing his own "responsible liberalism," Brown felt that it was time to show the country what California could achieve. He made ending housing discrimination his highest legislative priority. When the legislature reconvened in January 1961, he urged members to "extend our laws against discrimination in housing,"[40] and Assemblyman Hawkins introduced a comprehensive housing discrimination bill, AB 801.

Modeled on fair housing laws in several other states, AB 801 proposed to do two key things. First, the law would prohibit discrimination by homeowners, supplementing the Unruh Act's prohibition against discrimination by businesses such as brokers. A realtor could no longer claim to be simply following the owner's instructions. Second, Hawkins proposed an enforcement mechanism through the state's new Fair Employment Practices Commission (FEPC). FEPC could investigate, conciliate, and, if it found discrimination, order an owner to sell or rent a unit to the complainant. If the unit was no longer available, the owner was required to offer the minority family the next such unit (e.g., in an apartment house or subdivision) or pay damages up to $500.

Although these enforcement provisions reflected FEPC's standard procedures for business discrimination complaints, applying such provisions to ordinary homeowners gave the realtors a natural target to attack. As chairman of CREA's Legislative Committee, Charles Shattuck focused on the punitive aspects of the bill. AB 801 "would put property owners under the FEPC" and "adversely affect property owners in the state."[41] A Republican assemblyman "decried the extension of the FEPC['s] . . . Gestapo-like surveillance" to housing.[42]

The realtors enlisted editorial writers from throughout the state to lambaste FEPC's ordinary administrative procedures. The *Los Angeles Times* warned of "a quasi-judicial commission [that] can with threats . . . dragoon a property owner to dispose of his rights according to their judgment."[43] Bureaucrats would substitute their judgment for a property owner's, the *Times* argued, as if this had not been true of planning and zoning commissions for more than forty years. The *Sacramento Union* evoked the shadowy nature of government commissions: "These can be hard blows because they fall not in the open where they are subject to the roar of the crowd, the intervention of a referee, and the decision of a judge. They fall in alley darkness." The imagery conjured up that of Knowland's campaign against tyrannical government: "star chamber proceedings, usurpation of the rights of individuals, and punitive law."[44] The *Union* compared the needs for such punitive government action in California versus in the South: "California is not New Orleans nor Nashville. [It] does not need National Guard bayonets of Little Rock." Only "wild and hairy liberals" would "acclaim AB 801's controls on individuals—landlords, owners, other fiduciaries."[45]

Beyond their attacks on the FEPC, realtors launched a more

broad-based, more moderate-sounding campaign. Unlike Davis testifying at the U.S. Commission on Civil Rights the year before, CREA
and its allies now did not deny the existence of or defend discrimination. Instead they emphasized that "discrimination is an evil that must
cured but the best way is through education. We cannot force anybody
to behave like a good American."[46] "Nobody would quarrel" with the
aim of ending discrimination, but laws like this were not the way to go
about it.[47] Testifying in Sacramento, the San Francisco Real Estate Board
emphasized, "We are not against integration. . . . But . . . we are against
enforced integration by legislative action."[48]

From this position that discrimination was wrong, realtors and
their allies now argued that AB 801 in fact discriminated against the
white majority. "We cannot lift up one minority group by shoving down
another. . . . There can be no discrimination, racial or religious, in the
application of freedom. And it works both ways."[49] The San Francisco
Real Estate Board protested AB 801's "discrimination against the majority" and claimed that "forced integration" would give "minorities the
right to dictate to majorities and that is not the American way."[50] Precisely what this new discrimination consisted of the real estate board
did not make clear, as AB 801 prohibited discrimination against anyone,
minority or majority, based on race, religion, color, or national ancestry. Rather, the implication was that taking away a (presumably white)
owner's right to "exhibit preference in selecting buyers or renters"[51] was
discriminating against white owners. By calling this "discrimination,"
realtors were co-opting the language of civil rights and turning it against
the civil rights movement. Supporters of AB 801 called realtors on such
claims. The *San Francisco Chronicle* endorsed the bill, labeling discrimination "wrong and offensive to America's moral and constitutional principles." Fair housing advocates asked how the realtors' position was any
different from "that of Southern states" trying to stop school integration.[52]

Realtors lobbied furiously against AB 801. Although an assembly
committee passed the bill by a one-vote margin, it went no further. In
the governor's only major defeat of the entire session, a Senate committee sent the bill to an advisory commission for a two-year study. Far
from producing a resolution, the battle for an effective fair housing law

in California had only begun. Both sides anticipated that a version of AB 801 would be introduced at the next session in 1963 and that they would need to be fully prepared.

Moving quickly, liberal members of the assembly's Interim Committee on Governmental Efficiency and Economy therefore decided to investigate realtors' all-white membership policy. This policy might be especially subject to attack given the state's real estate licensing laws, the state's protection of the realtors' trademark, and the realtors' monopoly of the multiple listing service in each city.[53]

The dynamic of these fall 1961 hearings would therefore be very different from that of the AB 801 debate. There, realtors had claimed to be nobly and selflessly defending the freedom and property rights of owners throughout the state against new, punitive restrictions. In the fall hearings, by contrast, realtors would be put on the spot. They would have to explain the discriminatory practices they used to protect their own businesses, why LARB had no African American members,[54] and why such real estate boards and their members deserved continuing special protection from the state.

In answering these questions, Shattuck's blunt, old-school testimony before the Interim Committee in October 1961 provided powerful ammunition for liberals and fair housing advocates. It showed the vulnerability for realtors of centering their arguments on freedom of association. His testimony thus proved important in the evolution of CREA's ideology.

Shattuck, chairman of LARB's Race Relations Committee and former president of LARB, CREA, and NAREB itself, could hardly have been more direct. He skipped over any race-neutral language and emphasized realtors' obligations to neighborhoods and existing neighbors under the Code of Ethics. He ignored NAREB's subtle rephrasing. "We are not going to introduce people or uses into a neighborhood that will tend to destroy those neighborhoods. We believe in preserving neighborhoods and," Shattuck pointedly added, "having majority interests to look out for."[55]

Minority buyers had rights, of course, but these narrow legal rights did not give them the right to insist on moving into white neighborhoods, Shattuck continued, echoing Davis's testimony. "The Negro and other minority group citizens have and enjoy every single legal right you and I do,"[56] but "may not have as many social privileges"—the right to buy a home—"because they haven't earned them yet. They're on their way to earning them, but these things don't happen overnight." As a vice president of LARB had told the legislature in January, "This whole problem is a matter of the Negro people themselves educating the public. Essentially, it is their problem."[57]

"I'm not going to come up here and mealy-mouth because there are a number of them here in this room. I try to talk frankly," Shattuck declared. "I sympathize with all these minority groups but [at] the same time . . . they've got to be big enough to realize that the majority has some rights in this picture also."[58]

Each race had its own rights to have a place to live, but these rights were separate, Shattuck insisted. This was why realtors had adamantly opposed any African Americans becoming members. If an African American broker had access to the multiple listings for properties in white neighborhoods, he could find Black buyers and then hold owners accountable for his commission if they rejected such offers. "If those listings were going to circulate . . . where the owners . . . prefer to keep the neighborhoods white . . . then if it's on the multiple listing, we're in a lot of business difficulties." There would then be no way to keep a neighborhood all-white.

Brokers thus had to be racially separated to keep neighborhoods racially separate. Testifying immediately after African American brokers he had himself blackballed for membership in LARB, Shattuck recounted what he had told them. "Gentlemen, we have majority interests to look out for. I proposed they become their own separate board, requiring the Los Angeles Realty Board to cede part of their territory. [But] they didn't want that. They called that 'segregation.'" But segregation, in Shattuck's view, was essential. "They are primarily dealing with the Negro race and . . . those portions of the city . . . that . . . should rightfully be theirs. We would be glad" to give them their own territory, he explained, and "have them be realtors, but," Shattuck now added, "we are not going to be a party to the salt and peppering of the whole community."[59] Shattuck's words hung in the air and would long be remembered.

When assembly committee chairman Lester McMillan demanded

to know what he meant, Shattuck continued just as bluntly. "Birds of a feather flock together pretty much as a matter of nature." He swept aside the property-values argument realtors had used for decades. Realtors opposed African Americans moving into a district not because "of the change in values . . . that's not true. They do not hurt values."[60] White neighbors do not want to live next to them. When, after further testy exchanges, McMillan vowed legislation to prohibit racial or religious discrimination by any state licensee, Shattuck offered what might have been advice or a quiet warning or both: "You are not going to accomplish what you want except in the manner in which it has been accomplished up to this time."[61]

Within a week of Shattuck's testimony, however, Earl Snyder, president of the Home Builders Association of Los Angeles, Orange and Ventura Counties, usually a close ally of CREA, hurriedly wrote to chairman McMillan. Snyder wanted to disassociate the builders from Shattuck's argument. He wanted the hearing record to include a very different freedom-based argument. "If an owner, regardless of his wishes, must under penalty of fine and imprisonment accept as a purchaser or tenant a person he does not want, he is *not* free. This," Snyder insisted, "is the only issue."[62] Not segregation or integration, not freedom of association, not racial rights, but individual seller freedom of choice was at stake. This was why things had to remain as they were.

By the end of 1961, realtors in California and nationally, who had relied on a variety of such locally generated arguments against fair housing, recognized that they needed a more compelling way of presenting their case. They needed to redefine freedom to show that realtors were its guardians.

13.

Creating a Standardized Ideology of Freedom

> Today the rights and freedoms of the individual American prop-
> erty owner are being eroded. A renewed bill of rights to protect
> the American property owner is needed. It is self-evident that
> the erosion of these special freedoms may destroy the free enter-
> prising individual American.
>
> Property Owners' Bill of Rights, 1963[1]

By the end of 1961, Colorado, Connecticut, Massachusetts, Minnesota,
New Hampshire, New Jersey, and Oregon had passed fair housing laws.
Oregon's was especially troubling for realtors because it prohibited brokers from accepting discriminatory listings or discriminating even on
instructions from the owners. Rather than letting realtors say they were
acting on behalf of owners, the state sought to curtail discrimination by
the real estate industry itself.[2] These new state laws encouraged advocates in other states; with NCDH spurring them on, open-occupancy
committees organized across the country, growing from eighteen in 1959
to what would become four hundred by 1964 and over one thousand by
1965.[3] Realtor organizations in California, Illinois, Michigan, New York,
and Ohio all found themselves battling proposed legislation.

While civil rights advocates pressed their case for equal justice,
fairness, and freedom, realtors often seemed to be fighting a rearguard
action against changes in American values. For the first years of the war
against fair housing, from 1957 to 1961, realtors had not assembled a consistent ideology, nor found a convincing way to demonstrate that their
decades of segregating cities positively expressed America's deepest principles. Beginning in November 1961, however, NAREB began to take a

leading role in developing and distributing powerful and standardized arguments for realtors to fight fair housing everywhere.

"FORCED HOUSING"

On November 15, 1961, NAREB broke its long silence on racial issues and weighed in openly against fair housing. The stage could hardly have been more public. NAREB's president, O. G. "Bill" Powell of Iowa, spoke before five thousand realtors at their national convention. Powell attacked "forced housing by legislation and decree" as the "greatest challenge in American life today."[4]

From the moment that Powell labeled fair housing "forced housing," NAREB, state associations, local real estate boards, and realtor officials throughout the country adopted and consistently used this locution. "Forced housing," picked up by the nation's newspapers, suddenly became a common way to describe the civil rights movement's efforts to end housing discrimination. To provide balanced coverage, newspapers now needed to refer to both fair housing and forced housing.

Powell's phrase made fair housing menacing. While zoning, subdivision regulations, and real estate licensing—all of which realtors had helped create—were equally coercive, realtors had never spoken of forced zoning, forced subdivision regulations, or forced real estate licensing. But the "force" in "forced housing" conjured up more specific images as well: government forcing its way into one's private home and, perhaps more disturbing, forcibly inserting an unwanted minority into one's home, as if billeting enemy soldiers.

In his speech to realtors, Powell inveighed against forced housing as a moral peril. The "vicious and unrelenting campaign" for antidiscrimination laws threatened the country's deepest values, for forced housing elevated money above "dictates of conscience." Such laws would require "an owner to sell his property to any person who can pay the asking price." The implication was clear: forced housing put the market and money *above* racial loyalty, while realtors did not. Powell emphasized the sanctity of one's home: under these new laws, "a man's home may be his castle . . . but only until he tries to sell or rent it." Distinguishing legitimate "human rights" of property ownership from "so-called" civil rights, Powell declared that if the antidiscrimination movement is successful, "human rights [would] become the relic of another age."[5] Powell called for "an all-out attack" on government efforts to end racial discrimination.[6] Ending forced housing would be the highest priority for America's realtors.

The advantages of using "forced" to describe integration would soon be recognized by other groups in the North. "Forced busing" would be used for the first time two years after Powell's speech, as a rallying cry for a white parents' school boycott in New York.[7] The term quickly spread, for while school busing had been used for many decades, "forced busing," like "forced housing," suggested that opposition to integration —to overcoming the impacts of the segregated neighborhoods realtors had created—was not about race at all but was racially neutral opposition to government coercion.[8]

To buttress Powell's argument, NAREB enlisted prominent outside speakers at its convention to make forced housing a symbol of the dangers of state control. Conservative Republican senator John Tower of Texas compared forced housing to state slavery: "They accuse realtors of being more concerned with property rights than human rights, but one of the premises on which our society was founded is the right to own property and manage it for our own benefit. When the people abandon that right, they become slaves of the state."[9] Eddie Rickenbacker, a famous World War I ace fighter pilot and chairman of Eastern Airlines, predicted that "some day the American people will erect a monument to . . . Senator Joseph McCarthy." Reporters covering the convention noted the "militant conservatism" of the meeting, as speaker after speaker attacked the dangers of state control. Stateism was the enemy, as it had been for Charles Wallace Collins: an American version of communism. Indeed, Powell himself did not stop at forced housing in his speech, but attacked public housing as a "great Gargantuan economic Frankenstein . . . acting to destroy communities [and] miscegenate races." So-called forced housing was the leading edge by which stateism would destroy American freedom—"the seeds of the breakdown of a free America."

With Powell's speech, a giant seemed to awaken. Until now, state and local associations had wrestled with fair housing on their own, developing positions, lobbying, and testifying without any public word from their national organization. NAREB's *National Real Estate Journal* had not mentioned the subject. NAREB's archives, including minutes of its State Associations Steering Committee for dealing with state and local issues, do not mention the topic.

What then prompted NAREB in late 1961 to change gears and become so publicly engaged? News reports of Powell's speech suggest one key factor. As part of his attack on forced housing, NAREB's president warned against any possible federal executive order banning discrimination in the use of FHA or other federal housing programs: "Let us quit perverting the FHA into fields of social welfare. . . . Let FHA do the job it did so well for so many years—just simply insure mortgage credit."[10] NAREB wanted to push back against the possibility that President Kennedy would accede to the mounting pressure from liberals and civil rights advocates to issue the executive order he had promised during the campaign. The president, given his razor-thin election margin and reluctance to lose support from Southern Democrats for his legislative agenda, had been avoiding controversial actions on civil rights. Instead, he had been strengthening the advisory U.S. Commission on Civil Rights. Indeed, the *Washington Post* suggested, it was a new report on housing from this commission that spurred Powell's speech.

Although the *Post* focused on just one of its recommendations, that the government bar discrimination by real estate agents who receive federal assistance,[11] the scope of the commission's report was in fact far broader. It not only provided detailed documentation urging Kennedy to issue his long-promised executive order to end discrimination by FHA and VA, but weighed in on state and local fair housing laws as well. It emphasized the value of such laws in stopping FHA and VA discrimination.[12] Because organized real estate brokers, with few exceptions, "reflected, magnified, and sometimes . . . induced" property owners' prejudices, the commission identified how fair housing laws could potentially *restrict licensing of such brokers*.[13] Here was realtors' greatest potential vulnerability. The commission's sweeping report—with its focus on real estate brokers and linkage between fair housing and federal antidiscrimination rules—and a potentially imminent federal order that could undermine racially separate housing markets created a sense of urgency for NAREB.

For realtors, nondiscrimination laws and ordinances, now in effect in seventeen jurisdictions, were no longer merely a state and local threat but a national one. If the federal government was going to join in on the battle for fair housing laws, NAREB could not afford to remain on the sidelines. It was time for realtors to respond nationally as well.

COORDINATED MESSAGING

Following Powell's speech, NAREB swung into action. It took on a central role in coordinating and preparing messages for state associations and local boards to use in their particular battles against forced housing. Working primarily through its State Associations Steering Committee, which brought together presidents of state associations with national officials and staff, NAREB helped develop three documents in 1962 and early 1963 that provided the heart of the standardized arguments that realtors would use to systematically attack fair housing laws. These materials took many of the points that real estate boards had been making locally and assembled them into the powerful vision of American freedom that realtors would use in Proposition 14 and other campaigns throughout the country.

The first and weightiest of these documents, both intellectually and physically, consisted of the proceedings of a 1962 symposium featuring a national assemblage of outside lawyers and retired judges, almost all of whom were opposed to fair housing. The other two documents, approved by NAREB's State Associations Steering Committee in January 1963, were single-page statements that defined realtor beliefs: a "Property Owners' Bill of Rights," drafted by Spike Wilson as president of the California realtors, and NAREB's "Statement of Policy" on minority issues, drafted by the president of the Michigan realtors. All three documents aided realtors in their struggle to convince legislators and the public that they, and not civil rights advocates, were the ones truly in favor of freedom.

OPEN OCCUPANCY VERSUS FORCED HOUSING

The symposium book proposal came from outside the realtors and was welcomed as a major aid to their cause. At a Sunday meeting of the State Associations Steering Committee meeting in May 1962, the president of the Illinois association brought up as a high-priority item a request by Alfred Avins, an associate professor at Kent Law School in Chicago and an ardent critic of fair housing, to publish proceedings of a symposium "entirely devoted to forced housing." Having ordered one thousand copies of the proceedings to make publication feasible, the Illinois association asked for a national effort to publicize the work. With the committee's strong backing, NAREB arranged further purchases and national distribution through state associations and real estate boards[14] and touted the book as "covering every aspect of Forced Housing from the constitutional standpoint, the sociological, the psychological and especially with relation to the real estate industry."[15] Avins's *Open Occupancy versus Forced Housing under the Fourteenth Amendment*[16] provided the realtors the single most important intellectual source for their campaigns against fair housing. Many of the arguments realtors would use in their publications, state campaigns, and Forced Housing Action Kit distributed to local real estate boards would draw examples, phrases, and sometimes the smallest details from this book.[17]

Avins, a New Yorker, maverick law professor, and constitutional law expert, had long been a defender of segregation in the North as well as the South. He was a committed eugenicist, having helped establish the International Association for the Advancement of Ethnology and Eugenics for "encouraging research in the fields of race science" and making "the anti-integrationist position once again respectable." The reaction to the Nazis' crimes, Avins argued, was "almost as perverted as

Alfred Avins

the so-called 'scientific' foundation upon which these crimes were per-petuated."[18] In explaining his support for segregation, Avins argued that "ethnic differences are beneficial," that the "very diversity of these groups is a substantial benefit" to America as "a multi-cultural society," and that segregation helped perpetuate such vital differences.[19] As a later histo-rian ironically noted, Avins's insistence on the value of racial and ethnic differences might have been written by a "twenty-first century scholar of multiculturalism"[20]—except that Avins insisted on preserving racial barriers to maintain these differences.

Avins had therefore been outraged by passage of New York City's fair housing ordinance. In response, he formed a small nonprofit, the Association for the Preservation of Freedom of Choice, in February 1958 to challenge fair housing. Fair housing, he declared, "menaces the insti-tutions and foundations of a free society and tends to the creation of a totalitarian society devoid of the right of the individual to freely choose whom he shall associate with."[21] In April 1962, Avins had written to NAREB's executive secretary, Eugene Conser, to offer his organization's assistance in preserving "the right of individuals to freely choose their friends, neighbors and associates without government compulsion." Among his credentials, Avins highlighted an article he had written for the New York Law Forum against fair housing.[22] His timing in reach-ing out to the realtors, both through Conser and the Illinois association, could hardly have been better.

For the symposium, Avins solicited contributions from retired state supreme court and federal judges, conservative law professors and law-yers, a former U.S. senator, Eisenhower's former FHA commissioner, appraisers, and realtors. All of the forty-nine contributors strongly opposed fair housing except for Charles Abrams, a staunch civil rights advocate and founder of NCDH, whose inclusion provided nominal bal-ance. For NAREB, the symposium provided an all-star lineup of conser-vative legal experts who supported and expounded the realtors' position with the most sophisticated and effective arguments at their command.

Many of these conservative contributors were deeply opposed to the mainstream legal consensus that accepted the Warren Supreme Court's rulings against school segregation. Avins was a perfect example. His ini-tial efforts to incorporate the Association for the Preservation of Freedom of Choice had been denied by a New York judge who ruled the association a hate group,[23] and in fall 1962, the California attorney general's office cited this ruling as a precedent for threatening to revoke LARB's and other charters for excluding minority members.[24] After the symposium, Avins provided arguments for Senator Thurmond to use opposing the public accommodations provision of the 1964 federal civil rights bill on grounds of involuntary servitude.[25] He later attacked the voting rights bill for "diluting" the rights of white voters, and joined Thurmond's staff.[26]

Among other contributors, Nathaniel Weyl had just published a racist volume *The Negro in American Civilization*[27] and would go on to write *The Jew in American Politics*. Charles C. Tansill, a historian, had helped Avins cofound the eugenics association. Retired justice James B. McGhee of the New Mexico Supreme Court supported Southern courts' pushing back against integration.[28] The desire to turn back the legal clock was evident in many of the contributions. John Herbert Tovey's article quoted approvingly from the Supreme Court's *Plessy v. Ferguson* decision,[29] and Elmer Million's article summarized what had been learned from racial restrictive covenants "as if *Shelley* had not been decided."[30] Recently retired Washington State Supreme Court justice Joseph Mallery had notoriously ruled against Black parents who wanted to bury their dead baby in the white-only Babyland section of a Washington State cemetery.[31] His symposium contribution quoted from his own opinion: "It remains to be seen how resistant our ancient liberties of private association will be to the variety of mass pressures being mobilized by the NAACP. . . . Experience has shown that an aggressive minority can frequently exact special privileges from an indifferent minority. It may be that the realization of the Negro dream of compulsory total togetherness is just around the corner."[32]

Yet despite these authors' often highly unpopular and provocative views, realtors were able to adapt many of their arguments in campaigns that won the vast majority of votes in liberal-moderate states. In their campaign for Proposition 14, realtors would cite the symposium as their key legal and constitutional resource.

The thrust of the symposium was that fair housing violated freedom of association, and most of the articles offered a constitutional basis for such freedom. Avins's lead article attacked what he saw as the fundamental idea behind fair housing, expressed by New York's liberal Republican governor Nelson Rockefeller: "Every citizen should be able to live where his heart desires and his means permit."[33] To Avins, this simple-minded idea "completely ignored the interest of individuals to choose their fellow residents and neighbors and thus live in the kind of neighborhood that they desired." Prohibiting discrimination against minorities may sound costless in terms of American freedom, but by giving this new "right," government ipso facto took away the right of everyone else to live in a community of those one wanted to associate with.[34] Hence, the "'rights' [that fair housing laws] create must necessarily infringe on the freedoms of others by subjecting them to the exercise of those rights by minority groups."[35]

Here, in a single bound, Avins stated the fundamental claim that realtors would make throughout the Proposition 14 campaign. In the words of CREA, "Granting one group of citizens rights . . . necessarily takes equivalent rights away from the rest of the citizenry."[36] Realtors ceaselessly repeated this zero-sum view of freedom. As Spike Wilson put it, "Depriving one group of its basic rights . . . is not the proper way to embrace the rights of another group."[37] NAREB's president Daniel Sheehan insisted that "we cannot gain one freedom by destroying another."[38]

Fair housing advocates vigorously disputed the realtors' argument. The rights given to minorities were in no way "equivalent" to those being taken away. What fair housing took away was the right to discriminate and exclude others. What fair housing gave those others was the right to be treated equally. No one had or should have the "right" that fair housing took away. Such a "right" ran counter to American freedom itself.

Avins's proposition that forced housing "must *necessarily* infringe on the freedom of others" became an axiom for realtors, as simple and obvious as a problem in subtraction. Giving rights to someone must take rights away from someone else. They thus attacked the fundamental premise of King and the civil rights movement: that the freedom of whites "is inextricably bound to our freedom."[39] If realtors and their allies could persuade most white Americans that freedom was separable, that granting rights to minorities did not strengthen but diminished their own, it would become almost impossible for the civil rights movement to challenge segregation of all types in the North.

What was valuable to realtors about Avins's book was not merely the clarity and succinctness with which it summed up the case for freedom of association that local boards had improvised, but that the contributors anticipated each objection of opponents and provided a response. The contributors turned the constitutional, legal, and political weaknesses of the realtor cause into its most powerful strengths, by redefining what freedom meant. Contributors themselves explicitly asked and answered several questions that would be crucial to the realtors' cause.

How can freedom of association be fundamental to American freedom if it was never mentioned in the Declaration of Independence, Constitution, or Bill of Rights? Avins provided an answer so simple and disarming that realtors used it repeatedly. "The traditional rights of . . . freedom of association long thought so inviolate as not to require embodiment in constitutional or statutory law have now been . . . evaporated" by fair housing laws.[40] That a freedom was traditional but *not* mentioned in the Bill of Rights was thus proof of its importance.

Realtors, who repeated Avins's argument almost word for word,[41] frequently downplayed what was written in the Constitution compared to the tradition from which it was presumably created. Avins went further back still, as Charles Wallace Collins had done, invoking traditional rights of property going back "seven centuries . . . to the Magna Carta, the Statute of Westminster, the Petition of Right,"[42] in the same way Charles Wallace Collins had. Realtors would follow this approach, too, arguing that forced housing "rejects traditional and fundamental right[s] with roots in English common law," making them "anachronisms in the scheme of those who would determine for us the choice of our neighbors and our tenants."[43] Any legislative or judicial action that undermined traditional rights, as they defined them, was an attack on American freedom.

Symposium contributor Nathaniel Weyl further argued, in the vein of Chief Justice Roger Taney in the *Dred Scott* opinion, that America's founders believed in and assumed racial discrimination. The founders did not have to spell out the freedom not to associate with African Americans because they took it for granted. "When the court states that racial discrimination is contrary to the basic American philosophy," he wrote, "it forgets that none of the Founding Fathers considered the Negroes as citizens or as capable of being members of American society or as being persons to whom the safeguards of the Bill of Rights applied."[44] Whether this was historically true mattered little to those arguing this position. The "tradition" that realtors projected onto America's founding was one they had decided to find there.

How can the group rights of freedom of association be part of individual freedom? Avins insisted on calling "the right to decline to associate with another" a fundamental freedom of each individual: "an individual right, a natural right, a human right, and a civil right." Preventing an individual from exercising this right "threatens not only the rights and proper privileges of the individual but menaces the . . . foundations of a free society."[45] But Avins's description of freedom of association as an *individual right*, invoking American individual freedom, was words over substance. No one—not civil rights advocates nor the staunchest opponents of fair housing—ever denied an individual's right to go off on his own and avoid anyone else. What Avins and the realtors used freedom of association to mean, while calling it individual freedom, was the right of a *group*, and those within it, to create an exclusive environment.

Isn't freedom of association simply a way of justifying racial inequality? Wouldn't "equality of opportunity' and 'all men are created equal,' . . . go down the drain?" one contributor asked rhetorically.[46] The answer was simple. Contributors repeated Shattuck's 1947 argument that the right not to associate is an equal right of everyone regardless of race. Freedom of association was thus "not only compatible and consistent with the basic equality of all persons before the law . . . but a facet of the dignity of the individual and an indispensable prerequisite to full equality in such society."[47] The Supreme Court in *Shelley* had flatly rejected this idea: "it is no answer" to an African American denied equal treatment in buying a house to say that other African Americans can discriminate against whites.[48] But this response to the charge of inequality was so essential to their argument that contributors to the symposium and realtors continued to assert it.

"What about the Freedom of Choice of a Negro to live in the neighborhood he prefers?" John Herbert Tovey, a tax expert, asked and then answered his own question. "The opportunity to acquire real property is not a civil right," he wrote.[49] From a purely legal point of view, "the

Negro thus has the same rights as anyone else, no more and no less. That means he has no right to live in a particular neighborhood. His rights to purchase property are conditioned on the right and desire of the property owner to sell to him."[50] What was new and powerful in Tovey's argument was the way he narrowed the definition of freedom to support the realtors' position. A buyer's only "freedom" was to be able to execute a purchase contract with a willing seller. Since the law already provided this, everyone was already equal under the law. This became the core of the realtors' claim that they believed in equal rights.

Indeed, under this definition of freedom, no private discrimination, no matter how widespread or systemic, could deprive anyone of "freedom." Therefore, if government sought to expand these narrow buyer rights on behalf of minorities, if it protected minorities from discrimination, government would favor one race over another. Retired justice Mallery put the matter plainly: forced housing created governmental discrimination against white owners. "It strips the white man of the constitutional protection of his rights without due process," he declared. Far from being consistent with the Fourteenth Amendment's requirements for due process and equal protection of the laws, forced housing denied those rights to white owners.

Mallery's argument explained the otherwise seemingly ironic title of Avins's book: *Open Occupancy versus Forced Housing under the Fourteenth Amendment*. Fair housing advocates were not making any legal claim under the Fourteenth Amendment, which dealt with discrimination *by the state*. Rather, Avins, Mallery, and other contributors were trying to invoke the idea of fairness embodied by the Fourteenth Amendment to discredit fair housing. The realtors, having lost the covenant cases, now claimed that *they* were the ones dedicated to the Fourteenth Amendment, for white citizens as well as Black.[51]

But the real political dynamite lay elsewhere. Mallery's claim that "'forced housing' strips the white man . . . of his rights" was an argument that forced housing takes freedom away from those who have it to give special privileges to the Black minority. As Wilson would put it a year later, "Militant minorities have organized and vocalized for equal rights until 'equal rights' have almost become 'special privileges.'"[52] Mallery and Wilson's claim ignored the way fair housing laws were actually written.

As civil rights advocates constantly pointed out, a white buyer who was racially discriminated against could file a complaint, just as a minority could.[53] The claim that fair housing discriminated in favor of minorities was thus not a serious legal argument; no court overturned a fair housing law for racial discrimination. It was a political claim. Avins's contributors defined freedom so that what minorities were asking for was not freedom but special privileges.

Doesn't opposing fair housing mean being in favor of discrimination? This question had tripped up realtors in many of their local campaigns. They had blustered that discrimination did not exist or argued that minorities deserved to be discriminated against or conceded that discrimination was unfortunate but could only be changed by education. But the more realtors expounded such positions, the bigger the hole they dug for themselves. Unlike freedom, which could be defined to mean almost anything, discrimination was specific and concrete. As fair housing testers had shown, it could be proven. To speak about discrimination in any way, whether to dismiss or admit or excuse it, risked offending those who wanted to see themselves as racial moderates and whose support the realtors needed.

Tovey's answer was simplicity itself: "Discrimination means simply to make a choice. To discriminate you must be free to make a choice . . . to prefer one thing or person to another."[54] He thus equated discrimination and freedom. To restrict discrimination is to restrict freedom. And there he stopped. He did not try to explain why discrimination existed. He did not defend or excuse or justify it. The less said about it, in opposing fair housing, the better. The realtors made this less-said approach their mantra. When discrimination came up, they argued that "the issue is not one of discrimination . . ., but [whether] the government tells us to whom we should sell or rent our property."[55] The realtors turned any discussion of discrimination into a discussion about the dangers to freedom from forced housing. The more urgent and overwhelming such dangers, the less important any discrimination against minorities would seem to many whites.

Doesn't opposing fair housing mean being in favor of segregation? This was in many ways the crucial question politically. For realtors to appeal to racial moderates, they needed to distinguish themselves from die-hard defenders of the Southern "way of life." For while many of the symposium arguments would have justified Strom Thurmond's use of freedom of association, it was here that the symposium's arguments on behalf of the realtors diverged from those for Jim Crow.

Tovey asked and answered the question. "Certainly not. Segregation is a compulsory separation of the races by law. Like compulsory integration, it is a denial of Freedom of Choice."[56] Tovey, Avins, and the realtors thus recast fair housing as "compulsory integration." Fair housing advocates strongly disagreed; for them, fair housing simply prohibited discrimination by putting all buyers and renters on the same footing, regardless of race or religion; it did not compel anyone to sell his house or anyone to move anywhere. But the symposium contributors did not buy this. "The short of the matter is that, for all of its fancy trimmings . . ., a law banning discrimination in housing is, and is intended to be, a law compelling people to integrate who do not desire to do so."[57]

Calling fair housing "compulsory integration"[58] had great benefits for realtors. It evoked "penal sanctions" and government schemes to control where people lived. "To thus treat human beings as chess pieces, to be moved at the . . . whim of others who would like to plan their lives for them," Avins argued, "is as flagrant a violation of basic human rights . . . as can be found in the worst totalitarian system ever devised."[59] That fair housing did not require anyone to move was ignored. Avins looked behind such laws to what he saw as their ulterior purpose: to force people to change their behavior and beliefs, to give up their prejudices. He thus likened fair housing to "mass brainwashing in . . . Nazi Germany . . . Communist Russia." "In a democracy," by contrast, "people make up their own minds. A democracy has implicit in it, as an absolute, the freedom of association."[60] Such characterizations would naturally appeal to those on the right, including the 40 percent who had voted for Knowland's campaign of "freedom versus tyranny."

But the real benefit of calling fair housing "compulsory integration" was in appealing to the political center. For this label automatically set up a contrast between two putative extremes: compulsory segregation and compulsory integration. Realtors and contributors could say they were against both. They were moderate and reasonable, protecting American freedom from dangers on either side, from the extreme right and the extreme left, from Nazism and communism. By establishing this hypothetical "middle ground," realtors launched a highly successful effort to convince voters that the realtors' approach to dealing with race in housing represented the "civil rights program for moderates."[61] This extraordinary political achievement was crucial to their success.

In fact, realtors positioned themselves in the middle by picturing extremes that did not exist. Compulsory segregation of housing existed only in their rhetoric. Racial zoning had been unconstitutional since 1917. Nor, from results in other states, did fair housing laws lead to significant population shifts, let alone compulsory moves. Realtors therefore described initial fair housing laws as only the tip of the iceberg. Civil rights advocates would keep pushing for tougher laws to achieve integration, up to and including government quotas as to where people lived.[62] As Tovey put it, "In either segregation or compulsory integration, someone else makes the choice for you. Your freedom is gone."[63] The realtors were staking out the ground that Barry Goldwater would later seek to claim: "Our aim, as I understand it, is neither to establish a segregated society nor to establish an integrated society as such. It is to preserve a *free* society."[64]

Spike Wilson understood the power of this argument, stressing in his final editorial before the vote on Proposition 14 that only one issue mattered: the use of "the police power . . . to expedite forced integration."[65] The choice, Wilson made clear, was "forced integration" or freedom. *Open Occupancy versus Forced Housing* became a crucial tool for the realtors' cause.

But Wilson understood, too, what was even more basic: how to take all these ideas from self-acknowledged racial extremists—committed eugenicists, opponents of "the Negro dream of compulsory total togetherness" and of dead Black babies being buried next to white ones, lawyers who looked back fondly at separate but equal from 1896, and the author of the inflammatory *The Negro in American Civilization*—and turn them into popular, winning arguments in liberal states. The next step in this ideological effort would be his.

A NEW BILL OF RIGHTS

In late January 1963, the State Associations Steering Committee—after hearing reports from realtor leaders from Ohio, Pennsylvania, Nebraska, and Iowa that they were ordering Avins's book "in quantity"—was presented with two new documents. Each a page long, they were intended as fundamental public statements of the realtor case. Wilson handed out copies of his Property Owners' Bill of Rights.[66] A. R. Saunders from Michigan distributed a draft national policy on minority housing to help put NAREB out in front of criticisms of being racially prejudiced.

Developed independently, these two papers by state realtor presidents at the heart of battles over fair housing perfectly complemented each other. Jackson Pontius of CREA called them "a double-barreled suggestion."[67] The committee voted unanimously that NAREB's full board of directors adopt the Property Owners' Bill of Rights so that it could be published in newspapers nationally. The "Statement of Policy on Minority Housing" was more controversial because it clarified brokers' duties, but it too passed overwhelmingly.[68]

Although Wilson's bill of rights has often been seen as the realtors' political response to the new California fair housing bill introduced in spring 1963,[69] Wilson had drafted it in December 1962. Wilson had certainly known a legislative battle was coming. Governor Brown had made a new fair housing bill his top legislative priority. But what had spurred Wilson was Kennedy's executive order in late November 1962.[70] Seeing the attack on realtor practices at both the federal and state levels, CREA's new president wanted to lay out a clear and compelling list of owners' rights that, like the original Bill of Rights, government would be forced to respect.

After the unanimous vote from the State Associations Steering Committee, Wilson proposed that CREA sponsor a drive to include this new bill of rights verbatim in California's constitution.[71] If adopted by the voters, it would prohibit any new fair housing legislation—whether by the state or any of the cities where realtors had been fighting off local ordinances—and would exempt residential real estate from past state legislation such as the Unruh Act. It would provide a model for other states to stop fair housing. This approach of putting the Property

Owners' Bill of Rights on the ballot became in fact the strategy in Detroit by June 1963[72] and in Illinois. Thus, months before California passed Byron Rumford's new fair housing act in June 1963, Wilson and CREA had the idea not only of launching an initiative like Proposition 14 but also of what it would say. In the actual event, Wilson and CREA would decide on much more succinct and constitutional-sounding language for the ballot. Rather than serving as the text of Proposition 14 itself, the Property Owners' Bill of Rights was used instead to rouse support for the realtor cause. Local boards and state associations endorsed and published it in full-page newspaper advertisements in scores of cities.[73] It would become the national message of realtor opposition to fair housing for years to come.

Wilson's text, like much he wrote during the fair housing campaign, expressed the highly controversial points of Avins's contributors in bold, direct phrases that evoked both patriotism and common sense, drew on America's founding, celebrated immigrant striving and the promise of America, and manifested concern with equal opportunity for all races. The rights that Wilson was defending were the same ones set forth by Avins, Mallery, Tovey, and Weyl. But his tone, rather than pessimistic, attacking, sarcastic, or racial, conveyed that of the Preamble of the realtor's Code of Ethics: "The interest of the nation and its citizens require the highest and best use of the land and the widest distribution of ownership. . . . Such interests impose grave social responsibility and a patriotic duty."[74]

Wilson identified property owners and thus the real estate brokers representing them with the most virtuous qualities of Americans—"free enterprising," future oriented, investing in themselves and thus the country, concerned with family and neighbors, committed to individual freedom, and wanting the same fair laws to apply equally to everyone. In the same way that NAREB had asserted in 1947 that homeowners "are the nation's best citizens,"[75] Wilson's Bill of Rights thus identified the interests of the individual American owner with that of the country itself and the reason immigrants came to America—the promise of security, freedom, and opportunity.

By calling it "a renewed bill of rights," Wilson made clear that "the rights and freedom of the individual American property owner" that were being eroded were not new but implicit in the original covenant between America's government and its people. What distinguished Wilson's ten new rights, the same number as the original Bill of Rights, was that they guaranteed an owner's right to discriminate. Basic property rights—to own property, to not be deprived of property without due process or just compensation—had been included in the original Bill of Rights. Like Avins, Wilson suggested that his newly listed rights—to privacy, to choose one's own friends, to own and operate property according to one's own dictates, to enjoy the freedom to deal or not deal with others—had always been rights that Americans enjoyed. It was imperative to spell out freedom of association now because, for the first time, proposed laws threatened to interfere with it.

Wilson faced a similar problem as Avins: how to justify the racial rights of freedom of association in terms of traditional individual American freedom. Wilson's solution was to assert all rights in terms of the individual owner; "the right to choose his own friends" gave the homeowner the implicit right to choose who else could live in his neighborhood. Wilson then elevated this right of the seller by invoking, as had NAREB president Powell, the seller's right to follow "the dictates of his conscience." This phrase legitimized discrimination by linking it with freedom of religion. Infusing the sale of property with a moral obligation explained why a seller could not be required to sell to "any person who can pay the asking price."[76] More than money was at stake. Fair housing did not affect the seller's ability to realize the value of his home. Wilson therefore offered this higher reason, freedom of conscience, for why sellers must be allowed to discriminate.

Wilson applied the same solution for homeowners to landlords. The "right to maintain congenial surroundings for tenants" gave the landlord a right to exclude tenants of any other race. Indeed, this landlord right implied a landlord *obligation* to discriminate, to assure "congenial" surroundings for his tenants. Wilson thought this issue so important that he devoted another of the ten rights to it, making clear that "property owners should not be obligated to require their tenants to accept each other indiscriminately." Discrimination in rental housing was in fact where segregation was most severe. The U.S. Commission on Civil Rights in 1960 found that "the rental situation for Negroes and other non-Caucasians is even worse" than for home buying: "Even owners who will sell to Negroes will not rent to them. . . . Housing outside the Negro ghetto is denied Negroes regardless of his ability to pay, his character or his occupation."[77]

Beyond citing the direct rights of landlords and sellers, Wilson insisted on the right of neighbors to "the enjoyment of property"—that is, without minorities living nearby. Such neighbors' rights had been the principle behind racial covenants, remained fundamental to realtors' practice, and lay at the heart of this new bill of rights' justification of freedom of association. Finally, to protect brokers, Wilson included the absolute right of sellers to authorize brokers to discriminate on their behalf.

Wilson thus took all the discriminatory practices that realtors had been defending in their war against forced housing, standardized them as basic rights, and embedded them in a framework that Americans identified with their most precious freedoms. He placed freedom of association on a par with freedom of religion and freedom of speech. But unlike those original rights, which had been subject to centuries of judicial interpretation, qualification, and limitation, the rights Wilson asserted were new and absolute.

The absoluteness was crucial. For, as fair housing supporters argued, "you can't grant unlimited rights to some without infringing on the *basic* rights of others."[78] Wilson's strategy in the bill of rights was precisely to make the right to discriminate unconditional, so that government would never interfere with it.

Yet while Avins's contributors mentioned discrimination, segregation, or race in virtually every paragraph, Wilson's document never mentioned them. This was hardly accidental. A reporter would write about the wording of CREA's Proposition 14, "Nowhere in the title or text is there are any reference directly or remotely to race, creed or color."[79]

The Property Owners' Bill of Rights reflected a still larger silence. The ownership rights to be considered alongside freedom of speech and freedom of religion said nothing about the right *to* ownership. This absence was immediately mentioned by critics, such as District of Columbia commissioner Walter Tobriner, who noted that this bill of rights left out people's "equal access to a commodity as essential as housing."[80] Milton G. Gordon, California's director of real estate, dissented from the common realtor position and explained that "the right to hold property is preceded by the right to acquire property."[81] Thomas Pitts of the California AFL-CIO argued that the realtors were subverting "the rights of all people to acquire a decent home."[82] Indeed, Wilson's bill of rights listed only the rights of owners to *preclude others* from buying or renting property. Half the world of real estate, that of buyers and tenants, disappeared. Fair housing advocates quickly pointed this out: "Let's remember freedom to acquire property is fully as precious as freedom to sell it . . . the ancient legal right of people to acquire property . . . to house their families."[83]

To dispel any such suggestion that realtors only cared about the rights of some, Wilson always referred to discrimination in the language of equality. His bill of rights stressed the promise America had offered immigrants (while deliberately leaving out any reference to those brought here as slaves): "to live as free men with equal opportunity for all." Wilson often used immigrants in his rhetoric against forced housing. He related their quest to his personal story, which, like the Property Owners' Bill of Rights, linked America's founding with immigration: "All of my life," he said, "I have been aware of the importance of freedom. My mother was an immigrant. One of my great-great grandfathers, James Wilson, signed the Declaration of Independence."[84] He quoted a Greek immigrant boy he had met. "Here—I am a free man, I am a citizen. I own my home. No one comes to take it away. . . . Here— in America—what I build is mine—I have the same chance as any other American to be a free man!" Wilson then issued his warning: "But— unfortunately—the rights and freedoms this young Greek crossed the ocean to enjoy—are in danger of being lost by default! . . . Restrictive, coercive, paternalistic laws are eroding individual freedom."[85]

But focusing on immigrants in the Property Owners' Bill of Rights was also a political statement. European immigrants and their children and grandchildren represented many of the voters realtors would need. These included many of the union and other workers who had rejected Knowland: families that were often first-generation homeowners, many threatened by competition with African Americans for jobs or housing. More broadly, by speaking so positively about immigrants, Wilson conveyed the message that realtors were, in fact, inclusive, belying claims that they were prejudiced.

The bill of rights' emphasis on immigrants offered one other crucial payoff. Wilson's message was that hard work and savings were rewarded. America was the country of opportunity and potential upward mobility, and homeownership the proof that those who became owners were the ones who deserved it. If immigrants had worked their way up from nothing to become owners without asking for some special helping hand from government, the implication was clear. Groups asking for the special privileges of fair housing, insisting that government offer them protections no one else had received, were undeserving. That these immigrants and other white Americans had received FHA and VA loans almost entirely denied to African Americans, had been allowed to move into neighborhoods precisely because they were white, had spent far less for the same quality of housing as African Americans, and had benefited from all the privileges African Americans were deliberately excluded from was never mentioned in this story.

What those who had *not* been discriminated against wanted to hear, indeed what anyone wanted to hear, was that they deserved what they had. The more that realtors emphasized immigrants' success in their campaign against forced housing, the more realtors conveyed indirectly Shattuck's message that Blacks were not accepted because they were not acceptable. By this account, fair housing was not a way to level the playing field, reducing an enormous barrier against individual achievement, but a government handout to an undeserving group. Making it possible for a minority family to spend its own money to pay the asking price for a home was, in this view, a form of welfare.

Wilson further tapped into the American imagery of independence by speaking of "free enterprising" Americans. But even though free enterprise conveyed Wilson's idea of entrepreneurship and ownership free from government control, it suggested a free market and open competition that were the very opposite of the realtors' objectives. The entire purpose of the realtors' discriminatory system had been to limit where minorities could acquire property. As Loren Miller succinctly put it, "No man is free unless he has access to the open market."[86] Free enterprise also obscured the one point on which realtors were most legally vulnerable: their own restriction of the market. This point had worried several of Avins's contributors: that realtors had achieved near-monopoly power by controlling 80 percent of home sales and exercising that power to prevent sales to minorities. The imagery of free enterprise insulated realtors against government interference with *their own restriction* of the market for housing.

The final aspect of the American history lesson in the Property Owners' Bill of Rights was more subtle. Wilson invoked the promises of the Fourteenth Amendment of "equal protection for all," the civil rights movement's key argument for ending official segregation in the South. In doing so, the Property Owners' Bill of Rights seemed to be supporting and advocating equality for African Americans. However, Wilson's insertion, "but [the Fourteenth Amendment's] guarantees were for the protection of all," set forth Avins's case that the Fourteenth Amendment's guarantee of freedom protected white owners' right to discriminate. Far from seeking to overturn the Fourteenth Amendment as in 1948, realtors now claimed that it *precluded* laws limiting discrimination.

This new bill of rights thus represented a claim on history. Unlike the radical "new rights" of "forced housing" that Avins ridiculed as "unknown to American law and alien to fundamental constitutional norms,"[87] Wilson's proclamation "renewed" rights that Americans had always had and that were now threatened for the first time. The Property Owners' Bill of Rights was simultaneously a call to arms for realtors, a justification of freedom of association as patriotic, a claim that realtors believed in equal protection for all, and an assertion that realtors were concerned with the rights of ordinary Americans as opposed to "special privileges" for some.

Opponents denounced this new bill of rights as "an outmoded manifesto written by persons who actually wish to restrict fellow Americans from acquiring property."[88] Looking past its patriotic imagery, they called it "an attempt to justify continuance of segregation in housing, even though it uses words like 'freedom,' 'liberty' and 'conscience.'"[89] For Wilson's bill of rights did indeed seek to capture those words, along with equality, equal protection, and the country's founding purpose, all so that elected government could never interfere with the racial system realtors had created.

Property Owners' Bill of Rights, newspaper advertisement, 1963

With this proclamation as a statement of objectives, realtors no longer needed to remain on the defensive, justifying local practices—such as deliberately misleading minority buyers as to the availability or terms of homes—that might seem embarrassing or dubious. Instead, they were promoting an image of what America was for. Wilson printed the Property Owners' Bill of Rights in CREA's magazine in April 1963 while announcing that "it is time to launch a new crusade—a crusade for freedom to rescue the rights of the new 'forgotten man,'" the ordinary property owner, the average American.[90]

Touring California in early 1963, Wilson publicized this new bill of rights by stressing "the importance of renewing the rights . . . originally given to the citizens of this country." In Orange County, he went further back in history to the American Revolution, when citizens had to be roused to action against oppressive government. Wilson told assembled realtors that forced housing was "as bad as the Stamp Act in colonial days." When the Property Owners' Bill of Rights was published in full-page newspaper advertisements throughout the country, it showed a colonial patriot ringing a small bell for liberty.[91] In warning owners across the country that the government was threatening to invade their homes and deny them their rights, the realtors were the new Paul Reveres.

California realtors welcomed this new proactive approach. The nearly two thousand delegates to the state realtors' convention in Palm Springs in March voted unanimously to approve the bill of rights and to begin the initiative process to include it in the state constitution.[92] Whether or not Byron Rumford's new fair housing bill pending in the state capitol was enacted, California realtors had a way to move forward.

POLICY ON MINORITY HOUSING

To complement the Property Owners' Bill of Rights, NAREB adopted the Statement of Policy on Minority Housing[93] to demonstrate that NAREB was fully committed to racial equality—while maintaining racial discrimination. The policy thus offered a model for seeming racially unbiased in the civil rights era—and a way to deflect concerns of state licensing agencies—while protecting every tool realtors had used for years.

The key to this strategy was to shift responsibility for discrimination from realtors to owners. Realtors could then be absolved from discrimination—while insisting that owners must have the right to use realtors to discriminate. Thus, to oppose fair housing provisions such as Oregon's that held the realtor responsible for discrimination, this new policy made clear that as long as the realtor transmitted "all written offers," he was in no way responsible for the owner's decision. Requiring realtors to transmit such offers was a new policy, a seeming concession. But what it left out was that, as every survey and study showed, realtors used every approach possible—telling African American buyers that a house had just been sold, claiming the key was missing, avoiding appointments, telling newspapers which properties had to be advertised in the "restricted" columns—to avoid *ever taking* such a written offer.

The policy walked a similarly fine line by saying that no realtor should determine the racial eligibility of any buyer, while insisting that the realtors not only had the right but *the obligation* to let the seller know the race of the buyer. The buyer's race was factual information, and realtors must transmit all factual information. The policy also asserted, in opposition to fair housing provisions, that a realtor could freely advise a client about whether to sell to a minority in a transitioning neighborhood. Because the owner had the right to decide whom to sell to, the realtor could not be held responsible for encouraging discrimination.

Two new provisions were marketed as evidence of realtors' commitment to equality, without having any impact on what realtors did. "Each realtor should feel completely free to enter into a broker-client relationship with persons of any race"—which also meant that a realtor could freely choose not to work with a minority. If an offer from a minority was accepted, the realtor should, of course, "exert his best efforts to conclude the transaction."

But while asserting that realtors were racially neutral, the policy insisted that owners must have the right to discriminate. "Realtors may properly oppose any attempt by force of law to withdraw from property owners the right to freely determine with whom they will deal." Nor could rules on realtors be used to limit owner's "right of free decision." Why, if realtors were racially neutral, did they care so much about protecting this owner's right? The policy's only explanation was that, in accordance with the Property Owners' Bill of Rights, "the right of . . . owners to freely determine with whom they will deal is a right fundamental in the American tradition."

A NATIONAL CAMPAIGN

In formally adopting both the Statement of Policy on Minority Housing and the Property Owners' Bill of Rights in Washington, DC, in June 1963, NAREB unveiled its national campaign against fair housing. In announcing these policies, Spike Wilson explained to reporters that realtors were committed to equal rights and the owner's right to discriminate—and that both were essential attributes of freedom. "We plead for equal rights for all as guaranteed by the Constitution. In particular, and especially for the property owner, we seek to maintain the right of selection."[94] Here in new language was the same commitment to maintaining segregation.

NAREB's president Daniel Sheehan Sr. could thus "deplore the inequality which exists in this country . . . and sympathize with the desire and efforts to solve the problem," but also state, "Regardless of how we feel personally about . . . achieving better opportunities for minorities, . . . we can all agree that in tackling the problems of any group or individual it is folly to abrogate . . . traditional rights which have been the basis on which the country built its strength. We cannot gain one freedom by destroying another."[95]

In thus connecting the principles of Avins's contributors and Wilson's vision of freedom, Sheehan emphasized that whether minorities could acquire private housing depended on owners, not realtors: "The finger has been pointed erroneously at the broker. . . . I reiterate that brokers are legally the agents of sellers; they must and do reflect the attitudes and instructions of their principals, who are owners possessing the traditional freedom of choice in disposition."[96] While realtors, in their daily practice, made sure that owners in white neighborhoods were *not* free to sell to minorities, they could use the freedom of owners as both the rationale and shield for those same practices.

To reporters, realtors' claims that they were protecting freedom seemed disingenuous. A *New York Times* reporter called the realtors'

campaign "a curious effort on the part of organized real estate interests to promote the 'freedom' of property owners to select purchasers
without hindrance from anti-discrimination laws." The *Times* described
the purpose of the Property Owners' Bill of Rights in an extraordinary
understatement: it was "intended to relieve the profession of any obligation to promote open-occupancy housing."[97]

To those in favor of fair housing, what the realtors were advocating was not freedom at all, but its restriction. This presumed new bill
of rights had, as its single purpose, preventing minorities from ever
having freedom of choice.[98] Attorney General Robert Kennedy, secretly
working on what would become the president's civil rights bill focused
on the South, was more circumspect. Antidiscrimination measures, he
thought, "cannot be forced on the people, they are going to decide for
themselves." NAREB's position, however, "seems to be going a little too
far."[99]

The reaction that seemed to sum up best the enormous changes
occurring in people's attitudes of what was "too far" came from Frank
Luchs, former president of the Washington, DC, board of realtors. In
April 1962, he had staunchly opposed a fair housing bill in the District,
saying, "We would all be a lot happier if we didn't get a law shoved down
our throats." Confronted with news reports that African diplomats could
not find housing in the District—stories that embarrassed America's
position in the Cold War—Luchs said that discrimination against Black
diplomats "could be eased 'within 2 or 3 years' if the realtors were 'left
alone' [but] ventured no guess . . . as to when housing could be opened
up to American Negroes in Washington."[100] Now, little over a year later,
when Luchs was asked about the Property Owners' Bill of Rights, his
views were very different. "I think that this policy statement is made at
an unfortunate time in the history of this country, and I predict it will
have to be amended."[101] Luchs's judgment about both the times and the
country had changed.

For most realtors, however, this new bill of rights and policy statement were powerful tools to keep things the same. Even as he attended
NAREB's press conferences in DC, Spike Wilson was reading news reports
that CORE demonstrators in Sacramento were starting a "sleep-in'" in
the state capitol to demand fair housing legislation.[102] Having helped

create the realtors' new standardized national ideology of freedom, he foresaw that it would now be put to its crucial test.

Part Five.

A National Crusade in California:
June 1963–November 1964

The Property Owners' Bill of Rights was immediately seized on by local boards and state associations around the country in their own fights against fair housing. It offered, in a single page, a positive statement of ideals that realtors could selflessly proclaim on behalf of owners, an answer to the arguments of open-occupancy committees, a circular for legislators, a flyer for mass mailings to voters, a newspaper advertisement virtually everywhere, and, as Wilson had intended, a potential state constitutional amendment to end fair housing laws once and for all.

Realtors and homeowners quickly turned to this new bill of rights in the country's most public battles over fair housing: in Michigan, Illinois, Washington State, and California. In Illinois, when Chicago under Mayor Richard Daley approved a modest fair housing law, a South Side Property Owners' Coordinating Committee marched five thousand strong to city hall and then proposed a statewide referendum based on the Property Owners' Bill of Rights.[1] Although such a vote in Illinois would have been nonbinding, Governor Otto Kerner, who later headed President Johnson's commission on civil disorders, successfully asked the state supreme court to disqualify it, a legal maneuver that would inspire fair housing advocates in California.

Fair housing efforts in Michigan had been spurred by national publicity of a long-standing point system established by the brokers association in the high-end Detroit suburb of Grosse Pointe, which rated potential buyers on speech, dress, swarthiness, friends, and whether they were "typically American." In order to be accepted, Northern Europeans had to score 55 points, Southern Europeans 65, and Jews 85, and Negroes and Orientals were automatically ruled out. After efforts at state fair housing failed and a bill was introduced in Detroit's city council, a homeowners' right ordinance, virtually identical to the Property Owners' Bill of Rights, was proactively placed on the ballot in September 1964. Adamantly opposed by Mayor Jerome Cavanaugh, Governor George Romney, and most of the city's leaders, the ordinance passed 138,000 to 115,000 in a bitter contest, sweeping its sponsor Thomas Poindexter into the city council, before being nullified and ruled unconstitutional for "excessive vagueness."[2]

In both Seattle and Tacoma, the local real estate boards defeated fair housing in early 1964 referenda. Their campaigns, too, drew on much of the Property Owners' Bill of Rights. Seattle's "Save Your Rights Committee" sponsored newspaper advertisements asking, "Are you willing" "to vote away your personal decisions as to whom you will sell" to, "to vote away your neighbor's right to" choose whom to sell to, "to set up a social order of forced association," and as a renter "to sacrifice your choice of association?"[3]

But while these popular campaigns were viscerally charged and locally important, they did not match in significance the battle Wilson himself had returned to lead, this one against fair housing in California. NAREB would invest its own funds in the battle, and other state associations would join in. With a voter roll thirty times greater than Detroit's, the country's largest real estate market, over 170 local boards to coordinate, and the state's national political significance, Wilson was not exaggerating when he forecast that it would be the crucial battle in what he called "the great war" over fair housing.[4] Unlike these other contests that drew directly on the Property Owners' Bill of Rights, the battle in California would require Wilson and the realtors to change their emphasis from freedom of association to individual freedom of choice, and so create a new and powerful template for America's politics.

In this conflict, Wilson would confront Byron Rumford, sponsor of California's fair housing law, whose most basic ways of understanding problems were as different from Wilson's as their respective views of freedom. While Wilson had quickly crafted the Property Owners' Bill of Rights on his own, Rumford had fought long, hard, and slowly for ten years in the legislature, building enough votes to pass the fair employment law before turning to fair housing.

Rumford's path to the legislature itself and to owning a pharmacy in Berkeley had also been arduous. Growing up in a broken home, shuttling as a child between a small Arizona mining town, Tucson, Phoenix, Los Angeles, and back to Phoenix, he had shined shoes outside Goldwater's Department Store and attended a segregated Phoenix high school with four teachers, one of whom had attended UC Berkeley and inspired him to go there.[5] After UC's pharmacy school, when he applied to become an investigator for the state Board of Pharmacy, he was rejected multiple times at oral interviews where the only question he was asked was whether Joe Louis was a good fighter. During the Depression, when the director of an Oakland hospital, not wanting to hire a first African American professional, told Rumford, "You'd cause trouble," Rumford's immediate response was, "I've never caused trouble in my life."[6] He had always seen himself as trying to reduce barriers to understanding.

Similarly, Rumford's first government experiences, on a state-appointed rent control board and a Berkeley emergency housing committee during World War ll, were in trying to make peace between newly arriving African American and white war workers from the Dust Bowl. He had distanced himself from radical movements in the late 1940s, explaining that "I'd always felt that our problems were the problems that related to the established government and l was just not concerned with their type of movement." The issue that brought him to the state assembly, abolishing discrimination in the National Guard, required him to gradually convince reluctant, racially biased, older white legislators that fighting units should not represent a particular group or city.[7]

His effort to pass fair employment, inspired by the World War ll federal Fair Employment Practices Commission, had required overcoming similar barriers. "When we got the [state law] the whole thing changed completely! . . . When you go now, you see clerks in stores; you see them filling prescriptions. Nobody thinks anything about their color. The question [now] is: Do they have a license? Are they able to do it? . . . It was the law that did it. It made it possible for people to get a job largely based upon their ability to perform."[8] Rumford viewed fair housing in the same way, not as a matter of rhetoric but of changing rules to change what was possible.

Freedom in a democratic society was not, in Rumford's view, a matter of enforcing absolute rights, but of balancing rights. He candidly admitted that fair housing did, in fact, limit owners' rights. But "in making decisions about what rights property owners should have, it is necessary to weigh the advantages to the individual in having a right against the disadvantages to society. Not an easy task but . . . one that government must assume."[9] Here was a view of freedom, of looking at everyone's conflicting rights, that exactly contradicted Spike Wilson's.

These opposite views of freedom—whether certain individuals' absolute freedom of choice precluded any government role in balancing rights, or whether freedom in a society required government to limit rights in the interest of fairness—were precisely why California's battle over fair housing would have such long-term consequences for American politics. This battle could have been fought over very different issues: race, community, social stability, freedom of association. In the earlier battles over fair housing, these were precisely what realtors focused on. But as the conflict in California spread out over a year and a half, Wilson shifted what the realtors emphasized. He helped design a highly disciplined set of messages of racial moderation, color-blind freedom, and absolute freedom of choice to justify permanently protecting housing discrimination in the country's largest and, based on recent elections, largely liberal state.

Although only one measure would be on the ballot, voters would constantly be reminded that their choice for safeguarding American freedom was between the rhetoric of Wilson's Proposition 14 and the governmental checks and balances of the Rumford Fair Housing Act.

14.

A Constitutional Amendment to Permanently Protect Discrimination

> At the state convention of CREA directors . . . the party-line
> imposed from above by President "Spike" Wilson was ramrod-
> ded through and no effective hearing was allowed to the Real-
> tors for Fair Housing or to the pleas . . . urging a fair period of
> trial for California's Fair Housing Laws. . . . The wishes of the
> individual salesmen . . . were not even considered nor were they
> ever given a chance to vote.
>
> League for Decency in Real Estate, 1964[1]

On the floor of the California Senate on the night of June 21, 1963, an
hour and a half before the midnight end of the session, any possibility
of new fair housing legislation seemed to have died. The Rumford bill—
which Governor Brown had made his highest priority and had overwhelmingly passed the assembly—had been stalled in the same Senate
committee that blocked similar 1961 legislation. The Senate committee
chairman had cited the realtors' argument in refusing to schedule committee discussions or votes: "I'm against [fair housing] in principle. The
equal opportunities this bill seeks for all persons are already part of our
U.S. Constitution."[2] In protest, CORE demonstrators had spent the last
five weeks camped on air mattresses in the Capitol Rotunda. Now, on the
final night of the session, the realtors' most powerful ally, conservative
Democrat Hugh Burns of Fresno, controlled the agenda on the Senate
floor. Burns—longtime president pro tempore of the Senate and considered by Governor Brown to have more influence on legislation than any
governor[3]—had placed the Rumford bill, AB 1240, so far down the list

for discussion it could not possibly be considered in the session's final minutes.

Those who supported fair housing had believed 1963 would be different than 1961. Together with the governor and most legislators, Rumford considered "1963 . . . the year to take action":[4] to finally enact an antidiscrimination law "with teeth," enforced by the Fair Employment Practices Commission. The political climate had never been more favorable. Brown had easily defeated Richard Nixon for reelection. Condemning segregation as "the heritage of slavery," Brown insisted that "no man should be deprived of the right of acquiring a home of his own because of the color of his skin."[5] Liberals had increased their majorities in both houses. Public support for civil rights had grown throughout the North. In the last month alone, news coverage had displayed schoolchildren attacked by police dogs in Birmingham, George Wallace backing down over integration of the University of Alabama, President Kennedy's major speech on civil rights, and his proposal for a federal civil rights bill. Church and labor leaders provided major support for AB 1240.[6] Newspapers such as the *Sacramento Bee* strongly endorsed the Rumford bill. "There can be no logical objection [to it]. No one is deprived of any 'rights' through the achievement of equal treatment by a group of his fellow citizens. . . . No one has any 'right' to deny equal treatment because of racial prejudice."[7] Rumford's initial bill had passed the assembly 65 to 14.[8]

Compared to other fair housing legislation around the country, Rumford's bill—which had already gone through many amendments— was fairly moderate. His own focus for years had been passing fair employment. "If a man can't get a job, he can't work." The 1963 fair housing bill "was not my idea entirely. . . . Brown and some of the rest later wanted to say 'it was [my] bill,'" Rumford later laughed, "because of fright and fear."[9] Concerned about legal challenges, Rumford narrowed the bill to apply only to those single-family homes with government-backed mortgages (about 25 percent of all homes) and buildings with at least five units.[10] But unlike the existing Unruh and Hawkins Acts, the bill provided an administrative enforcement mechanism, using the new Fair Employment Practices Commission to hear cases, mediate, and set maximum damages of $500, instead of having to go to court.

But none of this made any difference to the old guard of the rural-dominated Senate. Burns had led opposition to fair employment since World War II, sponsored a failed 1946 effort to make the Alien Land Law against Japanese land purchasers part of the state's constitution, and led the Senate's committee on un-American affairs. Burns had so bottled up Rumford's bill that it had never even had a hearing in the Senate. Given the chamber's long-standing practices and Burns's control of the late-night agenda, it seemed that little would change with respect to housing discrimination in California until the next session in two years, if then.

At 10:30 p.m., however, liberal legislators tried a maneuver that had never been used. A little-known senator called for a point of order to challenge Burns's requirement that measures be taken up in the order he had established. Over Burns's fierce objections, the lieutenant governor —who months before had called fair housing the state's number-one priority[11]—ordered a vote on the procedural motion. By a narrow margin, the Senate set a hearing on AB 1240 for 11 p.m. After weeks of delay, the fair housing bill now proceeded at record speed. The hearing was conducted, and the Senate approved the bill and rushed it across the Capitol to the assembly. There, Speaker Unruh set a hearing at 11:40 p.m., and the lower house approved the bill at ten minutes to midnight.

Assemblyman W. Byron Rumford with the Rumford Act, 1963

When the vote was announced in the assembly, for the first time in its history there was a standing ovation.[12] The governor, waiting in his office in the capitol,[13] called the action "a historic step towards giving every Californian the right to live where he pleases."[14] In the Senate, the CORE demonstrators—moved, joyful, almost unbelieving after all the delays—began singing "The Battle Hymn of the Republic."[15] Few civil rights victories in California had seemed so historic or so hard won.

CREA'S RESPONSE

While liberals celebrated and civil rights leaders savored a rare rush of optimism, realtor leaders felt tricked and double-crossed, saying they had been "mouse-trapped" in those closing minutes. They had never gotten the chance they had been promised to make their protests before final votes.[16] In reality, although CREA sought to discredit the Rumford Act by citing how it had been passed—"rammed through" at the last minute[17] with demonstrators camping in the Capitol—CREA's response to the bill was not affected by how the law was passed, the scope of the bill, or how few complaints would actually be handled. Realtors objected to 1963 fair housing legislation in Seattle, Tacoma, Chicago, and California regardless of how each had been passed, whether it covered all private housing or only some, or whether its penalties were modest or severe. In each case, realtors immediately sought to overturn the legislation by going to the voters.

For realtors could no longer count, as they had for decades, on successfully lobbying friendly, well-placed legislators to protect them from social and political change. As the *San Francisco Chronicle* put it, "Passage of Rumford . . . was a bad defeat for leaders of the conservative, bi-partisan 'club' that has long controlled the upper house. When it was all over, the old guard had been dragged kicking and screaming . . . into the twentieth century. . . . Biggest fear now is that diehards will push the legislation to referendum setting the stage for a bitter election that could split California's citizenry."[18] No longer able to rely on senators stalling fair housing legislation, realtors now sought to convince the public at large.

Therefore, when California realtors considered their options for dealing with the Rumford Act, they focused not on its details but on how they could reverse the momentum for fair housing in general. CREA had a broad range of choices.

It immediately rejected the path of Massachusetts realtors, and then those in Colorado, of accepting the new legislation. A few of CREA's normal allies, including some home builders and members of the Los Angeles County Chamber of Commerce, had suggested this alternative path. A past president of the Los Angeles Apartment Owners Association urged landlords to "accept the fact that the anti-bias law is here" and to obey it: "If all other types of business can prosper under integration, why can't we?"[19] State officials, including the real estate commissioner, a Brown appointee and former realtor, urged realtors to simply give the new legislation a chance to see how it worked in practice. Realtors should be willing to accept government action that would make "the private market truly open."[20] Within CREA itself, at least some members believed it was time to end their long-standing opposition to racial integration. Ultimately, one past president, several directors of CREA, 14 of the 176 local real estate boards including San Francisco's, and modest numbers of individual realtors opposed CREA's campaign.[21]

CREA itself, however, had long been so committed to opposing fair housing in whatever form, it did not consider the possibility of working with and potentially seeking to amend the legislation in the future. Indeed, CREA's decision to resist fair housing by going to the voters had been made before the Rumford bill was even introduced, when the two thousand CREA delegates in March had approved a ballot drive to put the Property Owners' Bill of Rights in the state constitution.[22] Indeed, if there had been any question in Wilson's mind about going to the electorate, it was dispelled by the popular feedback when local boards published this bill of rights in newspapers across the state. In May, even as the assembly was passing the Rumford bill by a margin of 3 to 1, Wilson summarized the enthusiasm of property owners and homeowner associations. "Their joyful reaction at discovering old fashioned patriotism and a zeal for preservation of personal freedom [by] the real estate people of California is amazing."[23]

Now that the Rumford Act had passed, the more difficult question CREA faced was not whether to go to the voters but *what* to ask them for.

CREA had two choices. The common approach would be a referendum to overturn the new law before it went into effect; California's initiative system, established under reform administrations in the 1910s, allowed any newly passed bill to be challenged by referendum. The more difficult but far-reaching approach would be to amend the state's constitution itself.

Almost everyone outside CREA's leadership—the governor, Rumford, fair housing supporters, other members of the real estate industry, and opponents of fair housing—assumed that CREA would file for a referendum to repeal the Rumford Act. A referendum involved a simple yes or no vote as to whether the law should go into effect. Notice would have to be filed within thirty days of the law's passage, and 292,822 eligible petition signatures would have to be submitted from voters before midnight, September 16, when the law became effective. Before CREA made any decision, an organization backed by real estate interests in Berkeley, the Citizens League for Individual Freedom, quickly filed such a notice.[24] The Citizens League was a relatively new organization that refused to disclose its financial backers, but already had a successful record in overturning fair housing. It had been formed at the beginning of the year, when the Berkeley City Council adopted the first fair housing ordinance in the state. After a locally divisive campaign, the Citizens League prevailed 52%–48%. The Citizens League had worked with the Berkeley Real Estate Board on the Berkeley campaign and no doubt expected that CREA would join it in a similar statewide referendum to overturn the Rumford Act.

But within a few days of the Citizens League's announcement, CREA announced it would oppose the League's referendum. Simply overturning the Rumford Act, Wilson argued, would not stop fair housing. Indeed, getting rid of this new law would "open the door for further punitive state legislation,"[25] encouraging Brown and Rumford to change some aspect of the law and come back with additional bills at each session. Some bills would no doubt be more far reaching than the Rumford Act itself. And overturning the state law would simply encourage activists to promote local fair housing ordinances. Already in 1963, realtors had had to defeat such efforts in San Jose and Oakland, as well as Berkeley. There was no limit to the number of such proposals, and adoption of any one would create precedent for other cities. A referendum against the Rumford Act would "increase the number of laws of cities harassing the housing industry and the private property owner," thus requiring CREA and local real estate boards to fight nonstop campaigns.[26]

By contrast, a "properly drawn State constitutional amendment" would spell out "the private property rights and individual freedoms" that must be preserved. They would then "be forever protected from erosion by any city, county or State lawmakers," Wilson argued.[27] Through a single vote, the people of California would prevent any possible type of fair housing regulations that activists might ever devise.

While Wilson gave plausible public reasons for a constitutional amendment rather than a referendum, CREA had other reasons as well. A constitutional amendment would nullify not only Rumford but all existing antidiscrimination rules. As the dean of UCLA's law school quickly noted, such an amendment "vitiates" the 1959 Unruh Act. It would "carve out an exception for the real estate business from [an existing] civil rights law that continues to apply" to all other types of business. Sales "by real estate developers, the rental of housing by most landlords and . . . the . . . business of real estate brokers" would no longer be covered.[28] Such an amendment would thus not merely prevent the enforcement mechanism of the Rumford Act; it would eliminate the protections that minority buyers and renters *already had*.

In fact, an amendment would invalidate another new set of restrictions that received much less publicity, but which realtors had every incentive to eliminate. On July 24—less than a week before the realtors announced they would seek an amendment rather than join in the referendum campaign—the governor signed a sweeping code of fair practices that allowed the state to discipline and potentially revoke the license of any broker who discriminated.[29] A constitutional amendment would prohibit any such revocations.

An amendment would enable realtors to argue not merely against the actual provisions of the Rumford Act itself but against the most egregious forms fair housing could ever take. Realtors could invent any future governmental restrictions—criminal penalties for homeowners, inclusion of the three-quarters of single-family homes not covered by Rumford, neighborhood racial quotas—and use their amendment campaign to barnstorm against all such possibilities. The Property Owners' Bill of Rights had proven compelling to audience after audience, and having created such an effective document, Wilson must have been at least as anxious as the Michigan and Illinois associations to put it in front of the electorate, to ask who would vote against freedom.

Last, but not least, a constitutional amendment campaign offered far more time to spread the realtors' message. CREA's decision to put Proposition 14 on the ballot "was made after polls in 15 major cities."[30] Private surveys for CREA showed that the vast majority of California voters would oppose "a law restricting the rights of homeowners in disposition or handling of their property."[31] The typical disadvantage of a California amendment campaign—that it required 469,000 qualifying signatures to get on the ballot, instead of the 293,000 for a referendum—was not a concern for CREA. Unlike virtually any other sponsor who had to pay petition gatherers, the realtors could draw on a vast pool of volunteers. With forty thousand realtors in neighborhoods throughout the state, plus their former clients and the homeowners and neighborhood associations those realtors could contact, CREA would have no shortage of enthusiastic petition circulators. Indeed, the need to gather the higher number of signatures and the extra months to do so would be a key part of the campaign itself.

Local realtors would turn their offices into campaign headquarters and collect signatures in supermarket parking lots, receiving up to ten thousand signatures in a single day.[32] Asking voters to sign would be simple: Do you want to be able to decide whom you sell your house to? Phrased in this way, there would be little reason not to sign. And because they were building support for the proposition, the realtors would not stop when they reached the minimum number of signatures, but went far beyond. They submitted over one million signatures, the most that had ever been gathered in California.[33]

An amendment created one possible legal risk that would turn out to be crucial, but that CREA chose to ignore. Loren Miller immediately recognized that, however cleverly disguised, voters' approval of a state constitutional amendment would be "state action" "by the yardstick of the Fourteenth Amendment." It would "vest in the owner the legal sanction to use race" in disposing of his property.[34] If so, the Supreme

Court might conclude that an amendment providing constitutional immunity for racial discrimination violated the Fourteenth Amendment's equal protection clause. Realtors were opening themselves to the possibility that their own choice of a state constitutional amendment would come back to haunt them. By contrast, a referendum overturning a specific piece of legislation could not be legally challenged, because, as Rumford himself put it, no state is obligated to have any particular legislation.[35]

CREA's lawyers knew that the proposed amendment would be challenged as state action. CREA had engaged three of the state's leading law firms to help put together the amendment,[36] and the "state action" argument was the first point Loren Miller and attorneys made in claiming Proposition 14 was unconstitutional. CREA's lawyers could offer legal arguments to counter such a claim. Because the lack of fair housing laws had not violated the Fourteenth Amendment, surely the state could go back to the way things were without violating equal protection. CREA's amendment would only limit the kinds of laws the state could pass without going back to the voters for approval, so it changed only the relative powers of voters and legislators, not equal protection under law. But CREA's most fundamental argument was the simplest: its amendment did not prescribe or require discrimination by anyone; it did not designate any group to be discriminated against. The amendment, CREA claimed, "does not call upon the state to enforce private prejudice; it merely requires the state to remain neutral." It therefore "deprives no one of life, liberty or property."[37] But above all, whatever the legal arguments pro and con might be, CREA discounted the legal risk. Its leaders assumed that few courts would be willing to overturn a mandate by the voters themselves. It was a calculated, and dangerous, gamble.

For all these reasons, CREA decided to sponsor a constitutional amendment to prohibit all existing and possible future fair housing laws and regulations in California. In announcing the decision to the press, Wilson used the language of the Property Owners' Bill of Rights to launch the campaign: "We feel the voters, if given the opportunity, will once and for all [end] the erosion of individual freedom and property rights in our State. Our hope is that this . . . will help us all to start acting [as] the kind of dedicated free enterprising Americans we think we are."[38]

Such an amendment, Wilson argued, would reaffirm "rights to freedom and liberty and equal rights for all without the sacrifice of private rights and private freedom."[39] CREA thus linked freedom and equal rights as the reasons for the amendment, as it would throughout the campaign. In meetings of local real estate boards, this high-minded language of equal rights as the purpose of the amendment was sometimes put more crudely. An irate Japanese American realtor from Anaheim reported how the amendment's purpose was presented at the local board meeting: to stop "minorities in their asserted right to acquire property to pillage and rob the mass of the people of their basic rights of choice."[40]

Having decided on an amendment, the realtors immediately worried that the Citizens League's bid for a referendum might effectively preempt them. If the Citizens League placed a referendum on the ballot, it would dominate all discussion of fair housing. The realtors, having opposed the idea of such a referendum, would either have to reverse course and join in a sixty-day campaign initiated by others, or remain neutral and effectively maintain fair housing. Neither possibility was attractive. Thus CREA was likely even more pleased than fair housing advocates when, on the final day to submit petitions, the Citizens League conceded that it had collected only 250,000 of the 293,000 signatures needed.[41] Having stayed clear of the referendum drive and told realtors not to support it, CREA was now in a position where it could make the arguments it wanted, for a campaign it would run, for an initiative that would permanently ban fair housing in California.

On September 26, ten days after the referendum drive failed, Wilson spoke to the five thousand delegates at CREA's annual convention. In this setting, he formally launched the realtors' petition drive throughout California. Wilson announced that, although he had completed his one-year presidency of CREA, he would still lead the amendment drive that was crucial to realtors' future. He would head a statewide joint campaign committee that would include the Apartment Owners Association and California Home Builders Association (although in time the home builders would drop out). To help finance the campaign, Wilson announced a $10 surcharge on the dues of all realtors, creating a $400,000 initial kitty. The investment was well worth making, he argued, given the potential benefit: "A mandate from the voters . . . will provide a permanent settlement for the forced housing law. Such a mandate from the people will return control of private property once again to the individual home owners of California."[42] Local boards and members had no say in the surcharge. NAREB agreed to provide supplemental funds, and donations came in from other state associations around the country. The California battle would be a national one.

Wilson summarized the campaign's ideology by emphasizing equality as well as freedom. CREA believed in "equal rights and equal opportunity for all," which included minorities "but also . . . all other Americans." Because it believed in freedom and equal rights for all, CREA opposed "class legislation, special rights laws or special privileges . . . for any group or groups."[43] The realtors' cause, Wilson argued, was that of the public as a whole.

Wilson's themes were then echoed by CREA's featured speaker, the actor Ronald Reagan, who warned that government was growing and individual freedom shrinking. Reagan had been a star of past CREA conventions. The year before, delegates had offered "a polite but cool reception" to Governor Brown, while giving Reagan "a wild ovation"[44] for a speech in which he attacked the Kennedy administration and called the middle-of-the-road liberal "more dangerous than the outright Communist," at least on university campuses.[45] In the interim, General Electric had terminated Reagan's role as spokesman for GE Theater, and he was now on his own as a public speaker. At CREA's convention, Reagan gave his standard speech, "A Time for Choosing," that he would keep adapting and that would make him famous a year later when he delivered it on national TV for Barry Goldwater.

The stark choices Reagan outlined were especially suitable for the realtors' new campaign: "Two contrary philosophies divide us—either we believe in our traditional system of individual freedom with constitutional limits on the power of government, or we abandon the American revolution and confess that an intellectual elite in a far distant capital can plan for us better than we can plan for ourselves."[46] The themes resonated with the realtors, even if the far distant capital they most worried about was Sacramento.

Reagan thus offered the same general attack on "liberal philosophy" that he was making to many groups, but the realtors were about to turn his pieties about "government encroachment on personal and property rights" into a massive populist campaign about very particular personal and property rights. In doing so, realtors would need support from many voters who distrusted right-wing Republicans. Such voters supported and in many cases were members of unions; they had long believed in the New Deal, had overwhelmingly voted for Pat Brown, equally overwhelmingly rejected state right to work laws, and distrusted conservative Republican attacks, like Reagan's, on liberal government. Realtors needed to convince this far broader range of voters that the realtors' vision of American freedom was something they believed in. The realtors also needed to convince racial moderates throughout the state, both Republicans and Democrats, that voting for Proposition 14 and the right to discriminate was consistent with a belief in equal rights.

The realtors cheered Reagan's words, but it was up to them to define freedom and equal rights in ways that would be supported by millions of voters who did not see themselves as right-wing conservatives. The realtors—a business trade association and not a political party and without support from either party—would need to forge a political alliance that had never existed.

15.

Racial Moderation to Continue Segregation

> It is not true that the Real Estate Association opposes the Bill of
> Rights. We have pitched this thing from the standpoint that we
> stand for freedom for all.
>
> L. N. "Spike" Wilson, 1963[1]

> So much heat over . . . civil rights, it is difficult for the voice of
> reason, . . . of moderation, . . . of goodwill to be heard. . . . Yet,
> realtors . . . *must* speak and act with moderation and reason . . .
> for a solution most beneficial to the whole nation—not just one
> side or the other.
>
> Forced Housing Action Kit, 1964[2]

No event illustrated the realtors' central challenge in the Proposition
14 campaign better than the debate within the walls of the Los Angeles County Chamber of Commerce. The chamber had been one of the
realtors' closest ideological and political allies for sixty years. The first
realtor meetings in California took place in the chamber's offices. CREA
and the chamber had fought and won constitutional amendment campaigns against fair employment and public housing; they had jointly
supported Bill Knowland and the state Right to Work initiative, and
in 1962 collaborated on a failed proposition to ban members of subversive organizations from public employment. Yet when the chamber
met to consider endorsing Proposition 14, its subcommittee report supporting CREA was sharply opposed by board members. One noted the
opposition of churches and "moral leaders in the community" to the

proposition. Another worried that "the right we are giving up is the right to discriminate on the basis of race. Is that a right we want to bat for? . . . It is not a laudable right in the first place."[3] The chamber refused to endorse Proposition 14, the only one of seventeen state ballot initiatives on which it declined to take a position.[4]

The chamber's response exemplified the realtors' central obstacle. Could they persuade California voters in 1964 that it was moral and just to enshrine an absolute right to discriminate? No other state had ever had such a provision. It would exempt realtors from the Unruh Act, which had applied to all businesses for more than four years. As a former president of CREA and state fair employment commissioner asked, "Why does the real estate industry . . . [seek] a special privilege which no other business in the state enjoys—the privilege of segregating and discriminating in housing?"[5] Constitutional protection *for* discrimination was both new and radical. Moreover, the realtors were proposing this amendment in a state with a popular liberal governor who had made fair housing his highest priority in winning reelection, and a state assembly that had voted 3 to 1 for fair housing.

In embarking on Proposition 14, CREA was politically isolated. Virtually no prominent politician of either party endorsed the proposition. Caspar Weinberger, the state's Republican committeeman (and later a cabinet member for Ronald Reagan), reminded Republicans that the party's own platform supported laws to eliminate housing segregation. Weinberger underscored his point by reminding his party of the devastating consequences of supporting the 1958 Right to Work initiative.[6] Even Barry Goldwater, who voted with only four other non-Southern senators against the 1964 Civil Rights Act, refused to endorse Proposition 14. While adamantly calling for right to work laws in states across the county,[7] Goldwater dodged Proposition 14 by portraying it as a decision for Californians themselves to make.[8] He went out of his way to ask supporters *not* to display "Yes on Prop. 14" bumper stickers next to his own, to be certain his presidential campaign in California was not tainted by association.[9] Similarly, Ronald Reagan—who would afterward embrace Proposition 14 in his 1966 run for governor—remained silent about it during the campaign itself. The most enthusiastic support for the realtors in the Republican party would come from upstart, conservative activists, attracted in part by Proposition 14, who gained control of the volunteer California Republican Assembly and Young Republicans in early 1964 and turned those organizations to work for both Goldwater and Proposition 14.

Union and civic leaders throughout California opposed the realtors. Major churches and almost all prominent religious leaders, except for a few evangelical ministers, did as well.[10] Archbishop after archbishop condemned Proposition 14 as immoral and contrary to God's will.[11] Forced to defend themselves against charges that their opposition to forced housing laws was "un-Christian or at least un-religious,"[12] realtors took the offensive. Eugene Conser, NAREB's executive secretary, attacked "religio-political reformers who aim at the conversion of the human family through . . . legal enactment rather than through the methods followed by our Lord." By opposing fair housing laws, realtors "further the Christian principle of individual autonomy."[13] Conser's aim was legitimacy: not to convince the many pastors and archbishops who ardently opposed Proposition 14 but to provide voters a way to see realtors as at least equally religious.

No major business organization outside the real estate industry supported the realtors. Within the industry itself, even the home builders (part of CREA until the 1940s) backed away after offering initial support. Only the Apartment Owners Association remained allied with CREA. Their organization in Los Angeles was led by Howard Jarvis, who had run unsuccessfully against moderate-liberal Thomas Kuchel for Senate in 1962 and would later help spearhead the Proposition 13 taxpayer revolt.

Thus CREA had to make the case that its view of freedom was politically and morally acceptable largely on its own, while opponents decried the realtors' views as fundamentally at odds with the most basic principles of the country. As a Southern California Democratic club put it in opposing Proposition 14: "The right of any American to live where one pleases and to own property is fundamental to our free way of life; the right to exercise one's prejudices in order to limit the freedom of others is not."[14]

Moreover, realtors vividly recalled the hubris of William Knowland's 1958 campaign, when "freedom versus tyranny" arguments and the state Right to Work initiative failed dismally. In that election, Pat Brown had "effectively portrayed Republican opponents as atavistic extremists . . . out of touch with the state's liberal and forward-looking elector- ate."[15] This was what CREA had to avoid in 1964. CREA had one major potential advantage compared to 1958, when it had vigorously supported Knowland: instead of supporting one class of white voters over another in a right to work battle, CREA could now present itself as defending the rights of all white people. But such an argument, however tempting, could easily be viewed as racist and extremist, driving away both racial and political moderates. From CREA's point of view, this was the gravest danger of all.

A CAUTIONARY TALE

California realtors did not have to look far to see what would happen if they were seen as racially biased. A dozen years earlier, in 1952, a campaign for a California constitutional amendment for "Freedom of Choice" had failed for precisely this reason.

The Freedom of Choice amendment had been sponsored by Amer- ica Plus, Inc., founded by Aldrich Blake and former state senator Jack Tenney in the aftermath of *Shelley* and proposals for state fair employ- ment practices commissions. Both men were vocal anti-Communists. Tenney, for example, had headed the state senate's un-American activi- ties committee before CREA ally Hugh Burns, investigating communism in Hollywood, seeking to ban un-American school texts, and proposing loyalty oaths. Both, too, were firm believers in protecting the rights of white Americans. The *Plus* in the organization's title stood for property, liberty, unity, and strength, and the organization focused on property rights and race.

Based in Los Angeles, America Plus was active in fourteen states. Its avowed aim was amending state constitutions to nullify public accom- modation laws and state fair employment rules and to enable the major- ity of owners in a neighborhood to enter into occupancy agreements that would effectively serve the same function as racial covenants.[16] The stated purpose of the Freedom of Choice amendment was similar to

Proposition 14: "Restore these lost . . . property rights, correct the abuses which have resulted from coercive legislation and . . . reduce, not augment, racial tensions."[17]

Like CREA, America Plus had argued that freedom of choice "is not segregation; it is not discrimination, and basically it has nothing to do with race except as the issue is injected by those who oppose the right to choose." Also like CREA, America Plus had claimed that it was in favor of equal rights, that both Black and white owners would have exactly the same right to discriminate. Like CREA too, the group insisted that the "state can no more compel tolerance than it can compel people to be good. Not legal coercion, but only friendly enlightenment and gradual understanding can soften and perhaps in the end remove human friction."[18] America Plus further argued that its amendment was designed to help ordinary citizens who were "not bigots or racists, but just average Americans trying to live happy lives."

Like Proposition 14, the Freedom of Choice amendment was denounced by the NAACP[19]; by Pat Brown, then attorney general; and by the *San Francisco Chronicle*, which recognized that "the 'freedom of choice' label is, of course, window dressing. What the measure seeks to sell to the people of California is freedom to discriminate."[20]

What, then, drove the failure of the Freedom of Choice amendment? One problem was timing. The central idea of the amendment—of a majority of neighbors choosing who can live in the neighborhood— attracted enormous negative publicity when newspapers turned the Sing Sheng case in South San Francisco into a Cold War issue rather than a racial one. Tenney's support for Sheng's neighbors—"if people don't have the right to vote on their neighbors, they don't have the right to vote on their president"—was drowned out by anti-Communism.[21] A second problem was organization. America Plus had no organizational base of support; it did not have forty thousand realtors committed to circulating petitions and protecting their business practices.

Perhaps most fundamentally, Blake and Tenney were seen as outsiders who were virulent racists and, especially in the case of Blake, anti-Semites.[22] Although America Plus's literature spoke of "democratic liberties and property rights," Blake had personally argued that Negroes could not achieve "the high peak of equality with whites."[23] Blake and

Tenney were isolated by mainstream Republican party organizations who saw them and their campaign as embarrassing Governor Warren and presidential candidate Eisenhower. The amendment effort fell apart, failing to gain enough signatures to put it on the ballot.

The lesson for 1960s realtors was clear: what mattered most in obtaining popular support was not simply the cause being promoted, but *how voters saw those promoting it*. On a controversial issue, voters had to first believe in the legitimacy of its advocates.

CREA AND BIAS ACCUSATIONS

Realtors were indeed accused of bigotry, and their initiative was quickly dubbed "the Segregation Amendment" and "the Jim Crow Amendment." As the campaign heated up, realtors found themselves faced with what they condemned as "twisted charges"—that they were "bigots," that their "segregation initiative" would "set race relations back 100 years," and that "they only want to protect their right to discriminate."[24] Goldwater and Reagan thus had good reason to fear that supporting Proposition 14 might tarnish their reputations.

Realtors' own history of promoting racial covenants was thrown back at them. A fair housing committee compiled a sixteen-page pamphlet of racist quotes from *California Real Estate* magazine; they needed a small font to include as many as possible. This dossier started in 1927, with realtors reporting on the "color problem" and calling for "all Caucasian" districts. It quoted CREA's counsel on how to write covenants to exclude "mulattoes"; CREA's 1940 achievement award to a Los Angeles realty board for its "very energetic Race Restrictions Committee . . . doing a wonderful piece of work in the community"; CREA's 1946 advice to interpret covenants based on the "one-eighth rule which has received judicial interpretation in the Southern states" since there are few "pure Caucasians";[25] and a host of other baldly racist positions. All these made clear that, far from championing owners' right to choose whom to sell to, CREA had spent decades restricting that very right.

When realtors responded that the era of covenants was ancient history and that they had (modestly) reworded their Code of Ethics in 1950, opponents pointed to CREA's more recent history: a CREA magazine advertisement touting "Glendale: 100% Caucasian Race Community," a 1958 article reminding members not to sell homes to minorities, and a 1960 article urging realtors to insist on discriminatory listings.[26]

The most intense confrontation over CREA's past occurred at a public debate on Proposition 14. When Rumford displayed a copy of *California Real Estate* magazine's 1948 endorsement of LARB's proposed federal constitutional amendment to overturn the Fourteenth Amendment and place African Americans in separate districts by law, realtor leader David Robinson accused the assemblyman of using a "phony document" and "malicious" intent, then walked away.[27] The reaction of Robinson, who became the realtors' national president a year later, suggests how sensitive CREA was to charges of racial bias. CREA in no way wanted Proposition 14 to be linked to its own prior proposed amendment to address "the harm to our national social structure" caused by "the insistence of some Negroes upon moving into" white areas.[28]

More than CREA's history, however, what made CREA vulnerable to charges of current racial bias was Proposition 14 itself. A bar committee put the case as gently as possible: sponsoring Proposition 14 gave "aid and comfort, however unintentional, to the extremist element fighting to preserve racial discrimination."[29] Even the realtors' erstwhile allies at a junior chamber of commerce concluded unanimously that Proposition 14 was "inconsistent with the fundamental American ideal of equal opportunity for all."[30] CREA's magazine had to keep refuting charges that the amendment was based on hate and bigotry.[31] The state's attorney general called an amendment to protect discrimination "as extreme a notion as has ever been offered in our constitution."[32] He argued, "Proposition 14 would sanction [discrimination] and bring it out into the open. Signs would spring up around California saying 'No Negroes,' 'No Catholics,' 'No Jews.'"[33]

Opponents noted that California had long espoused ideals not only of racial openness but also of property rights that Proposition 14 threatened to reverse. The first article of the state's constitution, from 1849, specifically extended the universality of the Declaration of Independence to the acquisition of property: "All people are by nature free and independent and have certain inalienable rights, among which are . . .

acquiring, possessing, and protecting property."[34] The state had banned discrimination in public accommodations since 1897,[35] held antimiscegenation laws unconstitutional in 1948,[36] and enacted bans on employment and business discrimination in 1959. Proposition 14 would reverse this history of extending rights to minorities. Lieutenant Governor Anderson linked realtors to Southern segregationists and George Wallace's 1964 bid for president, saying, "What joy they must give to Governor Wallace of Alabama."[37]

The realtors disputed bias charges as "misleading or false,"[38] insisting that "NAREB is not opposed to civil rights"[39] and that realtors "deplore racial inequality."[40] The vehemence of the attacks against them, realtors argued, were in fact proof of realtors' willingness to stand up for American freedom—and that their opponents were the extremists,[41] trying to "debase [our] motives . . . to detract the people from the real issue."[42] Although realtors defiantly defended themselves, they were concerned enough by the attacks against them that they worked assiduously to appeal to racial moderates. The more reasonable they could sound on race, the more absolutist they could be about freedom. This would be a key to victory.

RACIAL MODERATION

CREA's effort to present itself as racially moderate began even before the campaign. The day after the Rumford Act had been approved, CREA announced two steps. First, it was creating an Equal Rights Committee "to inform and assist members in . . . giving equal services to all clients [and to] meet with leaders of any responsible group . . . to establish a cooperative and harmonious relationship in the field of property rights."[43] At public debates, throughout the campaign, CREA would often send a spokesman from the Equal Rights Committee. But the committee was little more than a façade. It met only once in its first nine months and took no action.[44]

Second, CREA proposed to amend its constitution to provide that "no . . . Board shall . . . impose any limitation upon membership because of race, color, creed or national origin."[45] But this reform, too, meant little. Because local boards often controlled membership through personal references and blackballed applicants with no reasons given, African American brokers continued to be excluded almost everywhere.[46] How could it possibly accept African American members, LARB's Southwest Branch explained to CREA, since any 5 of its 681 members could reject any applicant? CREA quickly backpedaled; it was "not really insisting that the . . . branch integrate but should include a letter of complaint on file as reason to reject."[47] Seventeen months after CREA's announcement, by the time of the vote on Proposition 14, only a handful of minorities were included among the state's forty thousand–plus realtors. Even those were mostly members at large of local boards, so they would not have access to the multiple listings. This did not stop Wilson from claiming throughout the campaign that "we accept anyone into our local boards regardless of race."[48]

These quick announcements, together with NAREB's releasing its new Statement of Policy on Minority Housing, enabled realtors to say they had no official policies against any race as they began circulating petitions for Proposition 14. But portraying themselves as racially moderate would require more than a few initial announcements. CREA made it a basic principle of its campaign to standardize and script what realtors said, lest they make any statements that opponents could portray as racially intolerant. "We must conduct ourselves in this campaign in such a way to bring credit to the property owner, our industry and the CREA," wrote CREA's president.[49] On the day CREA launched its petition drive, NAREB's public relations director recognized that to "uphold the human right of property ownership in states and cities . . . threatened by forced housing laws . . . realtors [must] follow . . . a course of moderation in the civil rights controversy."[50]

Wilson played an essential role in suggesting how realtors nationally could campaign forcefully against forced housing while consistently showing their moderation on civil rights. At a meeting of the State Associations Steering Committee in November 1963, he proposed that NAREB create a special kit to coordinate realtors' arguments against forced housing throughout the country.[51] The committee unanimously agreed, and NAREB staff worked urgently to assemble and distribute a confidential "Forced Housing Action Kit" to state associations and local real estate boards nationally.[52] Together with this kit, a staff was established by NAREB to "guide, coordinate and implement a nationwide defense against and positive alternatives to forced housing."[53]

The kit provided each local board a complete package of material for opposing fair housing. A hefty one-and-a-half pounds, it featured a hundred pages of instructions and recommendations; speaker scripts for a five-minute speech, a ten-minute speech, and a twelve-minute speech; questions and answers for debates with opponents; detailed drafts of sequential news releases; a publicity program against forced housing; and procedures for creating local civic and owners' associations to help in the drive. In addition to these specially prepared materials, the kit included a page of libertarian passages from Ayn Rand on the nature of freedom and numerous editorials and articles from newspapers throughout the country supporting the realtors' position. Realtors used the newspaper pieces to independently confirm realtor arguments and gave them to local papers to run similar stories. The kit was so comprehensive and detailed that running a campaign against forced housing did not require any new or original wording. Press releases had blanks for boards to fill in the name of the locality. Hearing of its existence, Proposition 14 opponents described the kit as NAREB's "passing the ammunition" to its members.[54]

The central message of the kit was *how* to present the realtors' position. The keys were "'moderation,' recognition that there are genuine problems, and determination to find just . . . solutions while branding coercion as unjust." Therefore, the kit stressed, "focus on freedom and coercion," that forced housing deprives all owners of their rights. Stress that the "civil rights of all" were equally important, the rights of the majority as well as the minority. Explain that, in opposing forced housing, realtors were not against any race, but in favor of all races. Indeed, the kit emphasized that since private housing had been left out of the civil rights bill before Congress, voters could be in favor of desegregating public accommodations in the South *and* against forced housing in their own state. There was no contradiction between the two. Both would protect individual rights.[55]

As the most important reminder for realtors dealing with the controversial issue of race, the kit prescribed a "moderate, conciliatory, firm tone." Remind voters that "'catch phrases' like 'fair housing . . .' and 'a moral issue' drown out the voices of fair-minded men who want to analyze the problem and [consider] all possible solutions thoroughly before . . . taking a blind step which may do more harm than good." Here was the central advice for making certain that realtors were not viewed as extremists opposed to racial equality.

The message of all these points was the same. Realtors were "fair-minded." They aligned themselves with "the moderate viewpoint of millions of Americans that certain injustices for minority groups should be corrected promptly by law." They were in favor of voting rights for African Americans in the South, but "social acceptance" of minorities was a different issue. Overcoming of prejudice "is intertwined with human emotions [and therefore] cannot be effected by laws [or] decrees." This erased the actual history in which Black residents had in fact lived among whites—until realtors created legal mechanisms to exclude them and organized neighbors not to accept them. This theme of social acceptance did two things. Echoing the chamber of commerce in 1946, realtors shifted the focus from discriminatory practices, which laws could change, to what was in people's hearts. Moreover, this emphasis on "social acceptance" reinforced the realtors' argument that all races already had the equal legal right to buy homes and that all that was missing, all that African Americans really needed or should want, was to be viewed differently by whites.

To show their evenhandedness, realtors recognized that "probably the greatest advancement of social acceptance for Negroes should come through education . . . for whites of tolerance, understanding and brotherhood and for the Negroes of responsibility, ambition, and moral standards. And this will not happen overnight. It will take time, despite the impatience of certain extremists."

Yet even while trying to sound racially neutral, that each race was imperfect and needed to change, realtors were suggesting that segregation was African Americans' own fault for lacking responsibility, ambition, and moral standards—not that realtors' organized racial discrimination had thwarted precisely their individual efforts at home-ownership. Instead of laws limiting discrimination, what was needed was "education of the Negro race so that they thoroughly understand the morals and ideals of the white community to which they aspire and earnestly endeavor to assume the responsibility and initiative which go hand-in-hand with freedom and equality."[56] How patronizing this was to African Americans mattered little to realtors. What realtors cared about was the moderate-sounding tone for their intended white audience, a tone of tolerance and good faith, in explaining why the state constitution needed to permanently protect discrimination.

The kit set out the opposite poles that Avins's symposium had suggested, portraying realtors as moderates who believed in neither forced integration nor forced segregation. "Always [present] a middle-of-the-road conciliatory attitude," the kit emphasized.[57] Realtors could thus assert that they were in the center and anyone in favor of nondiscrimination laws was an extremist.

Even more than laying out this position, the kit's greatest value was its spelling out, in detail, how realtors should respond to the questions and criticism they would receive on such a controversial issue. The greatest danger was that inflammatory, racist statements by individual realtors would be picked up by newspapers and undermine the entire cause. Such comments had often gotten realtors into trouble in the past. The possibilities for such racist statements in a statewide campaign were legion. These occurred occasionally. But considering the range of realtor opinions and the issues and emotions at stake, the kit largely did its work.

Not only did the kit provide safe answers to many of the questions that came up; it also forcefully reminded realtors what *not* to say. "Don't get involved in arguments or discussion on the pro's and con's of integration."[58] "Avoid . . . discussion of emotionally charged subjects such as mixed marriages, alleged . . . inferiority of races, and long-range social issues involved." "Whatever the local situation, extreme statements or [an] attitude of 'they shall never pass' will not win the argument." When controversial issues come up, talk about "how to assure the civil rights of all the individuals involved." Speak only about the absolute freedom of owners. All other issues—reasons for discrimination, how it had come about, how it was practiced, and its impacts—must be avoided.

Such advice did more than avert public relations disasters. By answering all questions with "firmness" and "moderation," realtors demonstrated their reasonableness. The more they were attacked as bigots and segregationists, the more frequently realtors repeated that they believed in freedom for all races. Their tone of reasonableness *was the message*: realtors were not ardent segregationists but moderate, thoughtful, if conservative, businessmen. With newspapers needing to balance coverage of each side, the continual repetition of the realtors' calm, middle-of-the-road tone gave them credibility and normalized their arguments. The purpose of all these racially moderate messages— the reason the realtors believed they were essential—was to promote a constitutional amendment that was not moderate in any way.

RACIAL MODERATION AND RACIST MESSAGING

Yet even as realtor spokesmen at the field level meticulously followed the kit's racial moderation script in debate after debate, CREA and NAREB made high-level decisions that violated this very posture. CREA reprinted on page 1 of its magazine an Asian American newspaper's editorial that Negroes "blame society for their womanfolks giving birth to illegitimate children and living on welfare checks . . . [and] all of their anti-social habits . . . on the 'unjust' community in which they live."[59] Having this come from a minority newspaper allowed CREA to say that it itself did not harbor prejudice. CREA quoted an evangelical pastor saying that forced housing was wrong because it violates "the commandment, 'Thou shall not steal.'"[60] While emphasizing the realtors' "moderate viewpoint" on civil rights, NAREB's president insisted that "social acceptance is something which is earned. . . . Some people enjoy it from more people than others. Some attain a greater degree of it as they mature and become more sophisticated."[61] The words, and racial denigration, were virtually identical to those of Charles Shattuck in his testimony to the California assembly.

Perhaps most notoriously, the Proposition 14 campaign hired as its campaign manager William K. Shearer, who had contributed racist articles to the *Citizen*, the national magazine of the Mississippi-based White Citizens Council. After touring Jackson in 1961, he demanded to know what integrationists' real objectives were. "Obviously their goal," he asserted, "cannot be adequate schools for Negroes. Nor . . . an opportunity for Negroes to . . . play golf, swim, live in decent neighborhoods or attend functions in a beautiful auditorium. All of these advantages are available to Negroes now." Their "true goal" must be "not to provide advantages to the Negro, but to force his association on the white people."[62] Shortly before he was hired for Proposition 14, he had likened President Kennedy to Hitler.[63] In a similar move, CREA refused to disavow support from the Los Angeles White Citizens Council.[64]

Indeed, in the midst of the Proposition 14 campaign, NAREB became the only business trade organization in the country to oppose the 1964 federal civil rights bill ending discrimination in employment and in hotels, restaurants, and other public accommodations. At an intense two-day internal meeting, representatives from state associations across the country argued over whether to take a position on the bill even though it specifically excluded private housing.[65] While opposing the civil rights bill might "alienate a great number of local boards" and undermine local and state fights against forced housing, realtors decided it would strengthen realtor morale in the Proposition 14 campaign. Wilson spoke passionately in convincing the realtors to oppose the federal bill. "California realtors have been facing civil rights legislation for the past 5 years and today have begun to enjoy increased public respect because of [their] courage and fortitude to initiate a referendum. A courageous stand by NAREB on the so-called civil rights bill would enhance the realtor image."[66]

Why did realtors work so hard to present themselves as racial moderates yet provide such racist arguments as well? Such positions were not slips from their careful position of racial moderation; they served a strategic function. CREA was appealing not to one audience but to multiple audiences at the same time. They were seeking the votes of racial moderates while mobilizing racial conservatives.

CREA succeeded in appealing to such different audiences because it was not concerned with political correctness. It never suggested that its past statements and positions on race had been morally wrong in any way. Any such apologies would have undermined its credibility with both racial moderates and conservatives, and its ability to argue for absolute freedom. By defining freedom aggressively, CREA saw no need to apologize.

Instead, under their big-tent approach that would enlist 75 percent of white Californians, realtors offered racially moderate voters a way to see themselves as unprejudiced. Given an idealistic reason to support Proposition 14—defending American freedom and their own rights while not attacking freedom for others—such voters could ignore the realtors' overtly racist claims for other audiences.

But if this approach were to succeed, realtors needed to define freedom itself in ways that would appeal to racial and political moderates while energizing racial and political conservatives. The redefinition of freedom Wilson devised to meet this challenge would provide a road map for moving American politics to the right.

16.

Redefining Freedom and America's Founding

> The problem is government.
>
> Forced Housing Action Kit, 1964[1]

If Spike Wilson and CREA's first great challenge was to make themselves and their campaign seem racially tolerant in an era of equal rights, their second challenge was in some ways even greater: how to define American freedom in a way that could be promoted as color-blind yet placed the right to discriminate at its heart.

Freedom of association—which realtors had used to defend discrimination for the past fifteen years, which had mobilized neighbors and brokers, which had been at the core of Alfred Avins's symposium and the Property Owners' Bill of Rights—was fatally flawed for this new task. It had been used again and again to defend Jim Crow and had been the rallying cry of Southern racists and the failed America Plus campaign in Califonia itself. More deeply still, a campaign based on one racial group's right to exclude another would inevitably subvert the realtors' carefully constructed message of racial tolerance and understanding.

Over the course of the Proposition 14 campaign, realtors shifted their emphasis from freedom of association to each individual owner's freedom of choice. They did this, however, without abandoning freedom of association. Rather, realtors employed individual freedom of choice to *express* freedom of association.

FROM FREEDOM OF ASSOCIATION TO
INDIVIDUAL FREEDOM OF CHOICE

CREA's important initial decision, the wording of the constitutional amendment itself, reflected the choice between these two different images of freedom. CREA's natural inclination was to use the Property Owners' Bill of Rights as the text of the amendment itself. This new bill of rights primarily emphasized freedom of association—the rights to choose one's friends, to not deal with others, to maintain congenial surroundings, and of neighbors to enjoy their property. Wilson had drafted this bill of rights only months before; it had been unanimously endorsed by NAREB and CREA, and it expressed the full range of rights that realtors believed that owners and brokers must have.

Yet rather than use this new bill of rights, Wilson worded Proposition 14 *solely* in terms of the individual owner's freedom of choice. This allowed CREA to frame the amendment in the august manner of the original Bill of Rights. Voters would be asked, "yes" or "no," whether to add these words to the state constitution:

> Neither the State nor any subdivision or agency thereof shall deny, limit or abridge, directly or indirectly, the right of any person, who is willing or desires to sell, lease or rent any part or all of his real property, to decline to sell, lease or rent such property to such person or persons as he, in his absolute discretion, chooses."[2]

By echoing the First Amendment's elevation of individual freedoms—that "Congress shall make no law respecting an establishment of religion, or . . . abridging the freedom of speech, or of the press"—the language of Proposition 14 suggested, as Avins and Wilson had argued, that an owner's right to choose a buyer had always been embedded in America's founding documents, that such a right was equally sacred. It portrayed the owner's selection rights—not previously mentioned in the nation's history—as a fundamental civil liberty,[3] along with religion and speech, in contrast to new "so-called" civil rights such as forced housing. By leaving out entirely the freedom of association provisions of the Property

Owners' Bill of Rights, realtors emphasized that Proposition 14 was essential to individual freedom.

Finally, the text was perfectly racially neutral. Nowhere did the amendment suggest that the "absolute discretion" being given to the owner was, in fact, the absolute right to discriminate. Nor did it suggest that putting this language in the state constitution would have any differential impact on any race. So noble and neutral sounding was the amendment's wording that in a poll of Black voters in Los Angeles, 60 percent of those who had the proposition read to them said they were in favor. Only when its impact was described did their opinion change.[4]

Indeed, Proposition 14 sounded like a civil rights bill. That the state shall not "deny, limit or abridge the right of any person," was precisely what civil rights leaders were asking for on such issues as voting rights, public accommodations, and employment. Many commentators at the time noted the confusing nature of the amendment. To vote for fair housing, one had to vote no, to reject individual rights. By contrast, the Property Owners' Bill of Rights had made its intent obvious. Its emphasis on congeniality, choosing one's friends, deciding whom to embrace or reject, choosing whether to accept one another, was clearly racial.

Having decided on the amendment language, realtors used both freedom of association and freedom of choice throughout the campaign, even though their meanings were diametrically opposite—the right of neighbors to control who could move into a neighborhood regardless of a seller's wish, and the absolute right of a seller to do as he wished. Regardless, realtors often linked these two ideas together. Wilson claimed in November 1963 that "massive approval of the initiative . . . will . . . fortify the right of all Americans to free choice, free association and to freely handle their own property."[5] In December 1963, CREA's legislative chairman complained at a public debate, "There has been no primary discussion of freedom of choice. We should always remain free to choose our friends, associates and neighbors."[6] A week before the election, a La Jolla realtor serving as publicity chairman for Proposition 14 argued that forced housing "tells us we have no right to pick our friends . . . that we have no right to rent or sell to anyone we please."[7] From the realtors' perspective, both types of freedom were important.

But while CREA spokesmen would continue to mention freedom of association at times, their advertising increasingly emphasized freedom of choice. Billboards on Los Angeles freeways proclaimed "FREEDOM to choose whom you rent or sell." Freedom to choose was the message "said by every person, who has [come across] this line over tv, radio, billboard, leaflet," an opponent of Proposition 14 lamented, explaining how hard it was to make any argument against Proposition 14 even heard.[8] "Red, white and blue pamphlets emblazoned with 'FREEDOM' . . . trumpeted the right to rent or sell to whom you chose."[9] Freedom of choice and yes on Proposition 14 became virtually synonymous.[10]

Making individual seller freedom of choice the tagline of the campaign offered a host of advantages for CREA. First, realtors and the voters they appealed to could say that they were in favor of neither segregation nor integration, that, as Wilson put it, "the law should avoid promotion of integration and abstain from promoting segregation."[11] Second, freedom of choice avoided some of the negative political connotations of freedom of association. Union leaders reminded their members that CREA had supported Knowland's Right to Work initiative based on freedom of association. Fair housing advocates reminded voters that Southern segregationists were the loudest voices for freedom of association; to resist school integration, Georgia governor Vandiver proposed to "guarantee each child his God-given right to freedom of association."[12] But individual freedom of choice did not carry this baggage.

Third, and perhaps most important, freedom of choice enabled realtors to make far broader and more resonant arguments based on individual freedom. These arguments would provide a template for conservative politics. The realtors drew on the long history of references to freedom in the Declaration of Independence and the Bill of Rights, in speeches by American presidents, in Cold War oratory against Communist totalitarianism. These always emphasized *individual freedom*, not the rights of groups. Realtors directly countered the civil rights movement's claims of freedom, while evoking the individual's right to his home.

By continually arguing that each individual had the right "to dispose of property as conscience dictates,"[13] realtors linked residential discrimination to freedom of religion. "Forced housing is like forced religion," Wilson argued.[14] "Freedom of choice is part of every American's life. He is not forced to observe only one religion."[15] Discrimination was a matter of conscience, then. Just as you did not have to agree with another's beliefs to defend his right to them—the fundamental basis of freedom of speech and religion—you did not need to see *yourself* as prejudiced to support Proposition 14. You only needed to believe that government had no right to interfere with the rights of others.

As the symposium's contributors had suggested, realtors made freedom of choice synonymous with discrimination, arguing that there can be no freedom without a right to make choices. Making residential segregation appear as simply the product of each individual owner's conscience, "freedom of choice" obscured the organized way that segregation worked: minorities excluded from real estate boards and access to multiple listings; realty boards deciding which homes were listed in newspapers as "white only" or restricted.[16]

At still another layer, realtors drew on the popularity of consumer freedom of choice. Consumer's freedom of choice, widely hailed in the Cold War as distinguishing the American system from Communist Russia, appealed across the political spectrum. New Deal administrator David Lilienthal, pilloried by Charles Collins for his belief in the individual, said that "by freedom, I mean essentially *freedom to choose*. . . . a maximum range of choice for the consumer when he spends his dollars."[17] James Jackson Kilpatrick, Virginia editor and *National Review* columnist who had defended Bull Connor's suppression of protestors in Birmingham,[18] used consumer freedom of choice to excoriate the public accommodations provisions of the federal civil rights bill. "The American system . . . rests upon the individual's right to [discriminate]. . . . When a housewife buys a nationally advertised lipstick, . . . she discriminates. When her husband buys an American automobile, . . . he discriminates. . . . In a free society, these choices—these acts of prejudice or discrimination—universally have been regarded as a man's right to make on his own."[19] Freedom of choice appealed not only to liberals and conservatives but also to those alienated from traditional politics, and only became more popular in the decades after World War II. By the 1970s, a Gallup poll asked Americans to rank their most important value. Freedom of choice was listed first, before such values as "following God's will," wealth, or a sense of accomplishment.[20]

Crucially, however, realtors used freedom of choice not to support the freedom of choice of consumers *but to limit it*, not to allow minorities to use their money to buy homes but *to prevent them* from doing so. When opponents insisted that realtors were ignoring "the freedom of choice of a Negro to live in the neighborhood he prefers," the Forced Housing Action Kit provided a ready answer. "The Negro has the same rights as any citizen. He should have neither more nor less.... To live in a voluntary society—not under dictatorship—we must be able to contract freely."[21] For racial moderates disturbed by the connotations of freedom of association, CREA stressed that Proposition 14 protected something they held dear: their individual freedom.

By speaking only of the freedom of choice of owners *in order to limit* that of buyers and renters, realtors had found a color-blind-sounding way of racializing freedom. If "withholding the presumption of equal humanity is the ultimate mechanism of racism in public life,"[22] realtors had been doing this since 1905 by withholding from millions of Americans the right to choose where to live. To perpetuate such exclusion, realtors had sought to withhold this presumption of equal humanity first in the domain of economics with their property-value ideology. Now they were withholding this presumption in the idea of American freedom itself.

But while individual seller freedom of choice—with its greater appeal to American history, libertarian values, individual conscience, and ownership and property rights—offered the realtors a more resonant way to appeal to many voters than freedom of association, freedom of association nonetheless remained in the background. Indeed, for some audiences, including racial conservatives and many white tenants, freedom of association was all that needed to be conveyed.

One of the most widely distributed pieces of campaign literature was a letter to tenants in all the white neighborhoods of Los Angeles, from Howard Jarvis's Los Angeles Apartment Owners Association. Signed "Your landlady," it began: "As manager of the apartment house in which you make your home . . . I constantly carry a deep feeling of responsibility for your safety and welfare. . . . I have the satisfaction of knowing that you can live here today in peace and comfort—and without fear." Not having government restrictions made it possible to "'size up' people" of any race and protect "the safety and well-being of children." Discrimination was essential. "We must discriminate every day of our lives in the selection of tenants, usually on the basis of the applicant's appearance and intuitions . . . through years of experience." This argument disclaimed any racial intent. Indeed, it asked plaintively, under forced housing, "How can I prove that my discrimination is based ONLY on individual lack of desirability, NOT on race, color or creed?" This letter was then printed as an advertisement in newspapers throughout the state.[23]

Even when freedom of association was not mentioned, *the purpose of freedom of choice*—the entire reason realtors were waging the Proposition 14 campaign, *the maintenance of all-white neighborhoods*—was always present. Freedom of Choice on billboards, on pamphlets, on commercials, conveyed a double message. Individual choice, the personal right to do what one wanted with one's own property, stood for community loyalty and tradition. This connection had been made crystal clear by John Gorsuch, grandfather of the Supreme Court justice, in 1962 in asking Colorado's supreme court to overturn fair housing: "Freedom of choice in the sale of one's property cannot be separated . . . from his freedom of association, his freedom to choose his surroundings, and the whole tenor of his life." Freedom of choice, Gorsuch admitted, had little to do with the seller's own interest: "It is true that, considering a single sale, the seller is no longer involved with the property." What the seller's freedom of choice *was crucial for*, what it assured and what mattered most, Gorsuch candidly explained, was the right to live in an all-white community. "It is still more true that . . . the liberty of a man to choose freely to whom he will rent or sell . . . has made it possible for him to choose the type of neighborhood in which he wishes to live and the associations he and his children will have."[24] Here was Proposition 14 in a nutshell.

Powerfully marketed, CREA's approach of using the individual owner's freedom of choice to stand for all-white neighborhoods proved brilliant. An African American opponent of Proposition 14 despaired at the power of the realtors' message. "It has been effective. I know . . . I've talked with many people, many one would expect to be unsympathetic to [Proposition] 14. We have allowed the opposition to gain the propaganda advantage. . . . Everybody arguing for 14 says he wants the right to choose." Proposition 14 had drowned out the reality that "we [African Americans] can only be free to choose without segregation" and that "fair housing

PROTECT[s] . . . PROPERTY RIGHTS: to a fair price for your property, to a stable neighborhood, to free choice of buyer or renter."[25] Instead, a right of sellers that had never been mentioned until fair housing was first proposed only a few years before—a right that had been least valued and most restricted by realtors themselves, a right whose only purpose was to exclude other races from a neighborhood—had become the reason that government should never limit residential discrimination.

LINKING FREEDOM OF CHOICE WITH AMERICA'S FOUNDING

But individual freedom as the right to discriminate was too isolated, novel, and questionable to be presented by itself. Opponents would attack such a vision of freedom as fundamentally at odds with the principle of the Declaration of Independence that all men are created equal. To bolster the acceptability and credibility of seller's freedom of choice, *to make it central to American values*, the realtors equated it with America's founding and the purpose of the American Revolution.

With the civil rights movement invoking the Declaration of Independence to justify its idea of universal, equal freedom, the realtors called their own campaign a "Re-declaration of Independence."[26] "From the moment the Declaration of Independence was signed," Wilson insisted, "the individual's right to acquire, control and dispose of property as he chose has been paramount."[27] Proposition 14 was essential to "reinstate that principle of freedom."[28]

More basically, and with far broader implications, the realtors characterized the American Revolution not as the creation of a new country with a government dedicated to securing the rights of all its citizens but as *a rebellion against government encroachment on owners' rights*. Forced housing was precisely such an encroachment and only the first step in government's taking rights away from its citizens. By asserting that the purpose of the American Revolution was to establish freedom *against* government, realtors took direct aim at a central tenet of the civil rights movement. For Truman's President's Committee on Civil Rights, the purpose of government in the Declaration of Independence was to protect individual rights within the society. "There is no essential conflict

WHY 'YES' ON PROPOSITION #14?

That Long, Long Arm of the Law—

YES Vote Will **restore** to California property owners the right to choose the person or persons to whom they wish to sell or rent their residential property.

YES Vote Will **abolish** those provisions of the Rumford Forced Housing Act of 1963 which took from Californians their freedom of choice in selling or renting their residential property.

YES Vote Will **amend** our California Constitution so that the only way future legislation could take away the freedom of choice in selling or renting of residential property would be by vote of the people.

YES Vote Will **halt** the State Fair Employment Practices Commission's harassing and intimidating the public and property owners in the exercising of their freedom of choice.

YES Vote Will **end** State police power over the selling or renting of privately owned residential property.

YES Vote Will **restore** rights basic to our freedom—rights that permit all persons to decide for themselves what to do with their own property.

The Rumford Forced Housing Act's police arm is long and strong.

It can reach almost any Californian—almost anyone who owns or rents a place to live. Owner. Tenant. Yes, and neighbor, too!

First, it reaches the owner. It takes away his right to choose his tenants or buyers.

Then it takes away a tenant's or buyer's right—the right to choose his neighbors.

If the owner insists on his freedom to choose, the long arm can reach out and make him pay a complainant up to $500; and further insistence by the owner can make him subject to contempt of court penalties.

If a tenant advises the owner to use freedom of choice, the long arm can reach the tenant with the same penalties.

In the matter of giving advice, even the neighbor must beware. That same long arm can put the neighbor in the same penalty box as the tenant!

14 SALES AND RENTALS OF RESIDENTIAL REAL PROPERTY. INITIATIVE CONSTITUTIONAL AMENDMENT. Prohibits State, subdivision, or agency thereof from denying, limiting, or abridging right of any person to decline to sell, lease, or rent residential real property to any person as he chooses. Prohibition not applicable to property owned by State or its subdivisions; property acquired by eminent domain; or transient lodging accommodations by hotels, motels, and similar public places. **YES** ✗

OWNERS! TENANTS! NEIGHBORS!

GET BACK YOUR RIGHTS!

VOTE "YES" ON PROPOSITION #14

Yes on Proposition 14, Committee for Home Protection, 1964

between freedom and government. Government . . . protects citizens against the aggressions of others seeking to push their freedoms too far. Thus to secure these rights, *governments are instituted among men*."[29] For civil rights advocates, therefore, Proposition 14 "violates one of the basic principles on which this country was founded . . . government . . . protection of the rights of each individual."[30] Realtors attacked this very premise; the Revolution had been fought not to have a representative government that would protect freedom but to defend individual freedom against government.

The realtors therefore defined the enemy as big government, not minority groups. By shifting attention away from individual minorities unable to buy homes, realtors changed the focus of the election. "The real issue is not one of civil rights," CREA claimed, "but . . . centralized government."[31] This definition of whom realtors opposed dovetailed perfectly with their claims to racial tolerance: Proposition 14 was not against any minority. As one of the campaign's weekly news flashes explained, in Wilson's usual patriotic language: "Proposition 14 is a Declaration of Independence by all of us—black—white—yellow—red and tan from those who would crush the Rights of all of us."[32]

CREA took this argument against big government even further, claiming that minority rights were only an excuse for expanding government power. "Strip off the mask of the Rumford Act," Charles Shattuck proclaimed, "drop the cloak of minority civil rights, and there stands the police state in the name of social justice, with a dagger poised directly at the very heart of freedom."[33] CREA thus made the individual homeowner the underdog. Talk of minority rights was only a cover; the real purpose of forced housing was to take away rights from each individual homeowner. Big government was attacking "YOU as an individual . . . the smallest minority on earth. Those who would trample on your rights cannot claim to be the defenders of minorities."[34]

To magnify the threat of government, realtors portrayed not what fair housing laws did but what they represented. The actual number of cases brought under such laws was miniscule: in the first year of the Rumford Act, the state FEPC dealt with eighty-two total complaints, only four of which involved homeowners; it had not ordered a homeowner to sell to anyone.[35] The Forced Housing Action Kit therefore instructed realtors not to talk about what had actually occurred under fair housing. Instead, "Emphasize first step,"[36] that any proposed fair housing law was just "a first step by government in attempting to deprive an owner of his right to . . . dispose of his property." Such a first step "can lead eventually to only one end—government assignment of quarters. As long as realtors stick to this principal point they are on solid ground."[37] Thus, the more modest the fair housing law, the more deceptive: "If the law fails in its purpose [of integration], people will look for stronger laws. The next logical step is to assign 'quotas' to apartment buildings and to neighborhoods."[38] "Remember," kit materials warned, "social and socialist regulations of property contributed to the rise of national socialism. Persecution followed those that owned property. . . . IT is done step by step."[39] What mattered was not the initial results of the Rumford Act but what it represented: "The Rumford Act is a dangerous step toward a police state."[40]

Presented as a last stand against government encroachment on individual freedom, Proposition 14 echoed Knowland's 1958 campaign of freedom versus tyranny, but in the context of a specific, immediate danger to the rights of ordinary white owners. If government succeeds in limiting this one right, realtors argued, it will soon go after all your personal freedoms. CREA made this a centerpiece of the campaign. Proposition 14 was the only way to stop government's relentless encroachment on personal liberty. As one Sacramento homeowner put it, she would "cast a big yes for Proposition 14. . . . We are fighting for our rights, and this, voters, is the only way we can do it. It appears to be our last chance!"[41]

Thus, rather than realtors arguing, as in the 1920s, that the "'Western Negro' is a menace" to property values,[42] or in their proposed 1948 constitutional amendment that "Negroes trying to live where they are not wanted . . . menace the family life of the nation as we have enjoyed it,"[43] realtors now described the menace as government's threat to individual freedom. The words changed, but the idea of theft remained the same.

In organizing citizens to resist this latest threat, realtors likened themselves to the Revolutionary patriot in advertisements for the Property Owners' Bill of Rights. Identifying realtors with "the Founders of Freedom in 1776," CREA proclaimed, "Let the people learn the TRUTH. Let the people know their individual FREEDOM is IMPERILED. And let them decide!"[44]

Howard W. Lewis Jr., a director of CREA who opposed Proposition 14 and would later say, "A racist initiative is what it was,"[45] put his finger on what the realtors accomplished with their campaign. Why, he asked, are "so many Californians planning on voting 'Yes'?" "Only part of the reason," Lewis explained, "is that some think fair housing laws took away a legitimate freedom of choice when selling or renting property (which they didn't). Only part of the reason is that some think fair housing laws 'eroded' property rights (whereas they really work to strengthen the institution of private property)." Lewis then sought to cut through CREA's interpretation of the purpose of America's founding. "Only part of the reason is that some (like the top leaders of CREA) have been fooled into mistaking a segregationist's mask for a patriot's dream."

This is when Lewis described the key to the realtors' campaign: "One basic reason some Californians will vote 'Yes' is because some of us *want* its false ideal to be established in our Constitution—to be told that what we have been doing to the minority members in our communities is right—is accepted—is morally good."[46]

17.

A Battle between Two Visions of Freedom

> We were never really asking white people to grant or give us any rights. Only to stop using their majority and power in preventing us from exercising our God-given rights.
>
> C. L. Dellums, c. 1970[1]

> A free nation needs free citizens who can freely acquire and sell property.
>
> Leonard Seeley, realtor opposing Proposition 14[2]

Liberals and civil rights advocates, led by a popular two-term governor and supported by almost the entire leadership of the state, organized a massive effort to defeat Proposition 14. But the greater their efforts—the more they sought to discredit the realtors and urge the reasonableness of fair housing and the indefensibility of discrimination—the more they found themselves on the defensive. The power of the realtors' vision of freedom was that those attacking it seemed to prove its case, that such high-minded arguments were designed to take away the individual freedom of ordinary citizens. Fully prepared to argue that fair housing would not lower property values, those opposed to Proposition 14 had a hard time responding to an ideal of freedom so unlike their own. They often treated CREA's idea as simply a cover for racial prejudice, both by the realtors and many of their supporters. The experience of the No campaign offered sobering lessons for liberal organizations for years to come.

CITIZENS AGAINST PROPOSITION 14

Governor Brown, the Democratic Party, and civil rights groups spared no effort in organizing Citizens Against Proposition 14, "CAP 14." Many of Brown's top aides resigned from state posts to play key roles, and the state's human rights commissioner, William Becker, monitored the effort daily for the governor. These men and other veteran organizers had helped Brown defeat the 1958 Right to Work initiative and the 1962 antisubversives initiative. CAP 14 worked with Catholic archbishops throughout the state, the California Council of Churches, the American Jewish Congress, the State Bar of California, unions, and hundreds of civic organizations and civil rights groups. Volunteers contributed hundreds of thousands of hours, participating in enthusiastic marches, meetings, rallies, dinners, and Hollywood Bowl fundraisers with leading movie stars.[3]

Donations roughly matched what CREA raised from its $10 assessment on all members plus gifts and loans from realtor organizations nationally. Several local real estate boards voted not to endorse Proposition 14, and dissident realtors formed Realtors for Fair Housing. Told he would be expelled by his board if he did not pay CREA's assessment to fight against what he saw as civil rights, one member yelled: "Then you can start expelling me."[4]

Hundreds of local evening debates were arranged between CAP 14 spokesmen and those for the Committee on Home Protection; all-day conferences took place at UC Berkeley and UCLA; and newspaper reports balanced arguments from each side. CAP 14 campaigners saw theirs as a major effort at public education, while realtor spokesmen repeated the phrases from the Forced Housing Action Kit. So intense was the public interest, one conference speaker joked at the size of the crowd: "Civil rights threatens to replace sex as the number one subject of conversation of our day."[5] To help CAP 14 have more time to convince voters, the Democratic secretary of state pushed back the vote from the June primary to the November election.

But the realtors' opponents found that however much time and effort they spent, their arguments made little headway or indeed seemed to back-fire. The fundamental issue from the beginning was the realtors' claim that the Rumford Act took away the fundamental rights of homeowners. One Brown aide noticed debate audiences sometimes beginning to agree with him on the need to end discrimination. But the moment his opponents began to "say 'you mean that you're going to let the government say that here you are living in this house and you've paid for it . . . and you have to rent it to them,' you could just see the faces take on a different look."[6]

Rumford and his allies had opened the door for realtors to use homeowners as "human shields." Rather than adopting Oregon's approach—"ignore the individual property owner and regulate the real estate industry"—the Rumford Act prohibited discrimination by both homeowners and brokers. Oregon's approach of banning only broker discrimination, by suspending or revoking their licenses, was the one realtors feared most; it gave owners a reason to sell properties themselves, to not use a broker at all. Politically, it would have been far harder for realtors to challenge such a law. The power of the realtors' campaign, starting with its one-million-signature petition drive, lay precisely in its appeal to homeowner rights, its claim that the state was taking away the freedom of ordinary citizens.

Early on, those opposed to Proposition 14 faced a major dilemma. Should they try to prevent the proposition from appearing on the ballot at all by asking courts to rule it unconstitutional, the approach that

No on 14 supporters with Tom Bradley, future Los Angeles mayor, 1964

had succeeded in Illinois? Tempting legally, this approach was politically dangerous. It would enable realtors to skewer liberals as elitists unwilling to let the people vote. But hoping to end the campaign before it began, CAP 14 challenged the measure in court. The outcome was in many ways the worst possible for Proposition 14 opponents. While the state supreme court expressed "grave" doubts about the proposition's ultimate constitutionality, the court demurred at not letting citizens vote on it first. The initiative remained on the ballot, and the lawsuit seemed to prove realtors' charges: Brown and Rumford cared more about expanding government and helping "militant minorities" than ordinary people. "LET THE PEOPLE VOTE!" a local newspaper proclaimed.[7] Shattuck declaimed on democracy: "Thoughtless persons . . . fearful of the voters of this state . . . maligned the CREA. How little they know of the history of California and the vision of it held by realtors."[8] The realtors—whose entire history had been antipopulist, including their national executive secretary's widely publicized 1949 view that "democracy stinks"[9]—had all the ammunition to campaign as populists.

No on 14, CAP 14, 1964

A more fundamental problem opponents faced was that they based their campaign almost entirely on discrimination being morally wrong. The No campaign's primary image showed two martyred presidents, Lincoln and recently assassinated John Kennedy, with a simple message: "Don't Legalize Hate." But this attack on discrimination was the argument CREA had worked so hard to prepare for. In describing discrimination as a matter of individual morality rather than systematic organized effort, CAP 14 strengthened the realtors' claims that liberals sought to impose their own beliefs on everyone else and would violate individual dictates of conscience. It made the campaign about homeowners' purported prejudices, not realtor-organized discrimination.

If the issue was in fact one of morality, then change could only come about, as the realtors constantly claimed, through education, not legislation. Echoing the Forced Housing Action Kit, realtors argued that "members generally consider discrimination immoral [but] it can't be legislated away." Realtors were against forced housing not because they believed in discrimination but because they believed in freedom. Voters could therefore see themselves as unprejudiced, indeed noble, in protecting the freedom of choice of all owners, not only themselves.

In the face of such responses, Proposition 14 opponents only ratcheted up their argument that Proposition 14 was based on bigotry, by portraying it as the work of Southern racists. "The CREA Amendment seeks to re-make California in the Southern racist image. The Amendment did not originate in California but is part of a campaign sponsored by NAREB. . . . The same sentiments motivated Alabama Governor George Wallace."[10] CAP 14 could point to NAREB's opposition to the 1964 federal civil rights bill, realtor publicity director William Shearer's support for the Mississippi White Citizens Council, and CREA's 1948 effort to have the U.S. Constitution authorize separate districts for "Negroes."

But the realtors' carefully orchestrated moderate tone, their claimed support for equal rights for all, and the unwillingness of most owners to see the local realtor who had helped them buy their home as any more prejudiced or racist than themselves, all led such attacks to backfire. When Governor Brown declared that the initiative reflected the "minority of the angry, the frustrated, the fearful," not California or its people, many homeowners saw this as an attack on themselves. Frustrated, and despite warnings from his aides, Brown only stepped up such attacks, calling Proposition 14 a "vicious" measure by a "vigilante committee" that would only strengthen "prejudice and bigotry"; those who supported it were themselves bigots. When Brown's press secretary urged him to soften his language, explaining that "most of the people we are talking to don't regard themselves as bigots, even if they do discriminate against Negroes," Brown acknowledged that he needed "to become more temperate." But the governor found it impossible to heed the advice.[11]

As a result, when the governor, Loren Miller, and others began to warn that Proposition 14's passage might lead to racial violence, to anger exploding in the African American community, this was taken by many not as a prediction but as a threat. To Brown's warning that the "problems of segregation and discrimination [would be] settled in the streets with blood and violence" if the proposition passed,[12] the realtors explained that they were not the ones arousing racial tensions, but rather those who had pushed for forced housing in the first place. Segregation would end peacefully through the efforts of men of good will and education, not through laws forcing social change at the cost of everyone's freedom.

Anxious to present the election as being about individual morality and to allay the fears of white voters, CAP 14 tended to downplay evidence of discrimination's extent and impact on minority communities. Rather than defend the need for the Rumford Act or suggest that fair housing was critically needed, CAP 14 emphasized how few complaints had been handled under the act, and thus how modest the impact of fair housing was likely to be.[13] This tended, however, to reinforce the views of many white voters that discrimination was not a real problem. Because those not subject to discrimination tended to minimize its existence, it was possible for many white voters to agree with the one state-elected official who supported Proposition 14, Republican secretary of state Frank Jordan. "We've never had any racial discrimination in California . . . I see no reason for the Rumford Act."[14]

When opponents claimed that realtors cared more about property rights than human rights, CREA was equally prepared. As instructed by the Action Kit, realtors explained that property rights *were* human rights, that freedom had long been based on the right to property, and that fair housing would take away owners' basic rights.

It would be left to dissident realtors to make the perhaps more effective argument against the realtors' idea of freedom, that fair housing was itself based on the importance of property rights, on the right to buy property in the first place: "Don't let them take your right to buy or rent a home!"[15] The state's real estate commissioner, a former realtor, explained that "a person who puts his home on the market says in effect he no longer desires that property," but rather dollars. "For him to prescribe racial . . . conditions to the purchase of that home would be depriving the prospective purchaser of the right to buy . . . that property."[16] But such arguments that fair housing was in fact essential to freedom of choice were drowned out by CREA's messages.

Brown's aides had discounted the realtors. "Never mind the real estate agents. Screw them. Who cared about them? They were a bunch of idiots. They were going to be against everything that they wanted to be against. But to be shocked that we had a minority position in this moral, upright, right thing, constitutionally, you name it, everything that you could name that was good . . ."[17] What such aides had discounted most was the power of the idea Spike Wilson had spelled out. Of voters who thought the central issue was "freedom of choice," 90 percent opposed the Rumford Act and supported the realtors.[18]

On election night, the extent of Proposition 14's victory became clear. It had won by thirty points. What made this so extraordinary was the contrast with the presidential results that same night. The traditional Democratic coalition had given Lyndon Johnson a landslide victory; staunchly in favor of civil rights, Johnson had swept Goldwater in California 4.2 million to 2.9 million votes. But on this same ballot, Proposition 14 won by even more: 4.5 million to 2.4 million. When it came to fair housing, the Democratic coalition had splintered apart.

Unions had been among the strongest opponents of the realtors. But white union *members*, who had voted overwhelmingly against Knowland's campaign of freedom versus tyranny, voted 82 percent for Proposition 14.[19] The realtors triumphed not only in then famously conservative Orange County but in Alameda County, with Berkeley and Oakland; in Los Angeles County; in every county up and down the Central Valley; in Santa Cruz and Santa Clara; and even in San Francisco, where only one out of three households were homeowners. Many of the future trends of American politics lay in these results.

Were there other approaches opponents could have taken? Were there ways they could have won? An extensive postmortem by NCDH asked precisely this. It identified things that could have been done better—more active efforts by union leaders to involve their members in the No campaign and better coordination with the civil rights movement. Later scholars such as Daniel HoSang and Mark Brilliant focused on lack of minority outreach and not describing the prevalence of discrimination.[20] But once the Rumford Act had made homeowners rather than realtors the perceived targets of the law, and realtors had effectively redefined American freedom as the issue at stake, the outcome, it seemed, was never in doubt. As dissident realtor Howard Lewis had suggested, CREA had needed only to provide white voters a way of understanding freedom as the right to the racially exclusive way of life they had invested in and come to take for granted.

AN OVERWHELMING VICTORY

There was, however, one approach not taken up by opponents, or taken up only occasionally by some of the dissident realtors. Unlike the struggle for civil rights and voting rights in the South, the effort to end housing discrimination was rarely cast of in terms individual freedom: the freedom to buy a house, to rent a home, to choose where to live. They almost always spoke of housing discrimination in terms of fairness, and thus inevitably morality, bias, and what was owed to minorities. Starting in the early 1950s, NCDH had argued for "fair housing" and drafted fair housing laws. CAP 14 did not sponsor billboards calling for "freedom of choice in housing." Their central argument was not that the real estate industry was limiting individual freedom.

Partly this had been a matter of strategy: the struggle against housing discrimination in the North had been seen as an uphill battle to convince moderate lawmakers, civic groups, religious leaders, and elite opinion-makers. The result, however, was that when it came to the political battle over housing discrimination, freedom—in newspaper stories, debates, advertisements, and the public mind—became the domain of those defining freedom as the right to discriminate.

For the million residents of California who learned that—no matter what they did, whatever law any city or the legislature might consider—housing discrimination could never be limited, that they and their children were to be permanently locked out of 95 percent of neighborhoods, the realtors' triumph was "a crushing blow." Belva Davis, the first African American television reporter on the West Coast, called it "devastating."[21] The doors of their prison clanged shut. Underlying all the debates and political and legal maneuvers to come was the simple fact that an ideal of American freedom—of freedom of choice—had been carefully designed, promoted, and popularized to restrict where Americans could live.

The consequences for residential segregation, for civil rights more generally, and for American politics would be far reaching. The idea that freedom meant the right to act in ways that limited others' choices, and that such freedom was one's sacred personal property, would begin to reshape the country's vocabulary. Proposition 14 had shown, at the very height of support for civil rights and American liberalism, how to make this case and how effective it could be.

Part Six.

An Earthquake: 1965–1968

On the morning after the 1964 election, Lucien Haas—Governor Brown's speechwriter, on loan to the No on Proposition 14 campaign for the past year—woke up with a single thought: My God, we've been hit by an earthquake.[1] Haas would later put this earthquake into words: The day Proposition 14 passed was the day "liberalism died."[2]

Haas's view was hardly that of most national commentators that November. In Lyndon Johnson's sweeping victory they saw the ascendancy of liberalism—a liberalism that would lead three-quarters of Americans to support his Great Society program and the Voting Rights Act of 1965.[3] James Reston of the *New York Times* declared that Goldwater "has wrecked his party for a long time to come." Many Republicans agreed.[4] *Time* proclaimed that the election had dealt "the conservative cause . . . [such] a crippling setback . . . they will not have another shot at party domination for some time to come." Not only had Goldwater lost 43 million to 27 million, but exit polls indicated that only 6 million had supported him because he was a conservative; the others had supported him solely out of party loyalty. Chet Huntley of NBC News considered those who had supported Goldwater politically marginal: "segregationists, Johnson-phobes, desperate conservatives, and radical nuts . . . the coalition of discontent."[5]

But what Haas recognized was the power of the realtors' "cause of freedom" to transform American politics. For decades, conservatives had viewed themselves as a minority and therefore opposed popular democracy and majority rule.[6] That this could change, indeed had changed, in California of all places, felt to Haas as if the earth had shifted. He was waking up in a California fundamentally different from what he, the governor, and their allies had assumed.

Realtors were emboldened in their efforts to defeat fair housing in states across the country. Fair housing advocates, focusing on Congress to avoid future referenda, found that Proposition 14's political shadow haunted their efforts there as well. In Berkeley, a student movement—ignited by CREA pressuring the university to shut down recruiting tables for volunteers against Proposition 14—created new fault lines and stereotypes in American culture and politics, ones that conservative politicians could seize on.

For families who remained trapped in areas like Watts because of their race, overwhelming approval of a constitutional amendment preventing any future fair housing law sent a message of despair. Loren Miller's fear of a violent explosion was soon realized, while realtors strongly denied any connection between the Watts rebellion and Proposition 14. Claiming that no law forces African Americans to live in Watts,[7] Reagan suggested that it was solely lack of ambition that prevented African Americans moving elsewhere, and therefore, if there was private discrimination, there was a basis for it.

The greatest political beneficiary of all these changes was Ronald Reagan. Adopting the realtors' language and cause helped him first crush Lucien Haas's boss, Pat Brown, to become governor of California, then almost overnight become a strong contender for the presidency. His bid for the 1968 Republican nomination helped lead to the grand bargain with Southerners for a national conservative party. Learning from the Goldwater debacle, this new Republican party would promote the realtors' vision of freedom as a unifying message to reset not only the state's but the country's agenda.

The spreading power of a new way to justify traditional social divisions in the name of freedom—this was what Haas experienced as an earthquake. The changes would be felt first in the politics of California, and then nationally.

18.

Reagan and the Realtors

> This has nothing to do with discrimination [but] with our freedom, our basic freedom.
>
> Ronald Reagan, 1966[1]

The small group of wealthy Southern California conservatives who first approached Ronald Reagan in February 1965 about running for office had been attracted by the "Time for Choosing" speech Reagan gave for Goldwater on television just before the presidential election. For auto dealer Holmes Tuttle, oil wildcatter Henry Salvatori, chairman of Union Oil Sy Rubel, Reagan's attorney William French Smith, and the others who put up the money, Reagan's speech provided a powerful attack on government control of the economy and people's lives. "We don't want [the Goldwater debacle] to be the demise of the Republican party," Tuttle told the others, suggesting they needed a new face to unify California Republicans.[2] The sincerity of Reagan's self-taught beliefs, winning demeanor, and ability, in Republican Paul Laxalt's words, to "convince himself and others that he was not really a politician, which inspired unbelievable trust in him,"[3] made him seem an ideal challenger against Pat Brown.

But as Reagan stumbled in his exploratory barnstorming around the state, the psychologists and researchers hired to advise him realized that Reagan had no knowledge or grasp of issues that would appeal in a state campaign. Reagan had put together "A Time for Choosing" from years of national news clippings that personally appealed to him, stored in an overflowing shoebox he had long drawn from in his appearances for corporate sponsors.[4] Reagan's shoebox of ideas, however, was just that: a compendium of anecdotes of government dysfunctionality, cost

Ronald Reagan,
meeting of San
Fernando Valley
voter registration
campaign, 1964

overruns, and absurdities together with principles distilled from
free-market economist Friedrich Hayek and the obscure nineteenth-
century thinker Frederic Bastiat's parable of French candlemakers
petitioning the government to block out the sun for unfair competition.
This collection of ideas—about government, free markets, the original
Constitution versus bureaucracy[5]—lacked the discipline and specificity
that the realtors had worked so hard to achieve. These qualities would
be essential to defeat seasoned politicians such as George Christopher,
Republican mayor of San Francisco, and Pat Brown.

The realtors' work on Proposition 14 provided the specifics of
homeowner rights, controlled messaging, ways of talking about racist
issues, and attracting Democratic voters—including union members—
that Reagan had initially lacked. Moreover, even before Reagan entered
the race, Proposition 14 had played a critical role in the political realignment of the state. When the state supreme court declared the proposition unconstitutional in the middle of the gubernatorial campaign, it
offered a hesitant Reagan a way to adopt the realtors' cause and helped a
handpicked candidate of the very wealthy become a successful populist.

REALIGNMENT

Proposition 14's impact on the state's political parties began during the realtors' campaign itself. The vast petition drive, starting in fall 1963, helped mobilize conservatives who then took over many California Republican party organizations that would support Goldwater. To such activists, Proposition 14 epitomized the conservative cause[6] and their vision of a new state GOP—one very different from the party that in 1962 had supported moderate Senator Kuchel over right-wing Howard Jarvis, and Richard Nixon over right-wing Joseph Shell. After those primary losses, Shell planned Operation Take-Over to wrest control of key party organizations, including the California Young Republicans and California Republican Assembly (CRA).[7] The new conservative members of these volunteer organizations got their first practical political experience circulating petitions for Proposition 14. The thrust of these organizations changed dramatically.

When longtime moderate members of the California Republican Assembly, calling themselves "practical Republicans," argued that Proposition 14 would embarrass the party, they were shouted down as "cowards."[8] For Proposition 14 was precisely what the new members of CRA believed the Republican Party should stand for. CRA's new conservative leaders thus issued some of the most forceful lines of the Proposition 14 campaign: "The essence of freedom is the right to discriminate."[9] "Freedom to discriminate means to make a free, discerning choice."[10] "Freedom to be unequal is really our national purpose."[11]

CRA's moderates did not go down without a fight. These new principles seemed antithetical to their idea of the Republican Party and the country itself. "Proposition 14 can surely not be defended upon the ground that bigotry is a national purpose or right. How can a nation which declared its independence with 'all men are created equal' have as its national purpose 'freedom to be unequal'?"[12] In response, the new conservative leadership denounced these officers for wanting "government-imposed equality" and ignoring the broader issue at stake. "We have slipped too close already to . . . state socialism and dictatorship. Let us return to the strength, vitality and honesty of freedom."[13] CRA's endorsement of Proposition 14 was the first time in its thirty-year history it had ever taken a position on a ballot measure.

California's Young Republicans followed the same path. New members vehemently supported Proposition 14. Many of them were drawn from Young Americans for Freedom—a national organization established at the Sharon, Connecticut, home of *National Review*'s William F. Buckley Jr. in 1960. The Young Republicans' new president attacked the Rumford Act as "socialistic" and having "nothing to do with civil rights or minority groups." He called Proposition 14 essential because African Americans had proven themselves "unacceptable" to white neighbors. The board of the Young Republicans endorsed Proposition 14 by a vote of forty-five to five.[14] In the same meeting, they applauded South Carolina's Strom Thurmond having just joined the Republican party.[15]

In the close and bitter California presidential primary in June 1964 that would decide the Republican nomination, these newly right-wing Republican organizations played a key role in helping Goldwater narrowly defeat Nelson Rockefeller. Goldwater's primary victory, in turn, forged a narrower, far more conservative Republican party both in California and nationally. The activism and momentum generated by the Proposition 14 campaign thus played a major role in shifting the national party.

At the same time, Proposition 14 persuaded many Democrats to oppose their own party's leaders in California. Democrats held a commanding 60%–40% margin in registered voters; this margin was similar to Brown's over Knowland in 1958 and Johnson's over Goldwater. A unified Democratic Party would have easily beaten back Proposition 14. But while almost all Democratic party leaders, from the governor on down, opposed Proposition 14, almost three-fifths of Democratic voters supported Proposition 14. Governor Brown was not on the ballot, but Democrats could show their displeasure by crossing party lines to vote against Pierre Salinger, President Kennedy's former press secretary, and for Republican actor George Murphy in the race for the U.S. Senate. In a sign of the future, over 80 percent of such crossover voters supported Proposition 14.[16]

The realtors' emphasis on white immigrants having earned the right to their homes—in the Property Owners' Bill of Rights and throughout the campaign—helped split the New Deal coalition. As one voter put it, accepting the realtors' implicit equation of nondiscrimination and welfare, "Let them earn their privileges, like other immigrants. . . . I never had a Cadillac."[17] The realtors' constant references to special privileges for minorities paid off; the vast majority of white voters came to see fair housing not as enabling African Americans to have the same right to buy a home at the market price as descendants of European immigrants, but as a handout.[18] Proposition 14 marked the first key rupture of the alliance of union members, Catholic Americans, Jewish Americans, Black Americans, and progovernment liberals who had been the mainstay of both the California and the national Democratic parties for thirty years.

The Proposition 14 campaign further contributed to political realignment through its impact on campus unrest. When Mario Savio and other leaders of what became the Free Speech Movement returned to UC Berkeley in September 1964 from Freedom Summer in Mississippi, they quickly recognized that the main threat to civil rights in California was Proposition 14. When these activists set up tables at Sproul Plaza to recruit students to volunteer against Proposition 14, realtor leaders reacted quickly. CREA's key leaders constituted University of California president Clark Kerr's real estate advisory committee.[19] They pressured the university administration to put a stop to such advocacy on its property.[20]

"Before the [university's] ban" on political activity, Savio recalled, "hundreds of people signed up to do precinct work against Proposition 14."[21] Once the university prohibited its facilities from being "used for the mounting of social and political action directed at the surrounding community," "there was just a trickle" of anti–Proposition 14 volunteers.[22] The free speech revolt, Savio explained, began as "an extension of . . . involvement in the struggle for civil rights," now brought home to California.[23] The realtors' campaign and their pressure on the university to shut down recruiting against Proposition 14 helped catalyze the protests—protests that would become the model for the student movement at campuses across the country in the late 1960s.

The highly publicized Berkeley demonstrations weakened support for Brown's "responsible liberalism" from those on the left and the right for years to come. Ronald Reagan, running against Brown for governor in 1966, would slam the university and the governor for insufficiently cracking down on the "filthy speech movement."[24]

Whether free or filthy, the student movement that quickly spread across the country from those tables on Sproul Plaza in the midst of the Proposition 14 campaign inspired a third vision of American freedom— one very different from that of *either* the civil rights movement or of the realtors and Ronald Reagan. Jack Weinberg, a twenty-four-year-old mathematics teaching assistant whose arrest by campus police triggered thousands of demonstrators blocking a police car for twenty-four hours and demanding "free speech" on campus, quickly recognized this new conception of freedom.[25] When he had chaired the student chapter of CORE, freedom meant equal rights. In the student movement, freedom meant the right to create one's own life against the dictates of society, to not be "treated as things . . . a cog in the machine." This vision of freedom as independence and nonconformity was very different from the civil rights movement's; indeed, Weinberg snapped out the generational motto "Don't trust anyone over thirty" when a reporter suggested that students were being "directed behind the scenes" by organizations with their own social agenda.[26]

But what the students meant by freedom was even more radically opposed to the realtors' vision. Freedom to not conform, to attack the values of established society—of what Weinberg called "the institutions, . . . managers of industry and the possessors of corporate wealth"—could hardly have been more different from the right to maintain social traditions and absolute rights of private property.[27] To supporters of Proposition 14, individual freedom belonged to those who deserved it through hard work, property ownership, and belief in traditional authority, precisely what the students mocked. These three radically different ideas of American freedom would play out over the years to come. Deriding student protests and lifestyles, conservatives blamed them, like fair housing, on liberal government's blurring the social boundaries that Proposition 14 had so forcefully reasserted.

Long before such attacks further weakened his position, Brown and many white supporters of fair housing felt "shattered" by the victory of Proposition 14.[28] They had assumed there was a growing consensus for civil rights and government efforts to end discrimination. They had felt assured at the beginning of the campaign; 90 percent of the "leadership class" of Californians was on their side, the realtors were trying to take the state backwards, and citizens only needed information and education to recognize that freedom could not consist of limiting opportunities for others. Yet the more information the No campaign provided and the more educated voters became, the greater the support for Proposition 14.[29] The overwhelming margin stunned and disillusioned white supporters of fair housing.[30]

WATTS

For African Americans, however, Proposition 14 confirmed their worst fears. From their point of view, the realtors' campaign was nothing new. The *Los Angeles Sentinel* reported in 1963 that "Negro real estate men and NAACP officials" viewed the Property Owners' Bill of Rights, with all its language about freedom and equal rights, as 'just another effort to legalize racial discrimination."[31] The realtors' campaign to maintain segregation and deny the modest promise of the Rumford Act fueled anger and bitterness. Calling it the "Segregation Amendment" and "the Jim Crow proposition,"[32] some considered it "the most serious insult to black men" since the era of the KKK.[33] "The single fact that emerges with crystal clarity," the *California Eagle* wrote, "is that, by and large white Americans . . . do not want to live next door to Negroes. No amount of rationalizing can submerge this truth."[34]

During the campaign, both white and Black civic leaders pointed out that restoring the legal right to discriminate might lead to civil unrest in the Black community—a prediction realtors angrily dismissed. Calling Proposition 14 "the greatest danger to the state and its tranquility and safety,"[35] Brown asked, "will we solve our ancient problems of segregation and discrimination through legal processes? Or shall they be settled in the streets with blood and violence?"[36]

In response, realtors attacked Brown as a fearmonger. "All this talk of . . . violence and bitterness," Proposition 14 campaign manager (and Mississippi White Citizens Council supporter) William Shearer suggested, "has come from . . . Governor Brown."[37] CREA derided the governor for "predicting that attempts to nullify the Rumford [Act] would cause . . . a 'racial war.'" There will not be violence if the Rumford Act is killed, unless it is stirred up [by] politicians and demagogues."[38] Indeed, CREA pointed out, "New York and Pennsylvania have some of the most stringent forced housing laws in the country—even stronger and more far-reaching than Rumford. Yet these are the very states that have had race riots. Obviously, these laws haven't relieved racial tension there."[39] Racial tensions in California were due not to segregation, the realtors argued, in line with many Southern segregationists, but to those who sought to change the existing system. "The present racial tensions will diminish . . .," Shattuck declared, "in direct ratio to the silence of demagogues, and to the ebb of the fear they create."[40] That segregation minimized racial tension had been a core tenet of realtors for fifty years. As far back as the 1917 Supreme Court case on racial zoning, *Buchanan v. Warley*, realtors had argued that maintaining racial separation would "promote the public peace by preventing race conflicts."[41]

By contrast, Loren Miller believed that segregation in Watts was breeding "racial frustration and despair" that would lead to "ever greater future conflicts." During the campaign, Miller wrote to the state attorney general's office that "violence in Los Angeles is inevitable."[42] Similarly, Mayor John Shelly of San Francisco argued against Proposition 14: "We must use law, not violence. We must use moderation, not extremism, in dealing with problems of human rights. But Proposition 14 is a repudiation of law . . . a rejection of conciliation and moderation."[43] The proposition's very purpose was to *prevent any law* ever enabling those discriminated against to move elsewhere. Like Brown, Shelly had thought of the Rumford Act as a form of moderation, a way to reduce polarization and the likelihood of violence—a prospect that in the wake of Proposition 14 seemed less and less likely.

When Watts erupted in violence ten months after passage of Proposition 14, realtors quickly insisted that "there is no evidence that Proposition 14 had anything to do with the Watts riot." After all, CREA argued, "there is no evidence that Proposition 14 has interfered with the Negro's ability to obtain housing." Indeed, CREA suggested, in line with its own campaign rhetoric, and regardless of 90 percent of African Americans voting against the proposition, they should have been happy with the results. "Freedom of choice in selling or renting their private property is now enjoyed by all Californians regardless of race, color, or religion." To justify their argument that Proposition 14 did not contribute to the inflammatory situation in Watts, realtors cited the executive director of the Los Angeles County Human Rights Commission, who doubted that 10 percent of rioters knew Proposition 14 existed.[44]

Many African Americans, however, believed that Proposition 14 was one of the causes behind the rebellion.[45] An activist noted that "the fight against Proposition 14 brought the issues of freedom and opportunity closer and more real. . . . Few got out and knocked on doors, but it was really important to people. . . . Even the [poorer] blacks who couldn't move anywhere discussed it . . . Everyone was angry that it even came up." The results made them angrier still: "Everybody in Watts was aware that they were being rejected by . . . somebody white."[46]

More fundamentally, as Loren Miller testified to the McCone Commission investigating Watts, the riots in Los Angeles and elsewhere were the direct result of residential segregation. "Such segregation," he said, "is an open invitation to conflict . . . it breeds conflict." Miller looked at why Watts was a ghetto in the first place. "The root cause of the 'Watts' riot of August 1965 was the social phenomenon that produced 'Watts': racial residential segregation. . . . The riot area . . . contains roughly 75% of the city's Negro population." Such segregation "did not just happen." It was not "an expression of spontaneous prejudice," but of years of concerted action with government approval. He recalled his statement at a debate on Proposition 14 a year before: "Government, which fanned this fire from individual sparks, must find its way to put it out." The vote on Proposition 14 had done the opposite. It "buttressed the feeling of rejection on the part of Negroes and played its part in fanning the hostility that flared out in Watts."[47]

What was clear from all these arguments was that realtors had little knowledge of or interest in how their campaign would affect the Black community. In the wake of the uprising, African American psychiatrist Alvin Poussaint recalled James Baldwin's description of the gap between white and Black perceptions of Los Angeles just two years before: "I doubt that a single Negro in Los Angeles would agree that conditions are improving. We don't walk down the same street. You may think the courts are the same, arrests are the same, getting insurance is the same. But it isn't. The real Negro leaders have been trying to speak to you for years. . . . You won't listen."[48] The realtors' campaign was based on ignoring the consequences of their own efforts to limit where African Americans could live. A classic example of such differences in perceptions occurred at a 1966 state hearing on antiriot legislation. Since unemployment was 40 percent in Watts, legislators asked a resident, why didn't people just move? The witness was astonished. CREA, he had to explain, "took care of that with Proposition 14."[49]

More broadly, the realtors had spent sixty years creating residential segregation in Los Angeles and across the country as if segregation had no costs, or costs they need be concerned with, or costs visible to most white Americans. Watts and similar conflagrations of the 1960s made these costs extraordinarily visible to all. For those committed to perpetuating housing segregation, it was therefore essential that these events be seen as justifying the walls they had instituted long before.

As a result, the events in Watts, like Proposition 14 itself, led to further polarization. For those living in the neighborhood, a UCLA survey found after the riot, 62 percent thought of it as a protest, 64 percent thought it was deserved, and 58 percent thought there would be favorable results.[50] But the violence reinforced the views of CREA and many whites to see Black Americans as a whole, not simply those arrested, as inherently violent and dangerous, and residential segregation as essential to protect the safety of white neighborhoods. William F. Buckley Jr. inveighed, "They all in the Watts district, or rather a substantial number of them, became animals." To ensure that the point was not missed, *National Review* editorialized: "Los Angeles is not the Congo. Or is it?"[51] Reagan, preparing to run for governor, likened urban streets to "jungle paths after dark."[52] These racist stereotypes long endured. Watts residents not yet born at the time felt, decades later, that they too were held as responsible as if they had thrown the first rock.[53]

Conservatives went further and blamed the rioting on the civil rights movement and its campaigns of civil disobedience. Poverty and frustration were not responsible for the riots, *National Review* argued, since "the living standards of Negroes in Los Angeles, bad as they are, would have seemed . . . near to heaven" to most of America's earlier immigrants. Not acknowledging the permanent barriers imposed on Black Americans that those immigrants did not experience—the barriers the civil rights movement had been protesting—*National Review* attributed the violence in Watts to the movement's tactics instead. "If you are looking for those ultimately responsible for the murder, arson, and looting in Los Angeles" [look to] "Martin Luther King and the high-minded, self-righteous 'children of light' of the 'civil rights' movement. They are the guilty ones, these apostles of 'non-violence.'" From *National Review*'s perspective, nonviolent protest had not been *an alternative* to violence, but its cause. "Their doctrine of 'civil disobedience' [has taught] hundreds of thousands of Negroes that it is perfectly all right to break the law . . . if you are a Negro-with-a-grievance. They have . . . called out their mobs on the streets, promoted sit-ins . . . taught anarchy and chaos by word and deed. . . . They have found apt pupils everywhere. . . . Sow the wind, and reap the whirlwind."[54] For *National Review*, it was essential that the country not lose the opportunity presented by Watts to delegitimize the civil rights movement—and the "politicians and bleeding hearts" who sympathized with it. "Shall we wreak our wrath upon . . . 'punks' and 'hoodlums'" rather than "the Martin Luther Kings, the inciters?"[55]

REAGAN, HOMEOWNERSHIP RIGHTS, AND THE RACE FOR GOVERNOR

If the causes and solutions to the violence in Watts were much debated, intensely polarizing, and extraordinarily far reaching, its immediate political implications were clear. By late 1965, both Los Angeles mayor Sam Yorty—a conservative Democrat seeking to challenge Brown in the primary for governor in 1966—and right-wing Republicans backing an expected Reagan campaign recognized that law and order was the number-one issue in the gubernatorial election. In a confidential poll for Brown, most Californians, when asked to name the single person most responsible for the violence, named the governor.[56]

In formally announcing his campaign in January 1966, Reagan insisted on his "deep commitment to brotherhood" and distanced himself from Proposition 14 by saying that he had taken no position on it, but in other ways echoed CREA's views from the Proposition 14 campaign. By complaining that voting blocs of hyphenated Americans, "Irish-Americans and Negro-Americans," were established so that "cynical men could make cynical promises in a hunt for votes," Reagan repeated, in a neutral-sounding way, CREA's charge that the political purpose behind forced housing was pandering to Black voters. To explain why the Watts riot had occurred, Reagan pointed to large numbers of African Americans from the South moving to Los Angeles expecting "streets paved with gold," promises in the just-started War on Poverty that could not be fulfilled, and "other elements with an axe to grind."[57] Reagan, in other words, did not look to the conditions of Watts, such as the 34 percent unemployment rate compared to 6 percent for whites in Los Angeles as a whole,[58] or the situation in which residents lived or the barriers to them moving anywhere else, but to those residents' newly inflated expectations. In the political environment of California in 1966, Reagan's message was clear. The "cynical promises" of "cynical men" hunting for Black votes, such as by passing the Rumford Act, were the problem, not the realtors' outlawing efforts to end racial discrimination in housing. Raising of hope had been the problem, not shutting the door on it.

Proposition 14 played an even larger role in the political transformation of California in 1966 than anyone expected at the beginning of the campaign. On May 10, a month before the gubernatorial primaries, the California Supreme Court declared Proposition 14 unconstitutional under the Fourteenth Amendment. The case that became *Reitman v. Mulkey*[59] had begun in 1963, when Lincoln and Dorothy Mulkey tried to rent an apartment in Orange County; the landlord, Neil Reitman, refused to rent any of the available apartments to them solely on the grounds of race. When Proposition 14 passed, a trial court held the complaint null and void, but the California Supreme Court took up this case and several parallel ones. One landlord evicted a tenant immediately following passage of Proposition 14, explaining that he no longer wanted to rent to African Americans.[60] Another evicted a white tenant when her new African American husband moved in.[61] None of the landlords disputed the facts: Proposition 14 allowed them to discriminate. But in a 5–2 ruling that stunned the state, the court held the proposition unconstitutional.

In all these cases, the landlords were represented by CREA's major outside counsel, Gibson Dunn and Crutcher, who had drafted Proposition 14. The lead attorney, William French Smith, while overseeing these discrimination cases for CREA, simultaneously served as Ronald Reagan's personal lawyer during his run for governor. Smith had been one of the small group of powerful Southern Californians who in early 1965 urged Reagan to run. Reagan relied closely on Smith, whose advice and guidance had enabled him to make his initial fortune on speculative land investments.[62] Smith served as informal chairman of Reagan's "kitchen cabinet," and, as governor, Reagan would rarely make an important decision without first asking, "Has this been cleared with Bill Smith?"[63]

William French Smith thus served as one of the main links between Proposition 14 and the rise of Ronald Reagan. Smith's argument for CREA to the California Supreme Court, and then to the U.S. Supreme Court, would become the cardinal principle of the civil rights division of the Department of Justice when Reagan appointed Smith attorney general. The department's philosophy under Smith would be crystal clear. Civil rights policies from the 1960s that depended on race-conscious government must be reversed; a government that tried to limit private discrimination would "favor some races over others."[64] Smith's unsuccessful constitutional arguments to defend Proposition 14 would become federal policy.

Ironically, however, in the 1966 campaign, Smith's defeat in his work for CREA proved a major boon to Reagan's election. The California Supreme Court rejected Smith's contention that, since the Fourteenth Amendment did not preclude private discrimination, "the People" of California certainly had a right to vote to allow private discrimination.[65] Indeed, as in *Shelley* and *Barrows v. Jackson*, the key question was not whether the Fourteenth Amendment prohibited private discrimination; all parties agreed that it did not. Nor was there any disagreement that Reitman's discrimination was private. Instead, the majority opinion focused on a single issue: Was state action—voter approval of Proposition 14—"sufficiently involved" in Reitman's ultimate private discrimination to constitute denial of equal protection? The answer, the court held, was yes. The State of California, which was not allowed to discriminate, had, by amending its constitution, "taken affirmative action . . . to make possible private discriminatory practices which previously were prohibited." The method by which CREA had done this, the court admitted, was ingenious. "If discrimination is thus accomplished" by voter enactment, "the ingenuity of those who would seek to conceal [discrimination] by subtleties and claims of neutrality" made no difference.[66] Proposition 14, in other words, was not neutral with respect to discrimination; it did not merely repeal the Rumford Act. Its purpose was "authorizing the perpetration of a purported private discrimination."[67]

If just before the court's decision, Proposition 14 had been a settled issue in California, both legally and politically, it suddenly became very much alive. CREA denounced the ruling as "a deliberate flaunting of the people's will"[68] and announced an appeal to the U.S. Supreme Court.[69] Reagan attacked the court's decision, identifying with millions of voters who asked, as one irate citizen put it, "How can a landslide be cancelled by the State Supreme Court?"[70] Spurred by the California court decision, Reagan shifted from his January position of neutrality on Proposition 14 to making it a central part of his campaign.

Like Goldwater, Reagan had initially sought to keep his distance from the proposition. He had said nothing during CREA's campaign and, in launching his own bid for governor in January 1966, had refused to state any sentiments about Proposition 14 whatsoever.[71] He had acknowledged the legitimacy of the government's prohibiting discrimination in publicly assisted housing, the same formula used by the Rumford Act. By late April, he had shifted. He now opposed both the Rumford Act *and* Proposition 14. He opposed the Rumford Act because it "set a very dangerous precedent," as the realtors had argued, while suggesting that Proposition 14 was not a "wise measure."[72]

Reagan's dance was a delicate one. As the *Los Angeles Times* noted, "Those in both parties . . . tell you that race relations can tip the scales against everything else, hurt the Democrats and help the Republicans—but only if the Republicans can find an effective way to bring it legitimately into political discussion."[73] Reagan, in other words, was dealing with the same dilemma Goldwater had faced: how to attract the support of those who favored Proposition 14 while projecting a nonracist image. It was very important to Reagan to see himself as someone who personally opposed discrimination. In March, at the Republican Black Caucus in Santa Monica, he stormed out of the room when his Republican rival

George Christopher, liberal-moderate former mayor of San Francisco, implied that Reagan had opposed the 1964 Civil Rights Act for racial reasons.[74] Reagan further worried that his having bought a house in 1941 with a racial covenant would eventually come out in the campaign, as it later did.[75] His initial approach on Proposition 14 was therefore to stake out an officially neutral position, while signaling that he understood the desires of white homeowners.

The California court decision changed Reagan's political calculus. He immediately took the side of those who voted for Proposition 14. "The people expressed their feelings in the 1964 election," he said. "All of us are the losers if we allow this [court] precedent to be established."[76] Insisting that he was "against restrictive covenants and anything that smacks of bigotry and discrimination," Reagan attacked the court ruling on the grounds of freedom, denouncing it as "an invasion of the individual's right to his . . . own property." Echoing the realtors, Reagan called the freedom to control one's property "as fundamental as freedom of press and freedom of speech." No court has the "right to take away" that freedom.[77]

The court ruling turned the Rumford Act, forestalled for a year and a half, into a political hot potato. Brown—worrying about the political ramifications of re-enforcing the Rumford Act in the middle of his reelection campaign—argued that because realtors would appeal to the U.S. Supreme Court, Proposition 14 would remain in effect. The Rumford Act would not be enforced.[78] Here was an ironic position for a governor who had fought passionately for the Rumford Act and against Proposition 14. CREA took an equally contrarian position. While absolutely opposed to the Rumford Act, the realtors insisted that it was now back in effect—since this would be "damning" to Brown's reelection.[79] Reagan took CREA's side. The court's ruling, Reagan insisted, required the governor to enforce the Rumford Act,[80] which Reagan, who had remained silent about it for years, now called an "infringement on one of our basic individual rights."[81]

Once Reagan handily defeated Christopher, and Brown defeated Yorty in the early June primary, Reagan, other Republicans, and CREA all worked together to embarrass Brown. CREA insisted that all candidates declare, yes or no, whether they would repeal the Rumford Act. Would they carry out the clear intent of four-and-a-half million voters or not?[82] Brown bobbed and weaved, explaining that, as he had said before Proposition 14 appeared on the ballot, he was open to amending the Rumford Act. Within a few weeks, an old face initiated a new Republican gambit to smoke out Brown.

Frank Doherty, who had led the chamber of commerce's successful 1940s campaigns against fair employment practices with his Committee of Tolerance, was now in his eighties, but as clever a strategist as ever. Doherty announced a new statewide group that would circulate petitions for an initiative to repeal the Rumford Act itself. CREA had rejected such a narrow referendum two years before, but now it served a different, subtler purpose. Even if Doherty's group gained enough signatures, its measure would not go before the legislature until 1967 and not get on the ballot until 1968. Doherty's aim, instead, was that "every candidate will be required to go on record whether or not he would abide by the will of four and a half million citizens."[83] As the *New York Times* recognized, "The real impact is to galvanize and polarize public opinion even more solidly than in 1964. Such polarizing of opinion could be a windfall to Reagan. One prominent Democrat remarked privately 'this could hurt us terribly.'"[84]

Reagan, for his part, now called for abolition of the Rumford Act, while claiming that his concerns and those of voters who had supported Proposition 14 were not racial ones. Rather, the fair housing law had provided a "precedent [that] can be used later to interfere with freedom in other ways."[85] At Reagan's specific insistence, the California Republican Party platform called for repealing or amending the Rumford Act "to protect the free choice and constitutional rights of all citizens."[86] The chairman of the platform committee made clear the importance of this move. "There are not that many registered Republicans in the state. . . . Many Democrats were obviously against Rumford and we want those Democratic votes for our candidates this November."[87] The aim of all these efforts—by CREA, Doherty, Reagan, and the Republican Party— was to not let Brown or the Democratic Party off the hook for having opposed Proposition 14.

The success of this strategy was measured by Brown's response. Once the forceful supporter of the Rumford Act, he now proposed a bipartisan commission to outline changes to the act or its replacement. He connected this approach with Watts, saying that it was "vital to the peace and security of our cities . . . that this political campaign reduce, not increase, the racial fears and tensions that have caused past violence."[88] African American assemblyman Willie Brown charged that the Democratic governor was now "talking like Reagan."[89]

Reagan, meanwhile, sought to appeal to the many Democrats who had voted for Proposition 14. On most issues, Reagan spoke, as one reporter noted, "in moderate accents, avoiding like the plague Goldwater's attacks on social security and the Tennessee Valley Administration."[90] He separated himself from Goldwater and Knowland by telling union workers at a steel mill that he had never supported right to work legislation; indeed, he had been a union member and president of a union, the Screen Actors Guild, for many years.[91] But on the Rumford Act, Reagan became more and more adamant as the campaign went on. Calling the governor's proposed bipartisan commission too little and too late, Reagan conceded that he no longer believed that government had the right to prohibit discrimination in publicly assisted housing. "I got myself tied up on this," he explained. He now argued that there was no possible case—including FHA lending—where open housing should ever exist.[92]

Far from his neutrality on fair housing issues at the beginning of the campaign, Reagan now adopted CREA's entire rhetoric from 1964. His vision of freedom was now theirs. "I have never believed that majority rule has the right to impose on an individual what he does with his property," he said. "This has nothing to do with discrimination. It has to do with our freedom, our basic freedom."[93] He charged that the Rumford Act had been "introduced into the Legislature in the last 6 minutes of the session and forced through hastily and without proper consideration." The claim was so factually exaggerated that even the pro–Proposition 14 *Los Angeles Times* noted that "records show [that the Rumford bill] was introduced early in the session and was the subject of extensive committee hearings."[94]

Speaking to CREA's annual convention, Reagan received standing ovations when he told the realtors that "forced passage of the Rumford Act"—paraphrasing the realtors' own term, "forced housing"—by "a big brother sitting in Sacramento" had "invaded one of our most basic and cherished rights—a right held by all our citizens—the right to dispose of property to whom we see fit. . . . No wonder that at the grass roots the people rebelled."[95] Like the realtors, he acknowledged that the Rumford Act had a humanitarian purpose, but blamed those who tried to end discrimination: "Who can measure the depth of bitterness that was the actual result." It was not Proposition 14 that had contributed to the violence in Watts, Reagan implied, but rather the Rumford Act.

Reagan repeated back to the realtors their own argument that racial discrimination cannot be solved by government. Insisting that we cannot give "one segment of our population rights at the expense of the basic rights of all our citizens," Reagan echoed the realtors' position that government could never protect anyone from discrimination, since that took away others' rights.[96] Never mentioned was that this "basic right" that fair housing took away—and, in Byron Rumford's words, "the only right the proposition confers"—was "the right to discriminate on the basis of race."[97]

Reagan gave Proposition 14 a noble purpose. Most of those who had voted for it, he insisted, "felt [that fair housing] laws violated a sacred constitutional right."[98] If some citizens voted for Proposition 14 out of racial prejudice, "I am sure that the majority did so because government was invading a constitutional right." At this, a reporter noted, "the realtors roared with approval."[99]

Reagan's taking up the realtors' message benefited both himself and the realtors. The realtors' arguments and vision of freedom, perfected during the Proposition 14 campaign, proved invaluable for the neophyte politician. For in starting out his candidacy, Reagan did not have a way of connecting to specific state or local issues that would appeal to California voters. Homeowners' rights had not been part of his vocabulary.[100] He did not yet know how to link race and freedom or appeal to Democratic voters, including union members and racial conservatives, on bread-and-butter issues.

Now, by focusing on and embracing homeowners' rights in his attacks on the Rumford Act, Reagan found a concrete way to appeal to ordinary white Californians. Fair housing was only one of the issues he stressed in his campaign, along with campus unrest, ghetto violence, welfare abuse, and others, but it was a central one. It was the issue on which Brown was most vulnerable. Brown had sought to prevent a vote in the first place, directly opposed the will of the vast majority of Californians, been successfully portrayed as violating their freedom, lost the support of 60 percent of the members of his own party, appointed the supreme court justices who flouted the popular will, and was now running for cover. Proposition 14 was Brown's "albatross."[101] By fall 1966, both parties' campaigns reflected the fact that "fair housing was driving the electorate,"[102] not only as an issue in itself but as a way for conservatives to show that liberal government had little interest in the hard-earned rights of responsible, taxpaying white citizens.

Perhaps most important, Reagan's defense of ownership rights helped him appeal to many Democrats who saw in him and his philosophy a new and more appropriate political home. Ethan Rarick has pointed to this cross-party appeal as "the real genius of the Reagan campaign—the recognition that Democrats were weakest where once they had been strongest." Republicans across the board, far outnumbered both nationally and in California, knew they needed the votes of Democrats and independents, but the question was how to get them. While Nelson Rockefeller tried to appeal to moderates, Reagan, "sensing an underlying anger and resentment among . . . blue-collar workers," appealed instead to this longtime "bastion of Democratic loyalty."[103] Reagan's success in attracting such voters helped cement what Mark Brilliant has called a "tectonic shift" in California, and American, politics that began with Proposition 14.[104]

To attract these voters, Reagan drew on the realtors' years of finding racially neutral ways to justify discrimination, on their arguments for color-blind freedom and freedom of choice that Reagan called "inseparable from . . . freedom itself."[105] He used the realtors' approach not only to attack forced housing but as a general philosophy. The Action Kit's methodology—espousing racial equality and equal rights while treating government protection of such rights as the greatest threat to individual freedom—paid off in Reagan's campaign speeches. "We all have the responsibility to work to end discrimination and insure equal opportunities for all," Reagan argued. "But I am opposed to trying to get this with legislation that violates basic tenets of individual freedom."[106] By embracing the realtors' vocabulary and narrative, Reagan concretized the two abstract philosophies that Americans must choose between in his "Time for Choosing." His opposition to fair housing translated his opposition to big government in general into a gripping and effective political strategy that could be used on many issues.[107]

Reagan proved an ideal champion of the realtors' ideas for the same reason he had been so reluctant to support Proposition 14 in the first place: his fear of appearing racially biased. Running for governor, he described "bigots" as "sick people."[108] "I worked for equality of opportunity," he recounted, "before it ever became the popular issue it is today. I could not consciously use prejudice. I would not patronize any business that discriminated against any human being on the basis of prejudice."[109] His hatred of prejudice had been lifelong, he told audiences. In Dixon, Illinois, with its Ku Klux Klan parades, his mother invited Black families for dinner.[110] He told of giving Black friends a place to stay when a hotel would not take them in.[111] This self-portrayal was not affected by and indeed enabled his indulging, in both public and private, in extraordinarily crude stereotypes of Black people as primitive savages.[112]

Reagan's belief in his own racial innocence, that he himself was not bigoted, had powerful impacts. He viewed discrimination as a matter of individual, moral conscience that could only change through education, not as something that was socially organized or changeable. If he had opposed the 1964 Civil Rights Act and the 1965 Voting Rights Act, it was on constitutional principle. If anyone implied otherwise, he became irate: "I resent the implication that there is bigotry in my nature. Don't anyone ever imply that I lack integrity. I'll not stand by and let anyone imply that—in this or any other group."[113] The California court ruling allowed Reagan to see fair housing as "not a racial issue" but as an "infringement on . . . individual liberty."[114] This, together with his belief in his own racial fairness, now allowed him to make increasingly blunt remarks that he viewed as simple truths: "If an individual wants to discriminate against Negroes or others in selling or renting his house, it is his right to do so."[115] When Reagan argued, on a visit to South Carolina during the campaign, that "No law says the Negro has to live in Harlem or Watts,"[116] this seemed ironic to fair housing supporters; what was Proposition 14 itself but a law preventing African Americans from moving out of Watts?

Reagan could ignore the racially differential impact of his statements and policies precisely because he saw himself as a man of good will.

For voters who did not want to consider themselves as bigoted while supporting a right to discriminate, Reagan embodied how they wanted to see themselves. Reagan understood this role. When a reporter asked, shortly before the 1980 presidential election, what Americans saw in him, Reagan answered, "Would you laugh if I told you that I think, maybe, they see themselves, and that I'm one of them?"[117]

In the 1966 general election, Reagan overwhelmed Brown. His margin, 58%–42%, reversed Brown's margin over Knowland eight years before and Johnson's over Goldwater in 1964. Democrats recognized the impact Proposition 14 had had on union voters. Brown, whose share of such votes dropped from 78 percent against Knowland to 57 percent against Reagan, considered Proposition 14 "a big contributing force" in his defeat.[118] Reagan's victory was widely seen as the most significant election result in the country, one that promised a new, widely appealing brand of conservatism. Like Proposition 14 and the Watts rebellion, Reagan's triumph was an earthquake. Each occurred along the same racial-political fault line in California. While portending new, enormous divisions in the state and country, these tremors reflected stresses that had accumulated for years.

As 1966 ended, realtors in California had reasons to be confident. William French Smith's brief to the U.S. Supreme Court laid out a powerful argument. Until the last few years, no government in America had ever considered interfering in the disposition of private property at all. Why should a state be prohibited from returning to the way things had always been? Upholding *Reitman* would impose an obligation on states to limit discrimination, vastly extending the domain of the Fourteenth Amendment. It would bring "virtually all conduct" of private parties "within the Fourteenth Amendment and subject to appraisal . . . by this Court. Such a holding neither is nor should be the law."[119] It was an argument that would appeal to many of the members of the U.S. Supreme Court.

But even if Smith lost, realtors had a saving grace. Californians had elected a governor who had campaigned against the reinstatement of the Rumford Act. The new governor's personal attorney and head of his transition team was William French Smith. While drafting CREA's appeal, Smith was overseeing establishment of Reagan's new administration in Sacramento, including the appointment of CREA's president as the state's new real estate commissioner. After the vote for Proposition 14 and then for Reagan, no one, and certainly no California legislator, could doubt where the vast majority of Californians and, by extension, Americans, stood on fair housing. CREA and its arguments had helped establish a new political reality.

One of the casualties of that new political reality was Byron Rumford, narrowly defeated in a state senate race during Reagan's 1966 landslide. Asked "Would you do it again?" about the law whose sponsorship had made him infamous for many—had led to his receiving death threats during the Proposition 14 campaign, being guarded on trips to Southern California by the California Highway Patrol, and telling his son to take care of the family "if something happens to me"[120]—Rumford responded simply, "Oh, sure. I think there is no substitute for right. Either we have a Constitution which protects all the citizens or we do not; and if we do not, then we do not have a democratic society. I think it is absolutely necessary that all people have the right to move about freely in this nation, to purchase and," he pointedly added, "to sell."[121] The idea that each right was equally important was what the Property Owners' Bill of Rights and the Proposition 14 campaign had been designed to combat.

Because of the new political reality of fair housing, the key debates on it escalated to the nation's capital, to both Congress and the Supreme Court. Having seen voters reject fair housing laws, advocates wanted a federal law not subject to ballot initiatives or referenda, while realtors took the arguments honed in California to seek a decisive defeat of forced housing.

19.

Realtor Victories against Fair Housing

> Those who are working hardest to repeal fair housing legislation
> are those who made it necessary in the first place.
>
> James K. Strong, 1963[1]

When Spike Wilson launched Proposition 14 as a "crusade for freedom,"
he had no doubt what its national impact would be. "The whole country
is watching," he declared. "And when they see that the people in the leading state in the nation had the courage to stand up and stop the erosion
of individual freedoms threatening this great country of ours . . . we are
going to be proud."[2]

The results of what Wilson labeled "Gettysburg 1964" exceeded
his prediction. Within three months of the vote on Proposition 14, the
Wall Street Journal concluded that "a civil rights campaign to promote
racial integration in housing through enactment of 'fair housing laws'
is shaping up as a failure." The *Journal* pointed to the votes not only in
California but also in Seattle, Tacoma, Akron, and Detroit.[3] For their
part, fair housing proponents, recognizing the vulnerability of all their
efforts, did not give up on state and local legislation but turned more
and more to the courts[4] and to lobbying for a federal open housing law
that would not be subject to referendum. Reeling after the vote on Proposition 14, NCDH telegrammed NAREB almost pleadingly to "appeal to
the realtors to halt the movement against fair housing."[5] Such a change,
indeed any compromise by the realtors, was hardly likely. A week after
the vote, NAREB's president told seven thousand cheering delegates at
their annual convention that NAREB would consider helping associations overturn fair housing laws in the fourteen states that had them.[6]

THE REALTORS' TWO-PART STRATEGY

Following the vote, CREA's president issued a warning to those who had opposed them. "This hard-won victory . . . might remind the Governor he is working for the majority as well as the minority. . . . The people . . . have spoken. For those who doubted this, take heed."[7] Alongside this political threat, CREA told those who had sought fair housing that they should instead work with the realtors in "a program of education" of owners generally to help reduce discrimination "on a voluntary basis, instead of by force and intimidation."[8] If their opponents were sincere, "the effort expended by the opposition . . . should now be directed toward working with CREA and property owners to correct inequities in some areas of our state."[9] CREA's voluntary initiative was a political one.

Realtors throughout the country quickly adopted this two-part strategy of unyielding opposition to "forced housing" together with voluntary "education." Their successful and devastating amendments to proposed fair housing legislation in Ohio illustrate their hard-line stance. NAREB touted these amendments nationally: prohibiting "testers" from ever posing as prospective buyers or renters to check whether discrimination existed, and requiring that anyone complaining of discrimination first post a bond equal to the value of the property.[10] Since such a law could never be practically enforced, NAREB declared that such changes made fair housing acceptable.

The realtors' voluntary programs were designed to complement and support such uncompromising lobbying. The State Associations Steering Committee celebrated the fact that "twenty state associations have started human relations programs and the primary object is to block forced housing laws while at the same time to see that voluntary programs are started or continued."[11] In the same spirit, NAREB sought an "accord" with major church organizations. The accord would commit all parties to ending racial discrimination in housing and enlist churches' support for realtors' voluntary efforts. NAREB's president highly publicly urged all real estate boards to adopt the proposed accord and announced that, having fought against forced housing, realtors had an obligation to solve the problem of open occupancy by voluntary means:

Perhaps we along with all of America are our own victims of long-established policies based upon "separate but equal." Those of my generation have been schooled . . . to believe in . . . racial covenants. . . . While it is difficult for us to reverse our thinking . . . this time has arrived. If we are to be able to save our business, our clients and our country from the ravages of . . . so-called fair housing laws . . ., we must take some positive actions.[12]

Together with this public plea, however, NAREB sent a private letter to local boards explaining that the accord was designed to co-opt church leaders and undercut their support for fair housing legislation, including a possible 1966 federal civil rights law. NAREB could hardly have been clearer: the accord "could be a powerful force in stopping the drive for . . . legislation."[13] When a copy of this letter was leaked, the churches immediately and publicly rejected the accord.

As the church leaders now recognized, the education efforts of realtors to end discrimination were largely for show. As head of Berkeley's board—and president of NAREB—Maurice Read touted to reporters that Berkeley board members "will not take a [racially] restricted listing." But asked if NAREB was pushing all local boards to drop restricted listings, Read demurred. "The time is not ripe for forcing all realtors to practice open occupancy." What was timely and important, NAREB's president insisted, was that NAREB was on record in favor of voluntary equal housing opportunities for all people.[14]

Thus, while proclaiming that "realtors . . . have experienced a complete turn of the wheel in the area of race relations" and that each realtor is "now on notice he should serve clients without limitation by virtue of race," NAREB claimed that it could hardly tell realtors not to discriminate. "To write [such a requirement] into the Code would raise the same questions as forced housing laws—circumscribe the member's right to follow the client's instruction."[15] Left out was the fact that, for more than thirty years, this same NAREB code had *required* every realtor in the country to discriminate.[16]

To show that realtors were not racially biased, Eugene Conser, NAREB's executive secretary, published a series of personal editorials in *Realtor's Headlines*. Conser, with his horn-rimmed glasses and light-colored hair, looked very much the part of a corporate executive—an Organization Man, in the parlance of the era. He framed his weekly columns like those of a skilled public relations executive at General Motors defending its dealers against Ralph Nader's charges, shifting ground as needed. Realtors had once opposed integration, he admitted, but that was long ago, before *Shelley*. While realtors "cannot deny our major responsibility," Conser explained away their actions. They had simply been "applying the then existing public policy of separate but equal" and carrying out neighbors' wishes as "World War I soldiers sought to spread out in to strange neighborhoods not yet prepared to admit 'foreign' appearing individuals."[17] Conser then absolved realtors of discrimination after *Shelley*. They only refused to help minority families because "the resistance of white home owners being at the time [1959] almost universally adamant." At no time, Conser argued in his revisionist history, had NAREB ever "taken a position" against Kennedy's 1962 executive order, ignoring NAREB president Powell's own forceful warning against it.[18]

Realtors, Conser insisted, now had no position against minorities—so long as owners chose to sell to them and, crucially, neighbors did not object. "As discussion of moral and ethical aspects of discrimination proceeds among neighbors," Conser stated, "additional families will sell on an open basis—realizing that if done with the knowledge of neighbors, it can be accomplished without damage due to an exodus from the area."[19] Put more directly, neighbors—whom realtors relied on for their future business—must always have a veto over minorities being allowed to buy in a white neighborhood. To any realtor reading these words, the message was clear: here in the language of discussion and morality and ethics was the same system of racial discrimination and steering realtors had used since *Shelley*. Nothing had changed.

Finally, Conser insisted on the purity of the realtors' motives. They had defended owners against forced housing not for racial reasons at all, but to protect "a right historically present in Anglo-Saxon common law . . . separate and far beyond the limits of any racial issue." Yet for simply standing up for others' freedom, realtors had "encountered the most formidable organized campaign of vilification."[20] Since "property owners and home owners are not organized," realtors "have been their spokesmen and protectors of their interests . . . choos[ing] to stand for freedom of thought . . . speech . . . contract."[21]

But while realtors depicted themselves as not being discriminatory, as only acting on behalf of owners, their own statistics showed how small a role the freedom of choice of sellers actually played. CREA had testified in the California Senate in 1963 that out of twenty thousand listings in the San Fernando Valley, only five owners restricted their listings.[22] A year after Proposition 14, to showcase the success of their voluntary education program, CREA asked all 176 local boards to report how many home listings under realtors' multiple listing service were racially restricted by owners. The answer was very few indeed, less than .6 of 1 percent. CREA reported these results glowingly as showing that "the owner is not using [Proposition 14's] freedom to discriminate against buyers of another race."[23]

But the results made clear that if owners were not discriminating, only two things were possible. Either residential discrimination had almost entirely disappeared in the state of California after Proposition 14 formally legalized it—or discrimination was being carried out not in obedience to owners' written instructions but by realtors *on their own*. CREA and NAREB argued that discrimination was almost nonexistent. "Discrimination Absent in Most House Sales, CREA Study Finds," *Realtor's Headlines* touted across the country.[24] The reality for African Americans was that discrimination had not disappeared; in many cases, it had become more blatant than ever, as the Reitman and other lawsuits starkly demonstrated.

Discrimination, as the tiny number of restricted listings made clear, was rarely initiated by the seller; this had always been true. Discrimination had been, and remained, the realtor's job. Beneath the cover of seller's freedom of choice was the right of realtors to discriminate. NAREB had said as much in celebrating its decisive victory in California: "We call [Proposition 14] . . . to the attention of other states where the freedom of real estate practice may be imperiled."[25] Here was the freedom that most affected realtors.

The importance to realtors of their freedom to discriminate became abundantly clear in their reactions to the civil rights bill that President Johnson announced in early 1966. For the battle that unfolded in

Washington in these years pitted the realtors' newfound political clout against a wily, powerful president committed to fair housing. It was a conflict in which each side would hold little back.

THE DEFEAT OF TITLE IV

Almost as soon as he became president after Kennedy's assassination in November 1963, Lyndon Johnson wanted to make fair housing a national priority. Having pledged to end housing discrimination in his first State of the Union address, Johnson wanted to introduce such provisions in the 1964 federal civil rights bill. His advisors and congressional allies warned him of the risks. To beat back filibusters by Southern senators and bring any civil rights legislation to the Senate floor, Johnson would need sixty votes for cloture from Northern senators. This would require broad support by both Democrats and Republicans. Active, mobilized opposition from realtors in virtually every Northern state, through both direct lobbying and the enlistment of neighborhood associations and legions of homeowners, would make it virtually impossible to obtain such support. Fair housing was therefore left out of the 1964 Civil Rights Act.

After the overwhelming vote for Proposition 14, Johnson's advisors, including Attorney General Nicholas Katzenbach, persuaded him not to pursue fair housing in 1965 but to concentrate instead solely on voting rights in the South. In 1966, despite Katzenbach's warning that a fair housing bill was unlikely to pass because many members believed they would lose their seats if they voted for it,[26] Johnson proceeded nonetheless. In his first State of the Union address after Watts, Johnson called on Congress to "declare resoundingly that discrimination in housing and all the evils it breeds are a denial of justice and a threat to the development of our growing urban areas."[27] As had Martin Luther King in his campaigning against Proposition 14, Johnson made the case for ending housing discrimination as a matter of freedom, stating, "We must give the Negro the right to live in freedom among his fellow Americans."[28]

The provisions of the 1966 civil rights bill challenged the realtors directly. Title IV aimed much of its focus at discrimination by brokers, including the realtors' multiple listing service. In response, NAREB and state associations mounted a full-court attack. NAREB issued a "Call to Action" on the front page of *Realtor's Headlines*, directly addressing members across the country: "You, personally, and your sales people, are threatened by a bill to impose restrictions against which you cannot protect yourself. . . . [The bill] could result in alienation of your clients, blasting of your reputation and destruction of your business. You will be prohibited from following your client's instructions to limit his tenant or purchaser to a certain racial . . . group."[29] Here was the danger realtors feared most: *they* would not be able to discriminate, but owners would be able to do so without them.

Moreover, as NAREB set in boldface, "any member of a minority group . . . would have a right of access to all multiple listing fields." Realtors would not be able to racially limit listings or prohibit minority brokers from joining local boards.[30] State associations lashed out at this provision: "'Discrimination' will be heard when an applicant for board membership is rejected. The public image of realtor is poured down the drain by being forced by government coercion to throw the doors open to any and all."[31] By focusing on real estate agents, NAREB argued, the bill was "more oppressive" than a total ban on housing discrimination.[32] NAREB therefore called on all realtors to "generate an immediate wave of indignation by all citizens" to defeat Title IV so decisively "as to end for all time any attempt to accomplish this objective through federal law."[33]

NAREB unleashed all its formidable lobbying power, arranging for a deluge of letters to members of Congress, testifying in both houses, and supplying arguments to Sam Ervin, chair of the Senate committee dealing with the bill, as well as Everett Dirksen, Senate minority leader.

NAREB sent out red, white, and blue flyers with a picture of an American eagle to millions of homeowners across the country, urging them to contact their legislators, that their rights were in danger: a federal court may order "you to sell or rent to a person not of your choice. It may also assess unlimited damages against you. . . . All because you want to defend your freedom of choice."[34]

NAREB repeated the arguments that had proven so successful in the Proposition 14 campaign. Realtors were "not against . . . equal opportunity"; "the real issue" was freedom.[35] They invoked freedom of religion to justify discrimination. Because citizens have "the right to accept or reject the Deity as their . . . convictions may dictate, [how can] government . . . compel the acceptance of one's fellow men in our private lives?"[36] Once more linking forced housing to the causes of the American Revolution, realtors pictured the attorney general about to "reach into a private home, unlatch the door and proclaim to the owner" whom he must sell to.[37] *"This must not be,"* NAREB declared.[38] "If this act is passed, we may as well repeal the Bill of Rights."[39]

While focusing on freedom of choice, realtors invoked freedom of association as well. Senator Ervin of North Carolina approvingly quoted the president of the Missouri realtors' association that "people of a given racial group tend to cleave to themselves. This is not a matter of bigotry or hatred."[40] Testifying on behalf of the right-wing Liberty Lobby, Alfred Avins dismissed fair housing as only helping the "relatively small percentage of Negroes who are in the upper income brackets . . . [the] social climbers. . . . Invoking such laws for their benefit is like enforcing minimum wage legislation for Elizabeth Taylor."[41] This ignored the fact that the beneficiaries of most fair housing cases were moderate-income renters.

Realtors took every opportunity to remind Congress of the vote on Proposition 14. Few members needed to be reminded. In the House of Representatives, with all members up for reelection in November, realtors were able to weaken the fair housing provisions considerably. An administration official hinted to the *New York Times* about its dilemma: "If we get the bill passed it's a fraud, but if we don't it looks like another racial insult."[42]

The battle now moved to the Senate. The senators who realtors most needed to convince were Northern Republicans. Realtors' arguments, the *Christian Science Monitor* noted, found "receptive ears in both Republican and Southern Democratic camps. Thus the old 'conservative coalition'—so seldom in fighting form in this 89th Congress—is shaping up once more." The realtors' claims were key to this alliance: "The tie that binds [the coalition] . . . is what . . . [a] realtor called 'this precious right that has always been held sacred—the right to buy and sell property as one sees fit.'"[43] If Republicans did not help end the Southern Democratic filibuster, the bill would die.

Victory or defeat therefore turned, as it had for the 1964 federal civil rights bill, on Republican Senate minority leader Everett Dirksen from Illinois, a business conservative who analyzed legislation closely and focused on his view of its constitutionality. While he had helped craft the ultimate version of the 1964 civil rights bill, and had similarly modified and ultimately supported the 1965 Voting Rights Act,[44] Dirksen had far more qualms about fair housing. He had closely followed the battle over Proposition 14[45] and quoted realtors' testimony: Title IV, he said, "seeks to take away rights from a large segment of the population and to vest minority groups with a special privilege." This was not why senators were elected, Dirksen insisted. "This Congress is [not] authorized under the Constitution, however piously or altruistically motivated, to dilute or take away the rights of one single American."[46] Although Dirksen had been willing to support the 1964 Civil Rights Act based on Congress's power to regulate interstate commerce, he was not going to use the commerce clause to restrict an individual homeowner. The Illinois senator famously declared, in words that would come back to haunt him, "If you can tell me what in interstate commerce is involved about selling a house fixed on soil . . ., I'll eat the chimney."[47]

With Dirksen and most Senate Republicans unwilling to vote for cloture, the 1966 civil rights bill was doomed. The Leadership Conference on Civil Rights summed up the difficulty: the mood of many Northern members was "one of apprehension and timidity"; they were anxious "about voter reaction . . . and the pressures of the real estate lobby."[48] Just as Proposition 14 represented Governor Brown's most devastating loss on any issue, Title IV gave President Johnson his "most crushing legislative defeat as President."[49] Both had come at the hands of the realtors.

20.

To Defeat the Realtors

> The Negro in America henceforth is a free man.
>
> *Realtor's Headlines*, 1968[1]

To defeat the realtors—with their ability to mobilize millions of homeowners and other constituents, their allies, lobbyists and lawyers, their appeal to freedom, and the specter of Proposition 14—would not be easy. Before they would accept fair housing, it would take multiple Supreme Court decisions, Lyndon Johnson's wiliness in lulling them into inaction, the impact of the Tet Offensive in Vietnam, Martin Luther King's assassination, and riots and rebellions in one hundred American cities. Machine gunners were stationed on the steps of the Capitol, and 13,600 federal troops occupied Washington when Congress decided the fate of federal fair housing.

This far-reaching battle over where Americans could live, which now reached its climax, was summed up in a 1967 debate between John Schmitz—Orange County's ultraconservative California state senator, John Birch Society member, and later congressman—and Rumford. Forced housing, Schmitz warned, "violates the right of contract, the soul of the free market economy." "There is an even greater contract," Rumford responded, "the contract under which we got this society together. This is a contract to treat everybody equally."[2]

LOREN MILLER'S VINDICATION

With the failure to pass Title IV in 1966, fair housing proponents and realtors turned to the pending battle in the U.S. Supreme Court, CREA's appeal of *Reitman v. Mulkey* in spring 1967. Loren Miller, who had conceived of the subtle constitutional argument against Proposition 14 before it was placed on the ballot, and that had prevailed in the California Supreme Court, lived to see the final outcome shortly before his death in July.

Realtors had argued from the beginning that the proposition was not state action since it "does not call upon the state to enforce private prejudice; it merely requires the state to remain neutral."[3] This was William French Smith and his colleagues' argument to the U.S. Supreme Court: Proposition 14 simply "authorizes . . . freedom of the property owner to act in accordance with his conscience."[4]

On questions of racial discrimination under the Fourteenth Amendment, the justices were split into a liberal wing, led by William O. Douglas, and a conservative one, whose most forceful advocate was John Marshall Harlan II. Although the grandson and namesake of the one Supreme Court justice who had dissented in the separate-but-equal decision *Plessy v. Ferguson* in 1896, Harlan was the strongest defender of states' rights and a narrow view of the Fourteenth Amendment. CREA had repeatedly invoked Harlan's argument against demonstrators sitting in at lunch counters in the South: "Freedom of the individual to choose his associates or his neighbors, to use and dispose of his property as he sees fit . . . are things all entitled to a large measure of protection from government interference. This liberty would be overridden, in the name of equality, if the strictures of the [Fourteenth] amendment were applied to governmental and private action without distinction."[5] Realtors especially cited Harlan's conclusion that "there are areas of private rights upon which the federal power should not lay a heavy hand."[6]

Given the split on the court, the decision turned on the views of Justice Byron "Whizzer" White, a former All-American football player and relatively conservative Democrat appointed by President Kennedy. White conceded that the state was "permitted a neutral position with respect to private racial discriminations." California was not bound by the Fourteenth Amendment to prohibit private discrimination. Simply repealing the Rumford and Unruh Acts would not have violated the Fourteenth Amendment.[7]

But Proposition 14 went much further, White pointed out. As Loren

Miller had argued three years earlier, Proposition 14 authorized and "announced the constitutional right" to discriminate. Under the realtors' sweeping amendment, private discrimination was "not only free from Rumford and Unruh but . . . enjoyed a far different status than before the passage of those statutes. The right to discriminate . . . on racial grounds, was now embodied in the State's basic charter, immune from legislative, executive or judicial regulation." White thus reached the crucial issue. "Those practicing racial discriminations," such as Reitman, "could now invoke express constitutional authority." California had thus authorized discrimination and made "the right to discriminate . . . one of the basic policies of the State."[8] By a 5–4 decision, the court ruled that Wilson and CREA had gone too far.

In his concurring opinion, Justice Douglas went out of his way to take the realtors to task for the role they played in establishing and maintaining segregation. Segregation had little to do with individuals discriminating, he said; "This is not a case as simple as the one where a man with a bicycle or car or . . . even a log cabin asserts the right to sell it to whomever he pleases, excluding all others whether they be Negroes, Chinese . . . Baptists or those with blue eyes." Proposition 14 was intended, like racial covenants, to effectively keep entire areas Caucasian. "Real estate brokers . . . are largely dedicated to the maintenance of segregated communities," rejecting minorities "who try to break the white phalanx." Proposition 14, Douglas concluded, "is a form of sophisticated discrimination whereby the people of California harness the energies of private groups to do indirectly" what, under *Buchanan v. Warley*, their government cannot.

Taking umbrage with realtor warnings that fair housing brings Americans "much closer to a centralized government in which ultimately the right to own property would be denied," Douglas pointed out that this right to own property is "already denied to many solely because of the pigment of their skin." Moreover, Douglas argued, the realtors who were effectively zoning "our cities into white and black belts" were in fact state licensees. Licensing private entities to practice racial discrimination, Douglas argued, constituted "state action in the narrowest sense" of *Shelley v. Kraemer*.[9]

CREA attacked Justice Douglas's image of realtors, calling his cynicism "disheartening." It was the same cynicism realtors had railed against in the campaign, "that cannot see unselfish motives for CREA's support of Proposition 14, even though our members spent countless hours of their time, effort and money for the benefit of property owners and not themselves." Douglas, not the realtors, was indulging in bigotry, CREA argued, to believe that the realtors' effort was "for the benefit of the white race only," since "the proposition gave the same freedom of choice equally to all."[10] CREA's argument was aimed not so much at Douglas or the Supreme Court but at the issue the court's decision had reopened in the California legislature.

THE RUMFORD ACT UNDER REAGAN

How would the legislature deal with the Rumford Act that realtors and millions of voters thought they had killed and the Supreme Court had revived? With Reagan as governor and legislators fully aware of the will of the vast majority of Californians, CREA seemed confident of their chances to either repeal the Rumford Act outright or at least remove any of its enforcement powers.

Hearings by the bipartisan Governor's Commission on the Rumford Act, which had been appointed by Brown after the state supreme court decision, reprised many of the issues of the campaign. Realtors who had opposed Proposition 14 came forth. Real estate listings do not preclude Communists, prostitutes, crime syndicate members, or child molesters, one dissident realtor pointed out, only Negroes.[11] The old textbook claim was wrong: white gangsters and madams would, in fact, have an easier time getting into a white neighborhood than a "colored man of means." Another dissident realtor argued that the Rumford Act was, in fact, "in harmony with the free enterprise system," while restrictive housing efforts thwarted free enterprise.[12] Howard Lewis, who had forcefully opposed Proposition 14, suggested that the Rumford Act should be amended to focus only on rental properties, since single-family homes are "the 'albatross' which conjures up visceral opposition and only 3% of complaints."[13] Here would be a way forward without the same political opposition.

The other side, however, voiced intense opposition to government coercion. Government should "listen to the voice of the people," and whom government should be listening to was clear: "Remember the taxpayer, the honest citizen." Along with realtors' racially neutral–sounding arguments about "everybody having equal rights and not taking them away to give to another,"[14] the Apartment Owners Association depicted American history as a fight for freedom of association: "Down through the ages, men have given their lives . . . to preserve their right . . . to choose . . . the associations they enjoy." If one wanted to end discrimination, what was needed was "a massive public relations effort to improve the image of ethnic people in the eyes of John Q. Public," suggesting that John Q. Public was different from ethnic people.[15] Few people's minds, it seemed, had changed since the battles over Proposition 14.

In the legislature itself, although many legislators who had voted for the Rumford Act had been chastened, if not defeated, remaining supporters were not willing to eliminate the provisions they had fought for. The result was a stalemate, one that Governor Reagan was unwilling to use any of his political capital to break. Reagan had ridden the issue into office and would continue to sound defiant when he spoke at CREA's convention in fall 1967, arguing that fair housing laws violated fundamental property rights.[16] But now that he was governor, and with an eye on the presidency, Reagan sought to avoid getting involved in the housing discrimination issue.

If, as Pat Brown believed, Reagan was "riding the backlash" generated by Proposition 14 and the Watts riot and was "contributing to it,"[17] it was that much more important to Reagan not to be seen as a segregationist or extremist. If CREA did not pursue the idea of a referendum to eliminate the Rumford Act, it was perhaps because there was neither a governor who would support such an effort nor one, as with Brown, whom CREA could run a campaign against.

The result was that the Rumford Act—which had triggered Proposition 14, driven two election campaigns, been the subject of landmark battles in both the California and U.S. Supreme Courts, and, in CREA's words, "relegated freedom" in California "to the history books"—simply remained in place. Realtors could take some comfort that, as a result of their campaign, California's fair housing law—limited in its coverage and modest in its penalties compared to many other states' laws—was not strengthened or supplemented as had happened in New York and other states. In applying the Rumford Act, the Fair Employment Practices Commission, chastened by the vote on Proposition 14, rarely invoked penalties.

If Spike Wilson and CREA had overreached themselves legally, they had created a new political and ideological reality. The Rumford Act might have been resurrected, but throughout the country many politicians believed it was dangerous and perhaps suicidal to support fair housing. New federal fair housing legislation would test this assumption in 1968.

JOHNSON AGAINST THE REALTORS, THE FINAL ROUND

The administration focused on a single problem in trying yet again to pass fair housing: How could they bring the bill forward before realtors could mobilize? How could they blindside the realtors?

The new strategy was therefore the opposite of that used for every prior civil rights bill. Instead of spending months outlining, announcing, and holding lengthy hearings on key provisions, and seeking passage in the House to build support before taking on a Southern filibuster in the Senate, the administration did just the reverse. The House passed a narrow civil rights bill limited to protecting the safety of civil rights workers in the South. The bill said nothing about housing. The Senate Judiciary Committee approved this House bill. Again there was no reason for realtors to organize. Then, once this bill was already on the Senate floor and being filibustered, Walter Mondale, Democrat from Minnesota, and Edward Brooke, Republican from Massachusetts, the only African American senator, suddenly added a broad, new, unrelated amendment prohibiting discrimination in selling or leasing property. By a quick vote, the bill for civil rights workers in the South suddenly became enormous, and Title VIII fair housing its primary purpose.

The question now was how to achieve sixty votes for cloture. Although Minority Leader Dirksen had opposed fair housing legislation in 1966 and now voted initially against cloture, he worked with the attorney general and the Democratic Senate leadership to create a compromise, "the Dirksen Substitute," that could then be passed with Republican and Northern Democratic support. This same approach had led to the victory of the 1964 Civil Rights Act. In that case, however, Dirksen's changes had left the key provisions intact.[18] His changes to fair housing were more substantive, providing exemptions for individual homeowners and weakening administrative enforcement.[19] After three unsuccessful efforts at cloture with its own version, the administration accepted Dirksen's substitute.

An astute observer of what was acceptable on Main Street and a gauge of the center of American public opinion, Dirksen had shifted his ground. Asked why he had changed his position from his unyielding opposition to fair housing only two years before, the senator replied tellingly, "One would be a strange creature indeed in this world of mutation if in the face of reality he did not change his mind."[20] Speaking a month after the Tet Offensive in Vietnam, he said, "I do not want to worsen . . . the restive condition in the United States. There are young men of all colors and creeds who are this night fighting 12,000 miles away. . . . They will return. They will have families. . . . Unless there is fair housing . . . I do not know what the measure of their unappreciation would be for the ingratitude of their fellow citizens."[21]

Others too who had fought strenuously against fair housing began to drop their opposition. The largest paper in Dirksen's home state, the staunchly probusiness *Chicago Tribune*, which had vociferously attacked the 1966 legislation, said nothing about the 1968 bill.[22]

Dirksen's sudden change of heart took realtors by surprise. They "had no idea the bill could go through the Senate," a Senate staff member reported. "The whole time we were debating the bill I didn't see a real estate lobbyist or any real estate mail." Compared to all previous civil rights legislation, the bill now moved with lightning speed. There had been no hearings on the fair housing provisions in either the House or Senate, and NAREB only began to lobby after cloture in mid-March.[23] The realtors had lost any chance of stopping the bill in the Senate.

If NAREB suddenly issued alarms—"A Time for Indignation—and Action" to combat "this tragic 'compromise' legislation"[24]—what disturbed realtors the most was Dirksen's *exemption* of individual owners while penalizing brokers who discriminated. The bill would apply to federally assisted housing immediately. Starting December 31, 1968, it would prohibit discrimination against minority brokers seeking to become realtors or accessing the realtors' multiple listing service. The even more crucial date was December 31, 1969. After that, homeowners could no longer use a broker if they wanted to discriminate.

Senator Harry Byrd Jr. of Virginia had desperately sought an amendment to allow brokers to continue to discriminate on behalf of a client, but had been defeated 38–56.[25] Thus, when the final bill was reported out of the Senate, NAREB was vitriolic. The "most amazing development" for realtors was "that a homeowner's right to dispose of his property to persons of choice will remain intact. However [the owner] can't employ an agent or broker." Realtors revived their cry from Proposition 14, but now it applied to themselves: "No better example of granting one person a right at the expense of another can be found than . . . in the so-called civil rights bill."[26] Instead of minority rights coming at the expense of white homeowners, they would come at the expense of realtors. The mask had slipped: instead of being able to claim they were defending the ordinary individual homeowner—the great power of their rhetoric in Proposition 14—realtors now had to show that they were nakedly defending their own self-interest.

However alarmed, NAREB was still confident that it would have an opportunity to stop the bill. The Senate bill sent to the House in late March was almost entirely different from the limited bill protecting civil rights workers that the House had previously approved. Realtors argued that the entirely new provisions required extensive hearings in the House.

But in the House, NAREB found that probusiness Republicans who had "voted against forced housing in 1966 have hesitantly indicated that perhaps 'political realities' now dictate a forced housing bill." Even as it warned congressmen of the political cost of supporting fair housing, of the "overwhelming views of American people in referendums," NAREB asked: "What . . . political realities? Should the rights of American homeowners be bargained away for the hope of political gain in the great urban centers?"[27]

Despite having been outmaneuvered and having hardly begun to lobby, realtors still believed they could garner enough support in the House to stop the lower chamber from simply accepting the Senate bill as its own. If the Senate bill went to conference with the House—almost always the case with entirely different pieces of legislation, where the central subject of one chamber's bill had not been considered by the other—realtors could weaken or strike the fair housing provisions.[28]

NAREB therefore hastily put together arguments that could be used in a full-blown debate and lobbying effort in the House. Drawing on Proposition 14, they cited coercion, "totalitarian concepts and total state control,"[29] and argued that the bill would "override liberty in the name of equality."[30] On March 27, to support its last-ditch battle, NAREB's Washington Committee decided on a massive grassroots letter-writing campaign—but one that would not be publicly linked to the real estate industry. NAREB made a special appropriation from its "Civil Liberties Reserve," established to fend off antidiscrimination legislation, to fund an outside group in the "enlistment to this cause of . . . the American people of all walks of life."[31] NAREB's key ally, Gerald Ford, House Republican minority leader and later president, had begun putting together a growing conservative coalition to oppose Title VIII,[32] when the House adjourned for its Easter recess for the first week of April 1968.

Before the week was out, however, King's assassination in Memphis electrified the country. Only a few weeks before the murder, the report of the Kerner Commission—the National Advisory Commission on Civil Disorders during the summer of 1967—had warned of a "system of apartheid" in the nation's cities, and of the country "moving toward two societies, one black, one white—separate and unequal."[33] No one, white or Black, now knew what the silencing of the leading advocate for nonviolent change would mean for this racial divide. In just a few days, violence consumed sections of one hundred cities. Twelve hundred buildings burned in the nation's capital alone; rioting had come within two blocks of the White House. Smoke, bitterness, and fear lingered in the air. On the day after King's death, President Johnson urged the House to accept the Senate bill immediately, partly as a memorial to King but, more important, as a way to address the anger and frustration in Black communities across the country.

Monday morning, the day after King's funeral, as troops and jeeps

Troops at U.S. Capitol, April 1968

stood guard outside the Capitol and as the House reconvened, the Rules Committee scheduled a floor vote on the Senate bill under extraordinary procedures: one hour for debate, no amendments. Walter Mondale, who had floor-managed the legislation in the Senate and called fair housing the most filibustered bill in history, reflected on this moment of crisis, "They didn't dare. They didn't dare hold it up."[34] Ford led the fight against the bill. He argued for a conference committee with the Senate, in which the fair housing provisions could be lobbied over, changed, or stripped out, giving realtors the time to mobilize across the country. He was arguing for normal procedures in what were extraordinary times. This key vote was relatively close, 225 to 196. The law passed the next day.[35]

VOWING TO FIGHT BACK

Realtors lambasted passage under these conditions, calling it surrender to lawless protest. Eugene Conser likened Title VIII itself to the riots that had helped bring about its passage. Both were attacks on private property as the foundation of American freedom. "This has been a sad ten days for America," he lamented. "We have awakened to find that 'it can happen here.' . . . The United States of America will never be the same after this week of violence. . . . Private ownership of property is under attack—subtly but vigorously."[36]

Conser condemned those who would take away the rights of private property: "Let us recognize that there are those who would make America worse. They may be subtle, clever, unscrupulous, audacious and intellectually rich, but they cannot overcome the mass of Americans who would make America better without tearing it apart or tearing it down. Beware of those who choose to tear it apart—irrespective of the label under which they march."[37] Even more bitterly, NAREB attacked the slain Martin Luther King, while acknowledging that realtors would have to obey the new law. "Unlike Martin Luther King, this Association holds that laws are to be observed. . . . [To not do so] violates the code of ethics."[38]

NAREB would not, however, accept the finality of the new law. Its editorial "Living with Law" was defiant. "This does not mean . . . that laws that are unfair or inequitable or unconstitutional should be allowed to stand without any effort to change, correct, or have them withdrawn."[39] NAREB issued a warning, not to those who might resist the new law, but to those who might seek to take advantage of it: "This is no time for agitators and extremists—hate-mongers on the left. . . . Not satisfied with federal law, [they] may try to get a law in every hamlet and village and state."[40] Realtors wanted to stave off any new state and local fair housing laws that would go beyond federal rules.

As their Washington Committee regrouped in May 1968, NAREB was determined to use all its resources to fight back: "We have lost the battle not the war." What troubled realtors most, however, was the compromise that had temporarily exempted homeowners and put the immediate burden on themselves. Worried that "many small brokers might well be out of business by the effective date of the Act," some local boards were urging NAREB to push for an open housing law that "covers everyone without exception." "[Put] the welfare of the brokers above that of the homeowner or at least on an equal basis."[41]

Placed in this political and economic bind, how should NAREB counter? Concerned about publicly pushing to penalize homeowners, the realtors' Washington Committee decided instead to support candidates in the November election who would repeal the "onerous provision which denies to a home owner the right of freedom of contract to employ the services of a real estate broker." That is, realtors could best support their own interests by presenting themselves as essential to the freedom of homeowners.[42]

ULTIMATE DEFEAT

But NAREB's resistance to Title VIII changed dramatically two months later. Realtors' warnings that they might challenge the law's constitutionality, seek to change or weaken it, or minimally comply with "the least disruption to the economic and social order," fell apart when the Supreme Court decided *Jones v. Mayer* in June 1968.[43] The court's ruling prohibited *all* racial residential discrimination in the United States, whether or not federal or state fair housing laws applied. It used a novel and entirely different basis for outlawing discrimination. The confined framework within which the legal and political battles over discrimination had been fought for the past fifty years, and the legal assumptions that realtors had relied on, suddenly seemed no more solid than a house of cards.

Jones v. Mayer tested a new legal theory for prohibiting private discrimination. When the Alfred H. Mayer Company, the largest developer in St. Louis, refused to sell a home in a new, major suburban subdivision to Joseph Lee and Barbara Jones because the husband was Black, the couple sued in federal court. They could not cite federal involvement in the project under Kennedy's executive order, nor had there been any state action under the Fourteenth Amendment.

Jones's attorney sued instead under the 1866 Civil Rights Act, a Reconstruction-era statute that had rarely been used, or even referred to, for ninety years. The 1866 act had been passed to implement the Thirteenth Amendment prohibiting slavery, and had never been repealed. It gave all citizens the same rights to acquire property as white citizens: "All citizens of the United States shall have the same right, in every State and Territory, as is enjoyed by white citizens thereof to inherit, purchase, lease, sell, hold, and convey real and personal property."[44] Jones's lawyer argued that the act thus prohibited discrimination both by private parties and by the state. Indeed, the 1866 act spelled out that it applied notwithstanding "any law, statute, ordinance, regulation, or custom," with custom presumably meaning any pattern of private economic behavior.[45]

Yet no court had ever interpreted the act to prohibit private residential discrimination. The reason lay in its complex origins and related Supreme Court rulings. The Thirteenth Amendment had declared, in two brief sentences, that "neither slavery nor involuntary servitude, except as a punishment for crime . . . shall exist within the United States" and authorized Congress "to enforce this article by appropriate legislation." As soon as this antislavery amendment was passed in 1865, however, Southerners devised a wide range of means to effectively reduce newly freed African Americans to serfdom. Owners refused to sell land to them, and employers refused to hire freedmen except under onerous contracts. Southern legislatures established local laws, "Black Codes," that made it illegal for freedmen to work for themselves or to not be employed under a contract by a white man; a freedman not under such a contract would be convicted of vagabondage and subject to forced labor by the state.

Outraged Northern Republicans passed the Civil Rights Act in 1866 to put a stop to these practices that vitiated the Thirteenth Amendment. When President Andrew Johnson vetoed the bill, it became the first major legislation ever passed over a presidential veto. After the Fourteenth Amendment was ratified in 1868, Congress re-passed the exact same Civil Rights Act, presumably to give it the protection of the Fourteenth as well as Thirteenth Amendments. After Congress passed a separate, additional civil rights law in 1875 to prohibit discrimination in public accommodations, the complaint of Loren Miller's granduncle Bird Gee for not being served in a hotel dining room went all the way to the Supreme Court. Striking down the 1875 law, in the Civil Rights Cases, the court ruled that Congress's power to prohibit slavery was limited to *state* acts of discrimination in accordance with the Fourteenth Amendment.[46] Here the matter had lain for ninety years. The 1866 act still remained on the books. It had not been ruled unconstitutional, but realtors and others had assumed that it added nothing to the Fourteenth Amendment.

In asking the Supreme Court to consider *Shelley v. Kraemer* in 1948, plaintiffs had applied for certiorari under both the Fourteenth Amendment, that judicial enforcement constituted state action, and under the 1866 Civil Rights Act, that Congress had prohibited private housing discrimination. The court granted certiorari only on Fourteenth Amendment grounds, without ever ruling on the Civil Rights Act.

By raising the 1866 act in *Jones v. Mayer*, attorney Samuel Liberman II, thirty-three years old and a new partner at his St. Louis law firm, was asking the federal courts to set an entirely new basis for banning *private discrimination* everywhere. His argument ran exactly counter to the realtors in Proposition 14: the 1866 act was intended to "create certain positive rights for Negro citizens which . . . it considered to be the fundamental rights of citizenship. . . . The right to enforce a contract in court would be valueless, if no one would contract with a Negro."[47] Although the case involved a major private developer, the same logic would apply not merely to organized discrimination but to every individual homeowner.

The stakes involved were not lost on Harry Blackmun, later a Supreme Court justice, when he ruled on the case for the Eighth Circuit Court of Appeals in Minneapolis in 1967. He wrote, "This case comes close to raising nakedly the question, whether in the absence of . . . open housing legislation, an owner of a home, . . . on the market for sale, may refuse to sell . . . to a willing purchaser merely because that purchaser is a Negro."[48] Given the enormous implications, the related nineteenth-century court decisions, and the lack of any favorable Supreme Court decision, Blackmun did not believe that a lower court could or should rule for the Joneses. But as he admitted to his colleagues, he *wanted* the Supreme Court to reverse him. "[I] spelled out precisely how the decision could be reached" and "served the issues up on a plate . . . for the Supreme Court to take."[49] Blackmun's opinion could hardly have been more specific: "It would not be too surprising if the Supreme Court one day were to hold that a court errs when it dismisses a complaint of this kind. It could do so by asserting that [the Civil Rights Act] was, because of its derivation from the 13th Amendment, free of the shackles of state action. . . . It could do so . . . on the ground . . . that Congress has acted through [the Civil Rights Act] to reach private discrimination in housing."[50]

By a 7–2 decision, the Supreme Court followed Blackmun's reasoning and therefore overruled his decision. Justice Potter Stewart, one of the conservative justices who had supported Proposition 14 in *Reitman v. Mulkey*, concluded that, unlike fair housers' efforts to stretch the state action provisions of the Fourteenth Amendment, the language of the 1866 Civil Rights Act was clear on its face. The act "bars *all* racial discrimination in the sale or rental of property and . . . the statute thus construed is a valid exercise of the power of Congress to enforce the Thirteenth Amendment." The statute itself, almost entirely ignored for all these decades, "in plain and unambiguous terms . . . grants to all citizens, without regard of race or color, 'the same right' to purchase and lease property as is enjoyed by white citizens." Therefore, and here was the crucial point, "whenever property is placed on the market for whites only, whites have a right denied to Negroes."[51] What realtors had been doing since 1905 was illegal.

The court's majority rejected Mayer's argument that the Civil Rights Act had only been aimed at state discrimination, that Congress had only been concerned with the Black Codes themselves. Congress "had before it an imposing body of evidence pointing to the mistreatment of Negroes by private individuals and unofficial groups . . . unrelated to . . . hostile state legislation."[52] The act meant what it said. The Supreme Court had, almost a century later, effectively overturned the Civil Rights Cases that had helped marked the end of Reconstruction.[53]

The realtors' very success, in installing and maintaining segregation in every major American city, was used against them. Liberman compared the language of the 1866 act to the divided housing markets that had since been created. "Congress did not intend to create an illusory right to purchase, dependent upon the will of the sellers in the market to sell. If such is the case, the Joneses have no real right to live anywhere in St. Louis County, or for that matter in the State of Missouri, or any of the States of the United States. If the sellers are allowed to exclude Negroes from one area, they are equally allowed to exclude Negroes from all areas."[54]

How, Liberman asked, could separate housing markets enforced by private discrimination be squared with the clear intent of Congress to eliminate the stigma of slavery? "Certainly Congress did not mean to allow the owners and sellers of real estate to create the two 'separate but equal' real estate markets," he argued.[55]

Justice Stewart recognized how sweeping the consequences of the decision might be. At the oral hearing, Liberman was asked whether his logic depended on the fact that Mayer was a major home developer whose decisions excluded not one minority but thousands. "Does [the Civil Rights Act] apply to an individual home seller?" Recognizing how controversial the rights of home sellers were likely to be, Liberman, on behalf of his client, tried to demur. "Your Honor, that question is not before the Court." The justice wanted a plain answer, however: "I know that; but in your view of the statute?" To this, Liberman could only answer, "In my view of the statute, it applies to the individual house-owner."[56]

When the justices met after the hearing, there seemed to be an easy and safe way to avoid such a provocative decision. They could rule for the Joneses simply by considering that the vast scale of Mayer's developments and their approval by local jurisdictions made such widespread discrimination effectively state action. Stewart and the other justices did not have to rule on private residential discrimination under the 1866 act.

But Stewart, apparently influenced by his law clerk Laurence Tribe, urged the court to adopt the broader interpretation of the 1866 act. As Stewart wrote in his opinion, joined by six of the other justices, the 1866 act applied to every sale and rental of property. There may be "revolutionary implications of so literal a reading," Stewart concluded, but Congress in 1866 meant "exactly what it said."[57] The internal vote on this far-reaching reading was taken before federal fair housing was passed; none of the justices could know whether Title VIII would be enacted.[58]

This broad interpretation was too far for Justices Harlan and White. In the dissent he published two months later, Harlan argued that it was unwise for the court to venture out on such broad grounds, effectively resurrecting a century-old statute, when Congress had just passed a fair housing bill.[59] That the new 1968 fair housing law, with its various exemptions, would not have helped the Joneses was, in the big picture, unimportant, Harlan declared. "I deem it far more important this Court should avoid, if possible, the decision of constitutional and unusually difficult statutory questions than that we fulfil the expectations of every litigant who appears before us."[60] Not surprisingly, Senator Sam Ervin of North Carolina, in an article in the *Vanderbilt Law Review*, chastised the court for "constitutional revision by judicial fiat," while critical law review articles claimed that the decision "border[s] on chutzpah."[61]

For realtors, the lopsided Supreme Court decision, coming on the heels of Title VIII, meant they had lost the war over fair housing. *Jones v. Mayer* erased the distinction realtors had long insisted on, between state discrimination and the private discrimination that realtors conducted, promoted, and defined as fundamental to American freedom. Nor was *Jones* limited to intentional discrimination.[62] The coverage exemptions in the 1968 act did not apply. Residential discrimination anywhere and everywhere violated the U.S. Constitution. Realtors could no longer defend discrimination.

A NEW REALITY

For NAREB, the Supreme Court decision was the end of road. Eugene Conser announced to realtors in the clearest possible terms that their legal and political reality had changed. *Jones v. Mayer* was "probably the most far-reaching action of the court in our time." Not only does it create open housing "throughout the country, but . . . bring[s] under it all property of every type."[63] Realtors had no choice but to change: "The opinion is clear-cut and positive. The Negro in America henceforth is a free man." In this single sentence, NAREB dropped its long-held argument that Black Americans had had exactly the same legal freedom as white Americans for over a century.

Further argument was pointless. "Or if there be any further impediment to that freedom in the future, the court noted the means by which it would be struck down. This is the message that every realtor should now know and understand. Yes, every citizen—whatever his attitude toward racial prejudice." For "those who oppose this view"—whether realtors or their customers—"should now understand that their position is forever negated. To believe otherwise can only lead to naïve and contentious frustration."[64]

The good news, Conser pointed out, was that, compared to Title VIII, *Jones v. Mayer* had improved their competitive position. The court decision leveled the playing field between realtors and owners. Because owners, too, could not discriminate, realtors could turn *Jones v. Mayer* to their advantage. Since "rejection [of a buyer or renter] cannot be made on the basis of race . . . clients will undoubtedly value the experience of realtors in qualifying individuals as buyers and renters capable of meeting the financial requirements . . . and require our assistance."[65] Realtors, in other words, could now play a more crucial role than ever by helping owners comply and avoid complaints and lawsuits. Implicit in NAREB's message, realtors could subtly reflect owners' concerns about whom they sold or rented to while protecting them from complaints. The New Jersey association urged government officials, starting with the governor, to "make it crystal clear that . . . home owners who sell without the professional services of a broker are liable for compliance with the law."[66] If Title VIII had threatened the business of realtors, *Jones v. Mayer* could be a way to increase market share.

NAREB stressed the importance of realtors showing they were complying with the new rules: "Local boards can do much to forestall the drive for more punitive legislation by publicly announcing adherence to 'the law of the land'—now a fact, irretrievable." Indeed, realtors could use the court opinion to argue that further state or local fair housing laws were unnecessary. NAREB suggested that local boards initiate public relations campaigns that would testify to their compliance, improve realtors' image, and make clear they were simply doing what everyone now had to do.[67]

After years of insisting to its members—as well as legislators, courts, and the public at large—that American freedom meant the right to discriminate, NAREB had to change its rhetoric. Moreover, because Title VIII allowed the Department of Justice to bring suits against organizations that engaged in broad patterns of discrimination, it was important to demonstrate that realtors no longer publicly supported discriminatory actions. NAREB therefore began to explain to its members that there was another way of viewing American freedom, one that was important to understand and begin to adapt to.

NAREB's executive secretary Conser thought the ideological reeducation of realtors so important, he began it immediately. Because the court's view of freedom was so different from the one that NAREB had been instilling in realtors for years, Conser laid out for every realtor the original congressional debate on the 1866 Civil Rights Act. He quoted what Congressmen had said more than one hundred years before: "Negro citizens North and South, who saw in the 13th Amendment a promise of freedom—freedom to 'go and come at pleasure' and to 'buy and sell when they please' would be left with 'a mere paper guarantee' if Congress were powerless to assure . . . the right to live wherever a white man can live." Here, in the pages of *Realtor's Headlines*, Conser quoted from the Reconstruction Congress: "The end is legitimate because it is defined by the Constitution itself. The end is the maintenance of freedom."[68]

To underscore this view of the freedom of minority buyers, the opposite of everything NAREB had stood for, Conser summed up the Supreme Court's judgment in two words: "The court said 'We agree.'" For realtors across the country, this description of American freedom was remarkable in a publication that had, week after week, so forcefully attacked the civil rights movement. "The question," Conser asked, "is what steps we take now to meet its mandate."[69]

Although, after 1968, realtors were no longer the public leaders of campaigns to defend American freedom, it took years before they would disavow their past views or suggest they had been wrong. NAREB accepted responsibility for realtors' past role in segregation by absolving themselves of having had any choice in the matter. Realtors had operated in and simply reflected a world of "separate but equal." In response to a 1969 *Saturday Review* article about realtors' role in creating segregation, NAREB's defense was categorical: "Realtors strongly deny . . . that they along with . . . others in the real estate field are largely responsible for the 'ghetto problem'. . . . The real reason why black people find it difficult to move into white neighborhoods [is] the attitude of the residents. It's not because of some sinister conspiracy of the real estate industry."[70]

Indeed, even in agreeing to comply with the new law and court decisions, NAREB still spoke of the freedom that had been lost. "In any event . . . after *Jones v. Mayer* and the Civil Rights Act of 1968 erased the traditional freedom of choice of the owner," NAREB wrote grudgingly, "we urge all realtors to comply." NAREB thus stated its new policy by redefending its old position that freedom included the right to discriminate. Realtors had nobly supported such freedom, but the courts and Congress had denied it to the American people. The realtors, their customers, and those who voted for Proposition 14 had not been wrong.

It took years for realtors to fully distance themselves from the arguments they had made in Proposition 14. Only in 1974, their internal history explains, "fourteen years after the United States government first used the term 'fair housing,' did the national realtors' organization first begin using it."[71] Until then, realtors treated fair housing as false propaganda for "forced housing." In 1975, Arthur Leitch, CREA's president during the final stages of the Proposition 14 campaign, in his new role as national president of the renamed National Association of Realtors, established its first affirmative marketing program. For the first time, all local boards would be required to support equal housing opportunity.[72]

America's realtors would no longer argue that freedom required the right to discriminate. But the lasting power of that message, of their redefinition of freedom, would shape the country for generations to come.

21.

An Ideology of Freedom for a
National Conservative Party

> The great political upheaval of the 1960s is . . . a populist revolt
> of the American masses who have been elevated by prosperity
> to middle-class status and conservatism. *Their* revolt is against
> caste, policies and taxation of the mandarins of Establishment
> liberalism.
>
> Kevin Phillips, 1969[1]

No longer tied to ongoing battles over the owner's right to choose, no
longer an argument over housing segregation, the realtors' vision of
freedom could now be used by the new national conservative political
party—the one first conceived by Charles Wallace Collins—as its central ideology. The first crucial political leader to recognize this and use
it to his advantage on a national stage was Richard Nixon, less than two
months after the realtors conceded defeat. The setting was the Republican National Convention in Miami in early August 1968.

"I've got it written in blood," Harry Dent, chairman of the South
Carolina Republican Party, told delegates from Southern states, referring to the pledge he and Strom Thurmond had extracted privately
from Nixon. As he looked out across the sea of Southern delegates in
an extraordinary closed-door meeting, Dent could see a new version of
the Solid South, not left behind in a national Democratic Party, but able
to decide who would be the presidential candidate of the Republican
Party—and to exert a grand bargain in exchange. Strom Thurmond had
just explained the terms of the deal to those gathered in the convention
center room. "I know you want to vote for Reagan, the true conserva-

tive," Thurmond had told them. "But if Nixon becomes president, he has promised that he won't enforce either the Civil Rights or the Voting Rights Acts. Stick with him." Dent confirmed the deal. If the Southerners stuck with Nixon, he would deliver.[2]

Goldwater's defeat haunted those in the room. They wanted a candidate they could trust to support states' rights, but they also wanted to win. Reagan's 1966 gubernatorial victory had quickly galvanized support for him among conservatives in the party, including many in the South. Reagan's approach and philosophy had enormous appeal to Southern Republican delegates, whose votes would be decisive at the 1968 Republican National Convention. Southern delegates provided more than 300 of the 671 votes needed to choose him. Even more important, unlike Northern states with Republican primaries, none of the Southern delegates were selected by primaries. The delegates gathered in the room could decide whom to vote for.[3]

The battle for these Southern votes was between Reagan and Nixon. Reagan had run an undeclared but increasingly visible campaign, and when he finally announced his candidacy at the convention itself, one governor likened it to "a woman who's eight and a half months pregnant announcing she's going to have a baby."[4] Nixon had a commanding lead going into the convention, but if the Southerners he had been courting, such as Thurmond, did not deliver their delegations, he could not come close to a first ballot victory. In the opening days of the convention, Reagan had been picking up support in Alabama, North Carolina, and Texas. Southern delegates were disturbed by Nixon's having supported the federal fair housing law just a few months before. They had been alarmed earlier in the day when Reagan's aides distributed three thousand copies of a newspaper story stating that Nixon would pick liberal Oregon senator Mark Hatfield as his running mate.[5] If Nixon lost on the first ballot, the convention's general lack of enthusiasm for Nixon as a two-time loser, to Kennedy in 1960 and to Pat Brown in California in 1962, could lead to a second-round ballot victory for Reagan.

Thurmond admitted to his fellow Southerners that he felt more comfortable with Reagan's philosophy than with Nixon's. But, so soon after Goldwater's decisive defeat, he doubted that, in the country as a whole, "the people were ready to jump that far." If Republicans were going to win the presidency, "we stood a better chance to elect Nixon." "Believe me, I love Reagan," Thurmond told Southern delegates, "but Nixon's the one."[6]

It was then that Thurmond revealed the commitments from Nixon to reassure Southerners, the ones "written in blood." In private meetings with Southern delegates, Nixon had promised that "I won't do anything that would hurt development of the 2-party system in the South," would not "use the South as a whipping boy," and would not choose a Northern liberal as vice president. "I won't take anybody that I have to shove down the throats of any section of the country."[7] Perhaps most important to Thurmond and Dent, he promised he would not press school desegregation. In a private meeting where the *Miami Herald* snuck in a tape recorder, Nixon had reassured Thurmond about why he had supported the federal fair housing bill. He had wanted the question of fair housing "out of sight," in order not to split the party over a platform fight.[8] Having taken a civil rights issue off the table (as with restrictive covenants), an administration uninterested in enforcement and anxious to defer to local values could assure that little might actually happen—while white owners, feeling that their rights had been taken away by the very existence of the law, would fuel conservative resentment. Such an approach would have political benefits for Republicans both North and South.

Dent and Thurmond proved convincing. With these delegates from the South, Nixon won on the first ballot by twenty-five votes. On each of these issues, Nixon proved as good as his word, choosing Maryland governor Spiro Agnew, who had harshly attacked Black protestors, as vice president. As president, Nixon would isolate and then push out his HUD secretary George Romney for promoting housing integration.[9] Nixon understood the central political importance of the deal he had struck. The threat of Reagan had pushed him to the right and helped seal the bargain Collins had envisioned twenty years before.

It was a key moment in the creation of an ever more conservative national political party. That party's rise and dominance, its power to shift the center of American public opinion, has been the central fact of American politics since Goldwater's stunning defeat and Proposition 14's even more stunning victory. While still using the same name, it bears little resemblance in either ideological or geographic loyalties to the

Republican party of Eisenhower and Dirksen, whose congressmen supported the 1964 Civil Rights Act by a far higher margin than Democrats.

Drawing on a careful analysis of voting patterns across the country during the months after the convention, Nixon strategist Kevin Phillips quickly laid out an approach for the national dominance of such a party. Written during the campaign itself to guide the party's efforts, *The Emerging Republican Majority* proved extraordinarily influential. The answer, Phillips recognized, was not a "Southern strategy" as it became known but rather a national approach that wrote off appealing to African Americans or Latinos while seeking white voters in middle-class and blue-collar suburbs.

Phillips viewed California and Reagan's 1966 victory there as a national model. The "rootless socially mobile group known as the middle class," like those in Southern California who have largely "risen to such status only in the last generation," deplore "further social (minority group) upheaval." This group, Phillips concluded, was "increasingly important . . . throughout the nation." Their "intense opposition to open housing"[10] offered a key to the emerging Republican majority, fueled by the "anti-establishment politics of South, West and Levittown."[11] The realtors' vision of freedom had appeal to precisely these "anti-establishment politics" in "'Middle-American' urban-suburban districts." It had been proven and tested, both in 1964 and in Reagan's gubernatorial run from which Phillips drew his lessons.

Most important, the realtors' vision of freedom offered a way to solve three structural obstacles to creating a majority and retaining it for generations to come: How to attract voters in the South without losing them in the North? How to appeal to both libertarians and social conservatives? And how to appeal to many white working-class and middle-class former New Deal supporters in ways that Goldwater had not, by showing that big government, rather than protecting their interests, was putting their deepest values at risk?

These three unifying conservative messages—designed by realtors out of necessity—offered a model that could be used by Republicans to appeal to a broad spectrum of voters, against the dangers of the federal government.

NONRACIAL LANGUAGE

If conservatives were to win a majority of the country as a whole, they would need a way of opposing civil rights that seemed acceptable in the North. The realtors' broadly popular, race-neutral argument for homeowner rights and freedom of choice had been precisely designed to do this.

At almost the same time, realtor arguments for color-blind freedom could now be attractive to white Southerners, whose bitterest legislative losses—the 1964 Civil Rights Act and the 1965 Voting Rights Act—had removed the last major obstacle to the creation of a national conservative party: official, state-sponsored white supremacy. So long as the South was seen as legally different from the North, conservatives could not appeal to Southern whites without seeming to defend white supremacy alongside them. Now that the 1964 and 1965 acts had given Black Southerners the same nominal legal rights as whites, astute Southern politicians, such as Sam Ervin, now spoke of freedom of choice, and formerly ardent segregationists adopted the realtors' racially neutral-sounding arguments.

To picture the realignment of America's political parties in the 1960s as solely a matter of Democrats shifting far to the left by avidly embracing civil rights leaves out much of what happened. The Republican party changed dramatically. Among Northern congressmen, a higher percentage of Republicans had voted for the 1964 Civil Rights Act than Democrats. Following Goldwater's defeat, the Republican party did not, as many analysts expected, move back to the center but embraced a view of American freedom and the role of government that could appeal to both a Southern and a national majority. Opposition to the 1964 act could now be treated as ancient history in the North, as the realtors had distanced themselves from racial covenants. That Reagan, like the realtors, had opposed the 1964 Civil Rights Act quickly became part of the past. What mattered to voters now was the future: Which party better understood and would better serve the freedom of "ordinary" Americans going forward? As with Proposition 14, "ordinary" Americans generally meant white Americans, without anyone having to say so.

The new strategy Nixon embraced, which limited federal efforts in integrating suburbs, school desegregation, school busing, and affirmative action, was quickly dubbed the "Southern Strategy." Nixon responded in 1972 that "it is not a Southern strategy. It is an American strategy. That is what the South believes in and that is what America believes in."[12] Kevin Kruse and others have argued that rather than Republicans having captured the South, it was the political strategies of the Southern suburbs, in effect, that captured the Republican party.[13]

An alternative and more illuminating picture is that the same political strategy that had worked in both California and in the suburbs of Atlanta enabled conservative Republicans to capture a national majority and not just a Southern one. For realtors had already dealt with the problem Southern Republicans now faced. The realtors' language and arguments—systematically honed to avoid references to racial superiority, speak of equal rights, and talk about freedom instead of race—provided a model for Southern Republicans' messages to be accepted nationally.

The same reasons that the realtor ideology of freedom of choice proved so helpful to this national party explain why the arguments of *National Review*—at the time the most prominent conservative publication in the country—were not acceptable to a national majority. *National Review* writers, who had largely founded modern conservatism, had spent the 1950s and early 1960s justifying denial of voting rights and crafting arguments to be as provocative as possible, not to win elections in liberal-moderate states.

National Review's editors had seized on the South's struggle to preserve white-only voting as a paradigm for what conservative intellectuals saw as their own battle against tyranny. Right-wing conservatives, a small minority in the 1950s, identified with the South. Not only were white Southerners a minority in America, embattled in their values since John C. Calhoun, but they were often outnumbered by African Americans in their own communities. Arguing against the 1957 civil rights bill in "Why the South Must Prevail," William F. Buckley Jr. asked: Is "the white community in the South entitled to take such measures as are necessary to prevail [where] . . . it does not dominate numerically?" Do whites have a right to prevent Blacks from being allowed to vote? "The sobering answer," Buckley wrote, "is *Yes*—the white community is

so entitled because, for the time being, it is the advanced race." Given
that "the median cultural superiority of White over Negro . . . is a fact
that . . . cannot be hidden by ever-so-busy egalitarians . . . the claims
of civilization supersede those of universal suffrage."[14] Nor did Buckley
leave it there. *National Review* in 1960 stated that "in the Deep South the
Negroes are, by comparison with the Whites, retarded. . . . Leadership in
the South then quite properly rests in white hands."[15]

That their support of official Southern segregation might seem
unpopular, antidemocratic, and provocative in most of the country only
enthused these writers. *National Review* articles followed Russell Kirk's
lead in *The Conservative Mind* in 1953, the founding text of American
conservatism. Kirk had honored Nathan Bedford Forrest, the first grand
wizard of the Ku Klux Klan, as that "magnificent, simple cavalryman,"[16]
and claimed that "civilized society requires orders and classes . . . and
sound prejudice."[17] In searching for a conservative tradition to build on
in 1950s and 1960s America, these founders of modern conservatism had
fastened on the legacy of the South.

In 1963, as public support swelled for federal action on civil rights,
Buckley called the March on Washington "a mob deployment" and "a
dangerous resort."[18] In response to the murder of four small girls in the
bombing of a Black church in Birmingham three weeks later, *National
Review* backhandedly blamed the murders on the civil rights movement,
stating, "Let us gently say the fiend who set off the bomb . . . set back
the cause of the white people there so dramatically as to raise the question whether . . . the explosion was the act of a provocateur—of a Communist, or a crazed Negro." Whoever set the bomb, the leading journal
of conservative opinion made clear where ultimate responsibility lay:
"Let it be said that the convulsions that go on . . . have resulted from
revolutionary assaults on the status quo . . . traceable to the Supreme
Court's manifest contempt for the settled traditions of Constitutional
practice."[19] Although in later years Buckley claimed the bombing was a
turning point in his view of civil rights,[20] at the time his position was adamant. Compared to *National Review*'s explicitly racial, hierarchical vision
of freedom, the realtors provided a more acceptable-sounding language
of equal rights and color blindness for a national conservative party.

TWO STRANDS OF CONSERVATISM

In the 1950s and early 1960s, conservative opinion was deeply divided on what kind of society conservatives were trying to achieve. Did conservatism mean maximizing individual freedom—the libertarian message of Goldwater's *Conscience of a Conservative*, ghostwritten by Buckley's brother-in-law Brent Bozell and the most popular political tract in American history? Or did conservatism mean the very opposite: restoring traditional social and religious norms? Such differences could splinter any conservative movement. Libertarianism and social conservatism pointed in seemingly opposite directions, whether the issue was abortion, sodomy, contraception, miscegenation, mandatory school prayer, public school dress codes, or government support for religious schools. The Proposition 14 campaign proved crucial to conservative thought by providing a model for linking individual freedom of choice to preservation of a community's way of life.

The belief that individual liberty was the highest value, "that personal freedom is inseparable from economic freedom,"[21] stressed by Friedrich Hayek, ran through much of Goldwater's *Conscience of a Conservative*. America, the book stated, should be based on "individual self-reliance,"[22] on each individual's right to his own beliefs, his own property, and his ability to make his own choices. In this atomistic view, society was nothing more than a set of individuals, and thus in itself has "no goals, interests or rights."[23]

By contrast, social conservatives thought of freedom not as an independent value or idea but as coming "from the adequate discharge of duties."[24] For Kirk, religious belief and the social fabric were the basis of conservatism, and the very opposite of individualism.[25] As to the libertarian "idea that men have the right to act anywhere according to their pleasure, without any moral tie, no such right exists."[26] Unlike libertarians, social conservatives thus saw government's role as essential: supporting what Kirk called the traditions and prescriptive ways of its people.

The tension between these conflicting values divided conservative thought.[27] By "the early 1960s, the already simmering pot boiled over," historian of conservatism George Nash has written. "On one side were

lists, many of them Catholic intellectuals: defenders of
us, morality, 'right reason,' religion, truth, virtue. On the
libertarians and classical liberals," many of them Prot-
...used on "individual liberty, laissez-faire, private property,
reason and individual liberty."[28] How could the coalition symbolized by
National Review itself even stay together, let alone provide a philosophy
for a coherent broad-based conservative movement? Efforts to create a
philosophy to fuse these two positions were unable to satisfy both sides,
leading scholars to conclude that "conservatives never fully resolved the
issue; indeed, given the . . . contradictory nature of the two languages,
they could not."[29]

The standard view is that these divergent believers dealt with their
fundamental disagreement by focusing instead on the success of the
movement and on political action against centralization of governmental power and communism.[30] As historian Lisa McGirr put it, "Despite
such disagreements and divisions on particular issues, libertarians and
social conservatives shared enough grievances against their common
enemy, the liberal Leviathan, to forge a political movement."[31] But while
a single conservative movement did emerge and grow, appealing alike
to free-market ideologues and to Catholic and evangelical social conservatives, this explanation leaves out a crucial feature of how it did so. It
leaves out the way that the conservative movement used—and continues
to use—individual freedom to justify traditional norms, the approach
realtors worked so hard to create.

The realtors themselves had long wrestled with the competing
values of social norms versus individual choice. They had spent half a
century establishing and carrying out community norms and traditions,
rules as to who could live where to create a "harmonious" social order.
But to appeal to a broad majority of voters, realtors had used freedom
of individual choice to maintain social control. Because they had had to
resolve a dilemma faced by the conservative movement as a whole, their
approach could provide a model for issue after issue that would emerge
over the years to come. This common approach helped assure that far
from splintering the movement, these separate causes only strengthened
it, adding to the case against liberal government.

LIBERAL GOVERNMENT AS THE ENEMY
OF ORDINARY AMERICANS

The realtors' final contribution to the ideology of a national conservative political party was, thus, the most far reaching. By describing as freedom what liberals were taking away from "ordinary" Americans, Proposition 14 made conservatism's abstract warnings about liberal government concrete and attractive to the vast majority of the public.

Proposition 14 was not the first postwar effort to portray liberal government as a dangerous, indeed ultimate, threat to American freedom. The menace of big government had been at the heart of the free enterprise campaigns of the National Association of Manufacturers (NAM) in the 1950s. William Grede—who helped expand NAM's political education efforts, cofounded the John Birch Society, and funded Freedom Schools—defined freedom as freedom from governmental intrusion, and liberal government as inevitably leading to socialism.[32] *Reader's Digest* had distributed more than ten million copies of NAM's "The Road Ahead." If not always going so far as Senator McCarthy, the Far Right and Right continually promoted the idea that the federal government and the Warren Supreme Court were the greatest domestic threats to American freedom.

But, as with Bill Knowland's 1958 California "crusade for freedom," these efforts to attack the mainstream consensus failed decisively. Although he had been a highly popular senator, Knowland only received 40 percent of the vote, his campaign for freedom seen by many union and working-class voters as little more than an attempt to roll back the social security, labor relations, and other benefits of the New Deal. In 1962, a California constitutional amendment against subversive organizations and teachers—backed by the Los Angeles County Chamber of Commerce, CREA, and Reagan's key funder Henry Salvatori—also received only 40 percent of the vote,[33] as did Goldwater in 1964. These failures suggested that, by the 1960s, Cold War accusations against liberal government—including Reagan's own "Time for Choosing" speech, perfected over years, delivered to rousing ovations from California realtors in 1962 and 1963, and presented on national television on behalf of

Goldwater in October 1964—appealed only to the already converted.

By contrast, the realtors brought abstract warnings about liberal government close to home. By speaking not about a general idea of freedom but of *your* rights, *your* property, *your* neighborhood, realtors showed that liberal government itself could no longer be trusted. "You have done more than any man in the history of the Democratic Party to drive me over to the G.O.P.," one voter wrote to Brown after Proposition 14.[34] Proposition 14 provided a road map for showing how liberal government was taking rights away from ordinary Americans. By redefining voters' interests not simply in material terms but in terms of their freedom, realtors offered a transcendent, almost existential vision of what was at issue in American politics.

Just as important, realtors showed how to make such an appeal to a broad majority. Unlike Goldwater, realtors did not welcome being seen as extremist, nor disdain those who "do not care for our cause,"[35] as Goldwater had in his acceptance speech. By working hard to establish their tone as reasonable and moderate, realtors created a sense of trust and credibility. Those who disagreed were the extremists and ideologues. Having made a radical proposal for California's constitution sound middle-of-the-road, their approach proved ideal for a party seeking to build and maintain a majority while proposing ideas that would have seemed far outside the mainstream only a few years before.

The realtors' vision of freedom offered to an increasingly conservative Republican party—one driven by the "antiestablishment politics" and electoral geography Nixon strategist Kevin Phillips had outlined—a unifying ideology that would prove more resilient and more powerful with each passing year. The realtors' impact had been practical as well. Their record-shattering petition drive—mobilizing activists who then helped Goldwater narrowly win the California primary and thus the nomination—made possible a Republican nominee who would oppose the 1964 Civil Rights Act, sweep Deep Southern states, and induce Strom Thurmond to forge the great alliance Charles Wallace Collins had laid out years before.

In offering a novice Reagan a way to appeal to a majority of voters, the realtors helped launch a politician who, like the realtors themselves, claimed to be outside politics. Like the realtors, Reagan conveyed the extraordinary double message that this conservative idea of American freedom was both as natural as common sense and threatened by apocalypse. Evoking both neighborliness and doomsday, this picture of freedom would shape the party's appeal, and American politics, to this day.

Part Seven.
American Legacy: 1969–

The realtors' efforts to create and justify residential segregation more than half a century ago continue to shape America today, dividing where Americans live and polarizing our politics. These two sets of divisions are deeply related. Residential segregation remains a central feature of American life because the rise of conservatism has made the governmental action to fully enforce fair housing and overcome past patterns politically infeasible. At the same time, the vision of freedom that the realtors created has helped shift America's politics more and more to the right, determining what is politically possible.

This shift of political power has been the central fact of American politics for the last fifty years. Ideas proposed by Richard Nixon, such as a guaranteed national income, seem unobtainable today. An increasingly conservative Republican party has dramatically shifted what is feasible even under Democratic administrations compared to the era of Lyndon Johnson. This general trend has continued for almost twice as long as FDR's New Deal coalition and has far outlasted any single leader. It has continued despite forces that the most astute observers half a century ago would have expected to strongly favor liberals: younger generations becoming voters, dramatic increases in the percentage of minority voters, rapid decline in church membership,[1] and increasing economic insecurity for the middle class and especially those without college degrees.

But among all the changes in the country and American politics over the last fifty years, one factor that has been constant at the heart of this rise, both before and long after Ronald Reagan's presidency, has been the persuasiveness of the idea that American freedom is threatened by liberal government. To understand the continuing power of this idea of freedom that the realtors helped define and why it has proven so effective, it is important to recognize how it builds on itself.

Whether the issue was taxes, new civil rights, economic regulation, abortion, gun control, perceived limits on religion, or attacks on community traditions, conservatives could follow the realtors' methodology. They could frame each issue as a principle of American freedom that went back to the country's founding, as an absolute value whose limitation in any way would jeopardize freedom itself. Each issue proved the same point, that freedom was an individual possession that liberal government, do-gooders, and outsiders were threatening to steal. Each issue only confirmed the urgency and relevance of this picture of freedom, and the illegitimacy of liberal government.

To understand how such a picture of freedom could have played this self-reinforcing role for conservatism as a whole, in ways that have only become stronger over the years, it is worth considering the work of two Stanford social psychologists. Two experts in educational intervention, Gregory Walton and Geoffrey Cohen, showed how offering individuals a new interpretation of their experience could have long-term cumulative effects by changing their mind-set, their picture of their relationship to society.[2] In an experiment Walton and Cohen repeated in multiple universities and reported in *Science*, students in the spring of their freshman year simply spent an hour creating a brief narrative of how their sense of isolation in the school was transient rather than fundamental; a control group spent the hour on study skills. This brief one-time experiment resulted, three years later, in tripling the percentage of African American students whose GPA was in the top 25 percent of their class. It reduced the achievement gap between African American and white students by 50 percent.

How could a one-hour experience, which few students even directly thought about three years later, have had such an effect? The answer was that creating such a narrative provided a new interpretive framework affecting how students saw their future ordinary daily experiences in class, on sidewalks, in dorms, with other students, and with professors. Daily experiences that might have reinforced minority students' sense of isolation could now be seen instead as part of the ordinary process of becoming adapted to the school.[3] In an article titled "Social-Psychological Interventions . . . They're Not Magic," the psychologists explained why such brief interventions worked. These, and lasting effects from similar interventions, came from targeting students' subjective experiences by offering a "persuasive yet stealthy" idea that tapped into recursive processes. Without in any way being told to do so, students took from that hour a framework that could be used to reinterpret experiences. Far from "a silver bullet," such interventions "rearrange forces" in the "tension system" in which students found themselves as they tried to define their identities.[4]

The Sacramento voter who had said she would "cast a big yes for Proposition 14" had found a new way to define her political experience. In her words, "We are fighting for our rights, and this, voters, is the only way we can do it. It appears to be our last chance."[5] The realtors had offered a new, carefully constructed way to see oneself in relation to liberal government that could be applied to issue after issue. Once freedom meant the right to maintain social traditions, threats to such traditions became threats to one's individual freedom. Once discrimination was defined to mean "simply to make a choice,"[6] limits on discrimination became restrictions to "freedom of choice." Once a particular narrow right became elevated as freedom itself, it could no longer be balanced against the rights of others. Such an approach could be applied to virtually any issue.

The more issues this idea of freedom was applied to, the more powerful it became. This picture of freedom created the opposite of the positive framework for interpreting one's ongoing experiences in the university experiment. Each action of liberal government became yet another attack on the tradition and community that one saw oneself belonging to—and on one's freedom to maintain that community. Walton and Cohen provided a framework that reinforced a sense of belonging; the realtors' vision of freedom provided an ongoing framework that reinforced liberal government's threat to people's sense of belonging. As a result, the *wider* the range of issues that conservatives applied this framework to, the more unifying and urgent its message became—the greater the sense that ordinary Americans were under attack.

Leading realtors themselves made precisely these connections across issues. In 1978, Howard Jarvis—who had led the apartment owners' efforts for Proposition 14—launched a statewide campaign to slash property taxes with Proposition 13, a cause that would quickly spread across the country. Reed Robbins, Spike Wilson's key lieutenant in 1964, dashed off a call to arms to his fellow CREA directors: "In this 'debate' on tax relief measures, if CREA does not support Proposition 13, we form a group 'Realtors for Proposition 13.'" Recalling the Boston Tea Party imagery of Proposition 14, Robbins called this effort the "Taxpayers Tea Party." Robbins understood precisely how the same image Proposition 14 had used—of brave individuals rebelling against government itself—could convince voters to roll back property taxes. When Reagan ran for president, Robbins started the "Realtors for Reagan Council." Prominent in Robbins's files was a quote from Reagan from 1967: "Freedom is based on the right of the individual to personal ownership of property and this basic human right cannot be infringed upon by majority rule." "No man better *presents* our philosophy," Robbins urged in 1980.[7]

At the heart of this idea of freedom that helped drive—and still drives—the conservative movement was the picture of the individual's right to restore a prior community, the picture realtors helped create in Proposition 14. To make this picture even more powerful—to place this idea of freedom and community on a plane above government or politics—conservatives have followed the realtors' lead in justifying the right to discriminate as freedom of religion. In Proposition 14, realtors had spoken again and again about fair housing violating "freedom of religion by forcing people of different religions to live in close proximity."[8] Religious expression might at first have seemed tangential to a campaign about residential racial segregation. But realtors invoked freedom of religion because it offered a nobler way to justify excluding others. More deeply still, realtors appealed to freedom of religion to make the right to discriminate an absolute right that could not be compromised—to place it above all politics. Over the last fifty years, freedom of religion has been used more and more to justify this conservative idea of freedom, with the right to discriminate at its heart. Claiming that religion was at stake enabled realtors, and conservatives in their footsteps, to embed ever more deeply—to sacralize—the self-reinforcing framework they had created for seeing liberal government as a threat to one's freedom.

22.

The Continuation of Residential Segregation

Residential segregation exerts a mighty influence on the ... attitudes and the actions of all of us, white and non-white alike. It lends credence to the popular belief that there are fundamental and irreconcilable differences between individuals based on race; it shores up the myth that certain sections of our metropolitan areas *belong* to defined ethnic groups.

Loren Miller, 1962[1]

Ultimately the fate of maintaining any area as integrated depends on establishing an open market in housing everywhere.

Reverend Donald Rowland, 1959[2]

Paradoxically, the realtors' defeat in the war over fair housing made their vision of freedom in Proposition 14 more broadly appealing to white voters rather than less. One reason is that the federal fair housing law had a larger impact symbolically than practically. Its passage suggested to whites that the issue of segregation had been resolved. The word *segregation* itself, as Massey and Denton noted, soon "disappeared from the American vocabulary."[3] If Black Americans still lived in Black neighborhoods after Title VIII, it was easy and convenient to believe that it was because they preferred to, or it was all they could afford; their living in the ghetto with other Black residents was "natural."

Title VIII's passage, realtors had warned, had a simple meaning for white Americans: the majority had forfeited their own rights for the special benefit of the Black minority. People's beliefs did not change because the law had. The fact that support for racial discrimination and segregation now had to be voiced sub rosa only enhanced the sense of white victimhood. Title VIII and *Jones v. Mayer*, far from ending the appeal of Proposition 14's vision of freedom, only enhanced it. Government's interference with homeowners' privacy, traditional rights, and expectations became part of the litany of what was dangerous about big government.

Realtors may not have ultimately prevailed in Congress or the Supreme Court, but they had effectively made their case to voters. That Congress and courts now chose to override the rights of ordinary citizens only underscored the realtors' argument: government was intent on taking away the rights of the majority to give special privileges to minorities. In the interest of social engineering, the federal government had violated individual freedom.

THE WEAKNESS OF TITLE VIII

While Congress's approval of Title VIII aroused powerful emotions and expectations on both sides and confirmed conservatives' fears of liberal government, it did little to change the day-to-day reality of where most people lived. Title VIII was unwieldy and impractical. This was inherent in its provisions. The shadow of Proposition 14, of overwhelming voter disapproval of fair housing, had shaped the legislation itself.

Indeed, for anyone looking to Title VIII to end racial discrimination, the legislation was flawed and weak. The Dirksen compromise had eliminated HUD's authority to conduct hearings, file complaints, or issue enforcement orders.[4] HUD's only power was to seek conciliation between the parties. Enforcement was up to the complainant, who would need to file a civil action in federal court.[5] The result was that during the law's first twenty-five years, "only about four hundred fair housing cases have been decided, compared with more than 2 million incidents of housing discrimination estimated to occur each year."[6] There were a wide range of exemptions, including six million units rented out by owner-occupants of two-to-four-unit buildings as well as units owned by religious organizations or private restricted clubs so long as race was not a criteria for membership. For the first twenty years after Title VIII, the law lacked an administrative enforcement mechanism, the same issue that led Byron Rumford to push for his bill in California in the early 1960s. HUD could not hold hearings or issue enforcement orders; few complainants could go beyond the HUD conciliation process to hire an attorney to actually seek resolution. These enforcement remedies were weak by design.[7] Even when the realtors lost, the chilling example of Proposition 14 helped set limits on what could be passed.

Even after the law was strengthened in 1988, its impact has been limited. Federal resources for enforcement have been meager compared to the scale of discrimination. Little has been done to deal with broad and systemic practices, pattern and practice cases, as opposed to individual complaints.[8] As one example, informal racial steering by real estate agents remained the same or increased in the decade after the law was amen-ded.[9] The law's ability to end widespread discrimination was thus more symbolic than practical.

Although the 1964 Civil Rights Act had quickly and effectively ended discrimination in public accommodations, housing was inherently far more intractable. It was easy to know whether a restaurant, movie theater, or motel accepted Black customers. Housing discrimination, especially after passage of Title VIII, often occurred almost invisibly behind the doors of brokerage offices, in driving around neighborhoods, in the differential assumptions brokers made about Black and white buyers, and in what they chose to emphasize. Sociologist Diana May Pearce documented the subtlety and effectiveness of continuing broker discrimination in the Detroit metropolitan area seven years after passage of Title VIII. Many white brokers consistently assumed that Black buyers had fewer resources than white buyers who presented identical assets and income. Brokers showed such Black buyers homes that on average were 10 percent lower in price and therefore mostly in lower-priced areas.[10] White customers were shown five times as many homes, on average, as Black customers who presented the same financial information.[11] Three-quarters of Black customers were not shown homes at all. These patterns were highly consistent in brokerages throughout the metropolitan area,[12] all of whom considered themselves in compliance with Title VIII. Unlike discrimination in public accommodations, housing discrimination could not be ended by one or two exemplary individual cases that quickly led to general national compliance.[13]

The idea that housing discrimination was a matter of individual cases was itself misplaced. Long after Title VIII, studies showed that discriminatory treatment in housing was not a matter of a few anomalous brokers who differed from their peers; rather, the more successful the broker, and often the more professedly "liberal" in racial attitudes, the more discriminatory.[14] Discrimination was institutional far more than it was individual. Yet unlike in school desegregation and employment discrimination cases, which had been approached on an institutional level, Title VIII only allowed individual complainants. Ten years after Title VIII and *Jones v. Mayer*, there had "not been even one large lawsuit about housing . . . affecting a significant number of people."[15] As a result, housing discrimination and segregation continued, but covertly rather than overtly.

White owners and voters who felt aggrieved by government taking away the rights of the majority still had the same largely exclusive neighborhoods to defend. That integration had not happened yet only made it more of a threat. Organizing around defending their interests against government—in battles over zoning, growth restrictions, NIMBY-ism, and property taxes—voters in these neighborhoods found the arguments about traditional American freedom more compelling over time. The realtors' presentation of such freedom as color-blind and race neutral had provided a compelling, politically acceptable model for expressing such beliefs.

The broader component of Title VIII that goes beyond nondiscrimination, requiring HUD and other federal agencies to "affirmatively further" fair housing, has been controversial from the start. Nixon quickly quashed the "Open Communities" efforts of his first HUD secretary George Romney to deny federal funding to cities and states whose zoning and other policies prevented racial integration. "Stop this one," Nixon ordered his domestic policy advisor, John Ehrlichman. Nixon then spelled out to his aides that he understood the consequences, using the realtors' terminology of "forced integration": "I am convinced that while legal segregation is totally wrong, that forced integration of housing or education is just as wrong. . . . I realize that this position will lead us to a situation in which blacks will continue to live for the most part in black neighborhoods."[16] Publicly Nixon acknowledged that while the "Federal

Government was not blameless in contributing to . . . the impairment of equal housing opportunity for minority Americans, . . . the persistence of racially separate housing patterns reflects the free choice of individuals in both the majority and minority communities."[17] Free choice meant discrimination against minorities.

When the Reagan administration entered office in 1981, committed to color-blind freedom, it took up the positions that the realtors had argued for years before. The Department of Justice under William French Smith—little more than a decade after he argued the realtors' case for Proposition 14 in the Supreme Court—systematically weakened enforcement of fair housing. Reversing the prior position of the Department of Justice, the Civil Rights Division argued that fair housing testers should be prohibited from filing suit under Title VIII. Just as important, despite broad court consensus allowing discrimination to be determined on the basis of outcomes rather than intent, the department refused to do so. Instead of the modest number of lawsuits the department had brought where there was a broad pattern of misconduct—averaging thirty cases per year under the Nixon, Ford, and Carter administrations—in its first year Smith's Department of Justice brought none, despite a dramatic increase in the number of housing complaints.[18]

HUD too, under the Reagan administration, sought to minimize the impact of fair housing. HUD revised its existing fair housing agreement with the National Association of Realtors to reduce the obligation realtors had previously agreed on to actively enforce Title VIII, and it prohibited local housing resource boards from using testers. HUD now made secret which local real estate boards had signed affirmative marketing agreements; this prevented minority home buyers from knowing whether local realtors had taken on such obligations.[19]

THE LASTING LEGACY OF HOUSING SEGREGATION

Virtually all studies show that at each income level, housing segregation of African Americans remains almost as intense as it was in 1968, when federal fair housing was first enacted.[20] By the late 1990s, almost 90 percent of white suburbanites lived in communities that were over

99 percent white.[21] Since then, more, rather than fewer, neighborhoods have become 90 percent Black.[22] Such segregation affects African American families regardless of income. In 2010, African Americans with incomes over $75,000 lived in neighborhoods that have a higher poverty rate than those of white Americans who earn less than $40,000.[23] Black middle-class households, with incomes in the $55,000–$60,000 range, live in neighborhoods with median incomes similar to those of white households earning $12,000.[24] This suggests the continuing power and impacts of racial segregation on where families can live and raise their children.

Real estate professionals have to some extent replaced open discrimination with informal racial steering. Brokers face continuing incentives and pressures to discriminate, and many white brokers see themselves as fully complying with fair housing, while showing far fewer homes to Black couples than white, offering less follow-up, showing homes in lower price ranges to families with the same income, and assuming that Black home buyers prefer preponderantly Black neighborhoods.[25] *Newsday*'s 2019 in-depth investigation of the real estate industry across Long Island demonstrated the extent of broker discrimination fifty years after it was prohibited by Title VIII.[26] When it comes to appraisals, significant differences have been described in valuations of the same home, depending on the assumed race of the owner.[27]

But underlying forces, set in place by realtors long ago to maintain all-white neighborhoods, are far more powerful than actions of individual brokers and appraisers. Redlining practices of lenders play out in new but often equally devastating ways, including the marketing to minority borrowers of subprime loans that wiped out household savings.[28] Local suburban governments, initially established to ensure segregation, naturally identify the public interest with their individual electorates, and often maintain single-family zoning, first designed by Duncan McDuffie to support racial exclusion, as a way to limit growth. Boundaries reinforce themselves over time. As the Federal Reserve Bank has definitively shown from its studies of former redlining maps in every metropolitan area, the blocks on either side of the disinvestment boundaries established during the Depression show far greater differences in property values, homeownership, and housing condition *today* than when they were drawn.[29]

The impact of past racial practices, in other words, has only increased over time. This compounding effect has been especially true of homeowner equity. A 2019 Duke University study estimated the equity lost by Black homeowners in Chicago alone in the 1950s and 1960s at $3 to $4 billion.[30] The Levittown homes that veterans lined up to buy in 1950 for $7,900 (with no money down and mortgage payments lower than typical rents)—homes no African American was allowed to buy—were worth fifty times that by the early 2000s.[31] The tenfold disparity in racial household wealth today is rooted in decades when African Americans were excluded from homeownership and had to pay 20 to 30 percent more for similar housing. This enormous disparity in wealth creates an even greater financial barrier as home prices continue to rise.

Prejudice against African Americans moving into white neighborhoods, inculcated by the real estate industry for decades, has dropped only slightly, while millions of incidents of housing discrimination each year go uninvestigated.[32]

But the very power of these forces makes clear the fundamental reason that segregation remains so widespread: strong government action would have been necessary to overcome them. Such action was precisely what the political impact of the realtors' arguments prevented. Indeed, the passage and existence of fair housing itself in this form provide an ongoing rationale for discrimination. That such a law exists, that government has already taken away the freedom of white Americans, is an argument against liberal government itself. And the fact that segregation continues despite such a law becomes proof for conservatives that discrimination is normal and natural. That some African Americans remain trapped in some of the worst neighborhoods in the country, neighborhoods that have had little or no reinvestment in generations, becomes evidence that this is all that they want or can afford.

Seen in this light, efforts to weaken fair housing by individual presidential administrations take on far greater significance. In summer 2020 when the Trump administration rolled back rules on local community housing goals—announced as "President Donald J. Trump Is Protecting Our Suburbs and Preserving the American Dream for All Americans"[33]—the action reflected more than current politics. Almost from its passage, Title VIII has offered a foil, a stage, to show that the realtors' vision of the freedom to discriminate was more important than ending discrimination.

From Nixon quashing Open Communities to protect "the free choice of individuals," to Reagan and William French Smith dramatically weakening enforcement, to Republican senators Lee, Rubio, and Enzi's 2015 effort to block the affirmative fair housing mandate because "every community should be free to zone its neighborhoods and compete for new residents according to its distinct values,"[34] to President Trump informing "all of the people living their Suburban Lifestyle Dream that you will no longer be bothered,"[35] the pattern has been the same. Fair housing has been a target. It has offered a tangible way to show that, even though King's speech at the March on Washington is widely honored and a holiday is named for him, his idea of American freedom is less important than the invisible walls realtors defended as freedom of choice. Indeed, the 2020 rule weakening fair housing was titled "Preserving Community and Neighborhood Choice," where choice has come to mean a community's right to maintain a certain way of life. Here was the realtors' legacy in a phrase: that freedom of choice meant freedom to zone. In all these efforts to limit fair housing, freedom meant not the right of those excluded to choose where to live but the right to exclude.

Although these particular new regulations may be rescinded, one thing is certain. Attacks on fair housing in the name of American freedom will continue. The specific issues, and thus the battle lines, may change from administration to administration. Analysts may question the continuing political benefits of such attacks as ways of appealing to "suburban housewives," as many suburbs become more diverse.[36] But such attacks serve a larger purpose. They offer a way for conservatives to demonstrate their commitment to this idea of American freedom, of the right to maintain a traditional community, that they have been articulating for fifty years.

Fair housing's continuing weakness and vulnerability have been part of the conservative vision of freedom's larger legacy for civil rights as a whole.

23.

A Legacy for Civil Rights

> If Martin Luther King could get up from the grave he would see
> that he'd have to start all over again raising hell.
>
> Elena Rocha, civil rights activist, 1988[1]

At his inauguration in 1981, Ronald Reagan offered a new presidential view of civil rights. He said little about what the federal government should do and much about what it should not do. He did not talk about the threat of communism. Instead he attacked the federal role and responsibility in local affairs set out by Truman's Committee on Civil Rights.

Reagan was emphatic on states' rights, the central tenet Collins had suggested for a national conservative party. Insisting on a constitutional claim that had been rejected by the Supreme Court for almost two centuries and had been used to justify Confederate secession,[2] he proclaimed, "the Federal government did not create the States; the States created the Federal government."[3] Reagan's aim, he made clear—as in the speech with which he opened his formal presidential campaign at the Neshoba County Fairgrounds in Philadelphia, Mississippi—was to return power to the states. In his inaugural address, he redeemed and reiterated the pledge he had made in that town of six thousand, known nationally for the Ku Klux Klan's murder of three civil rights workers. If elected, he had promised to the Mississippi fairgoers, "I'm going to devote myself to trying to reorder those priorities and to restore to the states and local communities those functions which properly belong there."[4]

In his inaugural address, Reagan drew heavily on the realtors' approach from Proposition 14. He spoke of equality and "equal

Ronald Reagan at Neshoba County Fair, Mississippi, 1980

opportunities for all Americans with no barriers born of bigotry or discrimination," while seeking to limit any federal intervention for "special
interest groups" based on "ethnic and racial divisions." While pillorying
those who had been discriminated against precisely because of such "ethnic and racial divisions," Reagan praised, as did Spike Wilson, the great
group "that has been too long neglected . . . that knows no . . . ethnic or
racial divisions, . . . 'We the people,' this breed called Americans."[5] He
evoked Wilson's image of the neglected "forgotten man," lauding America's taxpayers whose "patriotism is quiet but deep." Like the realtors, too,
Reagan suggested that such freedom had traditionally existed and now
needed to be restored. By limiting federal interference in the decisions
of local communities and private individuals, America "will again be the
exemplar of freedom."[6]

Although the most-remembered words from Reagan's speech are
short and simple—"Government is not the solution to our problem;
government is the problem"—Reagan insisted it was not government
per se that he objected to, but certain uses of government. "It's not my
intention to do away with government" but rather "the intervention and

intrusion in our lives that result from unnecessary and excessive growth of government." His target was federal policies that replace "self-rule" with "an elite group superior to government for, by, and of the people."[7] For Reagan—and the conservative national party he led to power— American freedom depended on limiting federal interference in local social arrangements. Ever since Collins's attack on the appointment of Truman's committee, this guiding idea drove the realignment of America's political parties.

Reagan described what he objected to as social engineering's interference with individual freedom. But from the point of view of Truman's committee, the reason for the federal government to intervene on any issue of civil rights had been far more fundamental. It had been to balance rights, to "protect citizens against the aggressions of others seeking to push their freedoms too far."[8] In the case of the realtors, these aggressions constituted the most detailed, organized, and—for generations— government-backed social engineering of where Americans could live. Government's very purpose, in the view of Truman's committee, was to protect basic rights against such aggressions. What Reagan was asserting, as the realtors had asserted in Proposition 14, was that government action to protect such rights violated a freedom that must remain absolute, one that government could not restrict.

The key, realtors had discovered, was to *elevate* such freedom as something that government could not limit or balance in order to protect the rights of others. This approach has continued to provide a model for conservatives long after Reagan's presidency. Conservative lawyers have argued that the dictates of conscience of an individual baker should override Supreme Court decisions on gay marriage. In *Burwell v. Hobby Lobby Stores*, they successfully asserted that organizations who object to the use of contraceptives should be able to exclude them from health plans for all their employees.[9] Starting in the late 1970s, the right to bear arms was redefined for the first time as an absolute individual right that government could not limit. Individual rights, including of the unborn, have been invoked to restrict abortions. An individual parent's right not to have his child exposed to scientific theories of evolution or learn about non-Christian religions has been used to limit teaching in public schools. In all these cases, American individual freedom has been invoked to maintain conformity. This view of freedom has created a sense of con-stitutional entitlement and has legitimized grievances about rights being taken away from the majority.

The difference between this conservative vision and that of Tru-man's committee was not over the importance of freedom, nor that government's primary responsibility was assuring freedom, nor that citizens should expect government to protect freedom. The very same governmental actions were seen by one side as the greatest protection for American freedom and by the other as the greatest threat to such freedom. The difference lay not in the governmental action but in what freedom consisted of.

We can now answer the question with which this book began. Why is freedom used so regularly and insistently by conservatives to oppose civil rights?

Since any expansion of civil rights inevitably restricts the right to discriminate, the question is why conservatives view this right as so essential to American freedom. Why do they reject the idea that the very nature of freedom requires limits—that, as Byron Rumford put it, "I must be restricted so that you can have freedom. Also, you must be restricted so that I may have liberty."[10]

What the realtors put into the language of color-blind freedom were two fundamental principles, designed together to protect the right to discriminate. First, those who seek protection from discrimination are asking for a special benefit. They are asking government for something that no one who is not discriminated against needs. To provide that pro-tection is to restrict the freedom of "ordinary Americans," the freedom they already enjoy and have historically enjoyed. The realtors drew a box around this ordinary, "traditional" American freedom and said that this, and only this, is the freedom America needs to protect. Second, having drawn this box, realtors argued that this "traditional" freedom, includ-ing the right to discriminate, must be absolute. Therefore, any effort to extend rights, to offer rights to those who have not enjoyed them, is an attack on American freedom itself.

Given these principles, anyone asking to be protected against dis-crimination—asking, as Rumford put it, "for the same rights as every-one else, the right to be treated no better and no worse than any other citizen"[11]—will take away existing rights *if those rights are defined as absolute*, ones that government cannot restrict. Here was a conception of freedom that could be invoked on almost any issue, by appealing to "ordinary Americans" that their freedom, the freedom they have always enjoyed, is at stake.

CLAIMING KING'S LEGACY

To drive home the point that there could be no other true meaning of American freedom, President Reagan invoked King himself. He did so at the very moment, on the first Martin Luther King national holiday in January 1986, when King was being presented as a national hero. Here was a president who had opposed all of King's ideas, from the 1964 Civil Rights Act through the Voting Rights Act and fair housing. Having argued strongly against the bill for a national holiday in King's memory, Reagan had signed the law only when faced with veto-proof majorities in both houses, and only after publicly questioning what King's FBI file would ultimately reveal and after telling a fellow conservative that he too had deep reservations about King, "but . . . the perception of too many people is based on an image, not reality."[12]

It was therefore striking when, on the first celebration of the holiday he had worked so hard to prevent, Reagan claimed that King's memory and words justified his own beliefs. "Martin Luther King believed, as I and so many Americans do," he said, "that our country will never be completely free until all Americans enjoy the full benefits of freedom. . . . We're committed to a society in which all men and women have equal opportunities to succeed, and so we oppose the use of quotas. We want a colorblind society, a society that, in the words of Dr. King, judges people 'not by the color of their skin, but by the content of their character.'"[13]

In citing King's words, Reagan did many things at once. He quoted King's dream of the ultimate outcome of government action—of government finally paying the promissory note of the Declaration of Independence, "the check that will give us upon demand the riches of freedom and the security of justice"[14]—to oppose government action to create such a society. Just as Spike Wilson had argued that government must be color-blind and therefore allow discrimination to continue—that limiting discrimination would benefit minorities and take away rights from white Americans—so Reagan was using color blindness to oppose affirmative action, which King had ardently supported. The message in both cases was the same: it was not King and the civil rights movement who were truly color-blind, but those who opposed them.

More broadly still, Reagan insisted, as he spoke about King, that there was no longer any need, or role, for government in expanding civil rights. "Blacks [are] doing better than ever before, and still not good enough," he said. "There's work to be done. But if we continue to allow the economy to expand and continue to work for a more perfect society, the people of all colors will prosper. And isn't that what Dr. King's dream and the American dream are all about?" The message was clear: there were no obstacles that government needed to remove "for all men and women to have equal opportunities to succeed."[15]

But Reagan's deepest message in speaking about King was the most important, a message not for African Americans but for whites. If even Martin Luther King believed in the same meaning of freedom as Ronald Reagan—that freedom meant the right to maintain one's traditions without being limited by government trying to assure freedom for others—then who could argue with this conservative vision of freedom as being unfair or racially biased? Reagan invoked King for the same reason that Spike Wilson had invoked Lincoln's Gettysburg Address twenty years before: to make this conservative vision of freedom, designed by America's realtors in the 1960s to oppose civil rights, seem like the *only* legitimate meaning of America's highest ideal.

The real question in these efforts to redefine American freedom was *whom* such freedom was for. At the heart of all the arguments over government and freedom was the question: Does freedom belong more naturally to some Americans than to others?

24.

Who Is Entitled to American Freedom

> I have great respect for the blue eyed and light haired races of
> America. . . . But I reject the arrogant and scornful theory by
> which they would limit . . . any . . . essential human rights to
> themselves, and which would make them the owners of this
> great continent to the exclusion of all other races of men.
>
> Frederick Douglass, 1869[1]

The realtors' most powerful contribution to modern conservative politics was an ideal of freedom that effectively prioritized the freedom of
certain Americans *without directly saying so*. The realtors' idea of freedom
appealed to a wide range of white voters because it protected and emphasized "our rights," meaning the rights of white Americans to continue to
discriminate—while claiming to support the equal freedom of all Americans. By defining freedom as they did, realtors did not have to say that
the freedom of some Americans was more important than that of others.
Rather, they redefined freedom so that this would be the result.

A key reason that realtors and conservatives succeeded in their
effort was that they used the same word as the civil rights movement
to mean something very different. Whenever they spoke about American freedom, freedom of choice, or rights, realtors presented freedom
as belonging to each person separately as a personal possession, so that
freedom for others diminished one's own. This legitimized one's right to
limit the freedom of others.

Distinguishing the realtors' definition of freedom from that of Truman's committee and the civil rights movement lets us grasp what was at
stake in these past and current political battles. We can summarize these

differences as two opposite, powerful, and far-reaching ideas of American freedom: the exclusive freedom that realtors envisioned to continue discrimination, in contrast with the inclusive freedom of the civil rights movement.

EXCLUSIVE VERSUS INCLUSIVE FREEDOM

In their deepest and most long-standing beliefs, realtors, conservative intellectuals, and white Southern leaders all saw American freedom not as an automatic and equal birthright but as a reward for those who deserved it, for those it truly belonged to. Realtors described rights as something that had to be earned: "All Californians must enjoy equal civil rights . . . but civil rights must include the assumption of civil responsibilities."[2] Fair housing took away "'human rights' from the vast majority of property owners . . . who . . . have earned the right to handle their own property as they choose."[3] Only those who had been allowed to own property, who could be admitted to certain neighborhoods, had earned such rights.

The idea that freedom depended on worthiness was implicit in the realtors' basic premise, that the right to discriminate was essential to American freedom. From the beginning, realtors had set standards of racial worthiness for who was entitled to live in a given area. Their methods of discrimination—and whom, which groups of Americans, they deemed worthy—evolved over the decades. What remained the same, however, was the realtors' fundamental idea that some people, from the moment of their birth, did not deserve to be able to freely choose where to live.

The Forced Housing Action Kit made this idea of deserving freedom explicit: "Those people who have struggled and sacrificed to make a decent social existence for their children . . . have won certain rights by virtue of their honesty and integrity. The most important of all their rights is their right to preserve their social identity, their community in which they find order and justice and freedom . . . and to preserve their community against newcomers."[4] Unstated, of course, was that realtors had set up racial barriers precisely to prevent other Americans, paying as much or more for housing, from ever attaining such "rights"—that the game of deserving rights had been rigged.

Like the realtors, leading conservative thinkers such as Russell Kirk spoke of rights depending on the individual's capacity to exercise such rights. Kirk attacked the idea of inalienable rights for confusing "rights with desires."[5] The idea of inalienable rights belonging to everyone was dangerous, Kirk insisted. He agreed with John Randolph—early nineteenth-century Virginia defender of states' rights and slavery—that "the principle that all men are born free and equal [is] . . . a most pernicious falsehood, even though I find it in the Declaration of Independence."[6] Kirk praised John C. Calhoun's assertion that "instead of all men having the same right to liberty and equality, liberty is the noblest and highest reward bestowed on mental and moral development."[7] Similarly, William F. Buckley Jr. in 1963 argued that Southern states must "defy the popular mania for the universal franchise."[8] In 1963, when few African Americans in the Deep South could vote, Strom Thurmond responded to the March on Washington, "No one is deprived of freedom that I know about."[9]

When realtors and conservatives dropped the language of racial entitlement and spoke about equal freedom, it was not to agree with the civil rights movement's idea of inclusive freedom but to oppose it more effectively. The idea that freedom must entail the right to discriminate meant that freedom was exclusive. For proponents of Proposition 14, the very purpose of freedom was the right to exclude.

Exclusive freedom already fully existed for everyone who deserved it; it did not have to be created or secured by government. Indeed, realtors insisted that American freedom preceded American government. It simply had to be defended against government taking away the right to exclude.

Seen in such a way, exclusive freedom was and had to be absolute. No conditions could be imposed on the right to sell or dispose of property; the owner must have "absolute discretion." Although absolute rights had never been part of freedom of speech, press, religion, or assembly, they were essential to the idea of exclusive freedom. Exclusive freedom eliminated the notion of government as referee, of freedom as something that had to be balanced and protected for everyone. By elevating certain rights as absolute, realtors and conservatives could argue that these particular rights were the very definition of freedom, while denying that such rights deprived anyone else of American freedom. Elevating these particular rights as the only ones that mattered allowed realtors and conservatives to cast aside any governmental protection of the rights others were deprived of, such as the right to buy a home in the first place. The purpose of absolute rights was to delegitimize the rights being suppressed. This was why realtors had to construct an idea of American freedom that would itself make the right to discriminate absolute.

Moreover, exclusive freedom hid within its seemingly neutral language *whose* rights should be absolute and whose should be ignored. The right to exclude contained a natural corollary, that freedom rightfully belonged to some Americans more than others. Providing minorities a right to not be discriminated against gave them an advantage—not because they were minorities, as realtors claimed, since fair housing gave everyone the same right to file a complaint, but because it *eliminated barriers*. It allowed minorities a social equality they had not "earned." The realtors had, since 1905, defined worthiness to live in a neighborhood in racial terms. What government threatened was the ability of entitled groups to limit freedom to those they deemed worthy of it—to themselves.[10]

Exclusive freedom was, inherently, the freedom of a group; its members could exercise their freedom because they were accepted as members of that group. Realtors and conservatives argued that the white majority was entitled to preserve its group rights—the right to maintain an exclusive sphere for its own group—partly by pointing to the civil rights movement itself as agitating for the rights of Black Americans.

Exclusive freedom differentiated those entitled to be treated *as individuals* from everyone else, who were treated only as members of an excluded group. This did not violate individual freedom in the eyes of realtors, because the essence of their whole system of segregation was that African Americans did not deserve to be treated as individuals. Rather, realtors wanted their collective organized discrimination to be seen simply as a series of separate decisions of individual white owners based on each one's conscience, as the freedom of those who deserved to be treated as individuals. Realtors thus made the conscience of each white individual sacrosanct while denying the individuality of those discriminated against. Discrimination, which by its nature meant denying individuality, was thus portrayed as the very purpose of individual freedom.

Realtors and conservatives then charged those seeking to end discrimination with seeing people only as racial groups. In accepting renomination in 1984, Reagan summed up this view: "Their government sees people only as members of groups: ours serves all the people of America as individuals. We believe in the uniqueness of each individual."[11] Such descriptions of his and his party's color blindness required Reagan to keep carefully private his own racist stereotypes. Kept private for almost fifty years was Reagan's 1971 call to President Nixon describing Tanzanian delegates to the UN: "to see those, those monkeys from those African countries—damn them—they're still uncomfortable wearing shoes."[12]

Civil rights advocates, by contrast, did not see fair housing and civil rights as claims for rights for Black Americans as distinct from those of other Americans; they were claims that individuals were entitled to the same rights regardless of race. "What rights? Special rights?" Rumford asked. "No. Only the same rights as everyone else has, the right to be treated no better and no worse than any other citizen."[13] For these advocates, there were no group rights, no "our rights" versus "their rights."

The difference between inclusive and exclusive freedom turned on a single question: Was freedom indivisible? If the answer was yes, as Truman's committee had argued, one's own freedom depended on others being free. If freedom meant equality of rights, the more freedom there was for everyone else, the more freedom each individual had. A country was free only if all of its citizens were. In Rumford's words, "Either we have a constitution which protects the civil and personal liberties of all people, or we do not."[14]

But if American freedom belonged separately as a type of private property to each individual, as the realtors vociferously argued, then giving rights to other citizens diminished and threatened the value of one's own. If American freedom was not inherently shared by all citizens, but something one possessed, like a house or piece of land, then its very exclusiveness was what made it valuable. And this exclusiveness had to be preserved for those who deserved it.

The vision of freedom needing to be limited to those worthy of it became part and parcel of conservative ideology. This conception of exclusive freedom underlies current arguments to prevent former felons from voting, to raise barriers to voting in general, to prevent undocumented immigrants from applying for citizenship, to build walls along our borders, and to limit refugees from certain countries. Conservative success was built on using the language of color blindness and equal legal rights to justify exclusive freedom. This was the precise formula realtors had developed for Proposition 14.

When Reagan spoke about freedom and equality, the language and arguments he used were those of the realtors, not of *National Review*. Reagan praised Russell Kirk as an "intellectual leader who shaped so much of our thoughts"[15] and created the "intellectual infrastructure of the conservative revival of our nation."[16] But Reagan would never have succeeded if, like Kirk, he had praised John C. Calhoun's view of "all men are created equal" as "so great an error"[17] and deemed the Declaration of Independence essentially un-American.[18] If, as some have argued, "the party of Lincoln . . . has become the party of Calhoun,"[19] it has done so not by citing Calhoun but, like Spike Wilson, claiming to be following Lincoln.

To argue for exclusive freedom after the 1960s—to win national elections based on freedom having at its very core the right to discriminate—conservatives needed to follow the realtors' example. They needed to quote the Declaration and the Gettysburg Address. They had to be in favor of freedom for all Americans while helping ensure that the benefits of such freedom belonged, by the very way they defined freedom, as if by the natural order of things, to some Americans more than others.

Conservatives needed above all to describe American freedom as separable. Proposition 14's vision of freedom enabled white Americans to vote to protect "our rights" as fully consistent with freedom for all Americans. White Americans heard over and over again that their own rights represented American freedom as a whole. The rights of "ordinary," "average," "forgotten" Americans, celebrated by Spike Wilson, Reagan, and a host of other conservative leaders, embodied that freedom. If those implicitly but indubitably white Americans were free, then Americans were free. This could only be true if American freedom was an individual possession, if one person's freedom did not depend on everyone else's.

What made the realtors' vision of freedom so politically success-ful, so divisive, and so emulated by modern conservatives was their use of individual freedom to defend the local social order. By convincing three-quarters of white voters that maintaining their own social tradi-tions was a matter of American individual freedom, realtors created a model for conservatism that went far beyond civil rights. Many, perhaps most, Americans came to believe that government efforts opposed to local social values were an attack on their individual freedom and there-fore on American freedom itself, as it had been so systematically defined and constantly promoted.

EXCLUDING COMMON RESPONSIBILITIES

Exclusive freedom carries with it one still deeper meaning that has made it especially powerful for conservatism overall: that freedom means the right to exclude public responsibilities. By locating freedom not in the nation itself but in each individual, exclusive freedom is inherently pri-vate. By picturing all freedom as a private possession—making "a per-son's house key the most sacred symbol of American freedom," in the words of the Forced Housing Action Kit—realtors and the conservatives who followed them suggested that freedom, like private property, was individually owned.[20] As a result, freedom meant the right to exclude not only others but the public sphere itself, to exclude what we owe each other.

Seen in this way, individual freedom meant the right to exclude the claims of society itself. Taxes, rather than a public duty, the price of the country's freedom, became instead an encroachment on one's individual freedom. Public education, rather than the way the country educated its citizens as the basis of the nation's freedom, became an intrusion on one's ability to raise and educate one's children in any way one likes. Pub-lic health measures became intrusions on the right not to vaccinate one's family. The commons—the common air, the common water, the com-mon climate—were not public responsibilities that government should protect on behalf of all its citizens. Such responsibilities could only limit one's individual freedom.

Because corporations have been defined as individuals and entitled to the same freedom, regulations on corporations were intrusions on their freedom. Food stamps, social security, a public safety net did not provide basic common protections but instead limited freedom. This same view of freedom helped shift the Second Amendment from the right to bear arms as part of a common militia to each individual's absolute right to weapons—the right to defend one's private sphere and to stand one's own ground. In the midst of the coronavirus pandemic, a shopper refusing to wear a face mask required by the store owner for the safety of customers and employees explained: "We have individual rights, we don't have community rights."[21]

This picture of exclusive freedom without a commons—without collective responsibility, without responsibility to others, and without government to balance these responsibilities—justified a fragmentary view of society. As British prime minister Margaret Thatcher, Reagan's ideological counterpart, put it, "They are casting their problems on society and who is society? There is no such thing! There are individual men and women and there are families."[22]

This isolating view of freedom was designed to serve a particular purpose. It was intended to maximize the rights and minimize the responsibilities of those who advocated it and whom they represented. The realtors used universal terms to protect a particular set of business practices. The language of individual rights, as the realtors had so carefully defined them, provided an ideal way for conservatives to argue that powerful businesses had no obligations; that regulations, rather than protecting the commons, inherently violated American freedom; that campaign contributions could never be limited; that there are no community rights.[23] Here was the basis of a political partnership, a grand alliance like that Collins had envisioned, between those seeking to expand their great wealth and tens of millions of voters for whom this idea of rights represented what they saw as their true and deepest interest: not the economic self-interest liberals told them was their true interest but their own freedom.

Because it was designed to protect the rights of some, the realtors' vision of freedom carried with it a particular emotional tone. Freedom became not a message of hope in a common future, in democracy, or in republican government—the animating message of the Revolution, the Union in the Civil War, or America in both world wars—but a way to express resentment, grievance, autonomy, and resistance. It was thus no accident that the more political power conservatives attained, the more central they made this message of resistance. Conservative presidents needed to demonstrate that they were really the leaders of the resistance, and that running the government was a battle against the enemy.

That it was the nation's realtors who contributed to this transformation of our politics, who successfully formulated a language of individual freedom to oppose "common responsibilities," exemplifies their changing role in the American dream. Rooted in progressivism, the realtor movement had been committed to regulation, progress, community, and social order. Realtors transformed appraisals and the very concept of value in real estate by emphasizing that a house had limited worth in itself, but derived its value from the surrounding neighborhood. Indeed, it was their belief in order, social stability, and the importance of the surroundings—not individual freedom—that led realtors to restrict whom owners could sell homes to. The American dream they marketed was of a family surrounded by those like itself. In all these efforts, they saw government as their natural ally, their partner in creating and institutionalizing this dream.

Only when government threatened this segregated dream in the name of common freedom did realtors redefine American freedom as an individual possession. To defend the racially exclusive neighborhoods they had worked so hard to create, they applied the language of exclusivity to freedom itself.

Beyond the realtors' idea of individual freedom, however, lay a desire to restore an idealized, narrow community. Glendale's realtors and officials had called theirs an "All-American City," with its "high standard of American citizenship," "smallest percentage of foreign population of any city in the state," and—proudly, as late as 1952—"100% Caucasian Race Community."[24] Individual freedom, in the realtors' 1964 campaign, referred to the individual's *right to such a community*, to be surrounded by those like oneself. The political power of the realtors' idea lay in invoking *individual freedom*—the right to choose one's own life, a right no government should limit—to insist on such lost, threatened, exclusive community.

In the half century since realtors designed this vision, as many Americans increasingly feel deprived of such a past community, the more this idea of individual freedom has driven the country's politics. Exclusive individual freedom is a claim that no shared, common, and equal rights of a broader community, of everyone, should stand in the way of the right to impose a past America.

These competing visions of exclusive and inclusive freedom are, as Lincoln suggested during the Civil War, fundamentally different visions of what the country should be.

CHANGING THE FUTURE

Recognizing the basic fact that our politics are being driven by two incompatible meanings of freedom provides a way to transform our political debates. This can be done in three complementary ways. Taken together, these approaches help challenge the way that the conservative vision of freedom has dominated much of our political landscape. Like the efforts to remove Confederate monuments by making plain that those heroic images—erected in the early twentieth century to redefine the meaning of the Civil War—were based on white supremacy, these approaches make plain that this ideal of American freedom raised to ennoble many conservative causes was based on excluding other Americans.

The first approach is to show, issue by issue, how this conservative vision of freedom has been developed and applied by advocacy groups, think tanks, state and national politicians, and conservative lawyers and judges to limit who is entitled to American freedom. Such work can show how the same techniques of elevating some rights and ignoring others have been applied across a wide range of issues that are usually thought of and fought over separately by separate constituencies.

For the conservative movement's ability to grow and thrive over many years through a seemingly disparate set of causes—opposition to abortion rights, gun control, gender rights, campaign finance restrictions, environmental regulations, taxes on homeowners, taxes on corporations, climate change initiatives, police reform, public schools—depended not on an adventitious alliance but on a unifying idea. At the heart of the rise of conservatism has been a new idea of freedom of choice designed to limit civil rights.

As the realtors showed, the success of this modern idea and of the causes it supports has depended on its being projected backward in time as America's original purpose. It has depended as well on freedom, communities, and the country itself being seen as rightfully belonging to some Americans more than others. The realtors understood that these two approaches—redefining our history and redefining whom freedom is for—are deeply entwined. They are versions of each other. At the heart of their original intent is an idea of whom the country was originally intended for.

Showing how these devices work, the assumptions they are based on, and their roots in the defense of segregation may be especially valuable for those who have been attracted, on at least one of these issues, by the appeal of this conservative vision of freedom.

The second approach is to positively assert that what is at stake in all these issues, what is indeed threatened, *is* American freedom, as the freedom of all Americans. Those who oppose this conservative vision can describe *their own objectives* as the defense of freedom: the freedom to marry, to choose where to live, to vote, to not be discriminated against by police or employers or retailers. All are part of an agenda of equal freedom.

Effectively challenging the causes in which the realtors' language has been deployed requires, not ignoring the importance of freedom, but redefining it. It requires the same insistence that American freedom is at stake in each issue. It requires understanding—as the realtors learned in switching from freedom of association to freedom of choice—what it is about freedom that resonates most deeply, that "freedom from" language has far less impact than "freedom to."

But it also requires challenging the realtors' underlying premise, that freedom is absolute. Rather, as Byron Rumford argued, anyone's freedom depends on everyone else's. Balancing and protecting such rights is the essential job and justification of government: "to assure to all equal freedom." If this history teaches anything, it is the power of a systematic appeal to freedom to reshape public debates.

The third approach is to systematically call these two opposite ideas of freedom *by opposite names*. Instead of *ignoring* these differences in how freedom is being invoked, of assuming that both sides are talking about the same general value or that these differences do not really matter—that they are simply justifications for self-interest and ways of appealing to each base—we can act. We can consistently and constantly call out these differences. When candidates or advocates talk about American freedom, we can insist on naming what is at stake. Rather than talk about freedom, we can spell out that what is being talked about is *exclusive freedom* or *inclusive freedom*.

Are these two terms, *exclusive freedom* and *inclusive freedom*, the best way to capture the differences in purpose, approach, and impact of these two ideas? There are other ways these differences can be described: as sovereignal freedom (freedom without respect for the rights of others) versus equal freedom, or as unequal versus equal freedom, or as separable versus inseparable freedom, or as libertarian freedom versus freedom as the right not to be dominated.[25] The terms exclusive and inclusive freedom have several advantages. They are simple and direct. They speak only about freedom itself. They distinguish what drives each of these different underlying ideas. They reflect the history of racial exclusion that led realtors to design a language of freedom to counter that of the civil rights movement. They remind us, whatever the issue, how mutually incompatible these ideas are. But whatever the terms, what is crucial is to name these differences.

By rigorously holding to such a standard, we can slowly begin to change the nature of our debates. No one provides a better model of how to do this than Ronald Reagan in his constant refrain throughout his debates with Jimmy Carter: "There you go again." The same approach can be used on every issue, on every level of debate: "There you go again, saying 'freedom' to justify exclusion." There will inevitably be resistance and risks. But there are graver risks in not doing so, in not challenging the way the word *freedom* is being used in our politics today.

ACKNOWLEDGMENTS

The idea for this book was triggered by a graduate seminar on human rights at Stanford University led by Professor David Palumbo-Liu, my son Andrew Slater's honors history thesis on another aspect of Proposition 14— its appropriation of Franklin Roosevelt's "the forgotten man" to splinter the New Deal coalition—and my work in affordable housing and neighborhood revitalization around the country.

James Campbell, professor in United States history at Stanford, was an extraordinary advisor as I developed these ideas first as a thesis for a master of liberal arts degree and then, with his encouragement, into a book. My meetings with Jim, his occasional "wows" and numerous "nopes," his decades of work on the history of civil rights, and his patiently and constantly pushing me deeper were invaluable. Linda Paulson and Peter Kline at Stanford offered excellent guidance and feedback.

Works by Daniel HoSang, Mark Brilliant, Aaron Cavin, Jennifer Burke, and Laura Redford suggested key archives. Hathaway Hester and Fredrik Heller at the archives of the National Association of Realtors in Chicago were very helpful. Their cooperation was essential to this project.

Affordable housing colleagues throughout the United States helped me see the connections between the history of residential segregation and the inequalities in housing patterns today. I also had valuable feedback from Simon Barsky, David Brodwin, Nazima Chowdhary, Bob Cornwell, Megan Haberle, Bob Harris, Michael Hindus, Bill O'Brien, and Lynn Withey.

Emmerich Anklam at Heyday was a keen, thoughtful, and stimulating editor, and the entire staff at Heyday was a pleasure to work with.

Both my sons, Andrew and Benjamin, living out my own dreams of becoming a schoolteacher, gave wise counsel throughout. My partner, now wife, Ayse Dogan, provided her centeredness and kind thoughtfulness.

This book is dedicated to Charles S. Johnson, Loren Miller, and Byron Rumford, whom I learned about in this research.

SOURCES

Many archives were crucial to this research and are noted as applicable for each item.

The archives of the National Association of Real Estate Boards are held by the National Association of Realtors in Chicago. The Los Angeles Realty Board's minutes and other documents are at the Charles E. Young Research Library, University of California, Los Angeles. The Reed Robbins Collection, from a key lieutenant to Spike Wilson, is at the Department of Special Collections at the University of the Pacific in Stockton.

The Edmund G. Brown papers and the William Byron Rumford papers are at the University of California, Berkeley's Bancroft Library. Proposition 14 campaign materials are also held by the Institute of Governmental Studies at UC Berkeley; by the Max Mont Collection, from a leading opponent of Proposition 14, at California State University, Northridge; and by the Stanford University News Service at the Department of Special Collections and University Archives of Stanford's Green Library.

Several valuable sets of materials are available online. An oral history of Rumford is part of the University of California's Earl Warren Oral History project, available at https://oac.cdlib.org/view?docId=kt5h4nb0wd&brand=oac4&doc.view=entire_text. The Loren Miller papers at the Huntington Library are available at https://hdl.huntington.org/digital/search/searchterm/Loren%20Miller. The Survey of Race Relations, including responses of local real estate boards throughout California in 1927, is available through the Hoover Institution at Stanford at https://purl.stanford.edu/px856nh3646. All the relevant California archives are listed at the Online Archive of California at https://oac.cdlib.org.

Dissertations are listed with the ProQuest identification number or the URL.

Magazine and journal articles include the URL where available. Important trade periodicals for this work are the *National Real Estate Journal* from 1910 to 1963 (with many of the early years fully available through Google Books), *Realtor's Headlines* from 1958 to 1968, and *California Real Estate* magazine (abbreviated as *CRE* in the notes) from 1920 to 1968. A crucial opposing voice was *Trends in Housing*, a newsletter published by the National Committee Against Discrimination in Housing, starting in 1956. Trade publication articles, except for several by leading realtors, are cited only in the notes, with date and page.

Newspaper articles (except those by key leaders or cited multiple times) are referenced only in the notes, with date and either page or URL. Many California newspapers are searchable for free through the California Digital Newspaper Collection (https://cdnc.ucr.edu), including editions back to the nineteenth century; minority-owned newspapers, including the *California Eagle* and the *Los Angeles Sentinel,* are especially valuable sources for this history. The *Baltimore Sun, Boston Globe, Chicago Defender, Chicago Tribune, Christian Science Monitor, Los Angeles Times, Pittsburgh Courier,* and *New York Times* are available through ProQuest. The *San Francisco Chronicle* is available on microfilm at Stanford, as is the *Oakland Tribune* starting in 1962.

NOTES

1. *Madera Tribune*, November 21, 1966, 6. Also see Longley et al., *Deconstructing Reagan*, 2007, 76.

2. Rumford, "Fair Housing and Proposition 14," 1966.

3. Frederick Douglass, "Our Composite Nationality."

Introduction: Gettysburg 1964

1. Lincoln, "Address at a Sanitary Fair," Baltimore, April 18, 1864, in *Washington Post*, December 28, 2015.

2. Younge, "Martin Luther King," 2013; Garrow, "King the Man, the March, the Dream," 2003. King confided "sort of a Gettysburg address" to African American journalist Al Duckett. See also Theo Lippman Jr., "The Making of a Dream," *Tampa Bay Times*, September 1, 2005, https://www.tampabay.com/archive/2003/08/24/the-making-of-a-dream.

3. King, "I Have a Dream," 1963.

4. King.

5. Younge, "Martin Luther King."

6. Younge.

7. Wilson, "Editorial," *California Real Estate*, July 1964, 2. Throughout the remainder of these endnotes, this publication is referred to as *CRE*.

8. Wilson, "Editorial."

9. Wilson, "The Fight for Freedom of Choice," *CRE*, June 1964.

10. HoSang, *Racial Propositions*, 2010, 53.

11. Stephen Grant Meyer, *As Long as They Don't Move Next Door*, 2001, 114.

12. Felker-Kantor, "Fighting the Segregation Amendment," 2014, 148–55.

13. Jimenez, "Fresno's Long Hot Summer," 2017, 41.

14. *San Bernardino Sun*, May 16, 1963, for Wilson's ancestry; *CRE*, April 1963, 5, 24, for Wilson's description of Greek immigrant dreams and the Property Owners' Bill of Rights.

15. *Los Angeles Times*, December 4, 1963, A1.

16. *Los Angeles Times*, A1.

17. Brilliant, *Color of America Has Changed*, 2010, 171; Reynolds, "An Institutional Study," 1964, 133.

18. U.S. Commission on Civil Rights, *Housing: 1961 Commission on Civil Rights Report*, 123.

19. King, "I Have a Dream."

20. HoSang, "Racial Liberalism," 2011, 198.

21. Jimenez, "Summer of 1967," 45.

22. Wolfinger and Greenstein, "Repeal of Fair Housing in California," 1968, 761f; Casstevens, *Politics*, 1967, 71–75.

23. Casstevens, *Politics*, 71–75.

24. Andrew Slater, "Race, Real Estate and the Forgotten Man," 2008, 31.

25. *Sacramento Bee*, October 28, 1964, 7, in Andrew Slater, "Race," 2008, 46.

26. Massey and Denton, *American Apartheid*, 1993, 200; National Fair Housing Alliance, "Fair Housing in Jeopardy," 2020, 32; Olatunde C. A. Johnson, "The Last Plank," 2011, 1192f.

27. Paul D. Kamenar, "Department of Justice." In Butler, Sanera, and Weinrod, 149–64, 155–56.

28. Foner, *Story of American Freedom*, 1999, 315.

29. Phillips-Fein, "Conservatism," 2011; Robbins, in John Denton, 1964.

30. Loren Miller, "Today and Tomorrow," May 23, 1957; National Committee Against Discrimination in Housing, "Housing and Civil Rights," 1959; and Robert Weaver, Address to NCDH, May 20, 1952, all in Loren Miller papers.

31. Lewis, "An Analysis of Proposition 14," 1964, 16.

32. Stephen Grant Meyer, *Don't Move Next Door*, 214.

33. Collins, *Whither Solid South?* 1947.

34. Edward Howden, "The Rumford Fair Housing Act and Proposed State Constitutional Amendment to Prohibit Such Legislation," speech to state convention of California Apartment Owners Association, October 1, 1963, Miller papers.

35. NAREB pamphlet, "Equal Opportunity in Housing." Cited in *American Israelite*, February 3, 1966, 1.

36. Lakoff, *Whose Freedom?* 2006, 73, 95.

37. Corey Robin, in "Reclaiming the Politics of Freedom," 2011, argues that "liberals and leftists" have failed to appreciate the power of the language of freedom in conservatism's appeal.

38. Foner, *Story*, xvi.

39. Kruse, *White Flight*, 2006, 6–10.

40. McGirr, *Suburban Warriors*, 2001.

41. Self, *American Babylon*, 2003; McGirr, *Suburban Warriors*. As one notable exception, Kevin Kruse, in *White Flight*, 2006, incisively showed how the use of color-blind language by suburban realtors around Atlanta helped create a political base for modern conservatism in the South and ultimately nationally. The present work expands on Kruse's approach, by looking at how such realtor arguments were first developed and why their use in California—a non-Southern, liberal state with a powerful, activist government and strong civil rights movement—proved especially influential.

42. Edsall and Edsall, *Chain Reaction*, 1992.

43. Sugrue, *Origins of the Urban Crisis*, 1996, and "From Jim Crow to Fair Housing," 2017; Self, *American Babylon*; Brilliant, *Color of America*, 2010.

44. King, "Other America," 1967, 5–6.

45. King, *Three Evils of Society*, 1967.

46. King, *Where Do We Go from Here*, 1968, 96.

47. King, "Other America," 7.

48. King, *Where*, 125–126.

49. Two of the best summaries of Proposition 14, by Mark Brilliant and Daniel Martinez HoSang, view the realtor arguments primarily in terms of the difficulties their opponents had in countering them. Brilliant focused on the political, legal, and especially interracial issues among Japanese, Hispanic, and African Americans, and thus viewed the realtors largely as an external obstacle for these groups. HoSang, in *Racial Propositions*, briefly but tellingly analyzed realtor arguments to show the difficulties liberals had in responding, including how liberals portraying discrimination as a matter of individual morality obscured realtors' organized discrimination. Like Brilliant, HoSang did not specifically focus on how realtors created their vision of freedom or its impact on conservatism.

50. *National Review* on "freedom-loving Americans," August 2, 2012, https://www.nationalreview.com/2012/08/where-have-heroes-gone-frank-miniter; Family Research Council's election summit to rally "freedom-loving Americans," September 18, 2020, https://www.prnewswire.com/news-releases/family-research-council-action-to-hold-virtual-values-voter-summit-to-rally-freedom-loving-americans-to-pray-vote-and-stand-301134026.html; House Minority Leader Kevin McCarthy on those who supported Republicans "voted for freedom," November 3, 2020, https://www.bloomberg.com/news/articles/2020-11-04/democrats-bid-for-senate-gets-early-test-as-first-polls-close.

51. See letter from William C. Carr of Pasadena Realty Board to Max Mont, January 10, 1960, Max Mont Collection, Box 3-10. Also see testimony before the U.S. Commission on Civil Rights, *Hearings*, 1960; McEntire, *Residence and Race*, 1960, 231f.

52. Letterhead of California Association of Realtors, 2021. For analyses of how realtors and the real estate industry generally have dealt with fair housing and discrimination since the passage of Title VIII, a vast topic of its own, see among many sources: Yinger, *Closed Doors*, 1995; Urban Institute, https://www.urban.org/features/exposing-housing-discrimination; Douglas S. Massey, "The Legacy of the 1968 Fair Housing Act," *Sociological Forum*, June 2, 2015, https://www.ncbi.nlm.nih.gov/pmc/articles/PMC4808815; "Long Island Divided," *Newsday*, November 16, 2019.

Part One. Limiting Individual Freedom for the Common Good: Early 1900s–Early 1920s

1. NAREB convention press release no. 57, November 15, 1961, NAREB archive.

2. *National Real Estate Journal*, May 10, 1910, 106.

1. Progressive Reformers of Real Estate

1. Pearl Janet Davies, *Real Estate in American History*, 1958, 52.

2. Keller, *Regulating a New Economy*, 1990, 93.

3. *National Real Estate Journal*, September 1917, 306. Quote from Herbert Cornish, president of the Los Angeles Realty Board (LARB) congratulating Garland on being elected president of NAREB.

4. These examples are from the *Los Angeles Herald*, January 26, 1899; June 19, 1902; January 25, 1899; June 12, 1903; June 17, 1903; and *San Francisco Call*, August 14, 1901; August 1, 1902; March 5, 1903.

5. Stults, "Brief History," 2015.

6. Pearl Janet Davies, *Real Estate*, 52.

7. McWilliams, *Southern California*, 1946, 118.

8. McWilliams, 120.

9. McWilliams, 133.

10. LARB archive; National Association of Realtors, "Garland"; "William May Garland," http://freepages.rootsweb.com/~npmelton/genealogy/lagar2.htm.

11. Babcock Ancestry, "William May Garland."

12. Redford, "Promise and Principles," 2014, 117. Garland's predictions, which he liked to point out were laughed at, proved remarkably accurate.

13. *National Real Estate Journal*, October 1917, 370. Speech by Garland to LARB.

14. Garland, "Civic Energy," 1921.

15. Garland.

16. Los Angeles Realty Board, "History," LARB archive.

17. *Los Angeles Times*, September 27, 1948, 1.

18. *National Real Estate Journal*, October 1917, 368. Speech by Garland to LARB.

19. *Los Angeles Herald*, June 4, 1904.

20. Los Angeles Realty Board, "History."

21. *Los Angeles Herald*, April 17, 1904.

22. *Los Angeles Herald*, May 31, 1903. Speech from Burdett to meeting of brokers at the Los Angeles County Chamber of Commerce.

23. Jonathan Club, "History," n.d. https://www.jc.org/history.

24. McGroarty, *Los Angeles from the Mountains to the Sea*, 1921, 152; *Los Angeles Times*, July 6, 1903, 6.

25. *Los Angeles Herald*, February 6, 1901; April 6, 1902; November 20, 1904.

26. Society page mentions of Garland and others who became LARB officials are from *Los Angeles Herald*, May 4, 1899; February 14, 1900; March 18, 1900; January 31, 1901; August 27, 1901; February 7, 1902. Altogether there were more than four hundred mentions of Garland in the society pages.

27. *Los Angeles Herald*, September 1, 1901.

28. Los Angeles Realty Board, "History."

29. LARB, "History."

30. McWilliams, *Southern California*, 1946, 133.

31. *National Real Estate Journal*, October 1917, 370.

32. *Los Angeles Herald*, May 26, 1904.

33. *Los Angeles Herald*, September 17, 1905.

34. *Los Angeles Herald*.

35. *Los Angeles Herald*.

36. Los Angeles Realty Board, "History."

37. *Los Angeles Herald*, April 23, 1903.

38. *Los Angeles Herald*, October 15, 1903.

39. *Los Angeles Herald*, May 30, 1903.

40. *Los Angeles Herald*.

41. Los Angeles Realty Board, "History."

42. *Los Angeles Herald*, June 28, 1904.

43. "Why the National Association of Real Estate Boards Is," *National Real Estate Journal*, January/February 1917, 1.

44. Nelson, "Real Estate Code of Ethics," 1925, 271.

45. Helper, *Racial Policies and Practices of Real Estate Brokers*, 1969, 149.

46. *National Real Estate Journal*, November 15, 1911, 262, describing Los Angeles as "no longer a boom city but a city of stability."

47. Krepleever, "Model Real Estate Board," 1911.

48. Frederick Law Olmstead Jr., quoted in Fogelson, *Bourgeois Nightmares*, 2005, 13.

49. Charles T. Male, *Real Estate Fundamentals*, 1932, 210–11. Quoted in Helper, *Racial Policies*, 1969, 208.

50. *National Real Estate Journal*, September 1917, 276. Speech at real estate convention by Lawson Purdy of the New York City Tax Department on restrictive covenants.

51. Hornstein, *Nation of Realtors*, 2005, 7; Redford, "Promise and Principles," 49.

52. *National Real Estate Journal*, April 1918, 226. "California License Law Adjudged Unconstitutional."

53. Redford, "Promise and Principles," 11, 48.

54. *Los Angeles Herald*, July 5, 1903.

55. *Los Angeles Herald*.

56. Nelson, "Real Estate Code," 1925, 270.

57. Nelson, 270.

58. *National Real Estate Journal*, August 2, 1920, 29. Quote from Paul Cowgill, Portland Real Estate Board.

59. Pearl Janet Davies, *Real Estate*, 55.

60. Redford, "Promise and Principles," 153.

61. *Los Angeles Herald*, September 12, 1903.

62. *Los Angeles Herald*, March 9, 1904.

63. Redford, "Promise and Principles," 89.

64. Weiss, *Community Builders*, 1987, 82–83.

65. Weiss, 85.

66. Claeys, "Euclid Lives?" 2004, 103–5.

67. Weiss, *Community Builders*, 10–11.

68. Weiss, "Urban Land Developers," 1986, 7.

69. *National Real Estate Journal*, May 8, 1922, 17. "Why Realty Interests Should Be Highly Organized," by Charles G. Edwards, New York Real Estate Board.

70. *National Real Estate Journal*, January 30, 1922, 10. "The Real Estate Profession."

71. *National Real Estate Journal*, June 15, 1910, 149, 150, 158; and July 15, 1910, 232.

72. *National Real Estate Journal*, January–February 1917, 1.

73. Krepleever, "Reform Movement," 1911.

74. Krepleever.

2. The Public Power of a Private Club

1. Krepleever, "Reform Movement," 1911.

2. *Los Angeles Herald*, July 5, 1903.

3. *National Real Estate Journal*, March 13, 1922, 15–18.

4. *Los Angeles Herald*, July 5, 1903.

5. LARB Articles of Incorporation, June 6, 1903, LARB archive.

6. Charles Shattuck, "Testimony," 1961.

7. *United States v. National Association of Real Estate Boards, et al.*, 339 U.S. 485 (1950).

8. *National Real Estate Journal*, October 15, 1911, 174.

9. Hornstein, *Nation of Realtors*, 2005, 16–17.

10. Weiss, *Community Builders*, 1987, 22–23.

11. *National Real Estate Journal*, November 1917, 440.

12. Krepleever, "Model Real Estate Board," 1911, 340.

13. Weiss, *Community Builders*, 1987, 26.

14. Krepleever, "Model Real Estate Board," 1911, 340.

15. Krepleever, 340.

16. Pearl Janet Davies, *Real Estate in American History*, 1958, 98.

17. Pearl Janet Davies, 98; National Association of Realtors, "Code of Ethics."

18. Pearl Janet Davies, 100.

19. Nelson, "Real Estate Code of Ethics," 1925, 271.

20. Parry, "Development of Organized Real Estate," 2004, 12.

21. *Riverside Daily Press*, November 9, 1921. Quote is from Riverside Realty Board.

22. Los Angeles Realty Board minutes, July 10, 1903, and "History of Los Angeles Realty Board, Inc. as of February 18, 1956," both in LARB archive. LARB's report citing increasing demands for its appraisals is from the *Los Angeles Herald*, June 5, 1904.

23. Pearl Janet Davies, *Real Estate*, 155.

24. Herbert Hoover, "Our Domestic Commercial Situation," *Chicago Real Estate*, June 1921, 1e.

25. *National Real Estate Journal*, March 13, 1922, 15.

26. Pearl Janet Davies, *Real Estate*, 39.

27. Hornstein, *Nation*, 3–5.

28. Redford, "Promise and Principles," 2014, 43.

29. *Los Angeles Herald*, September 25, 1908.

30. Hal G. Hotchkiss, "New President Lauds Realty Work," *CRE*, January 1928, 9.

31. Hornstein, *Nation*, 32, quoting *Chicago Tribune*, May 10, 1908, 14.

32. Krepleever, "Reform Movement," 237.

33. *Los Angeles Herald*, April 17, 1904.

34. Los Angeles Realty Board, "History."

35. LARB, "History."

36. Redford, "Promise and Principles," 21–22.

37. Redford, 24–25.

38. Redford, 23–24.

39. Charles Shattuck, "Testimony."

40. Shepherd, "No African-American Lawyers Allowed," 2003, 109. In 1914, the American Bar Association accidentally admitted its first three black members. Recognizing its mistake, it rescinded their admission, stating that "the settled practice of the Association has been to elect only white men to membership." It admitted its first African American member in 1943 when it waived its policy against two negative votes rejecting any applicant.

3. It's the Restrictions on Your Neighbors Which Count

1. Kurashige, *Shifting Grounds of Race*, 2008, 32–33.

2. Bunch, "Greatest State for the Negro," in de Graff, Mulroy, and Taylor, 143.

3. Flamming, *Bound for Freedom*, 2005, 66–68.

4. Massey and Denton, *American Apartheid*, 1993, 20.

5. Cutler, Glaeser, and Vigdor, "Rise and Decline of the American Ghetto," 1999, 463.

6. Taeuber and Taeuber, *Negroes in Cities*, 1965, 50. In Augusta, Georgia, 42 percent of all blocks in the city in 1899 were racially mixed.

7. Cutler et al., "Rise," 460, such as in Atlanta.

8. Cutler et al., "Rise," 463. In the decades since Taeuber and Taeuber first measured levels of racial spatial proximity versus isolation, scholars conducting more and more fine-grained analyses, both quantitative and historical, have shown that the level of segregation depends on the precise scale measured, such as John Logan and Matthew Martinez, "The Spatial Scale and Spatial Configuration of Residential Settlement Measuring Segregation in the Postbellum South," *American Journal of Sociology*, 123, no. 4 (2018): 1161–1203. But the broad trend of dramatically increasing segregation in cities in all regions in the early twentieth century remains.

9. Eventually passed as Chapter 241 in 1907. *Sacramento Union*, April 28, 1907.

10. *Los Angeles Herald*, August 12, 1909.

11. Buhai, "One Hundred Years of Equality," 2001; 1897 Cal. Stat., ch. 108.

12. Bunch, "Greatest State," 142.

13. Flamming, *Bound for Freedom*, 67.

14. Taeuber and Taeuber, *Negroes in Cities*, 485.

15. U.S. Commission on Civil Rights, *Equal Opportunity in Suburbia*, 1974, 16. Leroy Harris, in "The Other Side of the Freeway," 1974, 153–165, shows, in a detailed study of 1970 San Diego census data, that "if housing cost is a major factor in the concentration of Negroes into one section of the city, we would expect to find few if any other sections with housing costs as low or lower." In fact, because there were many such tracts with similar transportation and as low or lower costs but almost no African Americans, factors other than housing costs prevented them "from moving out of their present neighborhood." Similarly, the argument that African Americans remained concentrated in just a few census tracts out of choice was belied by studies showing how few properties were available to them elsewhere and how, unlike public accommodations, this had not changed in the decade since 1960. Looking at the nation as a whole, Kain and Quigley, *Housing Markets and Racial Discrimination*, 1975, 58, show that "Without exception . . . studies have determined that only a fraction of . . . black residential segregation can explained by low incomes or other measurable socioeconomic differences."

16. U.S. Commission on Civil Rights, *Equal Opportunity in Suburbia*, 16.

17. Weaver, *Negro Ghetto*, 1948, 6.

18. Taeuber and Taeuber, *Negroes in Cities*.

19. Berg, "Racial Discrimination in Housing," 1967, 87.

20. Nielsen, "Whiteness Imperiled," 2007, 120–124; Survey of Race Relations; Redford, "Promise and Principles," 2014, 107, shows that the original focus of restrictive covenants in Los Angeles had been against Mexican Americans and Japanese Americans.

21. Weiss, *Community Builders*, 1989, 1.

22. Fogelson, *Bourgeois Nightmares*, 2005, 161.

23. *Marin Journal*, December 30, 1915. Speech by McDuffie.

24. Worley, *J. C. Nichols and the Shaping of Kansas City*, 1990, 91.

25. Ivey, "Jesse Clyde Nichols," n.d.

26. Fogelson, *Bourgeois Nightmares*, 31.

27. Fogelson, 31.

28. Lorey, "History of Residential Segregation," 2013; Ivey, "Jesse Clyde Nichols"; Montgomery, "J. C. Nichols," 2016; Worley, *J. C. Nichols*.

29. Glotzer, *How the Suburbs Were Segregated*, 2020.

30. Weiss, *Community Builders*, 3.

31. Fogelson, *Bourgeois Nightmares*, 75.

32. Fogelson, 72.

33. Worley, *J. C. Nichols*, 82; Fogelson, *Bourgeois Nightmares*, 74.

34. Fogelson, *Bourgeois Nightmares*, 54.

35. Fogelson, 139.

36. Lorey, "History," 5.

37. Lorey, 8; Weiss, "Urban Land Developers," 1986, 13–19.

38. Hornstein, *Nation of Realtors*, 2005, 62.

39. Weiss, *Community Builders*, 3–10.

40. Weiss.

41. Worley, *J. C. Nichols*, 91.

42. Montgomery, "J. C. Nichols."

43. Steve Kraske, "I'm Still Talking about J. C. Nichols, Racism and Renaming the Fountain." *Kansas City Star*, June 30, 2017, https://www.kansascity.com/opinion/opn-columns-blogs/article158937604.html.

44. Mike Fannin, "The Truth in Black and White: An Apology from the *Kansas City Star*," December 20, 2020, https://www.kansascity.com/news/local/article247928045.html.

45. Fogelson, *Bourgeois Nightmares*, 73.

46. *California Outlook*, December 30, 1911, 17. Advertisement.

47. For Culver, see Weiss, *Community Builders*, 46–47; for Rush and Burck, see Redford, "Promise and Principles," 99–100.

48. Fogelson, *Bourgeois Nightmares*, 77–79, 102; Redford, "Promise and Principles," 96–97.

49. Fogelson, 161.

50. Redford, "Promise and Principles," 107.

51. Kurashige, *Shifting Grounds of Race*, 25.

52. Redford, "Promise and Principles," 111.

53. Kurashige, *Shifting Grounds of Race*, 25; Redford, 30.

54. Fogelson, *Bourgeois Nightmares*, 75.

55. Abrams, "Homes for Aryans Only," 1947.

56. Monchow, *Use of Deed Restrictions in Subdivision Development*, 1928, 47–51.

57. Kurashige, *Shifting Grounds of Race*, 25.

58. Gibbons, "Segregation in Search of Ideology?" 2014, 78.

59. Kurashige, *Shifting Grounds of Race*, 43.

60. Miller, "Race Restrictive Covenants and Democracy," 1946.

61. Davis, *City of Quartz*, 1992, 161.

62. Nielsen, "Whiteness Imperiled," 2007, 128.

63. Crimi, "Social Status of the Negro in Pasadena, California," 1941, 12.

64. Letter from William C. Carr, Pasadena realtor, to Max Mont, January 10, 1960, Max Mont Collection, Box 3-10.

65. Louis M. Pratt of Pasadena Realty Board, quoted in McMichael, *Real Estate Subdivisions*, 1949, 208–9.

66. Crimi, "Social Status," 21, 115, 119.

67. Crimi, 119.

68. Miles O. Humphreys, "Responsibility of the Smaller Cities of California." *CRE*, April 1927, 42.

69. *CRE*, July 1939, 56.

70. Fogelson, *Fragmented Metropolis*, 2005, 82.

71. Kurashige, *Shifting Grounds of Race*, 13.

72. Deverell and Flamming, "Race, Rhetoric and Regional Identity," 1999.

73. Deverell and Flamming, 127.

74. Sides, *L.A. City Limits*, 2003, 16; Redford, "Promise and Principles," 106. The rate was 93 percent in Santa Monica and 84 percent in Pasadena.

75. Sides, *L.A. City Limits*, 16.

76. Fogelson, *Fragmented Metropolis*, 72. "Their more ambitious friends" from these same states "departed for Chicago." Los Angeles and Chicago can be seen as two poles attracting immigrants, with those coming to Los Angeles drawn by

the climate and suburban prospects. Chicago also attracted those who had fewer resources and were looking for any work (Fogelson, 144).

77. Fogelson, 144.

78. Dana Barlett, Congregationalist minister, quoted in Fogelson, *Fragmented Metropolis*, 192.

79. Weiss, *Community Builders*, 79–82.

80. Fogelson, *Fragmented Metropolis*, 144–45, 191–92.

81. Fogelson, 213.

82. Abrams, *Forbidden Neighbors*, 1955, 144–46.

83. Fogelson, *Fragmented Metropolis*, 191.

84. Bartlett, *Better City*, 1907, 71–74.

85. Gibbons, "Segregation in Search of Ideology?" 92.

86. *Los Angeles Times*, September 7, 1924, D2. For graphic image, see http://michaelkohlhaas.org/wp/wp-content/uploads/2015/04/LA.times_.hollywoodland.ad_.png.

87. Quote from James Baldwin, in July 1963 file, Loren Miller files. From Baldwin, *The Cross of Redemption: Uncollected Writings*, ed. Randall Kenan (New York: Vintage International, 2011), 104.

88. *CRE*, February 24, 1924, 19.

4. Implementing Racial Exclusion

1. Flamming, *Bound for Freedom*, 2001, 153–54.

2. Glotzer, "Exclusion in Arcadia," 2015, 482.

3. McLain, "In re Lee Sing," 1990, 181f.

4. Kunai M. Parker, *Making Foreigners*, 2015, 141.

5. *National Real Estate Journal*, June 15, 1912, 288.

6. Cheng, *Cities of Asian America*, 2013, 26–27.

7. 49 Fed. 181, 182 (C.C.S.D. Cal. 1892).

8. Redford, "Promise and Principles," 2014, 103.

9. Redford, 105.

10. *Title Guarantee Trust Co. v. Garrott*, 183 p. 470 (Cal. Ct. App. 1919).

11. *Los Angeles Investment Company v. Gary*. 181 Cal. 680 (Cal. 1919), https://casetext.com/case/los-angeles-investment-co-v-gary. In effect, the court held that "once any set of bidders [for property] was excluded, it would be impossible to draw a line of reasonableness. . . . There would be no way to figure out whether the group of remaining bidders would be numerous enough." Brooks and Rose, *Saving the Neighborhood*, 2013, 60.

12. McGovney, "Racial Residential Segregation," 1945, 8.

13. 181 Cal. 680 (Cal. 1919).

14. Redford, "Promise and Principles," 105.

15. Ford, "Zoning Is So Logical," 1921, 46.

16. Davis, *City of Quartz*, 1992, 161.

17. Rarick, *California Rising*, 2005, 250.

18. Nielsen, "Whiteness Imperiled," 2007, 126.

19. Survey of Race Relations, 1927, 592.

20. Sides, *L.A. City Limits*, 2003, 16.

21. Bass, *Forty Years*, 1960, 96.

22. Nielsen, "Whiteness Imperiled," 126f.

23. Leroy E. Harris, "The Other Side of the Freeway," 1974.

24. Fisher, "Far from Utopia," 2008; Gage, "Creating the Black California Dream," 2015.

25. Ruffin, "Uninvited Neighbors," 2007; Cavin, "Borders of Citizenship," 2012.

26. U.S. Commission on Civil Rights, *Equal Opportunity in Suburbia*, 1974, 16.

27. Sanchez, "History of Segregation in Los Angeles," 2007, 7.

28. Hughes, *Chicago Real Estate Board*, 1979, 95.

29. Cheryl I. Harris, "Whiteness as Property," 1993.

30. Harris.

31. Philpott, *The Slum and the Ghetto*, 1978, 189–90; Freund, *Colored Property*, 2007, 87–93.

32. Philpott, 189–90.

33. Worley, *J. C. Nichols*, 1990, 150–52; Fogelson, *Bourgeois Nightmares*, 2005, 129. One developer, Hugh Prather of Highland Park in Dallas, defended selling to two or three whom he had "absolutely picked [as] . . . the best Jews in town" (Fogelson, 129). King Thompson of Upper Arlington in Columbus, Demarest of Forest Hills in Queens, and Bouton of Roland, near Baltimore, objected vehemently to the idea as "a perfectly ghastly mistake" (Worley, 151).

Part Two. Property Values:
Early 1920s–Late 1940s

1. Atkinson and Frailey, *Fundamentals of Real Estate Practice*, 1946, 34.

2. Atkinson and Frailey, 34.

3. Atkinson and Frailey, as quoted in Kushner, "Apartheid in America," 1979, 599.

4. Weaver, *Negro Ghetto*, 1948, 279.

5. *New York Times*, "Herbert Nelson, Real Estate Man," November 21, 1956, 27.

6. *New York Times*, "Real Estate Lobby Put under Inquiry," April 20, 1950, 19.

7. "Bristol's Most Famous [Unknown] Son," *Bristol Herald Courier*, December 17, 2017.

8. Gilpin and Gasman, *Charles S. Johnson*, 2003, 2.

9. Gilpin and Gasman, 1.

10. Bulmer, "Charles S. Johnson," 1981.

11. *Bristol Herald Courier*, December 17, 2017.

5. Undesirable Human Elements

1. Philpott, *The Slum and the Ghetto*, 1978, 196.

2. Survey of Race Relations, 1927, Napa, 622.

3. Survey of Race Relations, Madera County, 619.

4. U.S. Commission on Civil Rights, quoted in Darden, "Choosing Neighbors and Neighborhoods," 1987, 19.

5. Survey of Race Relations, 595.

6. Survey of Race Relations, Compton, 629; Riverside, 601f; Wilshire Development Association of Santa Monica, 623; San Jose, 606f; Pomona, 714; and Martinez, 620.

7. *National Real Estate Journal*, February 2, 1920, 28.

8. *National Real Estate Journal*, September 1919.

9. *CRE*, February 1937, 15, on the scientific nature of zoning.

10. *National Real Estate Journal*, April 1918, 199.

11. *New York Times*, April 20, 1950, 19.

12. Survey of Race Relations, Wilshire Development Association of Santa Monica, 623; Fresno, 633; San Pedro 729; Santa Maria, 731.

13. Redford, "Promise and Principles," 2014, 98; Cavin, "Borders of Citizenship," 2012, 180.

14. Kiang, "Judicial Enforcement," 1949, 3–6.

15. Survey of Race Relations, 736.

16. Fogelson, *Bourgeois Nightmares*, 2005, 123.

17. Nielsen, "Whiteness Imperiled," 2007, 98.

18. *U.S. v. Bhagat Singh Thind*, 261 U.S. 204 (1923).

19. Survey of Race Relations, 592.

20. NAREB, Code of Ethics, 1924.

21. Survey of Race Relations, Whittier, 593; Laguna Beach, 605; Bakersfield, 617.

22. Survey of Race Relations, San Jose, 607; Monrovia, 594.

23. Survey of Race Relations, Riverside, 601f.

24. Fisher, "Far from Utopia," 2008, 66, quoting *CRE*, July 1927.

25. Palmer, "Role of the Real Estate Agent," 1955, 66–78.

26. Helper, *Racial Policies*, 1969, 225.

27. Survey of Race Relations, Santa Barbara, 730.

28. Survey of Race Relations, 620.

29. Helper, *Racial Policies*, 118–120.

30. Helper, 121.

31. Survey of Race Relations, 601f.

32. Nelson, "Real Estate Code of Ethics," 1925.

33. *National Real Estate Journal*, January 30, 1922, 21. Article by A. C. McNurlin of Iowa.

34. Helper, *Racial Policies*, 118.

35. Nelson, "Real Estate Code of Ethics," 275.

36. *CRE*, January 1924, 25.

37. Survey of Race Relations, San Jose, 607f; Monrovia, 594.

38. Survey of Race Relations, 607f.

39. Survey of Race Relations, 594.

40. Survey of Race Relations, 599.

41. Abrams, *Forbidden Neighbors*, 1955, 155–67; Laurenti, *Property Value and Race*, 1960, 8–9; Helper, *Racial Policies*, 202–10.

42. Abrams, 155.

43. McMichael, *City Growth and Essentials*, quoted in Abrams, *Forbidden Neighbors*, 158–59.

44. Helper, *Racial Policies*, 202.

45. Babcock, *Appraisal of Real Estate*, 1924, 71.

46. Charles T. Male, *Real Estate Fundamentals*, 1932, 210–11, quoted in Helper, *Racial Policies*, 208.

47. John Spilker, *Real Estate Business as a Profession*, 1923, 128, quoted in Abrams, *Forbidden Neighbors*, 159.

48. Male, *Real Estate Fundamentals*, 210–11, quoted in Helper, *Racial Policies*, 208.

49. Abrams, *Forbidden Neighbors*, 166–67.

50. Elsie Smith Parker, "Both Sides of the Colored Line," 1943, 232–47.

51. McMichael, *Appraising Manual*, 1937, quoted in Helper, *Racial Policies*, 209.

52. Laurenti, *Property Value and Race*.

53. U.S. Commission on Civil Rights. *Hearings Held in Los Angeles*, 1960, 512–32.

54. U.S. Commission.

55. Weaver, *Negro Ghetto*, 268.

56. Laurenti, *Property Value and Race*, 20.

57. Hornstein, *Nation of Realtors*, 2005, 93.

58. Helper, *Racial Policies*, 25.

59. McMichael and Brigham, *City Growth and Values*, 1923, 181–82, quoted in Abrams, *Forbidden Neighbors*, 159.

6. Shaping Federal Housing Programs

1. Nelson, Testimony to House Select Committee, 1950, 21.

2. Kenneth Jackson, *Crabgrass Frontier*, 1985, 203.

3. Thurston, *At the Boundaries of Homeownership*, 2018, 41.

4. 1933 NAREB survey of its members, cited in Weiss, *Community Builders*, 1987, 28.

5. Henderson, *Housing and the Democratic Ideal*, 2000, 112.

6. Pearl Janet Davies, *Real Estate*, 1958, 178–79.

7. On the history of how this occurred, see Rothstein, *Color of Law*, 2017; Kushner, "Apartheid in America," 1979; Freund, *Colored Property*, 2007. Freund especially analyzes the underlying ideology.

8. Freund, "Marketing the Free Market," 17.

9. Berg, 1967, 38.

10. U.S. Civil Rights Commission, *Hearings*, 1960, 549.

11. Rothstein, *Color of Law*; Kushner, "Apartheid in America."

12. Nelson, Testimony, 21.

13. Pearl Janet Davies, *Real Estate*.

14. This war housing program was administered by Frederick Law Olmsted Jr., the eminent landscape architect who had designed Duncan McDuffie's and J. C. Nichols's subdivisions in the 1900s, and who, like them, was committed to racial exclusion. The hundred thousand units of war housing were racially segregated. Rothstein, *Color of Law*, 51.

15. McDuffie, "Interpretation of New Baking Regulations"; City of Berkeley, Landmark Application for Duncan and Jean McDuffie House, 2011.

16. Redford, "Promise and Principles," 2014, 44.

17. Redford, 178.

18. Hornstein, *Nation of Realtors*, 2005, 120.

19. Hornstein, 128.

20. Tillotson, "Risky Business," 2016, 32.

21. Tillotson, 34.

22. Foner, *Story of American Freedom*, 1999, 209.

23. Tillotson, "Risky Business," 20.

24. NAREB, Code of Ethics, 1924.

25. Weiss, "Richard T. Ely," 1989.

26. McMichael and Brigham, *City Growth and Values*, 1923, 356.

27. Homer Hoyt in 1933 on reduction in land values in Chicago, cited in Nicholas and Scherbina, "Real Estate Prices," 2013.

28. "President's Conference on Home Building," 1931.

29. Weiss, *Community Builders*, 143.

30. Pearl Janet Davies, *Real Estate*, 175–76.

31. Rothstein, *Color of Law*, 61, 82–83.

32. Rothstein, 61.

33. Johnson, *Negro Housing*, 1932, 35.

34. Johnson, 50.

35. Tillotson, "Risky Business," 54.

36. Weiss, *Community Builders*, 145–47.

37. Weiss, 145–47.

38. Pearl Janet Davies, *Real Estate*, 178–79.

39. Pearl Janet Davies, 44.

40. Nelson, Testimony, 1950, 21.

41. Weiss, *Community Builders*, 146.

42. *CRE*, February 1936, 10.

43. Weiss, *Community Builders*, 145–146.

44. Richard O. Davies, *Housing Reform*, 1966, 11.

45. Weaver, *Negro Ghetto*, 1948, 212.

46. *FHA Underwriting Manual*, 1935, sec. 233.

47. *FHA Underwriting Manual*, sec. 233.

48. Rothstein, *Color of Law*, 65.

49. Weaver, *Negro Ghetto*, 72; *FHA Underwriting Manual*, sec. 226.

50. *FHA Underwriting Manual*, 208.

51. Thurston, *At the Boundaries*, 108–10.

52. FHA's procedures for establishing maps are also far better documented than HOLC's, although it is largely HOLC's maps that have been preserved. FHA stopped using maps after the early 1970s in response to community investment concerns, and few of its maps are extant.

53. Light, "Nationality and Neighborhood Risk," 2010, 640.

54. Light.

55. Light, 647.

56. Kenneth Jackson, "Race," 1980, 451. "The deflation of real estate values in the 1930s, coupled with the view that there was a cycle of occupancy from the affluent to the poor, naturally made appraisers cautious. . . . The question was not whether a house or neighborhood would decline, but by how much and by when."

57. Hoyt, *Structure and Growth*, 1939, 121.

58. Aronson, Hartley, and Mazumder, "The Effects of the 1930s HOLC 'Redlining' Maps," 2017.

59. Federal Housing Administration, *Underwriting Manual*, 1938, sec. 909.

60. Jackson, "Race," 431.

61. Weiss, *Community Builders*, 147.

62. Weiss, 147.

63. Fogelson, *Bourgeois Nightmares*, 2005, 75.

64. *CRE*, September 1936, 16.

65. *CRE*, March 1940, 8.

66. Weiss, *Community Builders*, 153.

67. Sanchez, "History of Segregation," 2007, 6.

68. Gill, "'Decent Home,'" 2010, 337, 350.

69. Parson, *Making a Better World*, 2005, 56.

70. Gill, "'Decent Home,'" 358.

71. McEntire, *Residence and Race*, 1960, 249. As of 1945, according to NAREB, no real estate board in the country had an African American member.

72. Long and Johnson, *People vs. Property*, 1947, 2–3.

73. Long and Johnson, 8.

74. Atkinson and Frailey, *Fundamentals*, 1946, 61.

75. Thurston, *At the Boundaries*, 110–112.

76. FHA from 1949, cited in Rothstein, *Color of Law*, 86.

77. Rothstein, 94.

78. Helper, *Racial Policies*, 1969, 197.

79. Miles, "Hidden Hand," 2013, 25–26.

80. Rothstein, *Color of Law*, 94.

81. Rothstein, 65.

82. Freund, *Colored Property*, 14.

83. Weaver, *Negro Ghetto*, 72.

84. Weaver, 72.

7. Reconciling the War against Hitler with a New Racial Entitlement

1. Foner, *Story of American Freedom*, 1999, 237, 245.

2. Survey of Race Relations, 1927, Montebello, 601.

3. Abrams, *Forbidden*, 1955, 157.

4. Foner, *Story*, 238.

5. *Los Angeles Times*, July 19, 1943, 1.

6. Collins, *Whither Solid South?* 1947, 62.

7. Loren Miller, "Ghetto Is a Nasty Word," speech, c. 1945, Loren Miller papers.

8. Hassan, *Loren Miller*, 2015, 132.

9. Hassan, 143–145.

10. *Los Angeles Sentinel*, October 30, 1947, 1.

11. *Pittsburgh Courier*, October 9, 1943, 1, and November 27, 1943, 1.

12. *New York Times*, February 23, 1970, 26.

13. Kenneth Jackson, "Race," 1980, 437.

14. Elsie Smith Parker, "Both Sides of the Colored Line," 1943, 247.

15. Thurston, *At the Boundaries*, 2018, 127.

16. Thurston, 126–128.

17. Thurston, 113.

18. Freund, *Colored Property*, 2007, 127.

19. Tillotson, "Risky Business," 2016, 88.

20. Tillotson.

21. Tillotson, 34, 71.

22. Freund, "Marketing," 21; Freund, *Colored Property*, 19.

23. *CRE*, March 1924, 23.

24. Weaver, *Negro Ghetto*, 1948, 72.

25. Weaver, 72.

26. Loren Miller, "Address, March 14, 1955 to National Committee Against Discrimination in Housing"; "The House You Live In," California CIO State Convention, November 5, 1955, Miller papers.

27. Tillotson, "Risky Business," 59.

28. Tillotson provides an excellent exposition of this idea of theft and its use in the courts.

29. Vose, *Caucasians Only*, 1959, 84; *Hodge v. Hurd*, U.S. District Court, District of Columbia, 1945.

30. Rumford, Oral History.

31. Thernstrom and Thernstrom, *America in Black and White*, 1999, 60.

32. Schuman, Steeh, and Bobo, *Racial Attitudes in America*, 1965, 79, 106–107. In a 1963 National Opinion Research Center poll, 60 percent of whites agreed or strongly agreed that "whites have a right to keep blacks out of their neighborhoods if they want to, and blacks should respect that right." By contrast, a 1964 poll by the Institute for Social Research at the University of Michigan gave respondents a choice: Should blacks have the same right as whites to live where they could afford, or did whites have a right to keep blacks out of their neighborhoods? Given these options, 65 percent said blacks should have the same rights; 35 percent said whites had a right to exclude them.

Part Three. Freedom of Association: Late 1940s–Late 1950s

1. *Los Angeles Sentinel*, August 28, 1947, 1.
2. *California Eagle*, September 25, 1947, 1; *Los Angeles Sentinel*, October 9, 1947, 1.
3. *Los Angeles Times*, December 3, 2006, B2.
4. deGuzman, "'And Make the San Fernando Valley My Home,'" 2014, 132.
5. *Los Angeles Times*, September 27, 1964, O1.
6. Radkowski, "Managing the Invisible Hand," 2015, 148.
7. Hassan, *Loren Miller*, 2015, 13–20.
8. Loren Miller, "Song for a Suicide," poem, 1929, Loren Miller papers.
9. Hassan, *Loren Miller*, 152.
10. Hassan, 134.
11. Hassan, 159.
12. Hassan, 165.
13. Loren Miller, "Race Restrictive Covenants and Democracy," speech, Columbus, Ohio, October 10, 1946, Miller papers.

8. Defending Racial Covenants

1. Loren Miller, "Race Restrictive Covenants and Democracy," speech, Columbus, Ohio, October 10, 1946, Loren Miller papers.
2. Loren Miller, "Race Restrictive Covenants."
3. *Plessy v. Ferguson*, 163 U.S. 537 (1896), 544.
4. *Liberator*, May 31, 1839, 87.
5. *Smith v. Allwright*, 321 U.S. 649 (1944).
6. *Whitney v. California* (1929), 274 U.S. 357.
7. The Norris-La Guardia Act (1932), National Industrial Recovery Act (1933), and National Labor Relations Act (1935) established union members' freedom to associate together in a labor union; the Taft-Hartley Act (1947), passed over President Truman's veto, enabled states to pass right to work laws prohibiting union shops where new employees had to join the labor union. Perhaps the most pertinent use of freedom of association dealing with racial discrimination in the union context had come from the American Federation of Labor in 1943. The AFL had argued that fair employment laws interfered with their freedom of association as a labor union. The AFL executive council "does not believe that imposition of any policy, no matter how salutary, through compulsory government control of freely constituted associations of workers accords with basic rights of freedom of association." *Pittsburgh Courier*, October 16, 1943, 1. This argument to exclude other races was what the Supreme Court rejected, at least in the case of a political party organization, in *Smith v. Allwright* a year later, in 1944.
8. 163 U.S. 537 (1896).

9. *New York Times*, July 18, 1948, 2.

10. HoSang, *Racial Propositions*, 2010, 9–10.

11. HoSang, 34.

12. HoSang, 34–36.

13. Chen, *Fifth Freedom*, 2009, 127–31.

14. Chen, 127–31.

15. HoSang, *Racial Propositions*, 41–42.

16. Chen, *Fifth Freedom*, 127–129.

17. HoSang, *Racial Propositions*, 44.

18. Chen, *Fifth Freedom*, 124.

19. Chen, 75, 129.

20. Chen, 124.

21. HoSang, *Racial Propositions*, 39. Dellums's nephew, Ron Dellums, would be a long-serving congressman, a founder of the Congressional Black Caucus, and mayor of Oakland.

22. HoSang, 48.

23. *Los Angeles Times*, February 15, 1951, A1.

24. Richard O. Davies, *Housing Reform*, 1966, 40. At the end of the war, fewer than 15 percent of Los Angeles's 782,000 war workers left the city.

25. Sides, *L.A. City Limits*, 2003, 36f.

26. Housing and Home Finance Agency, "Housing of the Nonwhite Population 1940-1947," June 1948. Miller archive.

27. Robert Weaver in 1948, quoted in Mah, "Buying into the Middle Class," 2000, 62.

28. Elsie Smith Parker, "Both Sides of the Colored Line," July 1943, 247.

29. *California Eagle*, September 25, 1947, 1.

30. *Los Angeles Times*, December 3, 2006, OCB2.

31. *Los Angeles Sentinel*, August 14, 1947, 2.

32. *Los Angeles Sentinel*, June 19, 1947, 1.

33. *Los Angeles Sentinel*, July 17, 1947, 16.

34. *Los Angeles Sentinel*, February 3, 1947, 9, and October 2, 1947, 11.

35. Vose, "NAACP Strategy in the Covenant Cases," 1955.

36. Lawson, *To Secure These Rights*, 2004, 179.

37. Gardner, *Harry Truman and Civil Rights*, 2002, 16–17.

38. Andrew Myers, "Resonant Ripples in a Global Pond," 2002.

39. Roche, *Quest for the Dream*, 1963, 238.

40. Gardner, *Harry Truman*, 21.

41. Lawson, *To Secure These Rights*, 12.

42. Roche, 238.

43. Roche, 238.

44. Lawson, *To Secure These Rights*, 181.

45. Lawson, 181.

46. Lawson, 50.

47. Lawson, 50.

48. *CRE*, December 1947, 6.

49. Lawson, *To Secure These Rights*, 50.

50. Lawson, 102.

51. Lawson, 51.

52. Vose, *Caucasians Only*, 1959, 169.

53. 334 U.S. 23.

54. Ming, "Racial Restrictions," 1949, 203.

55. 334 U.S. 23.

56. Kurland and Capser, eds., *Landmark Briefs*, 1975, 543.

57. 334 U.S. 10.

58. Tushnet, *Making Civil Rights Law*, 1994, 93.

59. Tushnet, 94.

60. 334 U.S. 19.

61. Hassan, *Loren Miller*, 2015, 175.

62. Loren Miller, "Whose Civil Rights," March 1949, Miller papers.

63. *Los Angeles Sentinel*, May 6, 1948, 1.

9. Recommitting to Segregation after *Shelley*

1. Mikva, "Neighborhood Improvement Association," 1951, 118.

2. Weaver, *Negro Ghetto*, 1948, 236.

3. Mikva, "Neighborhood," 118.

4. *CRE*, September 1948, 4.

5. *Chicago Defender*, October 5, 1948, 5.

6. Mikva, "Neighborhood," 118.

7. *Pittsburgh Courier*, August 28, 1948, 5.

8. Mikva, "Neighborhood," 118.

9. Leo Kuper, "Sociological Aspects," 122–33.

10. Mikva, "Neighborhood," 118.

11. McKenzie, *Privatopia*, 1994, 77.

12. *CRE*, May 1951, 14.

13. McMichael, *Real Estate Subdivisions*, 1949, 206–208.

14. Brooks and Rose, *Saving the Neighborhood*, 2013, 6.

15. U.S. Commission on Civil Rights, *Hearings*, 1960, 715–19. Study by Dr. James H. Kirk and Elaine D. Johnson.

16. Rothstein, *Color of Law*, 2017, 89.

17. Abrams, *Forbidden Neighbors*, 1955, 184.

18. U.S. Commission on Civil Rights, *Hearings*, 248–62. Testimony of Loren Miller.

19. Loren Miller, *Petitioners*, 1966, 327.

20. Sanchez, "History of Segregation in Los Angeles," 2007, 1.

21. U.S. Commission on Civil Rights, *Hearings*, 258.

22. California Department of Transportation, "Tract Housing," 2011, 32.

23. City of Lakewood, "History," https://www.lakewoodcity.org/about/history/history.

24. *CRE*, February 1949, 6.

25. *Realtor's Headlines*, March 15, 1965.

26. *CRE*, September 1948, 4.

27. Gill, "'A Decent Home,'" 2010, 343.

28. *Los Angeles Times*, February 3, 2019, B1.

29. *Los Angeles Times*, B1.

30. Andrew Slater, "Race, Real Estate and the Forgotten Man," 2008, 12; *CRE*, June 12, 1948, 3.

31. *San Mateo Times*, August 3, 1948, 5.

32. Freund, *Colored Property*, 2007, 19.

10. Using Freedom of Association to Intensify Segregation

1. Helper, *Racial Policies*, 1969, 125.

2. Hecht, *Because It Is Right*, 1970, 4–5.

3. Cavin, "Borders of Citzenship," 2012, 357.

4. Helper, *Racial Policies*, 125.

5. Helper, 121–125.

6. Sanchez, "History of Segregation in Los Angeles," 2007, 8.

7. McEntire, *Residence and Race*, 1960, 241.

8. Kurashige, *Shifting Grounds of Race*, 2008, 238.

9. *New York Herald Tribune*, October 14, 1962, A1.

10. *New York Herald Tribune*, A1.

11. McEntire, *Residence and Race*, 239.

12. Palmer, "Role of the Real Estate Agent," 1955, 164.

13. Palmer, 66–67.

14. Palmer, 139.

15. Laurenti, *Property Value and Race*, 1960, 17.

16. U.S. Commission on Civil Rights, *Report*, 1961, 123.

17. Helper, *Racial Policies*, 292.

18. Helper, 212.

19. HoSang, "Racial Liberalism," 2010, 191.

20. U.S. Commission on Civil Rights, *Hearings Held in Los Angeles*, 1960, 111, 278–81.

21. Loren Miller, "Government's Responsibility," in Denton, *Race and Property*, 1964, 59.

22. Charlotte Brooks, "Sing Sheng v. Southwood," 2004, 463.

23. Brooks, 476.

24. Brooks, 488.

25. Loren Miller, "The House You Live In," speech at California CIO State Convention, Long Beach, November 5, 1955, Loren Miller papers.

26. Brooks, "Sing Sheng," 2004, 490–91.

27. Speech of California real estate commissioner Milton Gordon, quoted in Sullivan, "Letting Down the Bars," 2003, 304.

28. Sides, *L.A. City Limits*, 2003, 110, for Los Angeles suburbs; LeRoy Harris, "Other Side of the Freeway," 1974, 127–44, for San Diego.

29. Brilliant, *Color of America*, 2010, 171.

30. *New York Times*, July 9, 1962, 1.

31. Ethington, Frey, and Myers, "Racial Resegregation," 2001, 8.

32. Loren Miller, "Today and Tomorrow," speech, May 23, 1957, Miller papers.

33. Helper, *Racial Policies*, 233.

34. Helper, 233, for Chicago; Palmer, "Role of the Real Estate Agent," 53, for New Haven; Laurenti, *Property Value and Race*, for San Francisco; *Los Angeles Sentinel*, December 7, 1961, C6, for San Jose.

35. *Realtor's Headlines*, March 15, 1965, 2.

36. McEntire, *Residence and Race*, 241.

37. Fisher, "Far from Utopia," 2008, 246.

38. Daniels, "Berkeley Apartheid," 2013, 328.

39. Daniels, 235.

40. McEntire, *Residence and Race*, 247.

41. *United States v. Real Estate Boards*, 339 U.S. 485 (1950). NAREB's successor, the National Association of Realtors, was sued by and settled with the Department of Justice on antitrust grounds in 2013 and 2020, https://www.justice.gov/opa/pr/justice-department-files-antitrust-case-and-simultaneous-settlement-requiring-national.

42. *Los Angeles Sentinel*, September 4, 1947, 7.

43. Marcus, "Civil Rights and the Anti-Trust Laws,"1951, 210–14.

44. 333 U.S. 20.

45. Thurston, *At the Boundaries*, 2018, 115 ff.

46. Freund, *Colored Property*, 2007, 88.

47. Thurston, *At the Boundaries*, 116 ff.

48. Weiss, *Community Builders*, 1987, 147.

49. California Department of Transportation, "Tract Housing," 2011, 29.

50. Brilliant, *Color of America*, 171; Reynolds, "An Institutional Study," 1964, 133.

51. Berg, "Racial Discrimination in Housing," 1967, 132.

52. Loren Miller, "Government's Responsibility," in Denton, *Race and Property*, 67.

53. No. 97310, California Superior Court, Sacramento (1958).

54. *New York Times*, November 14, 1958, 46.

55. FHA letter to Walter White, December 29, 1944, quoted in Thurston, *At the Boundaries*, 114.

11. The Idea of a National Conservative Party

1. Crespino, *Strom Thurmond's America*, 2012, 68.

2. Driver, "Supremacies and the Southern Manifesto," 2014, 1070.

3. Collins, *Whither Solid South?* 1947, 257.

4. Collins, ix.

5. Collins, viii.

6. Collins, 282.

7. Russell, "*The Fourteenth Amendment and the States* by Charles Wallace Collins," 1914, 504.

8. Collins, *Whither Solid South?* ix.

9. Collins, ix.

10. Collins, 257.

11. Collins, 281.

12. Collins, vii.

13. Collins, 57.

14. Collins, 95.

15. Collins, 95.

16. Collins, 67.

17. Collins, 298.

18. Collins, 301.

19. Collins, 86.

20. Collins, 151.

21. Goldwater, *Conscience of a Conservative*, 1960, 12.

22. Collins, *Whither Solid South?* 257.

23. Chen, *Fifth Freedom*, 2009, 70.

24. Chen, 67–68. Quotes from Democratic representatives John Rankin of Mississippi, Samuel F. Hobbs of Alabama, and Jamie Whitten of Mississippi.

25. Chen, 136. Quote from Charles F. Hough, representing Associated Employers of Illinois in 1945 testimony to the Senate Judiciary Committee.

26. Chen, 129.

27. Critchlow and MacLean, *Conservative Ascendancy*, 2009, 5.

28. Lowndes, *From the New Deal to the New Right*, 2008, 26–30.

29. Hofstadter, "From Calhoun to the Dixiecrats," 1949, 148.

30. Lowndes, *New Deal*, 32.

31. Lowndes, 36.

32. Pach, "Dwight D. Eisenhower: Domestic Affairs," n.d.

Part Four. Freedom of Choice: Late 1950s–June 1963

1. Hoffman, "Like Fleas on a Tiger?" 1998, 3, 21.

2. Stephen Grant Meyer, *Don't Move Next Door*, 2001, 139.

3. U.S. Commission on Civil Rights, *Hearings,* 577; Tufte, "Civil Rights Movement," 1968, 112 f.

4. Sugrue, "From Jim Crow," 2017.

5. Miles, *Hidden Hand*, 2013, 36f; Rutledge, "Threat to the Great Society," 1965.

6. *Pittsburgh Courier*, August 28, 1948. Quote from LARB attorney Byron C. Hanna.

7. Massey and Denton, *American Apartheid*, 1993, 49. In a national survey in 1942, "84% of whites answered 'yes', 'Do you think there should be separate sections in towns and cities for Negroes to live in." By 1962, 61 percent of whites felt that "white people have a right to keep blacks out of their neighborhood if they want to, and blacks should respect that right." If Southern states were excluded, the figures would presumably be somewhat lower.

8. *Pittsburgh Courier*, August 28, 1948.

9. *Los Angeles Times*, January 13, 1963, 12, 26.

10. Palmer, "Role of the Real Estate Agent," 1955, 139.

12. Struggling for an Ideology to Defend against Fair Housing

1. Charles Shattuck, "Testimony," 1961.

2. Robison, "Fair Housing Legislation," 1968, 58.

3. *Pittsburgh Courier*, December 6, 1958, 5.

4. *Philadelphia Tribune*, December 16, 1958.

5. *Boston Globe*, October 6, 1963, A44.

6. *Boston Globe*, March 1, 1964, A34.

7. See, for example, *San Francisco Chronicle*, December 13, 1963, 7, on West Contra Costa Board of Realtors vote of 150 to 2 to support Proposition 14; *Los Angeles Times*, February 12, 1964, 3, on Realtors for Fair Housing who opposed Proposition 14; *San Francisco Chronicle*, December 4, 1963, on San Francisco Real Estate Board vote to oppose Proposition 14.

8. *CRE*, December 1960, 8f, quoted in Cain, "Absolute Discretion," 1964, 12.

9. Sara Marie Butler, "Partisan Pathways to Racial Realignment," 2015, 160–67. Taft, dying of cancer in 1953, supported Knowland's becoming Senate Republican leader. Syndicated columnist Joseph Alsop called Knowland the new "Mr. Republican." *National Review*'s editors considered endorsing Knowland for president in

their inaugural issue, but instead decided to do so later. After Eisenhower's heart attack, William F. Buckley Jr. urged Knowland to run.

10. Ambrose, *Eisenhower*, 1990, 334.

11. McGirr, *Suburban Warriors*, 2001, 115.

12. Sara Marie Butler, "Partisan Pathways," 178–180; Schuparra, *Triumph of the Right*, 1998. Knight had sought to avoid alienating labor. When he became governor in 1953, Knight vowed he would "never approve a law designed to punish labor or to discriminate against labor," continuing the largely centrist, pragmatic policies that had long allowed Republicans to dominate gubernatorial elections.

13. Andrew Slater, "Race, Real Estate and the Forgotten Man," 2008, 13.

14. Schuparra, *Triumph of the Right*, xvii.

15. Schuparra, xvii and 29.

16. Schuparra, 41.

17. Sara Marie Butler, "Partisan Pathways," 136.

18. McGirr, *Suburban Warriors*, 130.

19. Sara Marie Butler, "Partisan Pathways," 189. Knowland won 40.2 percent of the vote against Brown; the Right to Work initiative, Proposition 18, received an almost identical 40.4 percent.

20. Thomas L. Pitts, secretary-treasurer of California AFL-CIO, CBS radio script for September 20, 1964, Brown papers, Box 662:3 "Rumford."

21. *CRE*, February 1959, 5, 30.

22. Brilliant, *Color of America*, 2010, 173.

23. Andrew Slater, "Race," 15.

24. Brilliant, *Color of America*, 164, 173.

25. *CRE*, December 1960, 9.

26. *Newport Harbor News*, May 19, 1961, in NAREB, Forced Housing Action Kit.

27. Schiesl, "Residential Opportunity," 2013.

28. U.S. Commission on Civil Rights, *Hearings*, 1960.

29. U.S. Commission, 273.

30. U.S. Commission, 577.

31. Tufte, "Civil Rights Movement," 1968, 112.

32. *Hearings Before the United States Commission on Civil Rights*, January 1960, 577.

33. Tufte, "Civil Rights Movement," 128–130.

34. Radkowski, "Managing the Invisible Hand," 2015, 58.

35. Sides, *L.A. City Limits*, 2003, 110.

36. *Hearings*, 273–278.

37. *Hearings*, 274–276.

38. *Hearings*, 276–278.

39. Schiesl, "Residential Opportunity," 2013, 2.

40. Gill, "'Decent Home,'" 2010, 360.

41. *CRE*, May 1961, 8.

42. *Newport Harbor News Press*, May 19, 1961, in NAREB, Forced Housing Action Kit.

43. *Los Angeles Times*, April 7, 1961, in NAREB, Forced Housing Action Kit.

44. *Sacramento Union*, March 26, 1961, "An Iniquitous Measure," in NAREB, Forced Housing Action Kit.

45. *Sacramento Union*, March 26.

46. *Hollywood Citizen News*, May 20, 1961, in NAREB, Forced Housing Action Kit.

47. *Redondo Beach Daily Breeze*, May 13, 1961, in NAREB, Forced Housing Action Kit.

48. *San Francisco Chronicle*, April 11, 1961, 12, in NAREB, Forced Housing Action Kit.

49. *Sacramento Union*, March 6, 1961, in NAREB, Forced Housing Action Kit.

50. *San Francisco Chronicle*, April 11, 1961, 12, in NAREB, Forced Housing Action Kit.

51. *Los Angeles Times*, April 7, 1961, in NAREB, Forced Housing Action Kit.

52. Sullivan, "Letting Down the Bars," 2003, 275.

53. Radkowski, "Managing," 42. Testimony of assistant real estate commissioner G. E. Harrington that "anyone who uses the term [Realtor] without authority is subject to revocation of their license."

54. California Assembly, "Testimony of H. Jackson Pontius."

55. Shattuck, "Testimony," 1961, Loren Miller papers.

56. Shattuck, "Testimony."

57. *Los Angeles Times*, January 24, 1961, 2.

58. Shattuck, "Testimony," Miller papers.

59. Shattuck, "Testimony."

60. Shattuck, "Testimony."

61. Shattuck, "Testimony."

62. Radkowski, "Managing," 148.

13. Creating a Standardized Ideology of Freedom

1. *CRE*, April 1963, 6.

2. Robison, "Housing—The Northern Civil Rights Frontier," 1961, 116.

3. Rutledge, "Threat to the Great Society," 1965.

4. "NAREB convention press release no. 57," November 15, 1961, NAREB archive; *Los Angeles Times*, November 16, 1961, A1; *Washington Post Times Herald*, November 16, 1961, B7.

5. *New York Times*, November 16, 1961, 65.

6. *New York Times*, 65.

7. David H. Jaquith of the Conservative Party, letter to the editor, *New York Times*, February 22, 1964, 20.

8. Nikole Hannah-Jones, "It Was Never about Busing," *New York Times*, July 12, 2019.

9. *Los Angeles Times*, November 17, 1961, B10.

10. *Washington Post Times Herald*, November 16, 1961, B7.

11. U.S. Commission on Civil Rights, *Housing*, 1961, 150.

12. Commission, 142, 146.

13. Commission, 2, 123, 125 f.

14. State Associations Steering Committee, Notebook (including subcommittees), 1960–1967, May 6, 1962, and June 5, 1962, NAREB archive.

15. NAREB, Forced Housing Action Kit.

16. Avins, ed., *Open Occupancy*, 1963.

17. As one example, Avins in *Open Occupancy* cited an obscure New York City news story of a Black public housing authority tenant in Staten Island unable to move to a Manhattan project two hours closer to her job because the housing authority insisted on keeping both projects integrated. The story's only relevance to fair housing was to show the irrationality of government insistence on race-mixing. In the Proposition 14 campaign, a CREA leader and member of NAREB's board of directors cited the exact same story to make this point. Avins, "Anti-Discrimination Legislation," 1963, 30; Robbins, "Critical Analysis," 1964, 95.

18. Avins's pro-eugenics organization quoted in Jackson and Jackson, *Science for*

Segregation, 2005, 67.

19. Avins, "Anti-Discrimination Legislation," 38–39.

20. Jackson and Jackson, *Science for Segregation*, 66.

21. Jackson and Jackson, 67.

22. NAREB board of directors, minutes, 1962, and letter from Avins to Eugene Conser, April 20, 1962, NAREB archive.

23. Jackson and Jackson, *Science for Segregation*, 67.

24. Opinion of California attorney general 62/142, October 30, 1962, Loren Miller papers.

25. Landsberg, "Public Accommodations," 2016, 8.

26. *New York Times*, May 26, 1966, 29; Jackson and Jackson, *Science for Segregation*, 67.

27. Cooke, "Review," 1961, 622–23.

28. Mallery et al., "Comment on Martin"; Dickson, "State Court Defiance," 1994.

29. Tovey, "Discrimination," 64.

30. Million, "Racial Covenants Revisited," 90.

31. *Price v. Evergreen Cemetery*, 57 Wn. 2nd 352, P.2nd 702 (1960).

32. Mallery et al., "Comment on Martin," 205.

33. Nelson Rockefeller, quoted in Avins, "Anti-Discrimination Legislation," 4.

34. Avins, "Anti-Discrimination Legislation," 4.

35. Avins, 4.

36. California Real Estate Association, "Freedom of Choice," 1964.

37. *CRE*, May 1963, 1.

38. *Washington Post Times Herald*, June 19, 1963, A7.

39. King, "I Have a Dream," 1963.

40. Avins, "Anti-Discrimination Legislation," 4.

41. *CRE*, May 1964, 1. L. H. Wilson used this to describe a free economy.

42. Quote from Chicago Real Estate Board, January 1963, in Helper, *Racial Policies*, 1969, 277.

43. *Realtor's Headlines*, May 16, 1966, 2.

44. Weyl, "Comment on O'Meara," 192.

45. Avins, "Anti-Discrimination Legislation," 33.

46. Tovey, "Discrimination," 63.

47. Avins, "Anti-Discrimination Legislation," 34.

48. *Shelley v. Kraemer*.

49. Tovey, "Discrimination," 63.

50. Tovey, 64.

51. *CRE*, July 1963, 3.

52. *CRE*, April 1963, 24.

53. Statement of James K. Strong, Inglewood Human Relations Council, 1963, Miller papers.

54. Tovey, "Discrimination," 50.

55. *CRE*, February 1964, 5. Quote from Assemblyman E. Richard Barnes on gathering signatures for Proposition 14.

56. Tovey, "Discrimination," 50.

57. Avins, "Anti-Discrimination Legislation," 41.

58. Avins, 34. Avins described supporters of antidiscrimination legislation as "advocates of compulsory integration."

59. Avins, 41.

60. Avins, 33.

61. Trebilcock, "Civil Rights Program," 1963, in NAREB, Forced Housing Action Kit.

62. NAREB, Forced Housing Action Kit.

63. Tovey, "Discrimination," 50.

64. Lowndes, *From the New Deal to the New Right*, 2008, 74.

65. *CRE*, October 1964, 6.

66. For text, see *CRE*, April 1963, 6.

67. "Minutes for State Legislative Roundtable," January 26, 1963, and "State Legislative Report," January 28, 1963, in State Associations Steering Committee notebook 1960–1967, NAREB archive.

68. "State Legislative Report," NAREB archive.

69. *Los Angeles Times*, January 19, 1964, K1.

70. *Oakland Tribune*, March 17, 1963, 6.

71. *Oakland Tribune*, 6

72. Walker, "Fair Housing in Michigan," 365–67.

73. HoSang, "Racial Liberalism," 2010, 193, with respect to California boards; Burke, "National Association of Realtors," 2016, 50, on national endorsements.

74. NAREB, Preamble to the Code of Ethics, 1950 edition.

75. *CRE*, December 1947, 6.

76. *New York Times*, November 16, 1961.

77. U.S. Commission on Civil Rights, *Hearings*, 1960, 700–701.

78. TV script for Clive Graham, Brown papers, Box 662:3 "Rumford."

79. *Los Angeles Times*, September 20, 1964, 279.

80. *Washington Post Times Herald*, June 8, 1963, C2.

81. Gordon, radio script, c. 1964, Brown papers, Box 661:21 "Legislative: Rumford 1963–1964."

82. Pitts, radio script, September 20, 1964, Brown papers, Box 661:21 "Legislative: Rumford 1963–1964."

83. Reverend John Burt, "Questions and Answers about . . . the Initiative Against Fair Housing." ABC radio script, September 30, 1964, Brown papers, 661:21.

84. Burke, "National Association of Realtors," 45.

85. *CRE*, April 1963, 5.

86. *Los Angeles Times*, December 8, 1963, 11.

87. Avins, "Anti-Discrimination," 4.

88. Fisher, "Far from Utopia," 2008, 264.

89. Burke, "National Association of Realtors," 50.

90. *CRE*, April 1963, 24.

91. Burke, "National Association of Realtors," 45.

92. *Oakland Tribune*, March 17, 1963, 6.

93. *CRE*, July 1963, 5.

94. *Los Angeles Times*, June 9, 1963, 2.

95. *Washington Post Times Herald*, June 22, 1963, C6.

96. *Washington Post Times Herald*, C6.

97. *New York Times*, June 22, 1963.

98. *Washington Post Times Herald*, June 8, 1963, C2.

99. *Evening Star* (Washington, DC), June 7, 1963.

100. *New York Times*, April 13, 1962, 22.

101. *Washington Post Times Herald*, June 8, 1963, C2.

102. Rarick, *California Rising*, 2005, 264.

Part Five. A National Crusade in California: June 1963–November 1964

1. Landye and Vanecko, "Politics of Open Housing," 90–99.

2. Walker, "Fair Housing in Michigan," 358–62, 365–67.

3. Trevor Goodloe, "The 1964 Open Housing Election," Seattle Civil Rights & Labor History Project. https://depts.washington.edu/civilr/CORE_housing_media.htm.

4. L. H. Wilson, "Editorial," *CRE*, July 1964, 2.

5. Rumford, Oral History, 4–5; *San Francisco Chronicle*, "W. Byron Rumford Is Dead at 78," June 14, 1986.

6. Rumford, 6–9.

7. Rumford, 13, 28, 39f.

8. Rumford, 52.

9. Rumford, "Fair Housing and Proposition 14," 1966.

14. A Constitutional Amendment to Permanently Protect Discrimination

1. League for Decency in Real Estate, "Decency in Real Estate," 1964.

2. *Oakland Tribune*, May 4, 1963, 1.

3. *Los Angeles Times*, November 29, 1988, 3.

4. Rumford, "Fair Housing and Proposition 14"; Rumford, Oral History, appendix A.

5. Rarick, *California Rising*, 2005, 263.

6. Rumford, "Fair Housing Act."

7. Fisher, "Far from Utopia," 2008, 265–66.

8. Rumford, "Fair Housing Act."

9. Rumford, Oral History.

10. HoSang, *Racial Propositions*, 2010, 62.

11. Rarick, *California Rising*, 266.

12. Rumford, "Fair Housing Act."

13. Flamming, "Becoming Democrats," 298.

14. *Los Angeles Times*, December 5, 1963, F11.

15. Rarick, *California Rising*, 266.

16. *Los Angeles Times*, January 19, 1964, K1.

17. Rumford, "Fair Housing Act."

18. *San Francisco Chronicle*, June 30, 1963, 24.

19. *New York Times*, February 23, 1964, R1.

20. Sullivan, "Letting Down the Bars," 2003, 304.

21. *New York Times*, February 23, 1964, R1.

22. *Oakland Tribune*, March 17, 1963, 6.

23. *CRE*, May 1963, 3.

24. *San Francisco Chronicle*, July 25, 1963, 8.

25. *San Francisco Chronicle*, July 30, 1963, 8.

26. *San Francisco Chronicle*, 8.

27. *San Francisco Chronicle*, 8.

28. Maxwell et al., "Legal Opinion and Description of Proposition 14," c. 1964.

29. *Trends in Housing* (published by National Council Against Discrimination in Housing), July–August 1963, 5.

30. *Desert Sun*, October 5, 1964. Quote from Reg Dupuy of CREA.

31. *Los Angeles Times*, September 27, 1963, A1.

32. *CRE*, February 1964, 5. Also *CRE*, December 1963, 5.

33. Reed Robbins, untitled re Prop. 14, c. 1964, Reed Robbins Collection.

34. Loren Miller, "Memorandum on State Constitutional Issues Arising out of Proposed Initiative Amendment in Reference to Sale or Rental of Housing," c. 1963, Loren Miller papers.

35. Rumford, Oral History, 127.

36. *San Francisco Chronicle*, July 20, 1963, 5.

37. *Los Angeles Times*, September 20, 1964, 279.

38. *San Francisco Chronicle*, July 20, 1963, 5.

39. *CRE*, July 1963, 3.

40. Quote from Clarence Zishiu of Anaheim Board of Realtors from *Pacific Citizen*, October 16, 1964, 1, in Brown papers, Box 662:5.

41. *San Francisco Chronicle*, September 16, 1963, 16.

42. *CRE*, October 1963, 7.

43. *San Francisco Chronicle*, September 27, 1963, 14.

44. *San Francisco Chronicle*, October 10, 1962, 10.

45. *San Francisco Chronicle*, 10.

46. *CRE*, November 1963, 7.

15. Racial Moderation to Continue Segregation

1. *San Bernardino County Sun*, May 16, 1963, 30. Wilson speech to local realtors.

2. "Suggested Twelve Minute Speech," in NAREB, Forced Housing Action Kit.

3. HoSang, *Racial Propositions*, 2010, 73.

4. HoSang, 73.

5. Clive Graham, TV script for NBC television appearance, Brown papers, Box 662:3 "Rumford."

6. *San Francisco Chronicle*, January 6, 1964, 44.

7. Goldwater, *Conscience of a Conservative*, 1960, 48.

8. *Wall Street Journal*, September 11, 1964, in Stanford News Service archive.

9. Schuparra, *Triumph of the Right*, 1998, 107.

10. League for Decency in Real Estate, "Decency in Real Estate," 1964, 16.

11. League for Decency in Real Estate, 16.

12. *San Francisco Chronicle*, October 2, 1964, 11.

13. *Realtor's Headlines*, December 30, 1963, 2.

14. *Los Angeles Sentinel*, January 2, 1964, 8. Quote from letter from fifty-four members of Silver Spur Democratic Club in Palos Verdes.

15. HoSang, "Racial Liberalism," 193.

16. Mah, "Buying into the Middle Class," 2000, 155; American Jewish Committee, "Civic and Political Status," 1954, 75.

17. Brilliant, *Color of America*, 2010, 129.

18. *San Bernardino Sun*, December 13, 1951, 11.

19. *Philadelphia Tribune*, December 25, 1951, 16.

20. Brilliant, *Color of America*, 129.

21. Charlotte Brooks, "Sing Sheng v. Southwood," 2004, 477–78.

22. Robert E. Segal, "As We Were Saying: Of Peter Arno's Cartoon and Poor 'America Plus,'" *American Israelite*, February 28, 1952, 1.

23. Brooks, "Sing Sheng v. Southwood," 477.

24. *CRE*, June 1964.

25. Cain, "Absolute Discretion," 1964, 12.

26. Cain, 12.

27. *San Francisco Chronicle*, October 17, 1964, 2.

28. *CRE*, September 1948, 4.

29. *San Francisco Chronicle*, November 30, 1963, 2. Quote from Sunnyvale Bar Civil Rights Committee letter to Sunnyvale Real Estate Board.

30. *San Francisco Chronicle*, December 4, 1963, 1.

31. *CRE*, September 1964, 15.

32. *San Francisco Chronicle*, September 30, 1964, 2. Quote from Attorney General Thomas Lynch.

33. *San Francisco Chronicle*, 2.

34. "Constitution of the State of California," 1849.

35. Buhai, "One Hundred Years of Equality," 2001, 109.

36. *Perez v. Sharp*, 32 Cal. 2nd 711 (1948).

37. *Los Angeles Sentinel*, July 2, 1964, A6.

38. *CRE*, April 1964, 5.

39. *Chicago Daily Defender*, June 4, 1964. 1. Quote from Ed Mendenhall, president of NAREB.

40. *Washington Post Times Herald*, June 22, 1963, C6. Quote from Daniel Sheehan, president of NAREB.

41. "Suggested News Release 4," in NAREB, Forced Housing Action Kit.

42. *CRE*, April 1964, 5.

43. *San Francisco Chronicle*, June 27, 1963. Quote from L. H. Wilson.

44. For CREA's frequent publicity on its Equal Rights Committee, see *San Francisco Chronicle*, June 27, 1963, 13; *Los Angeles Times*, December 8, 1963, 11; *CRE*, July 1963, 5; *CRE*, January 1964, 3. However, nine months after forming, the committee did not list a single member in CREA's roster of committees. *CRE*, March 1964, 9. At the only meeting mentioned in *CRE*, chairman Clare Short explained that local committees had not formed due to "lack of understanding as to the objectives and purpose." *CRE*, May 1964, 26.

45. *CRE*, July 1963, 5.

46. *New York Times*, January 19, 1964, 76. Attorney General Mosk said, "Some realty boards used a secret 'blackball system' to keep Negroes and other minorities from membership."

47. Rumford papers, Carton 9, 73/1112 C 1:10 "Fair Housing, Jan.–Dec. 63"; "Report on Meeting of Members of Southwest Branch, Los Angeles Realty Board," November 4, 1963.

48. See, for example, *San Bernardino County Sun*, May 16, 1963, 30.

49. *CRE*, January 1964, 4. Quote from Art Leitch, president of CREA.

50. *Chicago Tribune*, September 26, 1963, E7. Quote from Edwin Stoll, director of public relations for NAREB.

51. NAREB, State Associations minutes, November 11, 1963, 3, NAREB archive.

52. NAREB, State Associations minutes, 3; also NAREB, Forced Housing Action Kit.

53. NAREB, State Associations minutes, February 3, 1964, 3.

54. San Francisco Labor, "The Realtors Attack Fair Housing Act," 4, Brown papers, Box 662.

55. The Realtors claimed that leaving private housing out of the federal civil rights bill proved that housing was inherently different from restaurants, movie theaters, and hotels because it involved long-term close social relationships. The reality was the other way around. Housing had been left out for purely political reasons. Because Northern states already required equality in public accommodations, a bill focused on them would not be controversial for congressmen from the North.

56. "Suggested Five Minute Speech," in NAREB, Forced Housing Action Kit.

57. "Suggested Five Minute Speech"; "Suggestions for a Publicity Program," in NAREB, Forced Housing Action Kit.

58. San Francisco Labor, "The Realtors Attack Fair Housing," 4, Brown papers, Box 662.

59. *CRE*, September 1963, 1.

60. *CRE*, January 1964, 4. Quote from David C. Brown, American Council of Christian Churches.

61. *Boston Globe*, October 1963, A44. Quote from Daniel Sheehan Sr., president of NAREB.

62. William K. (Bill) Shearer, "Jackson, Miss., Target City of the Freedom Riders. Eye Witness Report," August 30, 1961, 2, Brown papers, Box 661:21. "Legislative: Rumford 1963–1964."

63. *Los Angeles Times*, September 21, 1963, 12.

64. *Los Angeles Times*, August 4, 1964, 15.

65. NAREB, Realtors' Washington Committee minutes, April 8–9, 1964, 3–4, NAREB archive.

66. NAREB, Realtors' Washington Committee minutes, 3–4.

16. Redefining Freedom and America's Founding

1. NAREB, "Introduction and Questions Which You May Be Asked," Forced Housing Action Kit.

2. California Real Estate Association, "Freedom of Choice," 1964.

3. See L. H. Wilson, editorial, *CRE*, May 1964, 1.

4. Mann, "Matter of Rights," 2012, 65.

5. *CRE*, November 1963, 3.

6. *Los Angeles Times*, December 8, 1963, 11.

7. *Coronado Eagle and Journal*, October 29, 1964. Quote from Don Wiedmann.

8. Letter from Kenneth Bonnell to Charles Kenem of Californians Against Proposition 14, September 16, 1964, Brown papers, Box 662:6.

9. Schuparra, *Triumph of the Right*, 1998, 105.

10. Wolfinger and Greenstein, "Repeal of Fair Housing in California," 1968, 766.

11. *CRE*, November 1963, 3.

12. *New York Times*, January 10, 1961, 46.

13. *CRE*, March 1964, 1.

14. Wilson speech of February 20, 1964, quoted in HoSang, "Racial Liberalism," 2011, 198.

15. NAREB, Forced Housing Action Kit; Wilson, "Statement," 1963.

16. Self, *American Babylon*, 2003, 261.

17. Self, 261.

18. Hustwit, *James J. Kilpatrick*, 2013, 119–120.

19. Virginia Commission on Constitutional Government, "Civil Rights and Legal Wrongs," introduced in the record of U.S. Senate Hearings, 88th Congress, 405.

20. Foner, *Story of American Freedom*, 1999, 305.

21. NAREB, Forced Housing Action Kit.

22. Loury, *Anatomy of Racial Inequality*, 2012, 88.

23. Political advertisement in *Valley News*, October 27, 1964, and the *Fresno Bee*, October 30, 1964, 14.

24. Gorsuch and Ferguson, "Amici Curiae Brief," 1962.

25. *Los Angeles Times*, September 12, 1964, 34. Quote from George A. Beavers Jr.

26. Wilson, "Proposition 14 Fight for Freedom Approaches with Election Day," *CRE* September 1964, 6.

27. *CRE*, April 1964, 5.

28. *CRE*, 5.

29. Quote from President Truman's Committee on Civil Rights, in Lawson, *To Secure These Rights*, 2004, 51.

30. Lewis, "Analysis of Proposition 14," 1964, 13.

31. *San Francisco Chronicle*, September 28, 1964. Quote from Art Leitch, president of CREA.

32. *Flashes*, a weekly bulletin from the Committee for Home Protection, July 31, 1964, Max Mont Collection, Box 2-16.

33. *CRE*, May 1964, 8.

34. *Flashes*, July 31, 1964, Max Mont Collection, Box 2-16.

35. "News from FEPC," Brown papers, Box 662:6.

36. NAREB, Forced Housing Action Kit.

37. NAREB, "Introduction and Questions Which You May Be Asked," Forced Housing Action Kit.

38. NAREB, "Introduction."

39. Vincent L. Knaus, "Must Government Enforce 'Freedom'?" NAREB, Forced Housing Action Kit.

40. Statement from American Council of Christian Churches of America, Pasadena, December 17, 1963, in NAREB, Forced Housing Action Kit.

41. *Sacramento Bee*, October 17, 1964, 20.

42. Survey of Race Relations, 1927, 600.

43. Mikva, "Neighborhood Improvement Association," 1951, 118.

44. *CRE*, September 1964, cover and 3.

45. Gauvin, "Fair Housing Group's Roots," *Palo Alto Online*, July 26, 1995, https://www.paloaltoonline.com/weekly/morgue/cover/1995_Jul_26.ORIGINS.html.

46. Lewis, "Analysis," 16.

17. A Battle between Two Visions of Freedom

1. Radkowski, "Managing the Invisible Hand," 2015, 44.

2. "Leading East Bay Real Estate People Take Stand on Proposition 14," press release from Reggie Finney, Alameda County No on 14, October 28, 1964, Proposition 14 campaign materials, Institute for Governmental Studies, UC Berkeley. Quoting Leonard Seeley, past president of Southern Alameda County Real Estate Board.

3. HoSang, *Racial Propositions*, 2010, 75–80.

4. "Report on Meeting of Members of Southwest Branch," November 4, 1963, Rumford papers, Carton 73/1112.

5. Speech by Howard J. Jewel, assistant attorney general, at UCLA, May 13, 1964, Loren Miller papers.

6. Interview with William Becker, "The Governor's Office under Edmund G. Brown, Sr: Oral History Transcript," Bancroft Library, University of California, Berkeley, Banc MSS 81/164, 47.

7. *Hollywood Citizen-News*, quoted in Andrew Slater, "Race, Real Estate and the Forgotten Man," 2008, 41.

8. *CRE*, May 1964, 8.

9. *New York Times*, April 20, 1950, 19.

10. "The Facts about the Segregation Amendment Prop. 14," Brown papers.

11. Rarick, *California Rising*, 2005, 288–90.

12. HoSang, *Racial Propositions*, 82.

13. HoSang, 82.

14. *San Francisco Chronicle*, January 4, 1964, 10.

15. Pamphlet title, from Citizens Against Proposition 14, Brown papers, 661:21.

16. Gordon, "What Are the Obligations," 1963.

17. Interview with Lu Haas, "The Governor's Office under Edmund G. Brown, Sr: Oral History Transcript," Bancroft Library, University of California, Berkeley, Banc MSS 81/164, 75–76.

18. Wolfinger and Greenstein, "Repeal of Fair Housing in California," 1968, 766. The questions were about the Rumford Act rather than Proposition 14 directly.

19. Casstevens, *Politics, Housing and Race Relations*, 1967, 71–75.

20. HoSang, *Racial Propositions*, 85–86; Brilliant, *Color of America*, 2010, 205.

21. Doug Harris, *Fair Legislation*, 2016. Elihu Harris, later an assemblyman from Berkeley and mayor of Oakland, called it "a crushing blow."

Part Six. An Earthquake: 1965–1968

1. Dallek, "Time for Choosing," 1999, 158.

2. Brilliant, *Color of America Has Changed*, 2010, 225.

3. Edsall and Edsall, *Chain Reaction*, 1992, 47–48. Poll results from Harris polls in 1965. See also Rarick, *California Rising*, 2005, 61.

4. Menand, "He Knew He Was Right," 2001.

5. Goldberg, *Barry Goldwater*, 1995, 234–5.

6. McGirr, *Suburban Warriors*, 2001, 131. Goldwater, like the John Birch Society and Russell Kirk, all spoke of the country as "a Republic, not a democracy."

7. HoSang, "Racial Liberalism," 2011, 199.

18. Reagan and the Realtors

1. Perlstein, *Nixonland*, 2008, 91.

2. Holden, *Making of the Great Communicator*, 2013, 99.

3. Cannon, "Actor, Governor," 2004.

4. Holden, *Great Communicator*, 131.

5. Holden, 146–48.

6. Holden, 133.

7. Anderson and Lee, "1964 Election in California," 1965, 457.

8. *Boston Globe*, September 5, 1964, 13.

9. Schuparra, *Triumph of the Right*, 1998, 105.

10. *Los Angeles Times*, October 4, 1964, 88. Quote from Dr. Nolan Frizelle, president of CRA.

11. *Los Angeles Times*, September 29, 1964, 284. Quote from Nolan Frizelle, president of CRA.

12. *Los Angeles Times*, 284. Letter to the editor from "James Flournoy, Kurt Hahn and other officers of Los Angeles CRA."

13. *Los Angeles Times*, October 4, 1964, letter to the editor from Nolan Frizelle, president of CRA.

14. *Los Angeles Times*, September 21, 1964. Quote from Robert Gaston, president of California Young Republicans.

15. *San Francisco Chronicle*, September 21, 1961, 1.

16. Anderson and Lee, "1964 Election," 466.

17. Daniels, "Berkeley Apartheid," 2013, 334. The quote is from a voter during the March 1963 Berkeley referendum on fair housing.

18. Nationally, a Harris poll in 1964 of Northern "white minorities," e.g., of Eastern European ancestry, found that 61 percent felt that blacks were receiving special treatment their own fathers and grandfathers had not received. Thurber, *Republicans and Race*, 2013, 195.

19. Reed Robbins Collection. Members included Reed Robbins of Stockton and Robert Karpe of Bakersfield, both future presidents of CREA; Arthur Breed of Oakland; Dan Duggan of Coldwell Banker in Los Angeles; and John Glass of Los Angeles.

20. Oppenheimer, "California's Anti-Discrimination Legislation," 2009, 124–25.

21. *New York Times*, December 9, 1964, 1.

22. *New York Times*, 1.

23. Mukund Rathi, *Berkeleyside*, March 13, 2018, https://www.berkeleyside.com/2018/03/13/opinion-free-speech-movement-berkeley-defense-civil-rights-activism.

24. Holden, *Great Communicator*, 203–5.

25. Jack Weinberg, "The Free Speech Movement and Civil Rights," *Campus CORElator*, January 1965. http://www.fsm-a.org/stacks/weinberg.html.

26. Jack Weinberg quoted in the *Berkeley Daily Planet*, April 6, 2000, 1.

27. Weinberg, "Free Speech Movement."

28. Dallek, *Right Moment*, 2000, 61.

29. HoSang, *Racial Propositions*, 2010, 84, for California poll results during the campaign.

30. Dallek, *Right Moment*, 69.

31. *Los Angeles Sentinel*, March 14, 1963, 1.

32. Felker-Kantor, "Fighting the Segregation Amendment," 2014, 151.

33. Silvers, "Urban Renewal," 1969.

34. Silvers.

35. *Madera Tribune*, October 28, 1964.

36. Dallek, *Right Moment*, 58.

37. *Los Angeles Times*, January 3, 1964, A1, A2.

38. *CRE*, November 1963, 3. Quotes from radio station KNX manager Robert P. Sutton, included in Wilson's "President's Letter" to CREA members.

39. *Los Angeles Times*, October 4, 1964, 111. Quote from Art Leitch, president of CREA.

40. *CRE*, May 1964, 8.

41. 245 U.S. 61. (1917).

42. Loren Miller, "Testimony," October 7, 1965, 14, California Governor's Commission on the Los Angeles Riots.

43. Brown papers, Box 662:3.

44. *Los Angeles Times*, December 2, 1965, A4. Quote from H. Jackson Pontius, CREA executive vice president.

45. Theoharis, "'Alabama on Avalon,'" 2013, 48.

46. Stephen Grant Meyer, *Don't Move Next Door*, 2001, 182.

47. Loren Miller, "Testimony," California Governor's Commission, 4, 72.

48. Alvin Poussaint, "Testimony," California Governor's Commission.

49. Perlstein, *Nixonland*, 104.

50. Theoharis, "'Alabama on Avalon,'" 51.

51. *National Review*, September 7, 1965, 769.

52. Reagan, "Announcement on Candidacy for California Governor," January 4, 1966, *American Rhetoric: Online Speech Bank*; Boyarsky, *Rise of Ronald Reagan*, 1968, 92.

53. *Los Angeles Times*, August 11, 1985, B1.

54. *National Review*, September 7, 1965, 770.

55. *National Review*, 770.

56. *Washington Post*, October 3, 1965, A6.

57. *Los Angeles Sentinel*, January 6, 1966, A2.

58. *Washington Post*, October 3, 1965, A6.

59. 64 Cal 2nd 542 (1966).

60. *Hill v. Miller*, 64 Cal. 2nd 758 (1966). While holding Proposition 14 unconstitutional, in this case the court determined there was an inadequate factual record to support the plaintiff.

61. *Prendergast v. Snyder*, 64 Cal 2nd 878 (1966).

62. Richard Brownstein and Nina Easton, "The Culture of Reaganism," *New Republic*, October 24, 1982, 15–21.

63. *Washington Post*, October 30, 1990, B7.

64. Paul D. Kamenar, "The Department of Justice," in Butler et al., 149–64, 155–56.

65. HoSang, "Racial Liberalism," 210.

66. *Reitman v. Mulkey*, 64 Cal. 2nd, 543.

67. *Reitman v. Mulkey*, 544.

68. *Realtor's Headlines*, May 16, 1966, 1.

69. *CRE*, September 1966, 10.

70. Brilliant, *Color of America*, 2010, 221.

71. *Los Angeles Sentinel*, January 6, 1966, A2.

72. *Los Angeles Times*, April 22, 1966, A8.

73. *Los Angeles Times*, July 5, 1996, A4.

74. Holden, *Great Communicator*, 174–75.

75. Holden, 174–75.

76. *Los Angeles Times*, May 11, 1966, 20.

77. *Chicago Tribune*, May 12, 1966, 11.

78. *Boston Globe*, May 11, 1966, 30. Democratic attorney general Thomas Lynch, however, insisted that he would now begin to enforce the Rumford and Unruh Acts. *Los Angeles Times*, May 11, 1966, 20.

79. *Christian Science Monitor*, May 12, 1966, 1.

80. *Boston Globe*, May 11, 1966, 30.

81. *Desert Sun*, May 12, 1966, 1.

82. *Los Angeles Times*, June 25, 1966, H4.

83. *Los Angeles Times*, July 14, 1966, 3.

84. *New York Times*, July 17, 1966, 3.

85. *Los Angeles Times*, June 1, 1966, 3.

86. *Chicago Tribune*, August 8, 1966, B24.

87. *Chicago Tribune*, B24.

88. *Redlands Daily Facts*, August 13, 1966, 5.

89. *Boston Globe*, September 7, 1966, 36.

90. *Boston Globe*, 36.

91. *Los Angeles Times*, October 13, 1966, 3.

92. *Los Angeles Times*, October 31, 1966, 3.

93. Perlstein, *Nixonland*, 1.

94. *Los Angeles Times*, October 31, 1966, 3.

95. *Los Angeles Times*, October 7, 1966, 3.

96. *Los Angeles Times*, October 31, 1966, 3.

97. Rumford, "Fair Housing and Proposition 14," 1966.

98. *Los Angeles Times*, October 31, 1966, 3.

99. *Los Angeles Times*, 3.

100. HoSang, "Racial Liberalism," 199.

101. Radkowski, "Managing the Invisible Hand," 2015, 63.

102. Radkowski, 63.

103. Rarick, *California Rising*, 2005, 263.

104. Brilliant, *Color of America*, 225.

105. HoSang, "Racial Liberalism," 211.

106. Boyarsky, *Rise of Ronald Reagan*, 203.

107. Radkowski, "Managing the Invisible Hand," 66.

108. HoSang, "Racial Liberalism," 211.

109. Brilliant, *Color of America*, 222.

110. Holden, *Great Communicator*, 8.

111. Holden, 188.

112. See note 52 in this chapter and note 12 in chapter 24.

113. Holden, 175.

114. Radkowski, "Managing the Invisible Hand," 66.

115. Longley et al., *Deconstructing Reagan*, 2007, 76.

116. HoSang, "Racial Liberalism," 199.

117. Cannon, "Actor, Governor."

118. Brilliant, *Color of America*, 225.

119. Radkowski, "Managing the Invisible Hand," 68.

120. Harris, Fair Legislation, 2016; Rumford, Oral History, 123.

121. Rumford, Oral History, 128.

19. Realtor Victories against Fair Housing

1. Statement of James K. Strong of Inglewood Human Relations Council, 1963, Loren Miller papers.

2. Dallek, *Right Moment*, 2000, 51.

3. *Wall Street Journal*, February 1, 1965, 1.

4. *Wall Street Journal*, 1.

5. *New York Times*, November 11, 1964, 30.

6. *Los Angeles Times*, November 9, 1964, A1. Speech by Ed Mendenhall.

7. *CRE*, November 1964, 1.

8. *CRE*, 1.

9. *CRE*, 1.

10. *Realtor's Headlines*, August 9, 1965, 1.

11. NAREB, State Association Steering Committee minutes, January 31, 1966, 3, NAREB archive.

12. *Realtor's Headlines*, March 14, 1966, 1.

13. *Norfolk New Journal and Guide*, May 7, 1966, 15.

14. *Washington Post Times Herald*, November 15, 1965, B1.

15. *Realtor's Headlines*, March 29, 1965, 2.

16. Atkinson and Frailey, quoted in *Pittsburgh Courier*, October 9, 1943, 1. "At no time . . . may the honest . . . broker consider the wishes of his client without giving serious consideration to the possible influence . . . on the surrounding community."

17. *Realtor's Headlines*, March 1, 1965, 2.

18. *Realtor's Headlines*, March 15, 1962, 2.

19. *Realtor's Headlines*, March 22, 1965, 2.

20. *Realtor's Headlines*, February 22, 1965, 2.

21. *Realtor's Headlines*, April 12, 1965, 2.

22. *Trends in Housing*, May–June 1963, 4.

23. *CRE*, April 1966, 9.

24. *Realtor's Headlines*, December 6, 1965, 2.

25. *Trends in Housing*, January–February 1965, 7.

26. Lamb, *Housing Segregation*, 2006, 31–34.

27. *Journal of the House of Representatives*, Washington, DC: U.S. Congress, 1966, 465.

28. *Journal of the House of Representatives*, 465.

29. *Realtor's Headlines*, July 18, 1966, 1.

30. *Realtor's Headlines*, 1.

31. *Realtor's Headlines*, August 15, 1966, 1.

32. *Chicago Daily Defender*, September 7, 1966, 20.

33. *New York Times*, May 24, 1966, 29.

34. *Virginia Beach Sun*, June 3, 1966.

35. Display ad, "Civil Rights Bill of 1966," *Washington Post Times Herald*, June 7, 1966, A20, NAREB archive.

36. *Realtor's Headlines*, May 30, 1966, 2. Quoting from speech of Everett Trebilcock to the 1965 NAREB convention.

37. Emlen, "Forcing the Door," 1966.

38. *Realtor's Headlines*, June 13, 1966, 2. Quote from Jack Justice, president of NAREB.

39. *New York Times*, May 24, 1966, 29, quoting letter from a real estate agent in Pennsylvania.

40. *Congressional Record*, May 3, 1966, 9519.

41. Congressional Quarterly, 1966, 1147. ["1966 Civil Rights Act Dies in Senate," 1967].

42. Jenkins and Peck, "Congressional Action on Civil Rights," 2019.

43. *Christian Science Monitor*, June 18, 1966, 13.

44. Miles, "Hidden Hand," 2013, 83–84.

45. Miles, 83–84; Miles, "Art of the Possible," 2009, 110–11.
46. Miles, "Hidden Hand," 85–86.
47. Miles, "Art of the Possible," 111.
48. Miles, 114.
49. Lamb, *Housing Segregation*, 2006, 37.

20. To Defeat the Realtors

1. *Realtor's Headlines*, June 24, 1968, 1.
2. *San Francisco Chronicle*, March 16, 1967, Reed Robbins Collection.
3. *Los Angeles Times*, September 20, 1964.
4. *Reitman v. Mulkey*. 387 U.S. 375, oral argument.
5. *Peterson v. City of Greenville*, 373 U.S. 244 (1963).
6. *Peterson v. City of Greenville*.
7. *Reitman v. Mulkey*, 387 U.S. 375.
8. *Reitman v. Mulkey*.
9. *Reitman v. Mulkey*.
10. Jackson Pontius, president of CREA, letter to the *Los Angeles Times*, June 13, 1967, A4.
11. *Los Angeles Times*, May 30, 1967, 3. Quote from King Milligan, realtor from La Mesa.
12. *Los Angeles Times*, 3. Quote from William A. Robinson, member of the Los Angeles Realty Board.
13. *Los Angeles Times*, 3.
14. *Los Angeles Times*, 3. Quote from Mrs. Orpha M. Dohn, of Los Angeles.
15. Wilson, "Statement," 1963. Quotes from John T. O'Neill.
16. Radkowski, "Managing the Invisible Hand," 2015, 69.
17. Rarick, *California Rising*, 2005, 356.
18. Miles, "Art of the Possible," 2009, 103.
19. Miles, "Hidden Hand," 2013, 94.
20. Miles, "Art of the Possible," 115.
21. *Congressional Record* (Washington, DC: U.S. Congress, 1968), 4574.
22. Miles, "Hidden Hand," 97.
23. "Federal Fair Housing Requirements," 1969, 754.
24. *Realtor's Headlines*, March 11, 1968, 2.
25. "Federal Fair Housing Requirements," 752.
26. *Realtor's Headlines*, February 28, 1968, 2.
27. *Realtor's Headlines*, April 1, 1968, 2.
28. Miles, "Hidden Hand," 94.
29. NAREB, "Freedom of Choice v. Coercion: A Critical Analysis of Title VII of HR 2516, Providing for a Federal Open Occupancy Law," March 1968, NAREB archive.
30. NAREB, "Freedom of Choice v. Coercion."
31. NAREB, Realtors' Washington Committee minutes, March 27, 1968, subcommittee on civil rights legislation, NAREB archive.
32. Lamb, "Congress," 1982, 1126.
33. National Advisory Committee on Civil Disorders, 1968.
34. Hannah-Jones, "Living Apart," 2015.
35. Miles, "Art of the Possible," 116.
36. *Realtor's Headlines*, April 22, 1968, 2.

37. *Realtor's Headlines*, 2.

38. *Realtor's Headlines*, April 15, 1968, 2.

39. *Realtor's Headlines*, 2.

40. *Realtor's Headlines*, 2.

41. NAREB Realtors' Washington Committee minutes, May 4–5, 1968, NAREB archive.

42. NAREB Realtors' Washington Committee minutes, May 4–5, 1968.

43. 392 U.S. 409 (1968).

44. Darrell Miller, "White Cartels," 2008, 1019, citing act of April 9, 1866.

45. Miller, 1035.

46. Civil Rights Cases, 109 U.S. 3 (1883).

47. Miller, "White Cartels," 1015.

48. 379 F. 2nd 33 (8th Cir. 1967).

49. Miller, "White Cartels," 1011f.

50. Miller, 1013.

51. Miller, 1017.

52. Miller, 1019.

53. Estreicher, "Federal Power," 1974, 452.

54. Miller, "White Cartels," 1016.

55. Miller, 1016.

56. Miller, 1018.

57. Miller, 1018. See also Dubofsky, "Fair Housing," 1969, 165.

58. Belknap, *Supreme Court under Earl Warren*, 2005, 175.

59. Miller, "White Cartels," 1018. See also Dubofsky, "Fair Housing," 165.

60. Miller, 1020.

61. Miller, 1023.

62. Estreicher, "Federal Power."

63. *Realtor's Headlines*, June 24, 1968, 1.

64. *Realtor's Headlines*, 2.

65. *Realtor's Headlines*, 1. Quote from Lyn E. Davis, president of NAREB.

66. *Realtor's Headlines*, September 15, 1968, 3.

67. *Realtor's Headlines*, Quarterly Magazine Section, October 7, 1968, 1.

68. *Jones v. Albert H. Mayer Co.*, 379 F. 2nd 33 (8th Cir. 1967) and 392 U.S. 409 (1968), 391.

69. *Realtor's Headlines*, Quarterly Magazine Section, October 7, 1968, 1.

70. Stoll, "Realtors Reply," 1969.

71. "Fair Housing: The Evolution of National Association of Realtors' Perspectives and Policies," National Association of Realtors archive.

72. Heller, "Power of One Million," 2004.

21. An Ideology of Freedom for a National Conservative Party

1. Phillips, *Emerging Republican Majority*, 1969, 550.

2. Reichman and Wishart, *American Politics and Its Interpreters*, 1971, 148; "Chance to Lead," *Time*, August 16, 1968.

3. *Washington Post*, November 2, 1988, https://www.washingtonpost.com/archive/lifestyle/1988/11/02/uncle-strom-the-pragmatists-legacy/80bb7a1f-5412-4dff-a7c2-3e68a3fb51f5; *New York Times*, June 27, 2003, A1.

4. Moore, "Ronald W. Reagan's Campaign," 1992.

5. "Chance to Lead," *Time*, August 16, 1968.

6. Clymer, "Strom Thurmond," 2003; Perlstein, *Nixonland*, 2008, 299.

7. Clymer, "Strom Thurmond"; Perlstein, 299–300; Reichman and Wishart, *American Politics*, 148.

8. Reichman and Wishart, 148.

9. Kruse, *White Flight*, 2006, 255; Paul N. "Pete" McCloskey Jr., "The Republican Conventions of 1968 and 2016," *Huffungton Post*, March 31, 2017, https:/www. huffpost.com/entry/republican-conventions-1968-2016_b_9574256. Similarly, Nixon helped shut down efforts to integrate Southern public schools by then-Republican Leon Panetta at Health Education and Welfare.

10. Phillips, *Emerging Republican Majority*, 305, 477, 520.

11. Phillips, xiv.

12. Kruse, *White Flight*, 254.

13. Kruse, 255; Lowndes, *From the New Deal to the New Right*, 2008, 6. Lowndes treats this more generally as the "Southern capture of the Republican party."

14. *National Review*, August 24, 1957, 149.

15. Critchlow, *Conservative Ascendancy*, 2007, 74.

16. Kirk, *Conservative Mind*, 1953, 131.

17. Kirk, 4.

18. *Los Angeles Times*, August 19, 1963, A5.

19. Michael Miner, *Chicago Reader*, August 26, 2005, https://www.chicagoreader.com/chicago/look-back-in-anger-clueless-in-chicago/Content?oid=919716; *New Republic*, June 19, 2015.

20. Alvin Felzenberg, "How William F. Buckley, Jr. Changed His Mind on Civil Rights," *Politico*, May 13, 2017.

21. Brinkley, "Problem of American Conservatism,"1994, 417.

22. Goldwater, *Conscience of a Conservative*, 1960, 1.

23. Himmelstein, *To the Right*, 1990, 45.

24. Thorne, *American Conservative Thought*, 1990, 83–84. Quote from Donald Atwell Zoll.

25. Thorne, 142.

26. Kirk, *Conservative Mind*, 47.

27. Thorne, *American Conservative Thought*, 91.

28. Nash, *Conservative Intellectual Movement*, 2006, 264, 274–75.

29. Himmelstein, *To the Right*, 45.

30. Nash, *Conservative Intellectual Movement*, 275.

31. McGirr, *Suburban Warriors*, 2001, 164.

32. Connell, *Frank Zeidler*, 2011, 162 and 185.

33. Allswang, *Initiative and Referendum*, 2000, 69.

34. Brilliant, *Color of America Has Changed*, 2010, 221.

35. Goldwater, "1964 Acceptance Speech," https://www.washingtonpost.com /wp-srv/politics/daily/may98/goldwaterspeech.htm.

Part Seven. American Legacy: 1969–

1. Gallup News, April 18, 2019, https://news.gallup.com/poll/248837/church -membership-down-sharply-past-two-decades.aspx.

2. Walton and Cohen, "Brief Social-Belonging Intervention," 2011.

3. Walton and Cohen, 1447.

4. Yeager and Walton, "Social-Psychological Interventions in Education," 2011.

5. *Sacramento Bee*, October 17, 1964, 20, quoted in Andrew Slater, "Race, Real

Estate and the Forgotten Man," 2008, 39.

6. Tovey, "Discrimination," 50.

7. Reed Robbins, "Realtors for Reagan," c. early 1980, Reed Robbins Collection.

8. *San Francisco Examiner*, March 15, 1964. Quote from Robert D. Weinmann, Committee for Home Protection.

22. The Continuation of Residential Segregation

1. Loren Miller speech, "The Challenge of Democratic Living in Suburban Communities," February 23, 1962, Loren Miller papers.

2. Reverend Donald Rowland, "Report on Western Knolls Area," c. 1960, Miller papers; also summarized in U.S. Commission on Civil Rights, *Hearings*, 1960, 219.

3. Massey and Denton, *American Apartheid*, 1993, 1.

4. Massey and Denton, 192.

5. Dubofsky, "Fair Housing," 1969, 162.

6. Massey and Denton, *American Apartheid*, 200.

7. Olatunde C. A. Johnson, "The Last Plank," 2011, 1205.

8. Johnson, 1208.

9. Johnson, 1198.

10. Pearce, "Black, White, and Many Shades of Gray," 1976, 167f.

11. Yinger, *Analysis*, 1975, 329.

12. Yinger, 339.

13. 379 U.S. 241 (1964). Landsberg, "Public Accommodations," 2016.

14. Pearce, "Gatekeepers," 1979, 340.

15. Pearce, 340.

16. Hannah-Jones, "Living Apart," 2015.

17. Taylor, *Race for Profit*, 2019, 125.

18. Massey and Denton, *American Apartheid*, 207.

19. Massey and Denton, 208.

20. Massey and Denton; Yinger, *Closed Doors*, 1995; and Lee et al., "Residential Inequality," 2015, are representative of many analyses.

21. Foner, *Story of American Freedom*, 1999, 266.

22. Krysan and Crowder, *Cycle of Segregation*, 2017, 22.

23. Logan, "Separate and Unequal in Suburbia," 2014.

24. Reardon, Fox, and Townsend, "Neighborhood Income Composition," 2015.

25. Pearce, "Gatekeepers," 1979; Lacy, "Is Voluntary Residential Segregation Really Voluntary?" 2016; Yinger, *Closed Doors*.

26. "Long Island Divided," 2019.

27. Debra Kamin, "Black Homeowners Face Discrimination in Appraisals," *New York Times*, August 25, 2020; Troy McMullen, "For Black homeowners, a common conundrum with appraisals," *Washington Post*, January 21, 2020.

28. Thurston, *At the Boundaries of Homeownership*, 2018.

29. Aronson, Hartley, and Mazumder, "The Effects of the 1930s HOLC 'Redlining' Maps," 2017.

30. McCloskey and Orenstein, "Plunder of Black Wealth in Chicago," 2019.

31. Ruff, "Levittown," 2007.

32. National Fair Housing Alliance, "Fair Housing in Jeopardy," 2020, 32.

33. White House Fact Sheet, "Economy & Jobs," July 23, 2020; Hailey Fuchs, "Trump Moves to Roll Back Obama Program Addressing Housing Discrimination,"

New York Times, July 23, 2020.

34. "Preserving Community and Neighborhood Choice," a rule by the Housing and Urban Development Department, August 7, 2020, *Federal Register*, 86 FR 47899, p. 47901.

35. *New York Times*, July 29, 2020, https://www.nytimes.com/2020/07/29/us /politics/trump-suburbs-housing-white-voters.html.

36. Ben Zimmer, "What Trump Doesn't Understand about the Suburbs," *Atlantic*, July 31, 2020; Domenico Montanaro, "Trump Tries to Appeal to Housewives and White Suburbs, But His Views Seem Outdated," NPR, July 26, 2020, https://www. npr.org/2020/07/26/895228366/trumps-trying-to-appeal-to-real-housewives-and-white-suburbs-but-they-re-declini.

23. A Legacy for Civil Rights

1. *New York Times*, August 28, 1988, sec. 1, 20.

2. *Chisholm v. Georgia* (1793); *Martin v. Hunter's Lessee* (1816); *McCulloch v. Maryland* (1819); *Texas v. White* (1869).

3. Reagan, "First Inaugural Address," 1981.

4. Reagan, "Speech at Neshoba County Fair," 1980.

5. Reagan, "First Inaugural Address."

6. Reagan.

7. Reagan.

8. Lawson, *To Secure These Rights*, 2004, 51.

9. 573 U.S. 682 (2014).

10. Rumford, "Fair Housing and Proposition 14," 1966.

11. Rumford.

12. *New York Times*, October 23, 1983, 7; Tommy Christopher, "Watch: Ronald Reagan Opposed National MLK Holiday Right Up to Day He Signed It." *Media*, January 21, 2019.

13. Reagan, "Radio Address to the Nation," 1986.

14. King, "I Have a Dream," 1963.

15. Reagan, "Radio Address."

24. Who Is Entitled to American Freedom

1. Frederick Douglass, "Our Composite Nationality."

2. *San Francisco Chronicle*, September 7, 1964, 1.

3. *CRE*, January 1964, 1. Guest editorial from Henry C. MacArthur of Capital News Service.

4. *Chicago Daily Calumet*, April 5, 1960, in NAREB, Forced Housing Action Kit.

5. Kirk, *Conservative Mind*, 1953, 42.

6. Kirk, 138–39.

7. Kirk, 143.

8. *National Review*, June 4, 1963, 436.

9. Morgan Whitaker, MSNBC, August 28, 2013, https://www.msnbc.com/msnbc /back-the-day-what-critics-said-about-king-msna154716.

10. For conservatives' long-standing belief that freedom should be limited to those deemed worthy of it, see Kirk, *Conservative Mind*: "civilized society requires orders and classes," 8; praise of Edmund Burke and John Randolph's "strong love of personal freedom . . . and . . . strong caste feelings, in other words, devotion to their

own rights and those of their order" (quoting J. G. Baldwin), 13; opposition to in-alienable natural rights, 42; praise of Calhoun's attack on "all men having the same right to liberty and equality," 143; "liberty is a product of civilization and a reward of virtue, not an abstract right" 157; "for real liberty—the liberty of true distinction, not the fierce levelling freedom of envy," 381.

11. Reagan, "Remarks," 1984.

12. Elisha Fieldstadt, "Ronald Reagan Called African U.N. Delegates 'Monkeys' in Call with Richard Nixon, Audio Recording Reveals," *NBC News*, July 31, 2019.

13. Rumford, "Fair Housing and Proposition 14," 1966.

14. Conor Dougherty, "Overlooked No More: William Byron Rumford, a Civil Rights Champion in California," *New York Times*, August 7, 2019, https://www.nytimes.com/2019/08/07/obituaries/william-byron-rumford-overlooked.html.

15. McDonald, "Russell Kirk," 1999, 58.

16. *New York Times*, April 30, 1994, 13.

17. Kirk, *Conservative Mind*, 193.

18. Jaffa, "Calhoun versus Madison," n.d.

19. Sam Tanenhaus, "Original Sin: Why the GOP Is and Will Continue to Be the Party of White People," *New Republic*, February 9, 2013.

20. Rhode Island realtors quoted in NAREB, Forced Housing Action Kit.

21. *New York Times*, May 16, 2020, A11.

22. Margaret Thatcher, "Interview for *Woman's Own*," September 23, 1987, Margaret Thatcher Foundation, https://www.margaretthatcher.org/document/106689.

23. See MacLean, *Democracy in Chains*, 2017, with respect to the Koch brothers.

24. Cain, "Absolute Discretion," 1964, 12.

25. Patterson, *Freedom*, 1991, 3–4, drawing on Bertrand Russell on sovereignal freedom; Elizabeth Anderson, "Liberty," 2015, 1, contrasting hierarchical rights versus "a free society of equals"; Pettit, *Just Freedom*, 2014, xviii–xx, identifying non-domination as the key criterion for freedom that takes into account the effective rights of all.

BIBLIOGRAPHY AND WORKS CITED

Abrams, Charles. *Forbidden Neighbors: A Study of Prejudice in Housing.* New York: Harper Brothers, 1955.

———. "Homes for Aryans Only: The Restrictive Covenant Spreads Legal Racism in America." *Commentary,* January 1, 1947.

Aleinikoff, T. Alexander. "Racial Steering: The Real Estate Broker and Title VIII." *Yale Law Journal* 85, no. 6 (1976): 808–25.

Allswang, John. *The Initiative and Referendum in California, 1898–1998.* Stanford, CA: Stanford University Press, 2000.

Ambrose, Stephen E. *Eisenhower: Soldier and President.* New York: Simon & Schuster, 1990.

American Jewish Committee. "Civic and Political Status: Report on Civil Liberties in 1952 and 1953." 1954. http://www.ajcarchives.org/AJC_DATA/Files/1954_4 _USCivicPolitical.pdf.

Anderson, Elizabeth. "Liberty, Equality, and Private Government." Tanner Lectures in Human Values, Princeton University, March 4–5, 2015.

Anderson, Totton J., and Eugene C. Lee. "The 1964 Election in California." *Western Political Quarterly* 18, no. 2 (1965): 451–74.

Aronson, Daniel, Daniel Hartley, and Bhashkar Mazumder. "The Effects of the 1930s HOLC 'Redlining' Maps." Federal Reserve Bank of Chicago, August 3, 2017.

Atkinson, Harry Grant, and L. E. Frailey. *Fundamentals of Real Estate Practice.* New York: Prentice Hall, 1946.

Auble, Talmadge D. "Residential Appraisals in the Postwar Period." *Appraisal Journal,* January 1944, 42–49.

Avila, Eric. *Popular Culture in the Age of White Flight: Fear and Fantasy in Suburban Los Angeles.* Berkeley: University of California Press, 2004.

Avins, Alfred. "Anti-Discrimination Legislation in Housing: A Denial of Freedom of Choice." In Avins, 3–42.

———, ed. *Open Occupancy versus Forced Housing under the Fourteenth Amendment.* New York: Bookmailer, 1963.

———. "Racial Segregation in Public Accommodations: Some Reflected Light on the Fourteenth Amendment from the Civil Rights Act of 1875." *Case Western Reserve Law Review* 18, no. 4 (1967): 1251–83. https://scholarlycommons .law.case.edu/caselrev/vol18/iss4/10.

———. "Right to Be a Witness and the Fourteenth Amendment." *Missouri Law Review* 31, no. 4 (Fall 1966). https://scholarship.law.missouri.edu/cgi /viewcontent.cgi?article=1954&context=mlr.

Babcock Ancestry, "William May Garland." http://www.babcockancestry.com /books/garland/019williammaygarland.shtml.

Babcock, Frederick Morrison. *The Appraisal of Real Estate*. New York: Macmillan, 1924. https://catalog.hathitrust.org/Record/001894336.

Barraclough, Laura R. "Rural Urbanism: Landscape, Land Use Activism and the Cultural Politics of Suburban Spatial Exclusion." PhD diss., University of Southern California, 2006. ProQuest (AAT 3237185).

Bartlett, Dana W. *The Better City: A Sociological Study of a Modern City*. Los Angeles: Neuner Company Press, 1907.

Bass, Charlotta A. *Forty Years: Memoirs from the Pages of a Newspaper*. Los Angeles: Charlotta A. Bass, 1960.

Belknap, Michael R. *The Supreme Court under Earl Warren, 1953–1969*. Columbia: University of South Carolina Press, 2005.

Berg, Irving. "Racial Discrimination in Housing; A Study in Quest for Governmental Access by Minority Interest Groups, 1945–1962." PhD diss., University of Florida, 1967. ProQuest (AAT 6809511).

Bernstein, Shana. "From the Southwest to the Nation: Interracial Civil Rights Activism in Los Angeles." In Nickerson and Dochuk, 141–163.

Black, Charles, Jr. "The Supreme Court, 1966 Term—Foreword: 'State Action,' Equal Protection, and California's Proposition 14." *Yale Law School Legal Scholarship Repository*, Faculty Scholarship Series, 1967. https://digitalcommons. law.yale.edu/fss_papers/2591.

Boyarsky, Bill. *The Rise of Ronald Reagan*. New York: Random House, 1968.

Brilliant, Mark. *The Color of America Has Changed: How Racial Diversity Shaped Civil Rights Reform in California, 1941–1978*. New York: Oxford University Press, 2010.

Brinkley, Alan. "The Problem of American Conservatism." *American Historical Review* 99, no. 2 (1994): 409–21.

Brooks, Charlotte. "Sing Sheng v. Southwood: Residential Integration in Cold War California." *Pacific Historical Review* 73, no. 3 (2004): 463–94. doi:10.1525 /phr.2004.73.3.463.

Brooks, Richard R.W., and Carol M. Rose. *Saving the Neighborhood: Racially Restrictive Covenants, Laws and Social Norms*. Cambridge, MA: Harvard University Press, 2013.

Buckley, William F., Jr. *Flying High: Remembering Barry Goldwater*. New York: Basic Books, 2008.

Buhai, Sande L. "One Hundred Years of Equality: Saving California's Statutory Ban on Arbitrary Discrimination by Business." *University of San Francisco Review* 36, no. 1 (2001): 109–49. https://repository.usfca.edu/usflawreview /vol36/iss1/2.

Bulmer, Martin. "Charles S. Johnson, Robert E. Park and the Research Methods of the Chicago Commission on Race Relations, 1919–1922." *Ethnic and Racial Studies* 4, no. 3 (1981): 289–306.

Bunch, Lonnie G. "'The Greatest State for the Negro': Jefferson L. Edmonds, Black Propagandist of the California Dream." In de Graaf, Mullroy, and Taylor, 129–48.

Burke, Jennifer L. "The National Association of Realtors and the Fair Housing Mandate, 1961–1991." PhD diss., University of California, Santa Cruz, 2016. ProQuest (AAT 10140224).

Butler, Sara Marie. "Partisan Pathways to Racial Realignment: The Gradual Realignment of Race and Party in the Twentieth Century." PhD diss., University of California, Los Angeles, 2015. https://escholarship.org/uc/item/5pf8q447.

Butler, Stuart M., Michael Sanera, and W. Bruce Weinrod, eds. *Mandate for Leadership II: Continuing the Conservative Revolution*. Washington, DC: Heritage Foundation, 1984.

Cain, Leonard. "Absolute Discretion: The California Controversy over Fair Housing Laws." Sacramento Committee for Fair Housing, July 1964. Institute of Governmental Studies, University of California, Berkeley.

California Assembly Interim Committee on Governmental Efficiency and Economy. "Hearing in Los Angeles, Sept 28–29, 1961." Sacramento: California State Printing Office, 1962.

California Department of Transportation. "Tract Housing in California, 1945–1973: A Context for National Register Evaluation." Sacramento: CDOT, 2011. https://dot.ca.gov/-/media/dot-media/programs/environmental-analysis/documents/ser/tract-housing-in-ca-1945-1973-a11y.pdf.

California Governor's Commission on the Los Angeles Riots. "Transcripts, Deposition, Consultant Reports, and Selected Documents," 1965. Stanford Library Media & Microtext Center.

Californians for Fair Housing. "The Facts about the Real Estate Lobby's Ballot Proposition," 1964. Institute of Governmental Studies, University of California, Berkeley.

California Real Estate Association. Executive Committee minutes, January 5 and 6, 1967. Reed Robbins Collection, University of the Pacific, Stockton.

———. "Freedom of Choice vs. Forced Housing." Pamphlet, 1964. Institute of Governmental Studies, University of California, Berkeley.

Cannon, Lou. "Actor, Governor, President, Icon." *Washington Post*, June 6, 2004.

———. *Ronnie and Jesse: A Political Odyssey*. Garden City, NJ: Doubleday & Company, 1969.

Carter, William M., Jr. "Race, Rights and the Thirteenth Amendment: Defining the Badges and Incidents of Slavery." *UC Davis Law Review* 40, no. 4 (2007):

1311–79. https://lawreview.law.ucdavis.edu/issues/40/4/articles/DavisVol40No4_Carter.pdf.

Casstevens, Thomas W. *Politics, Housing and Race Relations: California's Rumford Act and Proposition 14, 1967.* Berkeley: Institute of Governmental Studies, University of California.

——. "The Defeat of Berkeley's Fair Housing Ordinance." In Eley and Casstevens, 187–236.

Cavin, Aaron I. "The Borders of Citizenship: The Politics of Race and Metropolitan Space in Silicon Valley." PhD diss., University of Michigan, 2012. https://deepblue.lib.umich.edu/handle/2027.42/93852?show=full.

Chen, Anthony S. *Fifth Freedom: Jobs, Politics and Civil Rights in the United States, 1941–1972.* Princeton, NJ: Princeton University Press, 2009.

Cheng, Cindy I-Fen. *Citizens of Asian America: Democracy and Race during the Cold War.* New York: New York University Press, 2013.

Claeys, Eric R. "Euclid Lives? The Uneasy Legacy of Progressivism in Zoning." *Fordham Law Review* 73 (2004): 731–70.

Clark, Tom C., and Philip B. Perlman. *Prejudice and Property: An Historic Brief against Racial Covenants, Submitted to the Supreme Court.* Washington, DC: Public Affairs Press, 1948.

Clausen, Donald N., and Richard T. Buck. "The Constitutionality of Antidiscrimination Legislation in Housing in Illinois." In Avins, 112–23.

Clymer, Adam. "Strom Thurmond, Foe of Integration, Dies at 100." *New York Times,* June 27, 2003.

Collins, Charles. *Whither Solid South? A Study in Politics and Race Relations.* New Orleans: Pelican Press, 1947.

Committee for Home Protection. "Comments on Questions and Answers from Fair Employment Practices Commission, September 25, 1963." Max Mont Collection, Box 3-17. California State University, Northridge.

Congressional Quarterly. "Negro Demands Bring Civil Rights 'Crisis.'" In *CQ Almanac 1963,* 19th ed., 334–57. Washington, DC: Congressional Quarterly, 1964.

——. "1966 Civil Rights Act Dies in Senate." In *CQ Almanac 1966,* 22nd ed., 450–72. Washington, DC: Congressional Quarterly, 1967.

Connell, Tula A. *Frank Zeidler and the Conservative Challenge to Liberalism in 1950s Milwaukee.* PhD diss., Georgetown University, 2011. ProQuest (AAT 3482057).

Constitution of the State of California, 1849. https://www.sos.ca.gov/archives/collections/constitutions/1849.

Cooke, Stuart T. "Review of *The Negro in American Civilization.*" *Western Political Quarterly* 14, no. 2 (1961): 622–23. doi:10.2307/443644.

Crespino, Joseph. *In Search of Another Country: Mississippi and the Conservative Counterrevolution.* Princeton, NJ: Princeton University Press, 2007.

———. *Strom Thurmond's America.* New York: Hill and Wang, 2012.

Crimi, James E. "The Social Status of the Negro in Pasadena, California." Master's thesis, University of Southern California, 1941. ProQuest (AAT EP65616).

Critchlow, Donald T. *The Conservative Ascendancy: How the GOP Right Made Political History.* Cambridge, MA: Harvard University Press, 2007.

Critchlow, Donald T., and Nancy MacLean. *Debating the American Conservative Movement: 1945 to the Present.* Lanham, MD: Rowman & Littlefield, 2009.

Culver, Harry H. "A Realtor's Viewpoint on Zoning, Present and Future." *Annals of the American Academy of Political and Social Sciences* 155 (1931): 207–12.

Cutler, David M., Edward L. Glaeser, and Jacob L. Vigdor. "The Rise and Decline of the American Ghetto." *Journal of Political Economy* 107, no. 3 (June 1999): 455–506.

Dallek, Matthew. *The Right Moment: Ronald Reagan's First Victory and the Decisive Turning Point in American Politics.* New York: Free Press, 2000.

———. "A Time for Choosing: Ronald Reagan, Pat Brown and the Political Contest That Shaped a Decade." PhD diss. Columbia University, 1999. ProQuest (AAT 9930701).

Daniels, Douglas Henry. "Berkeley Apartheid: Unfair Housing in a University Town." *History Research* 3, no. 5 (2013): 321–41.

Danielson, Michael N. *The Politics of Exclusion.* New York: Columbia University Press, 1976.

Darden, Joe T. "Choosing Neighbors and Neighborhoods: The Role of Race in Housing Preference." In *Divided Neighborhoods: Changing Patterns of Racial Segregation in the 1980s,* ed. Gary Tobin, 15–42. Newbury Park, CA: Sage, 1987.

Davies, Pearl Janet. *Real Estate in American History.* Washington, DC: Public Affairs Press, 1958.

Davies, Richard O. *Housing Reform during the Truman Administration.* Columbia: University of Missouri Press, 1966.

Davis, Mike. *City of Quartz: Excavating the Future in Los Angeles.* New York: Vintage Books, 1992.

de Graaf, Lawrence B. "The City of Black Angels: Emergence of the Los Angeles Ghetto, 1890–1930." *Pacific Historical Review* 39, no. 3 (August 1970): 323–52.

de Graaf, Lawrence B., Kevin Mullroy, and Quintard Taylor, eds. *Seeking El Dorado: African Americans in California.* Los Angeles: Autry Museum of Western Heritage, 2001.

deGuzman, Jean-Paul. "'And Make the San Fernando Valley My Home': Contested Spaces, Identities, and Activism on the Edge of Los Angeles." PhD diss., University of California, Los Angeles, 2014. ProQuest (AAT 3623291).

Denton, John H. *Apartheid American Style*. Berkeley, CA: Diablo Press, 1967.

———. "Perspectives on Race and Property." In Denton, 3–15.

———, ed. *Race and Property*. Berkeley, CA: Diablo Press, 1964.

Desjardin, Thomas A. "The Search for Meaning in Lincoln's Great Oration." In *The Gettysburg Address: Perspectives on Lincoln's Greatest Speech*, ed. Sean Conant, 300–21. New York: Oxford University Press, 2015.

Deverell, William, and Douglas Flamming. "Race, Rhetoric and Regional Identity: Boosting Los Angeles, 1880–1930." In *Power and Place in the North American West*, ed. Richard White and John M. Findlay, 117–43. Seattle: University of Washington Press, 1999.

DiAngelo, Robin. "White Fragility." *International Journal of Critical Pedagogy* 3, no. 3 (2011): 54–70. http://libjournal.uncg.edu/ijcp/article/view/249.

Dickson, Del. "State Court Defiance and the Limits of Supreme Court Authority: Williams v. Georgia Revisited." *Yale Law Review* 103, no. 6 (1994): 1423–81. https://digitalcommons.law.yale.edu/ylj/vol103/iss6/2.

Douglass, Frederick. *The Life and Writings of Frederick Douglass*, ed. Philip S. Foner. Vol. 4, *Reconstruction and After*. New York: International Publishers, 1952.

Driver, Justin. "Supremacies and the Southern Manifesto," *Texas Law Review* 92 (2014): 1053–135. http://texaslawreview.org/wp-content/uploads/2015/08/Driver-92-4.pdf.

Dubofsky, Jean Eberhart. "Fair Housing: A Legislative History and a Perspective." *Washburn Law Review* 8, no. 2 (1969): 149–66. https://contentdm.washburnlaw.edu/digital/collection/wlj/id/2616.

Edsall, Thomas Byrne, with Mary D. Edsall. *Chain Reaction: The Impact of Race, Rights and Taxes on American Politics, with a New Afterword*. New York: Norton, 1992.

Eisenstein, Diana. "The Free Speech Movement, University of California at Berkeley." Campus Americans for Democratic Action, 1965.

Eley, Lynn W., and Thomas W. Casstevens, eds. *The Politics of Fair Housing Legislation: State and Local Case Studies*. San Francisco: Chandler Publishing, 1968.

Emlen, Alan. "Forcing the Door: A Comment on Title IV—the Forced Housing Title—of the Proposed Civil Rights Bill of 1966—S. 3296." Testimony to the US Senate, June 13, 1966. NAREB archive.

Estreicher, Sam. "Federal Power to Regulate Private Discrimination: The Revival of the Enforcement Clauses of the Reconstruction Era Amendments." *Columbia Law Review* 74, no. 3 (1974): 449–527.

Ethington, Philip J., William H. Frey, and Dowell Myers. "The Racial Resegregation of Los Angeles County, 1940–2000." Public Research Report no. 2001-04, May 12, 2001. https://sites.usc.edu/popdynamics/race-and-ethnicity.

"The Federal Fair Housing Requirements: Title VIII of the Civil Rights Act." *Duke Law Journal* 18, no. 4 (1969): 733–71. https://scholarship.law.duke.edu/dlj /vol18/iss4/4.

Federal Housing Administration. *Underwriting Manual: Underwriting and Valuation Procedure under Title II of the National Housing Act.* Washington, DC: U.S. Government Printing Office, 1935 and 1938 editions.

Felker-Kantor, Max. "Fighting the Segregation Amendment: Black and Mexican American Responses to Proposition 14 in Los Angeles." In *Black and Brown in Los Angeles: Beyond Conflict and Coalition*, ed. Josh Kun and Laura Pulido, 143–75. Berkeley: University of California Press, 2014.

Fisher, Damany Morris. "Far from Utopia: Race, Housing, and the Fight to End Residential Segregation in Sacramento, 1900–1980." PhD diss., University of California, Berkeley, 2008. ProQuest (AAT 3388272).

Flamming, Douglas. "Becoming Democrats: Liberal Politics and the African American Community in Los Angeles, 1930–1965." In de Graaf, Mullroy, and Taylor, 279–308.

———. *Bound for Freedom: Black Los Angeles in Jim Crow America.* Berkeley: University of California Press, 2005.

Fogelson, Robert M. *Bourgeois Nightmares: Suburbia 1870–1930.* New Haven, CT: Yale University Press, 2005.

———. *The Fragmented Metropolis: Los Angeles, 1850–1930.* Berkeley: University of California Press, 1993.

Foner, Eric. *The Story of American Freedom.* New York: Norton, 1999.

Ford, George B. "Zoning Is So Logical and Reasonable That It Must Come Sooner or Later—It Is Inevitable." *National Real Estate Journal* 22, no. 20 (1921): 41–46.

"Free Speech Movement Chronology: Three Months Chronology of Events." *California Monthly*, February 1965. https://bancroft.berkeley.edu/FSM/chron .html.

Freund, David M. P. *Colored Property: State Policy and White Racial Politics in Suburban America.* Chicago: University of Chicago Press, 2007.

———. "Marketing the Free Market: State Intervention and the Politics of Prosperity in Metropolitan America." In Kruse and Sugrue, 11–32.

Gage, Kendra. "Creating the Black California Dream: Virna Canson and the Black Freedom Struggle in the Golden State's Capitol, 1940–1988." PhD diss., University of Nevada, Las Vegas, 2015. ProQuest (AAT 3730348).

Gainsborough, Juliet F. *Fenced Off: The Suburbanization of American Politics.* Washington, DC: Georgetown University Press, 2001.

Gans, Herbert J. "The Balanced Community: Homogeneity or Heterogeneity in Residential Areas?" *Journal of the American Institute of Planners* 27, no. 3 (1961): 176–84.

Gardner, Michael R. *Harry Truman and Civil Rights: Moral Courage and Political Risks*. Carbondale: Southern Illinois University Press, 2002.

Garland, William May. "Boom Danger Threatens City." *Los Angeles Times*, December 24, 1922, VI.

———. "Civic Energy, Foresight and Faith Impelling Factors in Development." *Judicious Advertising* 19, no. 12 (1921): 14–15.

———. "State's Development Monument to Pioneer." *Los Angeles Times*, May 28, 1922, VI.

Garrow, David J. "King the Man, the March, the Dream." *American History* 38, no. 3 (August 2003): 26–35.

Gibbons, Andrea. "Segregation in Search of Ideology? Hegemony and Contestation in the Spatial and Racial Configuration of Los Angeles." PhD diss., London School of Economics, 2014. http://etheses.lse.ac.uk/id/eprint/1049.

Gill, Andrea Marie Kathleen. "'A Decent Home in a Suitable Environment': The Struggles to Desegregate Public Housing in New York City, Chicago, and Los Angeles." PhD diss., University of California, Santa Barbara, 2010. ProQuest (AAT 3427841).

Gilpin, Patrick J., and Marybeth Gasman. *Charles S. Johnson: Leadership beyond the Veil of Jim Crow*. Albany: State University of New York Press, 2003.

Glotzer, Paige. "'Exclusion in Arcadia': How Suburban Developers Circulated Ideas about Discrimination, 1890–1950." *Journal of Urban History* 41, no. 3 (2015): 479–94.

———. *How the Suburbs Were Segregated: Developers and the Business of Exclusionary Housing, 1890–1960*. New York: Columbia University Press, 2020.

Goldberg, Robert Alan. *Barry Goldwater*. New Haven, CT: Yale University Press, 1995.

Goldwater, Barry. *The Conscience of a Conservative*. Shepherdsville, KY: Victor Publishing, 1960.

Gordon, Milton G. "Property Rights and Civil Rights: The Role of Government." In Denton, 42–57.

———. "What Are the Obligations of Government to Resolve Such Conflicts as Exist in This Area (Property Rights and Civil Rights)," November 22, 1963. Max Mont Collection, Box 2-16. California State University, Northridge.

Gorsuch, John E., and John L. Ferguson. "Amici Curiae Brief, Representing the Colorado Association of Real Estate Boards." In *Colorado Anti-Discrimination Commission v. Case*, 380 P. 2nd 34 (1962). http://dwightmurphey-collectedwritings.info/Ms2a-2-FairHousingBrief.htm.

Grayson, George W., Jr., and Cindy Long Wedel. "Open Housing: How to Get around the Law." *New Republic* 158, no. 25 (June 22, 1968): 15–16.

Guinn, James Miller. *A History of California and an Extended History of Los Angeles and Environs.* Los Angeles: Historic Record Company, 1915.

Hahn, Harlan. "Northern Referenda on Fair Housing: The Response of White Voters." *Western Political Quarterly* 21, no. 3 (1968): 483–95.

Hale, Myron Q. "The Ohio Fair Housing Law." In Eley and Casstevens, 149–186.

Hannah-Jones, Nikole. "Living Apart: How the Government Betrayed a Landmark Civil Rights Law." *ProPublica*, June 25, 2015.

Harris, Cheryl I. "Whiteness as Property." *Harvard Law Review* 106, no. 8 (1993): 1710–91.

Harris, Doug. *Fair Legislation: The Byron Rumford Story.* Produced for PBS, 2016, DVD. https://www.directv.com/tv/Fair-Legislation-The-Byron-Rumford-Story-QU04cHl2SE5QMGpIVll6OGInUlhIUT09.

Harris, Leroy E. "The Other Side of the Freeway: A Study of Settlement Patterns of Negroes and Mexican Americans in San Diego, California." PhD diss., Carnegie Mellon University, 1974. ProQuest (AAT 7426644).

Hassan, Amina. *Loren Miller: Civil Rights Attorney and Journalist.* Norman: University of Oklahoma Press, 2015.

Hecht, James L. *Because It Is Right: Integration in Housing.* Boston: Little, Brown, 1970.

Heller, Frederik. "The Power of One Million." *RealtorMag*, May 1, 2004. https://www.nar.realtor/rmomag.nsf/pages/featuremillionamay04.

Helper, Rose. *Racial Policies and Practices of Real Estate Brokers.* Minneapolis: University of Minnesota Press, 1969.

Henderson, A. Scott. *Housing and the Democratic Ideal: The Life and Thought of Charles Abrams.* New York: Columbia University Press, 2000.

Hernandez, Kim. "The 'Bungalow Boom': The Working-Class Housing Industry and the Development and Promotion of Early 20th Century Los Angeles." *Southern California Quarterly* 92, no. 4 (2010–2011): 351–92.

Himmelstein, Jerome L. *To the Right: The Transformation of American Conservatism.* Berkeley: University of California Press, 1990.

Hirsch, Arnold R. "Less Than *Plessy*: The Inner City, Suburbs and State-Sanctioned Segregation in the Age of *Brown*." In Kruse and Sugrue, 33–56.

——. *Making the Second Ghetto: Race & Housing in Chicago, 1940–1960.* 2nd ed. Chicago: University of Chicago Press, 1998.

Hoffman, Alexander von. "Like Fleas on a Tiger? A Brief History of the Open Housing Movement," 1998. Joint Center for Housing Studies, Harvard University. https://www.jchs.harvard.edu/sites/default/files/von_hoffman_w98-3.pdf.

Hofstadter, Richard. "From Calhoun to the Dixiecrats." *Social Research* 16, no. 2 (1949): 135–50.

Holden, Ken. *The Making of the Great Communicator: Ronald Reagan's Transformation from Actor to Governor.* Guilford, CT: Lyons Press, 2013.

Hormann, Matt. "When South Pasadena Was for Whites Only." *Hometown Pasadena*, September 15, 2014.

Hornstein, Jeffrey M. *A Nation of Realtors: A Cultural History of the Twentieth-Century American Middle Class.* Durham, NC: Duke University Press, 2005.

HoSang, Daniel Martinez. "Racial Liberalism and the Rise of the Sunbelt West: The Defeat of Fair Housing on the 1964 California Ballot." In Nickerson and Dochuk, 188–213.

———. *Racial Propositions: Ballot Initiatives and the Making of Postwar California.* Berkeley: University of California Press, 2010.

Hoyt, Homer. *The Structure and Growth of Residential Neighborhoods in American Cities.* Washington, DC: Federal Housing Administration, 1939.

Hughes, Everett Cherrington. *The Chicago Real Estate Board: The Growth of an Institution.* New York: Arno Press, reprinted 1979.

Hustwit, William P. *James J. Kilpatrick, Salesman for Segregation.* Chapel Hill: University of North Carolina Press, 2013.

Ivey, Mary Frances. "Jesse Clyde Nichols." *Pendergast Years*, n.d. Kansas City Public Library. https://pendergastkc.org/article/biography/jesse-clyde-nichols.

Jackson, John P., Jr., and John P. Jackson. *Science for Segregation: Race, Law, and the Case against Brown v. Board of Education.* New York: New York University Press, 2005.

Jackson, Kenneth. *Crabgrass Frontier: The Suburbanization of the United States.* New York: Oxford University Press, 1985.

———. "Race, Ethnicity and Real Estate Appraisal: The Home Owners Loan Corporation and the Federal Housing Administration." *Journal of Urban History* 6, no. 4 (1980): 419–52.

Jaffa, Harry V. "Calhoun versus Madison: The Transformation of the Thought of the Founding: A Bicentennial Celebration," n.d. Library of Congress. https://www.loc.gov/loc/madison/jaffa-paper.html.

Jenkins, David. "Moving beyond 'Drill, Baby, Drill.'" Jewish Policy Center, Fall 2010. https://www.jewishpolicycenter.org/2010/08/31/drill-baby-drill.

Jenkins, Jeffrey A., and Justin Peck. "Congressional Action on Civil Rights: The Fair Housing Act of 1968." Prepared for the Congress and History Conference, Harvard University/MIT, June 13–14, 2019. https://cpb-us-e1.wpmucdn .com/sites.usc.edu/dist/2/77/files/2019/06/FairHousingFullDraft.pdf.

Jimenez, Uriel B. "Fresno's Long Hot Summer of 1967: An Examination of Housing and Employment Discrimination." Master's thesis, California State University, Fresno, 2017. http://hdl.handle.net/10211.3/192461.

Johnson, Charles. *Negro Housing: Physical Aspects, Social and Economic Factors, Home Ownership and Financing.* Report of the Committee on Negro Housing. President's Conference on Home Building and Home Ownership. Washington, DC: National Capital Press, 1932. https://catalog.hathitrust .org/Record/006684531.

Johnson, Olatunde C. A. "The Last Plank: Rethinking Public and Private Power to Advance Fair Housing." *Columbia Law Review,* 2011. https://scholarship .law.columbia.edu/faculty_scholarship/1101.

Jones-Correa, Michael. "The Origins and Diffusion of Racial Restrictive Covenants." *Political Science Quarterly* 115, no. 4 (2000–2001): 541–68.

Kain, John F., and John M. Quigley. *Housing Markets and Racial Discrimination: A Microeconomic Analysis.* New York: National Bureau of Economic Research, distributed by Columbia University Press, 1975.

Katzenbach, Nicholas. "Oral History Interview 1." Lyndon B. Johnson Presidential Library. http://www.lbjlibrary.net/assets/documents/archives/oral _histories/katzenbach/KATZENB1.PDF.

Keller, Morton. *Regulating a New Economy: Public Policy and Economic Change in America, 1900–1933.* Cambridge, MA: Harvard University Press, 1990.

Kennedy, David M., and Thomas A. Bailey. *The American Spirit: U.S. History as Seen by Contemporaries.* Vol. 2, *Since 1865.* 12th ed. Boston: Wadsworth Cengage Learning, 2009.

Kiang, Yi-Seng. "Judicial Enforcement of Restrictive Covenants in the United States," *Washington Law Review,* February 1, 1949. https://core.ac.uk /download/pdf/267977283.pdf.

Kilpatrick, James Jackson. "Civil Rights and Legal Wrongs." *National Review,* September 24, 1963, 231–36.

King, Martin Luther, Jr. "I Have a Dream." Speech presented at the March on Washington for Jobs and Freedom, Washington, DC, August 1963. National Archives.

———. "The Other America." Speech at Stanford University, April 14, 1967. https:// www.crmvet.org/docs/otheram.htm.

———. "Three Evils of Society." Speech at National Conference on New Politics in Chicago, August 31, 1967. https://www.rimaregas.com/2015/08/08/martin -luther-king-jr-speech-the-three-evils-of-society-civilrights-on-blog42.

———. *Where Do We Go from Here: Chaos or Community?* Boston: Beacon Press, 1968.

Kirk, Russell. *The Conservative Mind: From Burke to Eliot.* Washington, DC: Regnery Publishing, 1953.

———. "Introduction." In *The Essential Calhoun,* ed. Clyde N. Wilson. New Brunswick, NJ: Transaction Publishers, 1992.

Koslow, Jennifer Lisa. *Cultivating Health: Los Angeles Women and Public Health Reform*. New Brunswick, NJ: Rutgers University Press, 2009.

Krepleever, L. M. "The Model Real Estate Board: Its Efficiency Based on the Multiple Listing Service and Exclusive Agency Contract." *National Real Estate Journal* 4, no. 4 (1911): 340–42.

———. "A Reform Movement in the Real Estate Business." *National Real Estate Journal* 4, no. 3 (1911): 235–37.

Kruse, Kevin. *White Flight: Atlanta and the Making of Modern Conservatism*. Princeton, NJ: Princeton University Press, 2006.

Kruse, Kevin, and Thomas Sugrue, eds. *The New Suburban History*. Chicago: University of Chicago Press, 2006.

Krysan, Maria, and Kyle Crowder. *Cycle of Segregation: Social Processes and Residential Stratification*. New York: Russell Sage Foundation, 2017.

Kuper, Leo. "Sociological Aspects of Housing Discrimination." In Denton, 122–33.

Kurashige, Scott. *The Shifting Grounds of Race: Black and Japanese Americans in the Making of Multiethnic Los Angeles*. Princeton, NJ: Princeton University Press, 2008.

Kurland, Philip, and Gerhard Capser, eds. *Landmark Briefs and Arguments of the Supreme Court of the United States: Constitutional Law*. Vol. 46, *Shelley v. Kraemer*, 539–60. Arlington, VA: University Publications of America, 1975.

Kushner, James A. "Apartheid in America: An Historical and Legal Analysis of Contemporary Racial Residential Segregation in the US." *Howard Law Journal* 22 (1979): 547–686. https://repository.law.umich.edu/mlr/vol79/iss4/32.

Lacy, Karyn. "Is Voluntary Residential Segregation Really Voluntary?" In *Race and Real Estate*, ed. Adrienne Brown and Valerie Smith, 49–63. New York: Oxford University Press, 2016.

Lakoff, George. *Whose Freedom? The Battle over America's Most Important Idea*. New York: Picador, 2006.

Lamb, Charles. "The Congress, the Courts and Civil Rights: The Fair Housing Act of 1968 Revisited." *Villanova Law Review* 27, no. 6 (1982): 1115–62. https://digitalcommons.law.villanova.edu/vlr/vol27/iss6/1.

———. *Housing Segregation in Suburban America since 1960: Presidential and Judicial Politics*. Cambridge: Cambridge University Press, 2006.

Landsberg, Brian K. "Public Accommodations and the Civil Rights Act of 1964: A Surprising Success?" *Hamline University School of Law's Journal of Public Law and Policy* 36, no. 1 (2016): 1–25. https://digitalcommons.hamline.edu/jplp/vol36/iss1/1.

Landye, Thomas M., and James J. Vanecko. "The Politics of Open Housing in Chicago and Illinois." In Eley and Casstevens, 65–104.

Lassiter, Matthew. *The Suburban Majority: Suburban Politics in the Sunbelt South*. Princeton, NJ: Princeton University Press, 2006.

Laurenti, Luigi. *Property Value and Race: Studies in Seven Cities: Special Research Report to the Commission on Race and Housing*. Berkeley: University of California Press, 1960.

Lawson, Steven F., ed. *To Secure These Rights: The Report of Harry S Truman's Committee on Civil Rights*. Boston: Bedford/St. Martin's, 2004.

League for Decency in Real Estate. "Decency in Real Estate," 1964. Institute of Governmental Studies, University of California, Berkeley.

Leavitt, Jacqueline. "Charlotta A. Bass, *The California Eagle* and Black Settlement in Los Angeles." In Manning and Thomas, 167–86.

Lee, Barret A., Glenn Firebaugh, John Iceland, and Stephen A. Matthews, eds. "Residential Inequality in American Neighborhoods and Communities." *Annals of the American Academy of Political Science* 660 (2015).

Levine, Robert A. "The Silent Majority: Neither Simple nor Simple-Minded." *Public Opinion Quarterly* 35, no. 4 (1972): 571–77.

Lewinnek, Elaine. *The Working Man's Reward: Chicago's Early Suburbs and the Roots of American Sprawl*. Oxford, United Kingdom: Oxford University Press, 2014.

Lewis, Howard, Jr. "An Analysis of Proposition 14, the CREA Amendment," 1964. Edmund G. Brown papers, Box 661:21. Bancroft Library, University of California, Berkeley.

Light, Jennifer S. "Nationality and Neighborhood Risk at the Origins of FHA Underwriting." *Journal of Urban History* 36, no. 5 (2010): 634–71.

Lockard, Duane. *Toward Equal Opportunity: A Study of State and Local Antidiscrimination Laws*. New York: Macmillan, 1968.

Logan, John R. "Separate and Unequal in Suburbia." Census brief prepared for Project 2010, December 1, 2014. https://s4.ad.brown.edu/Projects/Diversity/Data/Report/report12012014.pdf.

Long, Herman, and Charles S. Johnson. *People vs. Property: Race Restrictive Covenants in Housing*. Nashville, TN: Fisk University Press, 1947.

"Long Island Divided." *Newsday*, November 16, 2019. https://projects.newsday.com/long-island/real-estate-agents-investigation.

Longley, Kyle, Jeremy D. Mayer, Michael Schaller, and John W. Sloan. *Deconstructing Reagan: Conservative Mythology and America's Fortieth President*. Armonk, NY: M. E. Sharpe, 2007.

Lora, Ronald. *Conservative Minds in America*. Chicago: Rand McNally, 1971.

Lorey, Maya Tulip. "A History of Residential Segregation in Berkeley, California, 1878–1960." *Concord Review*, 2013. http://www.schoolinfosystem.org/pdf/2014/06/04SegregationinCA24-2.pdf.

Los Angeles Almanac. "Historic General Population, City and County of Los Angeles, 1850 to 2010." http://www.laalmanac.com/population/po02.php.

Los Angeles Realty Board. Articles of Incorporation and Minutes, 1903–1968. Los Angeles Realty Board records, 1904–1984. Charles E. Young Research Library, University of California, Los Angeles.

———. "History of Los Angeles Realty Board, Inc. as of February 28, 1956." Los Angeles Realty Board records, 1904–1984. Charles E. Young Research Library, University of California, Los Angeles.

Loury, Glenn C. *The Anatomy of Racial Inequality*. Cambridge, MA: Harvard University Press, 2012.

Lowndes, Joseph E. *From the New Deal to the New Right: Race and the Southern Origins of Modern Conservatism*. New Haven, CT: Yale University Press, 2008.

MacLean, Nancy. *Democracy in Chains: The Deep History of the Radical Right's Stealth Plan for America*. New York: Viking, 2017.

Mah, Theresa J. "Buying into the Middle Class: Residential Segregation and Racial Formation in the United States, 1920–1964." PhD diss., University of Chicago, 2000. ProQuest (AAT 9977054).

Maier, Pauline. *American Scripture: Making the Declaration of Independence*. New York: Vintage Books, 1998.

———. "The Strange History of 'All Men are Created Equal.'" *Washington & Lee Law Review* 56, no. 3 (1999): 873–88. https://scholarlycommons.law.wlu.edu/wlulr/vol56/iss3/8.

Mallery, Joseph A., James B. McGhee, I. Beverly Lake, and Robert E. Lee: "Comment on Martin: Changing Concepts." In Avins, 199–205.

Mann, Nick. "A Matter of Rights: Referendums, California and the Rise of the New Right." *Western Illinois Historical Review* 4 (Spring 2012). http://www.wiu.edu/cas/history/wihr/WIHRVolIV%20Mann.pdf.

Manning, June, and Marsha Ritzdorf Thomas, eds. *Urban Planning and the African Community: In the Shadows*. Thousand Oaks, CA: Sage, 1997.

Marcus, Philip. "Civil Rights and the Anti-Trust Laws." *University of Chicago Law Review* 18, no. 2 (1951): 171–217. https://chicagounbound.uchicago.edu/uclrev/vol18/iss2/2.

Massey, Douglas S., and Nancy A. Denton. *American Apartheid: Segregation and the Making of the Underclass*. Cambridge, MA: Harvard University Press, 1993.

Maxwell, Richard C., Orrin Evans, Frank C. Newman, Charles J. Meyers, and Richard R. Powell. "A Legal Opinion and Description of Proposition 14." c. 1964. Institute of Governmental Studies, University of California, Berkeley.

McCloskey, Sharon, and Bruce Orenstein. "The Plunder of Black Wealth in Chicago: New Findings on the Lasting Toll of Predatory Housing Contracts." Samuel Dubois Cook Center on Social Equity at Duke University, May 2019. https://socialequity.duke.edu/wp-content/uploads/2019/10/Plunder-of-Black-Wealth-in-Chicago.pdf.

McDonald, W. Wesley. "Russell Kirk and the Prospects for Conservatism." *Humanitas* 12, no. 1 (1999): 56–76. http://www.nhinet.org/humsub/mcdon12-1.pdf.

McDuffie, Duncan. "Interpretation of New Baking Regulations." *Cracker Baker*, February 1918.

McEntire, Davis. *Residence and Race: Final and Comprehensive Report to the Commission on Race and Housing.* Berkeley: University of California Press, 1960.

McGirr, Lisa. *Suburban Warriors: The Origins of the New American Right.* Princeton, NJ: Princeton University Press, 2001.

McGovney, D. O. "Racial Residential Segregation by State Court Enforcement of Restrictive Agreements, Covenants or Conditions in Deeds Is Unconstitutional." *California Law Review* 33, no. 1 (1945): 5–39.

McGroarty, John. *Los Angeles from the Mountains to the Sea: With Selected Biography of Actors and Witnesses to the Period of Growth and Achievement.* Vol. 2. Chicago and New York: American Historical Society, 1921.

McKenzie, Evan. *Privatopia: Homeowner Associations and the Rise of Residential Private Government.* New Haven, CT: Yale University Press, 1994.

McLain, Charles J. "In re Lee Sing: The First Residential-Segregation Case." *Western Legal History* 3, no. 2 (1990): 179–96. https://lawcat.berkeley.edu/record/1113811.

McMichael, Stanley. *Real Estate Subdivisions.* New York: Prentice-Hall, 1949.

McMichael, Stanley, and Robert F. Brigham. *City Growth and Values.* Cleveland, OH: Stanley McMichael Publishing Organization, 1923. https://catalog.hathitrust.org/Record/006567459/Home.

McWilliams, Carey. *Southern California: An Island on the Land.* New York: Duell, Sloan & Pearce, 1946.

Menand, Louis. "He Knew He Was Right: The Tragedy of Barry Goldwater." *New Yorker*, March 26, 2001. https://www.newyorker.com/magazine/2001/03/26/he-knew-he-was-right.

Meyer, Frank S. "Principles and Heresies: The Negro Revolution." *National Review*, June 18, 1963, 494–96.

Meyer, Stephen Grant. *As Long as They Don't Move Next Door: Segregation and Racial Conflict in American Neighborhoods.* New York: Rowman & Littlefield, 2001.

Mikva, Zorita Wise. "The Neighborhood Improvement Association: A Counter Force to the Expansion of Chicago's Negro Population." Master's thesis, University of Chicago, 1951. ProQuest (AAT TM99944).

Miles, Darren R. "The Art of the Possible: Everett Dirksen's Role in Civil Rights Legislation of the 1950s and 1960s." *Western Illinois Historical Review* 1 (2009): 86–119. http://www.wiu.edu/cas/history/wihr/pdfs/MilesWIHRSp09.pdf.

———. "A Hidden Hand of Oppression: The Real Estate Industry's Role in the Creation and Maintenance of Residential Segregation in Twentieth Century America." PhD diss., Western Illinois University, 2013. ProQuest (AAT 1544064).

Miller, Darrell A. H. "White Cartels, the Civil Rights Act of 1866, and the History of *Jones v. Albert H. Mayer Co.*" *Fordham Law Review* 77, no. 3 (2008): 999–1050. https://ir.lawnet.fordham.edu/flr/vol77/iss3/2.

Miller, Loren. "Government's Responsibility for Residential Segregation" In Denton, 58–76.

———. *The Petitioners: The Story of the Supreme Court of the United States and the Negro.* New York: Random House, 1966.

Million, Elmer M. "Racial Restrictive Covenants Revisited." In Avins, 90–99.

Ming, William R., Jr. "Racial Restrictions and the Fourteenth Amendment: The Restrictive Covenant Cases." *University of Chicago Law Review* 16, no. 2 (Winter 1949): 203–38.

Mohl, Raymond A. "The Second Ghetto and the 'Infiltration Theory' in Urban Real Estate, 1940–1960." In Manning and Thomas, 58–74.

Monchow, Helen C. *The Use of Deed Restrictions in Subdivision Development.* Chicago: Institute for Research in Land Economics and Public Utilities, 1928. https://catalog.hathitrust.org/Record/005299782.

Montgomery, Rick. "J. C. Nichols: Legendary Developer's Vision Went beyond the Plaza." *Kansas City Star,* January 15, 2016.

Moore, Glen. "Ronald W. Reagan's Campaign for the Republican Party's 1968 Presidential Nomination." Columbus, GA: Columbus State University, 1992. https://archives.columbusstate.edu/docs/gah/1992/57-70.pdf.

Morgan, Chester. "Presidential Elections: Mississippi's Voting History." *Mississippi History Now,* 2009.

Myers, Andrew H. "Resonant Ripples in a Global Pond: The Blinding of Isaac Woodard." Internet presentation, American Studies Association, Houston, TX, November 2002. http://www.historicwoolenmills.org/notes/myers.html.

Myrdal, Gunnar. *An American Dilemma: The Negro Problem and American Democracy.* Vol. 2. New York: Pantheon, 1944.

Nash, George H. *The Conservative Intellectual Movement in America since 1945: Thirtieth Anniversary Edition.* Wilmington, DE: ISI Books, 2006.

National Advisory Commission on Civil Disorders. *Report of the National Advisory Commission on Civil Disorders: Summary of Report.* U.S. Government Printing Office, 1968.

National Association of Real Estate Boards. "Amicus Curiae Brief, Shelley v. Kraemer." In Kurland and Capser, 539–60.

———. Forced Housing Action Kit, 1964. NAREB archive. National Association of Realtors, Chicago.

———. Realtors' Washington Committee minutes, 1960–1968. NAREB archive.

———. State Associations Steering Committee minutes, 1960–1968. NAREB archive.

National Association of Realtors. "The Code of Ethics of the National Association of Realtors."

———. "William May Garland." https://www.nar.realtor/william-may-garland.

National Fair Housing Alliance. "Fair Housing in Jeopardy," September 10, 2020. https://nationalfairhousing.org/wp-content/uploads/2020/09/NFHA -2020-Fair-Housing-Trends-Report.pdf.

Nelson, Herbert U. "The Real Estate Code of Ethics." *Journal of Land & Public Utility Economics* 1, no. 3 (1925): 270–75.

———. Testimony to House Select Committee on Lobbying Activities, April 18, 1950. In *Housing Lobby, Part 2 of Hearings before the House Select Committee on Lobbying Activities, House of Representatives*, 8–70. Washington, DC: US Congress, 1950. https://www.google.com/books/edition/Hearings _Before_the_House_Select_Committt/nwYkAQAAMAAJ?hl=en&gbpv =1&bsq=%22a%20joint%20undertaking%20by%20our%20group%22.

Nicholas, Tom, and Anna Scherbina. "Real Estate Prices during the Roaring Twenties and the Great Depression." *Real Estate Economics* 41, no. 2 (2013): 278–309.

Nichols, David A. *A Matter of Justice: Eisenhower and the Beginning of the Civil Rights Revolution*. New York: Simon & Schuster, 2007.

Nicolaides, Becky M. *My Blue Heaven: Life and Politics in the Working-Class Suburbs of Los Angeles, 1920–1965*. Chicago: University of Chicago Press, 2002.

Nickerson, Michelle, and Darren Dochuk, eds. *Sunbelt Rising: The Politics of Place, Space and Region*. Philadelphia: University of Pennsylvania Press, 2011.

Nielsen, Chris Stewart. "Whiteness Imperiled: Anti-Asian Sentiment in California, 1900–1930." PhD diss., University of California, Riverside, 2007. ProQuest (AAT 3298244).

Oppenheimer, David B. "California's Anti-Discrimination Legislation, Proposition 14, and the Constitutional Protection of Minority Rights: The Fiftieth Anniversary of the California Fair Employment and Housing Act." *Golden Gate University Law Review* 40, no. 2 (2009): 117–27. https:// digitalcommons.law.ggu.edu/ggulrev/vol40/iss2/1.

Pach, Chester J., Jr. "Dwight D. Eisenhower: Domestic Affairs." University of Virginia, Miller Center. https://millercenter.org/president/eisenhower /domestic-affairs.

Palmer, Stuart Hunter. "The Role of the Real Estate Agent in the Structuring of Residential Areas: A Study in Social Control." PhD diss., Yale University, 1955. ProQuest (AAT 6507526).

Parker, Elsie Smith. "Both Sides of the Colored Line." *Appraisal Journal*, January 1943, 27–34; July 1943, 231–49.

Parker, Kunai M. *Making Foreigners: Immigration and Citizenship Law in America,* 1600–2000. Cambridge: Cambridge University Press, 2015.

Parry, David. "The Development of Organized Real Estate in San Francisco." *Argonaut,* 2004. San Francisco: San Francisco Museum and Historical Society. https://150290062.homesconnect.com/AccountData/150290062 /DParticle.pdf.

Parson, Don. *Making a Better World: Public Housing, the Red Scare and the Direction of Modern Los Angeles.* Minneapolis: University of Minnesota Press, 2005.

Patterson, Orlando. *Freedom.* Vol. 1, *Freedom in the Making of Western Culture.* New York: Basic Books, 1991.

Pearce, Diana May. "Black, White and Many Shades of Gray: Real Estate Brokers and Their Racial Practices." PhD diss., University of Michigan, 1976. ProQuest (AAT 7708009).

———. "Gatekeepers and Homeseekers: Institutional Patterns in Racial Steering." *Social Problems* 26, no. 3 (1979): 325–42.

Perlstein, Rick. *Nixonland: The Rise of a President and the Fracturing of America.* New York: Scribner, 2008.

Pettit, Philip. *Just Freedom: A Moral Compass for a Complex World.* New York: Norton, 2014.

Phillips, Kevin. *The Emerging Republican Majority.* Princeton, NJ: Princeton University Press, 1969.

Phillips-Fein, Kim. "Conservatism: A State of the Field." *Journal of American History* 98, no. 3 (2011): 722–43.

Philpott, Thomas Lee. *The Slum and the Ghetto: Neighborhood Deterioration and Middle-Class Reform, Chicago, 1880–1930.* New York: Oxford University Press, 1978.

Powell, Richard. "The Relationship between Property Rights and Civil Rights." In Denton, 16–34.

"President's Conference on Home Building and Home Ownership 1931, Washington, D.C." https://snaccooperative.org/ark:/99166/w6qz7gvn.

Press Reference Library. *Being the Portraits and Biographies of the Progressive Men of the West.* Vol. 2. New York: International News Service, 1915.

Purdum, Todd S. *An Idea Whose Time Has Come: Two Presidents, Two Parties, and the Battle for the Civil Rights Act of 1964.* New York: Henry Holt, 2014.

Radkowski, Peter P.F., III. "Managing the Invisible Hand of the California Housing Market, 1942–1967." *Berkeley Law Review,* April 2015. https://www.law .berkeley.edu/wp-content/uploads/2015/04/radkowski-paper.pdf.

Rarick, Ethan. *California Rising: The Life and Times of Pat Brown.* Berkeley: University of California Press, 2005.

Read, James H. *Minority Rule versus Consensus: The Political Thought of John C. Calhoun*. Lawrence: University of Kansas Press, 2009.

Reagan, Ronald. "First Inaugural Address," January 18, 1981. American Presidency Project, University of California, Santa Barbara. https://www.presidency.ucsb.edu/documents/inaugural-address-11.

———. "Radio Address to the Nation on Martin Luther King, Jr., and Black Americans," January 18, 1986. Ronald Reagan Presidential Library and Museum. https://www.reaganlibrary.gov/archives/speech/radio-address-nation-anniversary-birth-martin-luther-king-jr.

———. "Remarks Accepting the Presidential Nomination," August 23, 1984. American Presidency Project, University of California, Santa Barbara. https://www.presidency.ucsb.edu/documents/remarks-accepting-the-presidential-nomination-the-republican-national-convention-dallas.

———. "Speech at Neshoba County Fair, Sunday August 3, 1980." *Neshoba Democrat*, November 5, 2007. https://web.archive.org/web/20110714165011/http://neshobademocrat.com/main.asp?SectionID=2&SubSectionID=297&ArticleID=15599&TM=60417.67.

Reardon, Sean F., Lindsay Fox, and Joseph Townsend. "Neighborhood Income Composition by Race and Income, 1990–2009." *Annals of the American Academy of Political and Social Science* 660 (2015): 78–97.

Redford, Laura. "The Promise and Principles of Real Estate Development in an American Metropolis: Los Angeles 1903–1923." PhD diss., University of California, Los Angeles, 2014. ProQuest (AAT 3622716).

Reft, Ryan. "Structured Unrest: The Rumford Act, Proposition 14, and the Systematic Inequality That Created the Watts Riots." *Tropics of Meta*, September 2, 2014. https://tropicsofmeta.com/2014/09/02/structured-unrest-the-rumford-act-proposition-14-and-the-systematic-inequality-that-created-the-watts-riots.

Reichman, Louis C., and Barry J. Wishart. *American Politics and Its Interpreters*. Dubuque, IA: William C. Brown Company, 1971.

"Report of Governor's Commission on the Rumford Act." Sacramento: The Commission, April 6, 1967. https://babel.hathitrust.org/cgi/pt?id=uc1.31210021617814&view=1up&seq=5.

Reynolds, Robert Eugene. "An Institutional Study of the California State Fair Employment Practice Commission 1959 to 1963." Master's thesis, University of Southern California, 1964. ProQuest (AAT EP63807).

Robbins, Reed. "A Critical Analysis of Anti-Discrimination Housing Laws." In Denton, 88–98.

Robin, Corey. "Reclaiming the Politics of Freedom." *Nation*, April 6, 2011. https://www.thenation.com/article/archive/reclaiming-politics-freedom.

Robison, Joseph B. "Fair Housing Legislation in the City and State of New York." In Eley and Casstevens, 27–64.

———. "Housing—The Northern Civil Rights Frontier." *Case Western Law Review* 13, no. 1 (1961): 101–27. https://scholarlycommons.law.case.edu/caselrev /vol13/iss1/8.

Roche, John B. *The Quest for the Dream: The Development of Civil Rights and Human Relations in Modern America.* New York: Macmillan, 1963.

Rothstein, Richard. *The Color of Law: A Forgotten History of How Our Government Segregated America.* New York: Liveright, 2017.

Rowell, George Presbury. *Rowell's American Newspaper Directory.* New York: Printers' Ink Publishing, 1898.

Ruff, Joshua. "Levittown: The Archetype for Suburban Development." *American History,* December 2007. https://www.historynet.com/levittown-the -archetype-for-suburban-development.htm.

Ruffin, Herbert G., II. "Uninvited Neighbors: Black Life and the Racial Quest for Freedom in the Santa Clara Valley, 1777–1968." PhD diss., Claremont Graduate University, 2007. ProQuest (AAT 3272793).

Rumford, W. Byron. "Fair Housing and Proposition 14." California State Junior Chamber of Commerce Seminar, March 17, 1966. Rumford papers, Carton 9, Speech File 1966m. Bancroft Library, University of California, Berkeley.

———. Oral History. Earl Warren Oral History Project. https://oac.cdlib.org /view?docId=kt5h4nbowd&brand=oac4&doc.view=entire_text.

Russell, John H. "*The Fourteenth Amendment and the States* by Charles Wallace Collins." *American Political Science Review* 8, no. 3 (1914): 5057. doi:10.2307/1946189.

Rutledge, Edward. "Threat to the Great Society: Anti-Fair Housing Referenda." *Journal of Intergroup Relations,* Autumn 1965. Max Mont Collection, Box 2:16. California State University, Northridge.

Sanchez, George J. "The History of Segregation in Los Angeles: A Report on Racial Discrimination," 2007. https://dokumen.tips/documents/the-history -of-segregation-in-los-angeles.html.

Santow, Mark. "Saul Alinsky and the Dilemmas of Race in the Post-War City." PhD diss., University of Pennsylvania, 2000. ProQuest (AAT 9989649).

Schiesl, Martin. "Residential Opportunity for All Californians: Governor Edmund G. 'Pat' Brown and the Struggle for Fair Housing Legislation, 1959–1963." Edmund G. Pat Brown Institute, August 2013. https://nanopdf.com /download/residential-opportunity-for-all-californians-governor -edmund-g_pdf.

Schuman, Howard, Charlotte Steeh, and Lawrence Bobo. *Racial Attitudes in America: Trends and Interpretations.* Cambridge: Harvard University Press, 1965.

Schuparra, Kurt. *Triumph of the Right: The Rise of the California Conservative Movement, 1945–1966*. Armonk, NY: M. E. Sharpe, 1998.

Schwizer, Peter, and Wynton C. Hall, eds. *Landmark Speeches of the American Conservative Movement*. College Station: Texas A&M University Press, 2007.

Self, Robert O. *American Babylon: Race and the Struggle for Postwar Oakland*. Princeton, NJ: Princeton University Press, 2003.

Shattuck, Charles B. "Freedom Is Ours—Lest We Forget." Address before Sacramento Real Estate Board, February 20, 1964. Max Mont Collection, Box 2-16. California State University, Northridge.

———. Testimony to California Assembly Committee on Governmental Efficiency and Economy, 1961. Loren Miller papers, 26:12. Huntington Library.

Shepherd, George B. "No African-American Lawyers Allowed: The Inefficient Racism of the ABA's Accreditation of Law Schools." *Journal of Legal Education* 53, no. 1 (2003): 103–56.

Short, Clare. "The Housing Industry's Need to Reconcile Property Rights and Civil Rights." In Denton, 77–87.

Sides, Josh. *L.A. City Limits: African American Los Angeles from the Great Depression to the Present*. Berkeley: University of California Press, 2003.

Silvers, Arthur H. "Urban Renewal and Black Power." *American Behavioral Scientist* 12 no. 4 (March 1, 1969): 43–46.

Slater, Andrew. "Race, Real Estate and the Forgotten Man: The Rise of Conservatism in California." Bachelor's thesis, University of California Berkeley, 2008.

Slayton, D. "Property Values in Changing Neighborhoods." In Avins, 282–85.

Stoll, Edwin L. "Realtors Reply." Letter to the editor. *Saturday Review*, February 22, 1969. NAREB archive.

Stults, Rachel. "A Brief History of Opening Our Homes to Total Strangers (aka the Open House)." *Real Estate News*, April 21, 2015. https://www.realtor.com/news/real-estate-news/brief-history-of-the-open-house.

Sugrue, Thomas. "From Jim Crow to Fair Housing." In *The Fight for Fair Housing: Causes, Consequences and Future Implications of the 1968 Federal Fair Housing Act*, ed. Gregory D. Squires, 14–27. London: Routledge, 2017.

———. *The Origins of the Urban Crisis: Race and Inequality in Postwar Detroit*. Princeton, NJ: Princeton University Press, 2005.

———. *Sweet Land of Liberty: The Forgotten Struggle for Civil Rights in the North*. New York: Random House Trade Paperbacks, 2009.

Sullivan, Deirdre. "Letting Down the Bars: Race, Space and Democracy in San Francisco, 1936–1964." PhD diss., University of Pennsylvania, 2003. ProQuest (AAT 3087471).

Sunstein, Cass. *The Second Bill of Rights: FDR's Unfinished Revolution and Why We Need It More Than Ever.* New York: Basic Books, 2004.

Survey of Race Relations, 1927. In "On Discrimination and Segregation of Orientals in U.S." Box 20-16. Hoover Institution Library and Archives, Stanford University. https://purl.stanford.edu/px856nh3646.

Taeuber, Karl E., and Alma F. Taeuber. *Negroes in Cities: Residential Segregation and Neighborhood Change.* Chicago: Aldine Publishing, 1965.

Tansill, Charles T., Alfred Avins, Sam S. Crutchfield, and Kenneth W. Colegrove. "The Fourteenth Amendment and Real Property Rights." In Avins, 68–89.

Taylor, Keeanga-Yamahtta. *Race for Profit: How Banks and the Real Estate Industry Undermined Black Homeownership.* Chapel Hill: University of North Carolina Press, 2019.

Theoharis, Jeanne. "'Alabama on Avalon': Rethinking the Watts Uprising and the Character of Black Protest in Los Angeles." In *The Black Power Movement: Rethinking the Civil Rights–Black Power Era,* ed. Peniel E. Joseph, 27–54. New York: Routledge, 2013.

Thernstrom, Stephan, and Abigail Thernstrom, *America in Black and White: One Nation, Indivisible.* New York: Simon & Schuster, 1999.

Thomas, Clarence. "Freedom and Obligation—2016 Commencement Address." *Imprimis* 45, no. 5/6 (2016). Hillsdale College. https://imprimis.hillsdale.edu/freedom-obligation-2016-commencement-address.

Thorne, Melvin J. *American Conservative Thought since World War II: The Core Ideas.* New York: Greenwood Press, 1990.

Tillotson, Amanda R. "Risky Business: Race, Risk, and Real Estate in the Development of the Home Ownership State." PhD diss., University of Michigan, 2016. ProQuest (AAT 10391812).

Thurber, Timothy N. *Republicans and Race: The GOP's Frayed Relationship with African-Americans, 1945–1974.* Lawrence: University Press of Kansas, 2013.

Thurston, Chloe N. *At the Boundaries of Homeownership: Credit, Discrimination and the American State.* Cambridge: Cambridge University Press, 2018.

Tovey, John Herbert. "Discrimination, Anti-Discrimination Legislation, and Freedom of Choice in Housing: A Dialogue." In Avins 50–67.

Trebilcock, Everett. "A Civil Rights Program for Moderates: Address to Michigan Real Estate Association," September 11, 1963. NAREB Forced Housing Action Kit. NAREB archive.

———. "Some Observations on Open Occupancy Housing." Presentation to the 1964 Annual Seminar of Real Estate Board Administrators, May 5, 1964. NAREB archive.

Tufte, Edward Rolf. "The Civil Rights Movement and Its Opposition." PhD diss., Yale University, 1968. ProQuest (AAT 6908449).

Tushnet, Mark V. *Making Civil Rights Law: Thurgood Marshall and the Supreme Court, 1936–1961*. Oxford, United Kingdom: Oxford University Press, 1994.

Uono, Koyoshi. "The Factors Affecting the Geographical Aggregation and Dispersion of the Japanese Residences in the City of Los Angeles." Master's thesis, University of Southern California, 1927. ProQuest (AAT EP68070).

U.S. Commission on Civil Rights. *Equal Opportunity in Suburbia*. Washington, DC: US Government Printing Office (GPO), 1974.

——. *Hearings Held in Los Angeles, California January 25, 1960, January 26, 1960, and San Francisco, California, January 27, 1960, January 28, 1960*. Washington, DC: US GPO, 1960.

——. *Housing: 1961 Commission on Civil Rights Report*, Washington, DC: US GPO, 1961.

——. *Report of the U.S. Commission on Civil Rights 1959*. Washington, DC: US GPO, 1959.

Vose, Clement E. *Caucasians Only: The Supreme Court, the NAACP, and the Restrictive Covenant Cases*. Berkeley: University of California Press, 1973.

——. "NAACP Strategy in the Covenant Cases." *Case Western Reserve Law Review* 6, no. 2 (1955): 101–45. https://scholarlycommons.law.case.edu/caselrev/vol6/iss2/4.

Walker, Jack L. "Fair Housing in Michigan." In Eley and Casstevens, 353–82.

Walton, Geoffrey M., and G. L. Cohen. "A Brief Social-Belonging Intervention Improves Academic and Health Outcomes of Minority Students." *Science*, March 18, 2011, 1447–51.

Ward, Jason Morgan. *Defending White Democracy: The Making of a Segregationist Movement and the Remaking of Racial Politics, 1936–1965*. Chapel Hill: University of North Carolina Press, 2011.

Weaver, Robert C. *The Negro Ghetto*. New York: Russell & Russell, 1948.

Weiss, Marc A. "The Real Estate Industry and the Politics of Zoning in San Francisco, 1924–1928." *Planning Perspectives* 3 (1988): 311–24.

——. "Richard T. Ely and the Contribution of Economic Research to National Housing Policy, 1920–1940." *Urban Studies* 26, no. 1 (1989): 115–26.

——. *The Rise of the Community Builders: The American Real Estate Industry and Urban Land Planning*. New York: Columbia University Press, 1987.

——. "Urban Land Developers and the Origins of Zoning Laws: The Case of Berkeley." *Berkeley Planning Journal* 3, no. 1 (1986): 7–25.

Weyl, Nathaniel. "Comment on O'Meara: Historical Inaccuracy." In Avins, 50–67.

Wheaton, William L.C. "The Evolution of Federal Housing Programs." PhD diss., University of Chicago, 1953. ProQuest (AAT T-02116).

Wheeler, Richard S. "Berkeley Discriminates." *National Review*, June 18, 1963, 497.

White, Lynell Hanzel. "Civil Rights Activists and California Politicians Challenge Housing Discrimination in Sacramento, 1950–1966." Master's thesis, California State University, Sacramento, 2016. http://csus-dspace.calstate.edu /bitstream/handle/10211.3/182744/2016WhiteLynell.pdf?sequence=1.

White, Theodore. *The Making of the President, 1964.* New York: Atheneum, 1965.

Whittemore, Andrew. "The Regulated City: The Politics of Land Use Regulation in Los Angeles, 1909–2009." PhD diss., University of California, Los Angeles, 2010. ProQuest (AAT 3441493).

Wiese, James Andrew. "Struggle for the Suburban Dream: African American Suburbanization since 1916." PhD diss., Columbia University, 1993. ProQuest (AAT 9412858).

Willard, Charles Dwight. *The Herald's History of Los Angeles City.* Los Angeles: Kingsley-Barnes & Neuner, 1901.

Wilson, L. H. "Statement before California Assembly Governmental Efficiency and Economy Committee," March 27, 1963. NAREB Forced Housing Action Kit. NAREB archive.

Wolfinger, Raymond, and Fred I. Greenstein. "The Repeal of Fair Housing in California: An Analysis of Referendum Voting." *American Political Science Review* 62, no. 3 (1968): 753–69.

Worley, William S. *J. C. Nichols and the Shaping of Kansas City: Innovation in Planned Residential Communities.* Columbia: University of Missouri Press, 1990.

Yeager, David S., and Gregory M. Walton. "Social-Psychological Interventions in Education: They're Not Magic." *Review of Educational Research* 81, no. 2 (2011): 267–301.

Yinger, John. *An Analysis of Discrimination by Real Estate Brokers.* Madison: University of Wisconsin-Madison, February 1975.

———. *Closed Doors, Opportunities Lost: The Continuing Costs of Housing Discrimination.* New York: Russell Sage Foundation, 1995.

Yohn, Susan M. "Will the Real Conservative Please Stand Up? Or, the Pitfalls Involved in Examining Ideological Sympathies: A Comment on Alan Brinkley's 'Problems of American Conservatism.'" *American Historical Review* 99, no. 2 (1994): 430–37.

Younge, Gary. "Martin Luther King: The Story behind His 'I Have a Dream' Speech." *Guardian,* August 9, 2013. https://www.theguardian.com/world/2013 /aug/09/martin-luther-king-dream-speech-history.

PICTURE CREDITS

Cover: *Ticky Tacky Houses in Daly City* (1968), photograph by Robert A. Isaacs, courtesy of the San José Museum of Art.

Endpapers: Home Owners' Loan Corporation maps, from Robert K. Nelson, LaDale Winling, Richard Marciano, Nathan Connolly et al., "Mapping Inequality," American Panorama, ed. Robert K. Nelson and Edward L. Ayers, https://dsl.richmond.edu/panorama/redlining.

Opposite title page: Officers, San Fernando Valley Board of Realtors, 1958, Valley Times Collection, Los Angeles Public Library.

Opposite p. 1: Martin Luther King at March on Washington, 1963, Getty Images.

Opposite p. 1: L. H. "Spike Wilson," President, California Real Estate Association, 1963, in the California Digital Newspaper Collection, Center for Bibliographic Studies and Research, University of California, Riverside.

p. 25: William May Garland, public domain.

p. 47: California State Realty Federation, 1905, reprinted with permission from California Real Estate Magazine, copyright 1942 by the CALIFORNIA ASSOCIATION OF REALTORS®, all rights reserved.

p. 59: Duncan McDuffie of Berkeley, National Archives.

p. 59: Advertisement for Claremont Court, Berkeley, 1907, public domain.

p. 61: Country Club District, Kansas City, 1912, public domain (per the State Historical Society of Missouri).

p. 61: J. C. Nichols of Kansas City, courtesy of the Johnson County Museum, Overland Park, Kansas.

p. 84: Herbert U. Nelson, Executive Secretary, National Association of Real Estate Boards, National Association of REALTORS® Library & Archives.

p. 84: Charles S. Johnson, Scurlock Studio Records, Archives Center, National Museum of American History, Smithsonian Institution.

p. 136: Charles B. Shattuck in 1946, Valley Times Collection, Los Angeles Public Library.

p. 136: Loren Miller in the 1930s, University of Southern California Digital Library, Library Exhibits Collection.

p. 156: Ethel Shelley of St. Louis reads about Supreme Court decision, 1948, *St. Louis Post-Dispatch* / Polaris.

p. 162: Westlake Improvement Association, Daly City, California, 1950s, courtesy of the Daly City History Guild Museum & Archive.

p. 172: Sing Sheng and family, seeking to buy a home in South San Francisco, 1952, courtesy of the San Mateo County Historical Association.

p. 183: Charles Wallace Collins, public domain.

p. 183: Strom Thurmond at Democratic National Convention, 1948, courtesy of the Strom Thurmond Institute of Government and Public Affairs, Clemson University.

p. 198: U.S. Senator William F. Knowland, Biographical Directory of the United States Congress.

p. 198: California Governor Edmund G. "Pat" Brown, San Francisco History Center, San Francisco Public Library.

p. 216: Alfred Avins, from Widener University Delaware Law School.

p. 233: Property Owners' Bill of Rights, newspaper advertisement, 1963, reprinted with permission from California Real Estate Magazine, copyright 1963 by the CALIFORNIA ASSOCIATION OF REALTORS®, all rights reserved.

p. 245: Assemblyman W. Byron Rumford with the Rumford Act, 1963, courtesy of William B. Rumford Jr.

p. 278: Yes on Proposition 14, Committee for Home Protection, 1964, public domain, in the Max Mont Collection, Special Collections and Archives, Oviatt Library, California State University Northridge.

p. 284: No on 14 supporters with Tom Bradley, future Los Angeles Mayor, 1964, Los Angeles Public Library.

p. 285: No on 14, CAP 14, 1964, public domain, in the Max Mont Collection, Special Collections and Archives, Oviatt Library, California State University Northridge.

p. 294: Ronald Reagan, meeting of San Fernando Valley voter registration campaign, 1964, Bob Martin, Valley Times Collection, Los Angeles Public Library.

p. 333: Troops at U.S. Capitol, April 1968, Warren K. Leffler / Library of Congress.

p. 369: Ronald Reagan at Neshoba County Fair, Mississippi, 1980, Jack Thornell / AP.

INDEX

Note: Bold numbers indicate images.

ABOUT THE AUTHOR

Gene Slater has served as senior advisor on housing for federal, state, and local agencies for over forty years. He cofounded and chairs CSG Advisors, which has been one of the nation's leading advisors on affordable housing for decades and has structured more than $70 billion of financing for first-time home buyers, mixed-income apartments, neighborhood revitalization, and improved public housing.

Slater helped design and implement major housing strategies for Chicago, Denver, Los Angeles, New Orleans, Philadelphia, Phoenix, Pittsburgh, San Diego, San Francisco, Seattle, Washington, DC, and Wichita, and assisted a wide range of small towns and suburbs. His work designing Pittsburgh's home improvement loan program, which rehabilitated 18,000 of the city's 72,000 single-family homes, became the Department of Housing and Urban Development's national model for housing rehabilitation. He has advised the state housing finance agencies of California, Colorado, Connecticut, Illinois, Massachusetts, Minnesota, New York, Virginia, Washington State, and many others. His projects have received numerous national awards, and in 2009, in the aftermath of the financial crisis, he helped design the program by which the U.S. Treasury financed homes for 110,000 first-time buyers and 40,000 affordable rental units.

Slater received a BA from Columbia University *summa cum laude*, a traveling fellowship to the London School of Economics, a master's in city planning from MIT, and a master's from Stanford University. A midcareer Loeb Fellowship in Environmental Design from Harvard University, awarded to ten planners and architects from around the world each year, enabled him to study capital markets for housing at the Harvard Business School and create the first joint Harvard-MIT seminars on financing public-private partnerships. In 2020, he gave the American Institute of Architects' first national webinar on the history of housing segregation.

Growing up in Brooklyn—in the only assembly district in New York State to vote for Barry Goldwater—he helped start what became CSG Advisors in a rural Wisconsin farmhouse by the Mississippi River, and has also lived and worked in New York, Boston, Chicago, and the San Francisco Bay Area, where he currently resides.

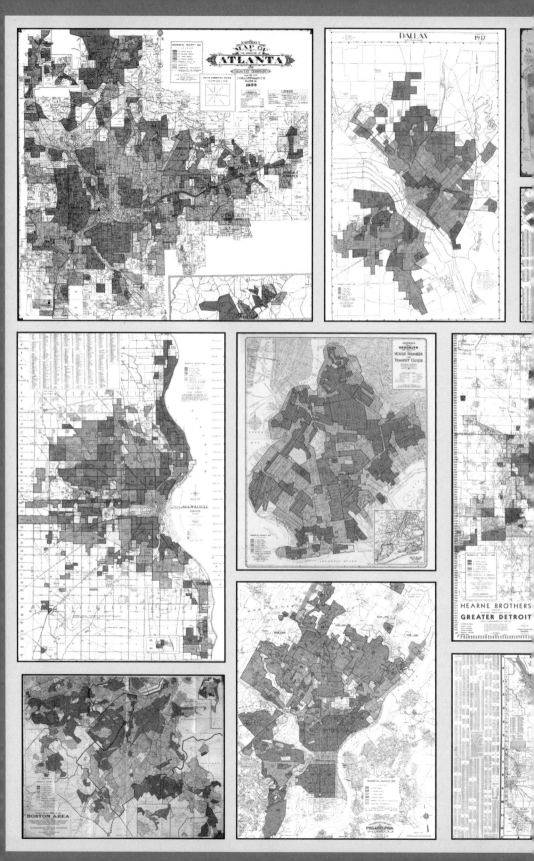